# Linguistic Content

UNIVERSITY PRESS

Great Clarendon Street, Oxford, OX2 6DP,
United Kingdom

Oxford University Press is a department of the University of Oxford.
It furthers the University's objective of excellence in research, scholarship,
and education by publishing worldwide. Oxford is a registered trade mark of
Oxford University Press in the UK and in certain other countries

© the several contributors 2015

The moral rights of the authors have been asserted

First Edition published in 2015

Impression: 1

All rights reserved. No part of this publication may be reproduced, stored in
a retrieval system, or transmitted, in any form or by any means, without the
prior permission in writing of Oxford University Press, or as expressly permitted
by law, by licence or under terms agreed with the appropriate reprographics
rights organization. Enquiries concerning reproduction outside the scope of the
above should be sent to the Rights Department, Oxford University Press, at the
address above

You must not circulate this work in any other form
and you must impose this same condition on any acquirer

Published in the United States of America by Oxford University Press
198 Madison Avenue, New York, NY 10016, United States of America

British Library Cataloguing in Publication Data

Data available

Library of Congress Control Number: 2014946090

ISBN 978-0-19-873249-5

Printed and bound by
CPI Group (UK) Ltd, Croydon, CR0 4YY

Links to third party websites are provided by Oxford in good faith and
for information only. Oxford disclaims any responsibility for the materials
contained in any third party website referenced in this work.

# Linguistic Content

*New Essays on the History of Philosophy of Language*

EDITED BY
Margaret Cameron
and Robert J. Stainton

# Contents

| | |
|---|---|
| List of Contributors | vii |
| Introduction<br>Margaret Cameron and Robert J. Stainton | 1 |
| 1. Method, Meaning, and Ontology in Plato's Philosophy of Language<br>Deborah Modrak | 16 |
| 2. Names, Verbs, and Sentences in Ancient Greek Philosophy<br>Francesco Ademollo | 33 |
| 3. On What is Said: The Stoics and Peter Abelard<br>Margaret Cameron | 55 |
| 4. Philosophy of Language in the Medieval Arabic Tradition<br>Peter Adamson and Alexander Key | 74 |
| 5. Those 'Funny Words': Medieval Theories of Syncategorematic Terms<br>Joke Spruyt and Catarina Dutilh Novaes | 100 |
| 6. Semantic Content in Aquinas and Ockham<br>Gyula Klima | 121 |
| 7. Meaning and Linguistic Usage in Renaissance Humanism:<br>The Case of Lorenzo Valla<br>Lodi Nauta | 136 |
| 8. Medieval Theories of Signification to John Locke<br>E. Jennifer Ashworth | 156 |
| 9. Locke on the Names of Modes<br>Benjamin Hill | 176 |
| 10. Herder's Doctrine of Meaning as Use<br>Michael N. Forster | 201 |
| 11. Thomas Reid on Language<br>Patrick Rysiew | 223 |
| 12. Meaning in Action: Anton Marty's Pragmatic Semantics<br>Laurent Cesalli | 245 |
| Name Index | 267 |
| Subject Index | 269 |

# List of Contributors

PETER ADAMSON, Ludwig-Maximilians-Universität München

FRANCESCO ADEMOLLO, Università degli Studi di Firenze

E. JENNIFER ASHWORTH, University of Waterloo (emerita)

MARGARET CAMERON, University of Victoria

LAURENT CESALLI, Université de Genève

MICHAEL N. FORSTER, University of Bonn/University of Chicago

BENJAMIN HILL, Western University

ALEXANDER KEY, Stanford University

GYULA KLIMA, Fordham University

DEBORAH MODRAK, University of Rochester

LODI NAUTA, University of Groningen

CATARINA DUTILH NOVAES, University of Groningen

PATRICK RYSIEW, University of Victoria

JOKE SPRUYT, Maastricht University

ROBERT J. STAINTON, Western University

# Introduction

*Margaret Cameron and Robert J. Stainton*

## 1. Preliminaries

The present volume treats linguistic content across the history of Western philosophy of language, from Plato through Brentano's student Marty. As befits careful and cautious history of philosophy, in addressing this broad topic our contributors go where their chosen texts and historical figures lead them. The summaries of the chapters—presented at the end of this Introduction, and designed to help readers decide which dovetail most closely with their interests—will make this clear. Nonetheless, while we are wary about anachronistically reading the historical texts as overtly and directly answering them, there are two questions that emerge repeatedly as unifying themes. These will be our focus in most of what follows:

Q1: What varieties of linguistic content did the author or period countenance?
Q2: What metaphysical groundings for linguistic content were considered?

In this Introduction, we will clarify Q1–Q2 by surveying some highly simplified (and mostly ahistorical) answers to them. We then highlight a range of answers from the figures and texts addressed herein.

## 2. Ahistorical Answers to Q1 and Q2

There are two ways of understanding Q1, and we are interested in both. The first is robustly metaphysical, taking as its starting point views according to which meanings are: *mental* things, whether representations or acts, in the same family as pains, tickles, and beliefs; *concrete physical* items, in the same family as rocks; *abstracta*, in the same family as numbers; and *social performances* such as promising and betting.

---

We would like to thank our Advisory Board for the History of Philosophy of Language for their generosity in advising us on this and other related projects: Rachel Barney, Ray Elugardo, Benjamin Hill, Henrik Lagerlund, Martin Lenz, Claude Panaccio, Jeff Pelletier, Lisa Shapiro, and Martin Tweedale. We are also grateful to the Social Sciences and Humanities Research Council for its support.

The question then is which ontology of contents, or which combination of ontologies, was embraced? Since we take that sort of debate to be quite familiar, our focus will be on explaining another reading of the question, more focused on the details and complexities of languages.

In this light, consider caricature versions of Russell and Frege. Meanings for Russell, in the very early years of the twentieth century, were entities external to the mind. Meanings were to be sharply distinguished from mental states or processes. Similarly for Frege. Within that general rubric, and crucially for our purposes, Russell countenanced several varieties of such externalia: particular objects such as Mont Blanc; propositions, such as that Mont Blanc is snow-covered; and functions from an object to a proposition, such as that picked out by '$x$ is snow-covered'. The foregoing shows already that, to discover an author's view on the broad ontological category to which meanings belong, is not yet to have completely sorted out "the varieties of meaning" he allows for. The range of variation possible is driven home if we consider that Frege proposed a taxonomy that closely paralleled Russell's, but at two levels. Again very roughly: at the level of reference, Frege introduced objects, truth-values, and unsaturated functions from the former to the latter; at the level of sense, he posited individual concepts (that is, modes of presentation of objects), his Thoughts, and (something like) properties. The lesson is, when it comes to the general-ontological-rubric aspect of Q1, Frege and Russell are in the same ballpark, but they nonetheless differ on essential details.

Here is another way at the same point. Two semantics $A$ and $B$ could adopt the caricatured Russellian view above, not only in terms of taking meanings to belong to the broad family *concrete and abstract externalia*, but even in assigning objects, propositional functions, and propositions as meanings for names, predicates, and declarative sentences respectively—yet still disagree about other varieties of linguistic content. Regarding logical connectives, $A$ might take them to stand for functions from two truth-values to one (or, in a Fregean vein, to refer to a function from two truth-values to one while having some rather peculiar mode of presentation as sense). Thus, for $A$, 'and' might stand for a function from <T, T> to T, and from every other pair of values to F. $B$, meanwhile, instead of assigning an entity to 'and', 'or', 'if', and so on, might take logical connectives to express a syncategorematic rule (as per Davidson–Tarski). On this view, the meaning of 'and' is given as follows:

*Sentences of the form "p and q" are true iff p is true and q is true.*

So understood, there is no "thing" that 'and' refers to. (The same basic idea is captured by the *Tractarian* proposal that the meaning of logical connectives is given entirely by the truth tables for them.) Similarly, $A$ and $B$ could embrace the same general ontological rubric yet disagree about quantifiers. $A$ might propose that words such as 'something', 'nothing', and 'everything' express second-order properties of sets: the first is true of non-empty sets, the second is true of empty sets, and so on. $B$ could urge, to the contrary, that these are syncategorematic. Another meaning theorist *C* might even deny that quantifiers introduce a different variety of content, proposing instead that they are simply names for abstract particulars, namely SOMETHING, NOTHING, and EVERYTHING. (Put in the formal mode, in terms of varieties of meaningful expressions, all three agree that names, predicates, and sentences are distinct logico-linguistic categories. *A* and *B* agree that quantifier-words are another one. *C* denies this.)

To be clear, the question about sub-varieties of meaning is not specific to the Frege–Russell tradition. Those who take meanings to belong in the general family of mental states and processes are prone to distinguish among the linguistic contents of names, sentences, and logical connectives just as much as the Frege–Russell tradition does. For instance, a familiar line of thought has it that a name corresponds to an idea of an individual, and predicates to mental concepts, while natural language sentences correspond to mental sentences, or judgements. Use theorists, for whom meanings are potential social performances, also distinguish among names (which are governed by conventions for referring) and sentences (which are governed by conventions for various speech acts: stating, promising, commanding).

One could explore this topic at much further length. One could, indeed, devote an entire book-length survey of philosophy of language and philosophical semantics to it. For present purposes, we rest content with clarifying what our first unifying theme is: both what general ontological famil(ies) linguistic contents belong to, and what sub-categories are required within them.

The other question that arises throughout, and unifies the chapters, is Q2: the origin of meaning, in the sense of its metaphysical grounding. In explicating the desired sense of 'origin' and 'grounding', the usual parallel is with metaethics. Even when all hands concur that torturing babies for fun is wrong, philosophers can disagree about why this ethical fact obtains. Is it because it reduces the overall number of hedons; because it treats the infant as a mere means; because God forbids it; and so on? This is not a question of the *cause* of the fact, so much as what lower-level facts constitute it. In the same vein, whereas Q1 pertains to what sort of thing linguistic content is (or, maybe better, what sort*s* of thing*s* content*s* are), Q2 asks, instead, in virtue of what linguistic expressions mean what they do. For instance, assuming the meaning of 'Bertrand Russell' is simply the person so named, the question remains: what makes this the case? Or again, what more basic facts undergird the semantic fact that 'cow' has a meaning at all, and has the particular meaning it does?

There are three familiar options here. The relation of resemblance, in some sense of that term, seems a natural candidate for metasemantic grounding: what makes it the case that 'cow' means what it does is that the symbol is similar, in the right sort of way, to cows. Equally familiar is the suggestion that meaning emerges from causal–historical links: what makes it the case that 'cow' means what it does is that tokens of this form have been reliably caused by cows. (Or something like that.) Finally, the way that the expression is used by a group is an obvious source of its meaning: what makes it the case that 'cow' means what it does is that the appropriate group of people use it to talk about cows.

As with Q1, settling on one of these general conceptions is not the end of the story. Whichever path one pursues, there are further choice points. A first is whether the meaning of "linguistic sounds" is grounded directly, or whether they are directly paired with something else (typically something mental), and then an additional metasemantic story is told about the latter. Consider, in this light, the resemblance theory. Though Plato toyed with the idea that spoken words resemble what they stand for, or anyway that an ideal language would have this feature, this view has found little favour. In contrast, as will become clear below, it has been extremely common from Aristotle's *De interpretatione* forward to suppose that (i) mental representations have the content that they do because they are images, or likenesses, of their external world reference and (ii) that public words are paired with mental representations by some non-resemblance mechanism. Similarly, tokens of the spoken word 'cow' are not reliably caused by cows. (Thankfully so.) Possibly, however, the mental concept COW is so caused, thereby having its meaning grounded—and then the English word is connected to that concept by some non-causal mechanism.

Another choice point is whether the theorist takes the origin/grounding to be natural or conventional. There is a link between this and the direct/indirect contrast. Though some philosophers have been tempted by the idea of a natural connection between public language words and their meanings (with *natural resemblance* being a preferred case in point), this strikes most as far-fetched. The mere fact of massive cross-linguistic variation—English 'cow' versus Greek 'agelada' versus Spanish 'vaca'—militates strongly in favour of a merely conventional connection. On the other hand, a natural connection (for example, an innate one) between at least some concepts and some of their referents has been taken very seriously both historically and nowadays.

One last clarification before we move on. Though we present Q1 and Q2 as orthogonal, this overstates things. It is important not to run them together, and there do not seem to be entailments from one to the other. Nonetheless, if one takes meanings to be, say, imagistic mental representations, almost inevitably one will think that both the mental and resemblance will have a key role to play in metasemantic grounding. And, if one takes meanings to be, say, use-potentials, almost inevitably one will think that usage does the fixing of meaning facts. Such interconnections show up repeatedly in the historical studies included here.

In sum, we have surveyed very briefly and schematically two questions about linguistic content, clarifying each by presenting postage-stamp answers. Q1 pertains both to the general ontological family to which linguistic contents belong (mental, physical, abstract, use-theoretic?) and to which sub-varieties are required (for names, predicates, sentences, logical connectives, quantifiers?). Q2 pertains to the general issue of what grounds linguistic content (resemblance, causation, use?) and to various sub-options for each (direct or indirect, natural or conventional?).

## 3. Q1 and the History of Philosophy of Language

In addressing Q1 historically, we begin with the broad ontological family to which meanings are held to belong. Looking for a figure who took meanings to be abstract, a candidate is not hard to find: the original Platonist, the Plato of the later works. Granted, to pigeonhole any historical figure, cleanly and unequivocally, within one of our categories is a mistake. Then again, the contrasting ontological categories are useful for getting an overview of the philosophical terrain, and taken with that important grain of salt, if we ask which category the meanings of 'justice', 'piety', or 'goodness' belong to for Plato, the natural answer is that they stand for Forms.

As for an arch Mentalist, Locke comes immediately to mind. To quote the famous passage from book III of the *Essay*: "Words, in their immediate signification, are the sensible signs of his ideas who uses them." And yet, as Hill explains in his contribution, Locke's position is also far more subtle and complex than a cursory reading would suggest. (The same holds for much of the Early Modern period: what looks to be crude Mentalism about meaning in everyone from Descartes and Hobbes, through Hume and Berkeley, emerges as something more sophisticated below the surface.) In particular, Locke seems to have held that ideas are merely the *immediate* signification, while the ultimate signification of a word is something external that corresponds to the idea. The same point applies to what look to be Mentalist theories in the later Medieval period. What is most characteristic of theories of meaning in, say, Aquinas, Ockham, and Buridan is the postulation of a mental language, and the suggestion that public language words stand for representations therein. However, as Klima explains, if one asks what the items in the *lingua mentis* mean in their turn, they stand for concrete particulars in the external world. Thus the actual views are something more like a hybrid of Mentalism and Physicalism about the broad ontological category of meanings. In this, all take a leaf from what may be the single most important passage in the history of Western philosophy of language, at the very outset of the *De interpretatione* ($16^a3$–8):

Now spoken sounds are symbols of affections in the soul, and written marks symbols of spoken sounds. And just as written marks are not the same for all men, neither are spoken sounds. But what these are in the first place signs of—affections of the soul—are the same for all; and what these affections are likenesses of—actual things—are also the same.

If one were to boil down the debate about the metaphysics of meanings up to the Renaissance, it would be tempting to describe a contest among Mentalists. Platonism in the contemporary sense of human-independent meanings in a "third realm" was essentially unheard of. And thoroughgoing Physicalism was rare. Being staunch Materialists, the Epicureans had to reject any role for the mental, and for the abstract, but this approach had little sway. (See Cameron's chapter on the Stoics for more.) A radical departure from this consensus appears with Valla, and re-emerges with Reid and Herder. As explained in the chapters by Nauta, Forster, and Rysiew, one begins to find the idea, reminiscent to a degree of Ordinary Language Philosophy, that meanings are not "things", either inside the mind or in the third realm, but are instead quotidian social action-potentials.

Having canvassed examples of the four broad categories, we turn now to exploring sub-varieties of linguistic content within the history of philosophy of language. Rather than trying to flag every place in which the topic arises in the chapters that follow, we will focus on three innovative varieties: propositions, syncategoremata, and use-theoretic contents.

At the risk of embracing an overarching narrative of philosophical advancement, there is a tale to be told about a progressive move away from a name-centred theory of linguistic contents. The obvious initial view, possibly not held in all seriousness by anyone, is what has become known as the 'Fido'–Fido theory, according to which every word stands for an object. (This is the view Wittgenstein targets at the start of his *Philosophical Investigations*.)

A very first insight into the varieties of linguistic contents is that not all words work this way. Put otherwise, the insight is that there *are* varieties. The recognition that languages have, roughly speaking, both names and predicates was, of course, already present in Ancient Greece. A closely related insight, but one that is nonetheless more hard won, is that these distinct parts—the Greek's *onomata* and *rhemata*—can sometimes come together to form a unity. *Rhemata* can blend with *onomata*, to yield something complete, namely the complex sentence—so that there is a difference between, for example, a list consisting of the name 'Theaetetus' and the predicate 'flies', and the sentence 'Theaetetus flies'. As Francesco Ademollo explains, Plato addresses this mystifying union in the *Sophist*. Deeper still, though merely a glimmer in Ancient Greek philosophy, is the idea of a meaning-glue (rather than just a name–predicate glue), and a meaning-complex (rather than just a name–predicate complex). Aristotle's fascinating take on this, argues Ademollo, involves time. Crudely put, the meaning-complex, which we would now call a proposition or a state of affairs, is a matter of something-now-holding. The *onomata* and *rhemata* jointly contribute the something-which-may-hold. That which joins these expressions together, namely tense, provides that crucial "now" as meaning-glue.

This line of thought comes to fruition, as Margaret Cameron explains, in the Stoics. They stress the notion of the sayable—which, importantly, is mind-independent yet is not a Platonic Form, consonant with their deflationary metaphysics. Cameron also describes how the same notion re-emerged independently with Abelard, who shared many Stoicist motivations.

Denying that predicates are names for (peculiar) objects, for example, Forms outside space and time, and instead have a *sui generis* variety of linguistic content, represents a crucial step away from the 'Fido'–Fido picture. Greater progress still is to recognize meaningful expressions that simply do not have meaning-relata—to recognize, that is, syncategoremata such as 'if', 'or', 'only', and 'necessarily'. Spruyt and Novaes survey and contrast medieval accounts of these "funny words". They do not stand for anything. Yet, as they stress, syncategoremata cannot be dispensed with, since they are absolutely crucial to argumentation (for example, because of the logical connectives) and to metaphysics (for example, because of the meaning of modals like 'necessarily'). As they explain, in making sense of these words, the medieval tradition built on the Aristotelian theory of meaning. When combined with the idea of an entire mental language, of the sort mentioned above, an ingenious new option opens up. Unlike names or predicates, 'or' and 'if' cannot correspond to ideas that then represent some external thing. Indeed, 'or' does not seem to be a symbol of any "affections or impressions". However, syncategoremata can correspond to mental operations/processes on the *lingua mentis*. In fact, they are mental acts rather than mental items. A final innovation is underscored by Hill. According to him, Locke treats mixed modes as a *sui generis* kind of linguistic content, a sort of meaning-idea unlike any other in terms of how simple ideas get combined therein. Specifically, it is the attachment of a name to a complex cluster of ideas of various sorts that *creates* a meaning!

In sum, the texts and figures discussed in this volume represent a wide range of answers to Q1. There are differing answers with respect to the broad ontological rubric to which meanings belong: abstracta in Plato, mental representations (at least in the first instance) in Locke and Ockham, physical entities in the Stoics, uses in Valla, Herder, and Reid. And, with respect to the sub-varieties, one can see progressive richness and diversity across time, for example, with the addition of special meanings for predicates, declarative sentences, and logical connectives.

## 4. Q2 and the History of Philosophy of Language

In Section 2 we encountered three choice points with respect to the origins/grounding of meaning facts:

- direct or indirect?
- natural or conventional?
- resemblance, cause, or use?

We now revisit these with an eye to history.

Our discussion has already made clear that very many figures, taking off from Aristotle, endorse an indirect link between public words and external things. The immediately mental/derivatively external approach can be found from al-Farabi and Ibn Adi, to Ockham, to Locke. (See the contributions by Adamson and Key, Klima, and Hill respectively.) Starkly contrasted to it, is that associated with Plato's *Cratylus*. Plato's view there seems to be that linguistic sounds are directly correlated to external things.

Plato is also usually cast as a proponent of a natural connection between linguistic sound and linguistic content. However, as is by now well known, this misses the nuances and complexities of Plato's view. At a minimum, Plato supposed that an ideal language should work like this, and that actual spoken languages had degenerated from this ideal. Deborah Modrak presses the complexities and nuances still further, proposing that there are actually two contrasting notions of metasemantic grounding in Plato. There is a normative, prescriptive issue, which pertains to what words are "groping for" in their confused way—that is, to true underlying natures rather than mere appearances. What grounds the latter transcends humans, and it is this latter that involves resemblance. On the other hand, there is a descriptive issue, which pertains to the superficially observable meanings of words, found in ordinary, confused usage. These kinds of semantic facts are grounded by actual talk and convention. (As Modrak stresses, it is essential to contrast these twin notions, because the latter is a very poor tool for the philosopher: one might say that it is the linguistic counterpart of sensory observation. And she paints Plato's evolving philosophical methodologies across the *Phaedo*, *Sophist*, and *Thaetetus* as diverse attempts to bypass the superficial/conventional/descriptive, to arrive instead at the underlying/natural/prescriptive.)

One might also propose, with some reason, that philosophers like Ockham embrace a natural connection too, this time between mental representations and their denotations—the connection being natural because it rests on brute world-to-idea causation. Contrast this, for instance, with the Lockean idea that certain meanings have to be created by the active powers of the human mind: that the world, acting on its own, cannot furnish such ideas.

Speaking of causation, consider the resemblance–cause–use choice point. The former two have been illustrated already, by Plato on the one hand, at least with respect to "ideal" grounding, and by Ockham et al. on the other. We have also flagged several use theorists: As Lodi Nauta explains, Valla happily grounded meaning in nothing more than custom of usage. So did Herder—though, both of them recognized that, in some cases, it is how a word ought to be used that gives it its meaning. What is more, not all uses are of equal weight: for example, the *hoi polloi* do not fix the meaning of specialized terms within a genre, and contemporary vulgar usage does not fix what Latin words meant in Ancient Rome.

The most pervasive position of all is some kind of hybrid among the options canvassed above. Most salient here is Aristotle. Unpacking the quotation from *De interpretatione*, Aristotle brought to light three stages for metasemantics:

Written Words ▶ Spoken Words ▶ Affections/Impressions of the Soul ▶ External Objects

His view, taking these from right to left, was that the mental impressions represent external objects by means of likeness. The former are, in a sense proprietary to Aristotle's hylomorphic conception of the soul, copies of the latter. The connection is natural, rather than conventional, and is to be found across humankind. Spoken words are then signs, in the first instance, of these impressions, and only derivatively signs of the corresponding external objects. This connection, being highly variable, cannot be natural, but must rather be conventional. Presumably, then, it does not involve resemblance (though what it does involve is left unsaid). At the final step, written words are signs of spoken words. What more basic facts ground this connection is also left open, but, given that Greek orthography was not the only possible one, Aristotle might easily have supposed it to be non-natural. Putting this all together, and continuing with our prior example, the written words (as we might have it, the orthographic forms) 'cow', 'agelada', and 'vaca' signify the spoken words (presumably, as we would now put it, the linguistic sounds) /cow/, /agelada/, and /vaca/ respectively. These are all "primarily" signs of cow, the mental symbol. The semantic object of the latter is the animal itself.

Reid's position was a sophisticated hybrid as well, as Patrick Rysiew explains. Reid agrees with Plato, and with Aristotle, that there is an important role for "natural signs". But what Reid has in mind are not internal images that naturally stand for externalia (consonant with his rejection of the way of ideas), nor sounds that are somehow like what they mean, but rather "natural signs" like facial expressions and automatic gestures. These, for Reid, play a role in grounding what he terms artificial languages, like English: the former allow us, by a process of bootstrapping, to enter into social compacts or agreements about the conventional signs of spoken tongues. Precisely this, by the way, allows Reid to provide a metaphysical grounding for the meaning of general terms without appealing to "general ideas" as an intermediary (the latter being anathema, as they were for Berkeley).

Finally, Cesalli's article introduces a twist on the use-theoretic grounding story that will be familiar to contemporary readers. For Marty, what makes 'Cows moo' mean what it does is, very roughly, that it is used *to induce the belief* that cows moo. Thus, anticipating Grice, Marty took the mental to be an intermediary, but in a very different way from "the way of Ideas".

## 5. Chapter Summaries

**Deborah Modrak** looks at the different ways that Plato investigates what words mean and how they should mean. Plato's project is both descriptive and prescriptive, and throughout his dialogues he explores the ways in which linguistic meanings can and should express the true natures of the things they name, even though they fail at their task. Beginning with the *Phaedo* Modrak identifies a process of determining linguistic meaning similar to the Socratic method of prompting a variety of 'ambiguous and confused linguistic definitions' among his interlocutors to find the correct (that is, normative) one. The quest for an explanation for the correctness of names is taken up explicitly in *Cratylus*, where the etymologies of names are explored for their descriptive content, and 'correctness of a name is a function of its describing the intended referent correctly'. But Socrates and his interlocutors encounter a problem—a recurring problem, as it turns out—that words or even word-parts (which Plato considers to have a certain meaningfulness) for things in the sublunary world with changing natures fail to get a 'linguistic fix' on reality. Modrak identifies in *Sophist* that the new method for ascertaining definitions by means of division provides a sort of improvement, since the method of division along generic and specific lines provides a 'conceptual framework in which to comprehend the actual nature' of a thing, and this gives a better ontological footing for linguistic meaning than that 'implied by ordinary language'. Finally, in *Thaetetus*, in which there is a long (and unresolved) investigation of the nature of knowledge and belief, it once again emerges that, given the instability of perceivable objects by which we come to many of our beliefs, language turns out to be inadequate to the task of fixing the natures of potential objects of knowledge. In the end, it seems that for Plato words do not achieve what they should, which is to express reality as it is. Modrak is aware that contemporary philosophers might not recognize their interests in linguistic meaning in Plato's philosophy, although she rightly points out that the differences are not so great after all: there remains a driving interest in achieving conceptual clarity by means of linguistic analysis. But, whereas Plato begins with ordinary words and tries to find in their meanings the expression of transcendent reality (that is, the Forms), 'the modern solution is to stipulate meanings and then in light of the stipulated meaning determine the reference of the term'. It is a difference of starting point, but not of overall aim.

**Francesco Ademollo** starts out examining Plato's and Aristotle's claim—whose interpretation is controversial—that there are two kinds of basic components of a simple declarative sentence, *onoma* and *rhema*. He argues that in both authors these are primarily two distinct word-classes, 'name' and 'verb', but that, from Plato's *Cratylus* to his *Sophist*, and from this to Aristotle's *De interpretatione*, we can trace the emergence and refinement of the notion that these two word-classes play different syntactic roles and that, in particular, part of the function of verbs is to signify predication. Ademollo also shows how in the *Sophist* this idea carries with it another, connected one—namely that a sentence has a signification of its own over and above that of its components, and how in Aristotle this might take the form of a glimmer of recognition that what is signified by a sentence is a propositional item. The post-Aristotelian aftermath of this recognition, Ademollo suggests, must have been 'momentous'. One piece of that aftermath is preserved in the writings of the Stoics, taken up in the next chapter.

**Margaret Cameron** takes up this new type of meaning—propositional meaning— in the Stoics and Peter Abelard (1079–1142). Abelard developed a theory of propositional meaning without, apparently, access to the work of the ancient Stoics, and while working strictly within an Aristotelian logical context. Both the Stoics and Abelard introduce the notion of a 'sayable', a kind of content that is mind-independent and has as its meaning some sort of state of affairs or way things are. Cameron's chapter outlines the ways in which the Stoic theory might have evolved out of a critical response to Plato's philosophy, since the Stoics seemed adamant to eschew the view that linguistic meanings are Platonic Forms. Abelard introduces the idea that sayables are the content of what is said by spoken utterances, and they correspond and are made true by what he calls *status*, or ways that things are according to their natures (or, as God made them). Both the Stoics and Abelard restrict their focus to natural kind terms, and both seem to have been motivated by a desire for a deflationary metaphysics.

**Peter Adamson and Alexander Key** present, through a vivid retelling and reconstruction of a debate between a tenth-century Arabic philosopher (a logician) and a traditional Arabic grammarian, the site of encounter, conflict, and resolution between two traditions. Although the traditions seem on the surface to hold two different theories of linguistic content (a bipartite theory from grammar, and a tripartite theory from Aristotelian logic), the authors show that at root the two traditions are not in such conflict, and in fact share many of the same features. The Arabic grammatical tradition was deeply suspicious of Greek philosophy, regarding logic as a foreign tool, subject to the conventions of the Greek language; but these were complaints of a cultural sort. The deeper criticism was that, by prioritizing the mental over the verbal, the logical analysis of language was unprepared to deal with problems of polysemy and synonymy, and the grammarians urged that only a greater attention paid to the art of eloquence could properly capture the relation between what we think and what we say. In response to the public debate over this issue, which portrays that the philosophers lost the argument, philosophers such as al-Farabi and Ibn Adi redescribed the mental content associated with spoken language in terms of its being a kind of mental language, a 'discourse' (along the lines described by Plato) that is not in any particular language. But what continued to drive debate between these two traditions was, at base, the competing claims to truth: the logicians believed that logic was the path to divine understanding, whereas the grammarians insisted that hermeneutics, the poetical interpretation of revealed Scripture, was the only way. For the latter, context and linguistic interpretation were paramount. Adamson and Key explain that, in the end, it was the work of the great logician Avicenna who provided the means for the two traditions to begin to coalesce, and he did so by constructing an Arabic, as opposed to an Aristotelian (Greek), logic; Avicennian logic was then reapplied back to poetics and literary theory.

There are particular sorts of words that do not seem to have their own linguistic content. **Joke Spruyt and Catarina Dutilh Novaes** take up this issue in their chapter on the medieval study of syncategorematic terms, such as 'if', 'because', 'or', 'only', and 'necessarily'. Medieval authors were keenly interested in these sorts of terms, not just because of their role in argumentation and the study of fallacies, but also because of deeper metaphysical concerns (such as how modal terms such as 'necessarily' and 'contingently' function, or what 'one' means in the sentence 'Only one is'). Syncategoremata are difficult to characterize, and little help on this front is given by medieval thinkers themselves. Logically, they do not have complete signification, but in some way or other rely on their combination with other meaningful terms to function. Grammatically, they cannot be used as either the subjects or the predicates of sentences. Some logicians described syncategoremata as 'affects of the intellect', such as 'if', which is not itself a concept, but instead functions to order components such that one follows another (for example, 'If Socrates is running, he is moving'). Syncategoremata are tracked into the tradition, beginning in the fourteenth century, of mental language, in which they are considered to be mental 'acts and operations'. Spruyt and Dutilh Novaes consider, but then reject, the suggestion from others that syncategoremata can be thought of as logical constants. While there is a widespread belief that the boundaries of logic are demarcated by the class of logical constants, the authors explain that this cannot be how syncategoremata were considered: what was considered 'logic' in the Middle Ages was far more expansive than it is today (including, for example, epistemology), and there were different senses in which logic was thought to be formal.

In the wake of contemporary turns to externalist theories of mind and language, historians of philosophy have re-evaluated philosophical theories of linguistic content from the past. Motivated in part by the frequent mischaracterization of most pre-twentieth-century theories as 'internalist', locating linguistic content somehow 'in the head', scholars point to philosophers such as the fourteenth-century Franciscan philosopher William of Ockham (c.1287–1347), who seem to have certain externalist commitments about linguistic (and mental) content. **Gyula Klima**'s 'Semantic Content in Aquinas and Ockham' elaborates upon this characterization of Ockham, first given by historian of philosophy Claude Panaccio. If Ockham is a semantic externalist, then Thomas Aquinas (1225–74)—and a host of philosophers before him—ought to be characterized as 'hyper-externalists'. To elucidate this characterization and to compare it to the nominalist-variety of externalism espoused by Ockham, Klima examines how these thinkers explain the relation between concepts and their objects. Klima argues that it was an Ockham-style nominalism about semantic externalism that rendered possible the 'Demon scepticism' famously entertained by Descartes.

**Lodi Nauta**'s chapter focuses on the linguistic views of Lorenzo Valla (c.1406–57), the great Renaissance humanist, and in addition provides a broad characterization of the humanists' approach to language and meaning. Along the way, Nauta helpfully corrects the over-embellished comparison of Valla to various contemporary movements in the philosophy of language, while carefully noting points on which they do bear comparison. Nauta explains that, for Valla, it is linguistic *custom* that grounds meaning: he explains, 'linguistic usage should sanction the rules of grammar and the meaning of words'. Valla's emphasis on ordinary usage of language is meant in part as a contrast to the Scholastic tradition of philosophy of language grounded in Aristotelian logic, specifically the *Categories*, in which terminology is taken out of its usual context and grossly adulterated. Valla's ordinary language was Latin, which might strike us as a strange choice on which to base his common-sense ontology. But the Latin Valla endorsed was not the language of the elite and educated, nor the garbled Latin of the Scholastics, but the language as it was spoken by ancient Romans, which Valla attempted to recover by his study of ancient texts. For Valla, using Latin as a vernacular also provided him with a powerful interpretative and critical tool 'for sifting spurious from authentic works and forgeries from real documents, and hence a weapon for attacking established philosophical and theological dogmas and practices', as Nauta shows. Linguistic study was practical, not theoretical, and it is interesting in so far as it represents a movement towards the social and pragmatic use of language.

For most of the history of philosophy, philosophers did not talk about *meaning* or *linguistic content*, but about *signification*. As E. Jennifer Ashworth reminds us in 'Medieval Theories of Signification to John Locke', to signify cannot readily be explained in terms of modern theories of meaning. Ashworth spends time in this chapter usefully examining the texts that help illuminate what philosophers meant by 'signification'. Signification is a property of a word, best characterized as a psychocausal property in so far as it gives rise to some understanding. For example, as the fourteenth-century Peter of Ailly clearly states, 'to signify is to represent something, or some things, or in some way to a cognitive power by vitally changing it'. Ashworth takes us through the variety of theories of signification espoused by Thomist-inspired realists, nominalists, and other eclectic thinkers from the period before Locke. These thinkers enquired how humans first came to use spoken language, which they recognized to be an instrument for communication. Names are imposed on things in some way or another, they held, but how did this happen? The conventionality of spoken and written language was recognized by all those following the lesson given in Aristotle's so-called semantic triad, although Ashworth spends time to clarify that the imposition of names *ad placitum* is not helpfully translated as 'conventional imposition', but rather in terms of the imposition being agreeable, given that in the Aristotelian triad concepts are taken to be 'the same for all' (even if the spoken and written words vary from culture to culture). On this former point, as is well known, Locke expressed disagreement. Ashworth then carefully examines the philosophical views of Aquinas, Ockham, John Buridan (1295/1300–1358/61), and a host of (to us) lesser-known but influential Scholastic thinkers such as Domingo de Soto (1494–1560) and Martinus Smiglecius (1564–1618), on the three elements of Aristotle's triad: the concept, the thing, and the relation between the concept, thing, and name. Philosophical trends in theories of signification during this period can be distinguished according to the variety of ways the relata of the semantic triad were organized.

**Benjamin Hill**'s chapter takes up the topic of John Locke's (1632–1704) naming of modes (simple and mixed), and more specifically the naming of our ideas of modes. What modes are for Locke is a subject for considerable discussion—since he includes contemplation, dreaming, love, murder, jealousy, running, habit, and many others not so obviously related to one another—but at root they can be distinguished from substances, which enjoy independent existence, because of their dependent status. Hill begins with Locke's metaphorical explanation of how modes exist: 'in mixed Modes 'tis the Name that ties the Combination together, and makes it a Species.' To understand what Locke means, Hill pursues the thesis that Locke is here creating a 'brand-new kind of linguistic act', according to which the act of naming in fact *creates* the very idea of a mode. Modes, unlike qualities, do not inhere in substance, and thus their unity needs explanation. For example, what unifies the mixed mode Beauty, itself compounded out of the simple ideas of colour, figure, plus the relation of causing a perceiver's delight? Hill proposes that it is the activity of naming—that is, the linguistic act. But Locke's writing is ambiguous, and Hill finds support for the expression of two readings of this thesis: the mental reading (MR) and the linguistic reading (LR). The former is supported by texts in which Locke suggests that the mind first unites the various simple ideas under a single cognition, which is then named; the latter by texts suggesting that the linguistic activity of naming is what generates the very idea of the mode. The priority of naming over cognizing—a feature of later theories of meaning—is thus (first?) presented by Locke to account for the ideas of mixed modes. These ideas then play a regulative or archetypal function, regulating predications and property attributions, via the normative, conventional use of names.

According to **Michael Forster**, it is J. G. Herder (1744–1803) who makes the first explicit commitment to the doctrine that meaning is use. Forster's chapter provides a history of the development of this idea within the German tradition, beginning with Herder and extending through to L. Wittgenstein. Although there is the suggestion of a historical connection between Herder and Wittgenstein, Forster is primarily interested in the motivations that were driving this doctrine of meaning. Although Herder never explicitly justifies this doctrine, he is, according to Forster, emphatic about what meaning is *not*: it is not the referent of a name, nor a Platonic Form, nor a subjective mental 'idea'. Forster outlines possible sources of inspiration for Herder, including Spinoza and Ernesti, and tracks the development of the doctrine in the work of his successors. Although there is no single doctrine according to which meaning is use, Forster wonders whether it is possible to determine which of them is the best version to hold. To answer this question, Forster takes up four topics: a comparison of an atomistic versus a holistic version of the doctrine, the role and character of rules of usage, the role of society in constituting meaning, and the role of psychological processes. In the end, Forster prefers the less theoretically developed but, to his mind, the more plausible version of the doctrine found in Herder.

**Patrick Rysiew** takes on another philosopher whose work has been characterized as anticipating a number of movements in contemporary philosophy of language, Thomas Reid (1710–96). Rysiew tempers the comparison somewhat by emphasizing that Reid's interest was primarily in understanding the human mind, and his interest in language was in service of that goal. Reid's philosophy of language is pragmatic and, like Valla's, focused on the use of terms in their ordinary acceptation. Famously, Reid denied the prevailing theory of ideas, and his theory of meaning needed to be consistent with the denial of ideas. To do so, Reid observes that different languages share many common features, which leads him to recognize a kind of universality underlying linguistic use. He takes up a sign theory, or semiotics, akin to that used by

Augustine, in which natural language is distinguished from artificial language. The 'natural language of mankind', for Reid, is immediately understood by all humans and includes facial expressions, gestures, and the like. These natural signs permit other forms of communication, since they provide the compact or agreement that enables the development of artificial signs, consisting of spoken, conventional languages. Reid's great achievement, according to Rysiew, was his recognition of the social operations of mind and the linguistic expressions of them. This allowed Reid, as Rysiew argues, to account for the meaningfulness of general terms: since Reid denies there are general ideas (since he denies there are ideas), he instead accounts for them in terms of being the result of a 'social process' by which we learn from others 'how to indicate to others our recognition of the fact that attributes are common to multiple objects'.

**Laurent Cesalli**'s chapter on Anton Marty (1847–1914) is an absorbing one for a number of reasons. Marty was active just before G. Frege, taken to be the 'father of linguistic philosophy' by many. Perhaps for this reason, Marty and other members of the phenomenological tradition were eclipsed. But their work reaches back to the rich Scholastic tradition of philosophy of language to generate a new theory of meaning based on speaker meaning. Although this tradition exploits the technical terminology of Scholasticism, its primary interest in that period seems to have been its focus on spoken language as a means of communication. Language is, Marty thought, essentially spoken, and can be understood only 'as a specific type of human action'. Language is not a 'natural, spontaneous emanation of the mind', but rather a *conscious* process of language formation with the goal to communicate (an 'empirico-teleological' conception of language, according to Cesalli). As it is for H. P. Grice, Marty's theory of meaning is rooted in intentions, and what is meant is what the speaker intended. Cesalli helpfully explains some of the technical distinctions in Marty's philosophy of language, while connecting this theory of meaning both to the past and to contemporary theories.

# 1

# Method, Meaning, and Ontology in Plato's Philosophy of Language

*Deborah Modrak*

Many of the texts presenting Plato's theory of ideas in its canonical form begin with a discussion of what we mean when we use words such as 'beauty' or 'good' or 'equal' and end in arguments for ideal exemplars of the attributes under discussion. Semantic considerations not only drive the ontology of forms in the middle period dialogues but also play an important role in Plato's later, critical writings. The importance of having an adequate account of linguistic meaning is evident in Plato's deliberations about ontology and knowledge throughout his career. This will be an attempt to sketch his evolving conception of meaning and its role in his larger project of identifying the metaphysical grounds of meaning and knowledge.

From the Socratic dialogues on, Plato underscores the importance of clearly defined concepts for meaning and explanation. The concepts to be defined are linguistic, but ordinary language definitions are repeatedly found wanting. Socratic elenchus establishes the need for more satisfactory definitions. It is devastatingly effective in showing what is wrong with accepted definitions of moral concepts. As a philosophical method, elenchus proves inadequate for discovering definitions of the right sort. The search for philosophically perspicuous definitions and the failure of elenchus to discover them prompts Plato to look to transcendent, ideal objects (Forms) to furnish satisfactory definitions. Besides also trying out and rejecting traditional philological analysis, Plato later develops a method of conceptual analysis—namely, the method of division—as a tool for clarifying concepts and determining whether a definition is adequate.

To generalize, Plato makes certain normative assumptions about definition, which he then applies to linguistic definitions and the ontology presupposed by ordinary language. The outcome for Plato is a two-tiered account of definition and reference. The first tier consists of names and senses as expressed in linguistic definitions and the referents of words; the second tier consists of the same names and their philosophically adequate definitions, which modify the ordinary senses of the words, ideal exemplars as the primary referents of the names and ordinary objects (that is, those the words are typically taken to refer to) as the secondary referents of the names.

## Socratic Definitions

Moral concepts and the problematic character of the accepted linguistic definitions of moral terms are topics that Socrates explored on the streets of Athens. Plato's early dialogues paint a vivid picture of Socrates' practice of elenchus, which is a dialectical method for scrutinizing the beliefs of the person to whom Socrates is speaking. As presented by Plato, Socrates typically began by querying his interlocutor with a disarmingly simple question: "What is virtue <justice, courage, moderation, etc.>?" Socrates would then ask a series of questions about the implications of the answer. These questions would often reveal inconsistencies in the interlocutor's beliefs and thus undermine the cogency of their position or the proffered answer would be rejected because it failed to meet some other criterion such as unity.[1]

MENO: ...If you want the virtue of a man, it is easy to say that a man's virtue consists of being able to manage public affairs and in so doing to benefit his friends and harm his enemies... There is a virtue for every action and every age, for every task of ours and every one of us... SOCRATES: I seem to be in great luck, Meno; while I am looking for one virtue, I have found you to have a whole swarm of them. (*Meno* 71e–72a)

Not only are answers rejected because they provide lists instead of precisely formulated statements of the nature of the entity being defined, but Socrates also rejects answers that admit of counter-examples. In *Republic* I, Cephalus' common-sense definition of justice as speaking the truth and paying one's debts is rejected on the basis of a hypothetical example. It would not be just, Socrates and Cephalus agree, to return weapons to a friend who has gone mad or to tell him the whole truth (*Rep.* 331c). Yet another criterion of definition is introduced in the *Euthyphro*, when Socrates argues that, even if the pious is always god-loved, being god-loved does not provide an adequate account of piety (9e–11a). The characteristic of being god-loved does not capture the essence of piety, because it does not explain why the gods love piety. In this instance, even a simple, unified definition that holds of all and only instances of piety is rejected on the grounds of a failure of explanatory adequacy.[2]

Taking the Socratic dialogues all together, it seems clear that Socratic elenchus proceeds in accordance with several implicit criteria of definition.[3] A definition will be rejected if it fails to apply to all and only instances of the concept in question; a definition will also be rejected if it lacks unity and simplicity or it fails to capture the

---

[1] For instance, at *Laches* 190d–e the question 'what is courage?' is initially posed; by 194b Laches has given up his attempt to give an answer that meets Socrates' objections and at 200b Nicias also gives up in frustration; at *Charmides* 159a the question 'what is moderation?' is posed and at 162b Charmides, who has given three answers, all of which have been shown to be inadequate, gives up.

[2] See Cohen (1971).

[3] Dancy (2006) identifies three conditions of Socratic definition that are met by Forms—namely, substitutivity, the paradigm requirement, and the explanatory requirement.

essential nature of its object. It seems likely that Plato develops his mature metaphysics with an eye to conceptualizing basic objects that could ground definitions of moral terms and do so in a way that would meet Socrates' criteria for adequacy. Socratic elenchus implicitly distinguishes between the linguistic definition of a moral term and a philosophically perspicuous one; the latter but not the former expresses knowledge of the concept in question.[4] A philosophically perspicuous definition is one that meets the Socratic criteria of definition by providing a precise account of the object of the definition that captures its essence. Because it articulates the essence, the definition will pick out only appropriate referents of the concept properly understood. A philosophically perspicuous definition is prescriptive as well as descriptive; it provides a basis for criticizing the corresponding linguistic definition(s).[5] Plato agrees with Socrates about the importance of possessing a perspicuous definition and about the criteria an adequate definition must meet. He develops a metaphysics that will provide the right kind of objects for definition—ones that will yield perspicuous definitions of moral terms. Ideal objects, which are independent of human minds but are grasped by them, are uniquely singular, completely unified, and are just what they are. Plato emphasizes the contrast between the Ideal and the sensible particulars that possess the characteristic in question. There is only one form of Beauty but there are many beautiful things. Beauty Itself does not admit the not-beautiful, but beautiful things do because they are not beautiful in every respect at every time. Plato's resolution of the problem posed by Socrates' failure to reach perspicuous definitions expressing knowledge is to stop trying to find such definitions in the physical world but to look for them in an ideal realm. In order to define beauty in a way that would meet the Socratic criteria for definition, Plato posits an ideal exemplar to Beauty to ground the definition of 'beauty'. Since the content of the perspicuous definition of beauty expresses the nature of Beauty Itself, it would be insulated from the vicissitudes of the sensible objects to which the word 'beauty' applies.

## Plato's Solution: Theory of Ideas

In the *Symposium*, Plato describes the mind's ascent to a cognitive grasp of Beauty Itself. The description is given in a speech by Diotima, who is instructing Socrates on the nature of love. She introduces her topic by making a point about how we use the word *eros*.

Why don't we say that everyone is in love?... It is because we divide out a special kind of love, and we refer to it by the word that means the whole, love, and for the other kinds of love we use other words... Out of the whole of poetry we have marked off one part, the part the Muses give us with melody and rhythm, and we refer to this by the word that means the whole. For this

---

[4] Robinson (1971: ch. 6).
[5] For the sake of brevity, a philosophically perspicuous definition will be called a perspicuous definition in this chapter.

alone is called 'poetry'... That's also how it is with love. The main point is this: every desire for good things or for happiness is 'the supreme and treacherous love' in everyone. But those who pursue this along any of its many other ways... we don't say that these people are in love and we don't call them lovers. It is only when people are devoted exclusively to one special kind of love that we use these words that really belong to the whole of it. (*Symposium* 205b–d)

This discussion of the misuse of language is prompted by Socrates' question why if love is just the desire for happiness we do not describe everyone as in love. In order to gain clarity about the nature of the object, in this instance love, we have to be clear about our use of language. Unless we are clear about how we are using the word 'love' and to what it refers, we cannot even begin an analysis of the emotion. It is also noteworthy that there are two issues on the table—first, the linguistic meaning, that is, how Plato's contemporaries use the word *eros* and its cognates and, second, how the word should be used. It is the latter concern that motivates Plato to posit ideal exemplars to ground the meanings of our terms and thus enable us to use words in an epistemically perspicuous manner.

Later in her speech Diotima says that all beautiful things participate in Beauty Itself (211b). This makes the possession of beauty a function of the object's standing in a particular relation to the form of beauty. The object's beauty falls short of the form of Beauty, which is beauty "itself by itself with itself and single in form existing always [*auto kath' hauto meth' hautou moneides aei on*]" (211b). Many factors contribute to this failure; the object is typically beautiful only for a certain finite period of time; the object may be beautiful from one perspective but not from another; or its beauty may be qualified in some other respect.[6] Because the character of beauty as instantiated by objects in the physical world is subject to a number of liabilities, the linguistic meaning of *kalos* (beautiful) in both its adjectival use and its substantive use, *to kalon* (beauty), is hard to pin down and must be such that a number of different instances are covered. The criteria for the correct use of *kalos* seem to include many diverse factors. The considerations prompting the description of a sculpture as beautiful are not the same as those prompting the description of a chorus as beautiful. Although linguistic meanings may provide an adequate basis for everyday communication, they fall short (Plato believes) as tools for understanding mind-independent natures. They reflect the shifting character of the world as perceived. A term, in order for its use to further understanding, must have a unitary and clearly defined meaning.[7] Intelligibility requires an ontology of unchanging objects, the characteristics of which are captured by perspicuous definitions. This is why the philosopher, the lover of truth, cannot simply rely on ordinary language but should attempt to bring the meanings of our terms closer to the realities they

---

[6] This is not intended to be an exhaustive list of the factors that apply in the case of beauty and that distinguish the instantiations of beauty in the observable world from the Form.

[7] Cf. Socrates' insistence that an adequate definition of a moral concept be unity and basic (*Charmides* 161d–162b; *Meno* 71e–72a; *Euthyphro* 6d–e).

primarily represent. Diotima proposes a strategy for getting clear on the nature of beauty, the object of love, that involves a cognitive ascent through more and more truly beautiful objects, from bodies to souls to activities and laws and customs, to forms of knowledge, to the apprehension of Beauty in itself. At every stage, the lover of beauty clarifies her conception of beauty and this clarification serves as a corrective for how she uses the term *kalos*.

The importance of the clarification of the concept of beauty becomes even clearer in *Republic* V. Two types of cognitive enquiry are distinguished there: philosophy, the love of wisdom, and aesthetic appreciation, the love of sights and sounds (475c–480a). In both cases, the love of beauty motivates the search for and study of appropriate objects. The aesthete, however, confuses manifestations of beauty with Beauty Itself (476b). This confusion undermines the search for beauty and makes it impossible for the aesthete to have knowledge of the beautiful. The philosopher, by contrast, recognizes the limitations of beauty as instantiated in external objects and strives to comprehend beauty as it is in itself. The philosopher grasps something that always is, whereas the aesthete attempts to hold on to something that is always becoming.

Putting the two texts together, it is clear that for Plato, if there is a genuine nature to be grasped of beauty or anything else, it must be single, unified, and actual.[8] This is the object to which the term in question primarily refers, even if we confusedly misuse the term, attributing a variety of meanings to it, and conflate its secondary reference to objects in the sensible realm with its primary reference to an ideal object. Its proper meaning just is the nature that is grasped when the mind comprehends beauty as it is in itself.

Sometimes the process of unpacking a meaning involves the recognition that the way in which we employ a term implies that we possess concepts (meanings) that we could not have derived from experience. As part of an argument in the *Phaedo* to establish that the soul exists before it becomes embodied, Socrates appeals to the doctrine of recollection and offers as a proof of it our conception of Equality in itself. He argues that the concept of Equality is such that, when we perceive that two sensible objects are equal, we recognize that these objects aim at but fall short of instantiating perfect equality. This establishes that we are able to employ a concept of Equality that we could not have derived from the experience of perceptible instances of equality. The concept of perfect equality is evident in how we categorize our experience but must be brought by the mind to the experience. Although the concept of Equality Itself is initially grasped by the mind before embodiment, the active knowledge of it in this life requires effort and dialectical investigation (75d).

In the *Phaedo*, perception prompts the recollection of the normative concept. In *Republic* VI and VII, the mind's progression from perceptible to intelligible objects is

---

[8] Plato frequently emphasizes the reality of the Ideas; similarly, in the Socratic dialogues, Socrates is portrayed as getting the agreement of the interlocutor that the object under discussion (e.g. virtue) is something real. See, e.g., *Protagoras* 330c.

described in a series of contexts. First Socrates draws a line in the sand and divides it into sensible and intelligible realms in which cognitive states are paired with their objects; imagination with images and so forth (509d–513e). These stages are portrayed far more vividly in the image of a cave with prisoners reduced to looking only at shadows on the wall (514a–517c). This is followed by a detailed account of the education of the philosopher rulers; the goal of the educational programme is to enable successful students to grasp the highest and most intelligible objects. Although definition is not the primary focus of this discussion, what enables the mind to progress is its grasping ever more abstract concepts. When one crosses the line between perceptible and intelligible objects, one is *ipso facto* crossing the line between linguistic definitions that express the varying natures of sensible objects to accounts expressing the essences of invariant objects. The transition in each case is from the shadowy representations of inherently unstable objects, the many, to the clear representation of a single, fixed object.

Doesn't each <sense> rather do the following: The sense set over the hard is, in the first place, of necessity also set over the soft, and it reports to the soul that the same thing is perceived by it to be both hard and soft?... And isn't it necessary that in such cases the soul is puzzled as to what this sense means [*semainei*] by the hard, if it indicates that the same thing is also soft, or what it means by the light and the heavy, if it indicates that the heavy is light, or the light, heavy? (*Rep.* 523e–524a)

When the mind is confronted by such perplexing perceptual reports, it is prompted (Plato believes) to ponder the nature of the characteristic in its own right: what is the hard? the soft? The mind seeks to conceive hardness in a way that is unlike its sensible manifestations. If a thinker is successful in this effort, she arrives at a conception of hard that is unitary, is just what hardness is and does not admit softness. In short, the mind has grasped the Hard Itself. This knowledge of the hard is expressed in the perspicuous definition of 'hard' that the thinker is now in a position to articulate. This cognitive process is one that begins with confused perceptions that summon the mind to ponder the characteristics in question, to separate opposites from one another, and ultimately to achieve understanding (*Rep.* 523b–525a). Although Plato does not explore this point, his description of the process is such that it could easily be extended to the case of the mind's confronting ambiguous and confused linguistic definitions such as those offered by Socrates' interlocutors and its being summoned to seek normative definitions of the sort that Socrates sought.

## A Different Strategy in the *Cratylus*

Plato also explores the possibility of grounding meanings not in transcendent ideal objects but in linguistic practice and the relationship between words and physical objects. This task is taken up in the *Cratylus*, which only briefly mentions Forms in the final pages. Prompted by worries about whether names are correct by nature or by convention, Socrates and his interlocutors set out to discover the connection between a word and its referents that ensures that the word is a proper tool for conceptualizing the thing to which it refers. The meaning of the word should be such that it captures the nature of the object. This investigation is carried out primarily with respect to objects in the physical world—words, linguistic meanings, relations between words and physical entities that the word names or describes. Normative considerations are reduced to the requirement that the word be an accurate tool for dividing reality up (389d–390e). A philological strategy for establishing correctness is adopted as appropriate to an enquiry into the correctness of linguistic meanings. Socrates and Hermogenes look to the words themselves for clues about their referents. Initially the discussion seems to follow a standard rhetorical practice, which consists of identifying the descriptive elements in proper names and then considering whether the description fits the referent of the name. For instance, Astyanax, the son of Hector, is correctly named in that the components of his name, *anax* (master) and *asty* (city), are appropriate; Hector is also rightly named because his name means holder (*hector*), an alternative descriptive term for a ruler. It should be noted that this type of philological analysis does not require that each object named have a unique name or that the name have a unique spelling.

Whether the same thing [*to auto*] is expressed in one set of syllables or another makes no difference; and if a letter is added or subtracted, that does not matter either, as long as the essence [*ousia*] of the thing is made clear by the name. (393c–d; cf. 399a)

This principle enables Socrates to give similar explanations of the meanings of synonymous yet phonetically distinct words, while holding on to a notion of correctness that is grounded in the nature of the extra-linguistic world. Because the names of humans are often given for the wrong reasons and thus fail to capture the nature of the bearer of the proper name, Socrates proposes that they turn their attention to eternal natures (397b). This leads to a meandering discussion first of the names of gods, then of the names of daemons, the names of humans and mind and body, and finally a long discussion of the names of deities (397c–408d). This is followed by a discussion of the names of astral bodies, elements, and virtues (408d–421c). Throughout, it is assumed that reference is secured by description; in the etymologies, names are not construed as purely denotative but as also having a descriptive content. The correctness of a name is a function of its describing the intended referent correctly. The discussion ranges over both proper names and common nouns. How proper names refer stands in need of some explanation, because the relationship between a proper noun and its referent appears to be arbitrary. If, instead, the name is a disguised description, there is a non-arbitrary relation between the name and its object. Etymology as practised in the *Cratylus* provides a way to explain how a seemingly arbitrary proper name refers to its object in a systematic way. Having shown that reference is secured by description in the case of proper names, Plato is then in a good position to extend this model to the case of common nouns.

The same strategy is attempted on smaller units than words; it is applied to what Socrates calls the primary names, which are the phonetic units making up a word (422a–427d). The difficulty here is that phonetic units do not appear to be disguised descriptions. However, Socrates argues that they are. The sound describes by imitating its referent. That is, one might say that, while both elements and words are meaningful, the way in which they possess meaning and secure reference is sufficiently different to allow us to distinguish between two levels of meaning bearing objects. Socrates' actual procedure calls into question any distinction of this sort between the two levels.

In this way we, too, shall apply letters to things, using one letter for one thing, when that seems to be needed, or many letters together, making up syllables, as they are called, and from which nouns and verbs are composed. (424e–425a)

Socrates leads Hermogenes in a search for the meanings of the primitive names—that is, what each phonetic element imitates. They begin with *rho* (426c–e). This consonant is expressive of motion because the tongue is particularly active in pronouncing it. Not surprisingly, it is found in many words for motion. After a few examples of this sort, Socrates suggests that all letters could be shown to have imitative characteristics appropriate to their correct use as elements of syllables. In short, a name is correct just in case its elements are such that it fixes reference to the right objects. Since elements indicating motion and change far outnumber those indicating rest, the philological investigation fails to ground meanings on stable objects (436e; cf. 437d).

We must look for something else, not names, which will make plain to us which of these two kinds are the true names, which of them clearly show the truth of things. (438d–e)

This leads to a brief attempt to get behind words and their changeable, physical referents to unchanging ideal objects such as Beauty Itself (439d). If it should turn out that what is, is in a constant state of flux, then the language-user would be unable to express knowledge in words.

Then again it can't even be known by anyone. For at the very instant the knower-to-be approaches, what he is approaching is becoming a different thing, of a different character, so that he can't yet come to know either what sort of thing it is or what it is like (439e–440a; cf. *Theaetetus* 183a–b).

In the end Socrates expresses pessimism about using words to express unchanging natures of the sort required for knowledge (440b–c).[9] The goal of grasping the things

---

[9] While it is possible to read this discussion as a rejection of linguistic representation full stop—i.e. the cognitive grasp of a real nature is ineffable and inexpressible—on balance the textual evidence counts

that are is to ensure that our linguistic concepts fit what is real. Linguistic definitions have been shown to belong to the world of flux, and words with fluctuating meaning cannot be vehicles for truth. The pessimism about linguistic representation expressed in the *Cratylus* is a product of the method used to discover the correct meanings of terms. The philological investigation has revealed the shortcomings of assuming that meanings can be deduced from linguistic tokens. The challenge, however, remains to explain the mind's grasp of realities that are expressible in language but are not created by language. Plato continues to seek ways to test and secure meanings in later dialogues. The *Sophist* discusses the method of division at length as a device for establishing perspicuous definitions. The *Theaetetus* illustrates the limitations of attempting to do epistemology without appealing to the method of division or to the ontology of Forms while equipped only with linguistic definitions and assumptions. The philological method explored in such detail in the *Cratylus* is abandoned and other strategies used in its place, most notably the method of division.

## The Method of Division in the *Sophist*

The *Sophist* is an extended attempt to arrive at a dialectically acceptable definition of the term 'sophist'. The main speaker, the visitor from Elea, calls our attention to the vagueness and ambiguity of the term as used in common parlance.

> Now in this case you and I only have the name in common, and maybe we have used it for a different thing. In every case, though, we always need to be in agreement about the thing itself by means of a verbal explanation [*dia logon*], rather than doing without any such explanation and merely agreeing about the name. (218c)

In order for a discussion to further understanding, any crucial term used in the discussion must be used with the same sense by all speakers. This is a minimal condition, but another and more familiar Platonic requirement is lurking in the wings—that the definition be the one that states what the object referred to by the word is. The Eleatic Visitor then proceeds to demonstrate the method to be employed to determine the correct definition of the term. Owing to the difficulty of answering the 'what is a sophist' question, he first illustrates the method, which we (following Aristotle) call the method of division, using the term 'angler'. The method is one in which the definition of the term is arrived at by finding the most general terms under which it falls, in this instance, art, and then dividing that kind (*genos*) into two types (*eide*), production and acquisition. These in turn are sub-divided into two types, and the process continues until at last one reaches a division that applies uniquely to angling. The definition of the angler's art is:

---

against doing so. At the end of the dialogue Socrates voices reservations about a language that presupposes a Heraclitean ontology, but he makes no attempt to generalize this claim to any language whatsoever (440c–d).

One half <of art> was acquisitive; half of the acquisitive was taking possession; half of possession-taking was hunting; half of hunting was animal-hunting; half of animal-hunting was aquatic hunting; all of the lower portion of aquatic hunting was fishing; half of fishing was hunting by striking; and half of striking was hooking. The part of hooking that involves a blow drawing a thing upward from underneath is called... angling. (221b–c)

At this point, the discussants not only have a name in common but have also agreed about the *logos* (definition) stating what the thing is (221a–b). The *logos* is such that it maps the conceptual relations among the various components of the definition. For instance, angling is but one species of the acquisitive art, which is also true of hunting, but hunting is a more general species. The definition orders the component concepts from most general to most particular. The first attempt to apply this method to the term 'sophist' generates not one but six definitions of the sophist's art. In the same spirit as Socrates' critique of Meno's offering many definitions of virtue, the Visitor rejects the initial definitions of 'sophist' and begins the process anew. In order to complete the division, he is forced to make conceptual space for negation. But, prior to looking at the final perspicuous definition of 'sophist', we should look at the conceptual grid that displays the relations between the first six putative definitions (see Figure 1.1).

The initial steps in this illustration of division are the same as for the angler. Art is divided into productive and acquisitive; acquisitive into conquest and exchange; conquest into (*a*) combative conquest and (*b*) hunting; exchange into selling and an unnamed kind; selling is divided into selling products made by others, which is divided into (*c*) selling wholesale and (*d*) selling retail and (*e*) selling one's own products. It turns out that, when additional suitable specifications are made by further divisions, a clearly recognizable form of sophistry is delineated under each of (*a*)–(*e*). Besides these five definitions, a sixth is found by conducting divisions of types of discrimination (which is presumably a kind falling under the complement of selling). It is clear by the end of this exercise that each of the six definitions is such that it fits historical examples of people called sophists by Plato's contemporaries.[10] These definitions are linguistic definitions that fit common parlance. The method of division has been shown to be a useful tool, if we want to clarify the conceptual relations underlying our use of a particular term.

If our goal is the modest one of better understanding linguistic concepts as found in our language, division correctly used will provide clarity about the meaning and use of a term. Although valuable, increasing our understanding of language as spoken is not enough for Plato, just as it did not satisfy Socrates. The ultimate goal for Plato is a perspicuous definition—that is, one that concisely and precisely expresses a meaning in a way that captures reality. It is the definition of 'sophist' that will apply to all and only genuine sophists. The final division results in a perspicuous definition. It

---

[10] *Pace* Brown (2010), who argues that the multiple definitions of 'sophist' are evidence that 'sophist' does not name a genuine kind and thus does not have a single definition discoverable by division.

The first six definitions arrived at by division (components in bold type)

(Definition 5) (Definition 1) (Putative definition 6) (Definition 2) (Definition 3) (Definition 4)

Figure 1.1

proceeds by dividing productive arts into divine and human; human into producing originals and producing copies. The latter kind after further subdivisions (specifications) results in a definition of sophist that applies to all individuals falling under the first five linguistic definitions but not to those falling under the sixth (namely, Socrates).[11] At this point, the Visitor has laid out a conceptual framework in which to comprehend the actual nature of sophistry. The method of division unlike either elenchus or philology enables the philosopher to go beyond linguistic definition and grasp actual natures. Its limitations, however, are also illustrated by the various attempts at defining 'sophist'. The method of division does not guarantee its own

---

[11] Following Plato, modern scholars often distinguish between Socrates and other individuals called sophists. Socrates' contemporaries, however, grouped them all together, as is clear from Aristophanes' comedy *The Clouds*.

success as a method for discovering perspicuous definitions, because a particular application of division is only as sound as the assumptions governing the selection of kinds, species, and sub-species to divide.[12]

Having illustrated the limitations of the method of division in the initial series of definitions, the Visitor turns to a discussion of the Great Kinds (Forms). That is, the search for perspicuous definitions requires, Plato believes, a far more secure metaphysical foundation than the ontology implied by ordinary language. It also requires an ontology that allows us to make sense of relations. We cannot simply view each object in isolation without thinking about it in relation to other ideal objects. This becomes clear in the *Sophist* when the topics of negation and falsity are broached. While the logical possibility of both has been implicit in the theory of forms all along, the differentiation of Forms from particulars tended to obscure these issues. Forms were said to be just what they were—for example, Beauty, Justice, and so on— whereas particulars were shown to be simultaneously beautiful and not beautiful, just and unjust, and so on. Negation like falsehood seemed to belong to the sensible realm alone. In the *Sophist*, the Visitor points out that Being is not the same as Motion or any of the other Great Kinds. That is, not only is it true that Being is the same as itself but it is also true that it is not Motion or Rest or even Sameness or Difference. The philosopher, the expert in dialectic, is the person who is able to discern the relations that hold among Forms.

<The philosopher> will be capable of adequately discriminating a single form [*idean*] spread out through many things, each of which stands separate from the others. In addition he can discriminate forms that are different from each other but are included within a single form that is outside them, or a single form that is connected as one thing throughout many wholes or many forms that are completely separate from others. (*Sophist* 253d–e)

Just as the *Cratylus* designated the dialectician as the person who would be capable of determining when a term is correctly defined (390c–d), the *Sophist* makes the ultimate decision with respect to the adequacy of the method of division the task of the dialectician/philosopher. This person is able to grasp the actual relations among Forms and use that knowledge to guide the application of division to a particular concept. The nature of sophistry is such that, in order to define it by division, the philosopher must have an understanding of Forms and their relations that provides a basis for understanding negation and the falsity of sentences.

Being different from becomes the ontological underpinning for true negations. As Plato points out, "what we call not beautiful is the thing that is different from nothing other than the nature of the beautiful... The not beautiful turns out to be, by being both marked off within one kind of those that are, and also set over against one of those that are" (257d–e).

---

[12] Aristotle makes this criticism (*An. Post.* 91$^b$17–23; *Met.* VII.12 1037$^b$29–1038$^a$36).

Just as 'beautiful' finds its proper signification and reference in Beauty Itself, 'not beautiful' finds its proper signification and reference in all those realities (Forms) that are different from Beauty Itself. This ontological foundation allows the negation of the true claim 'A is beautiful' made about a sensible beauty also to be true because the beauty of A is such that A, unlike Beauty Itself, is beautiful in one respect and not beautiful in another respect. Having explicated the nature of negation, the Visitor turns to the issue of falsehood. This too, he believes, can be explained in a similar way.

But if someone says things about you, but says different things as the same or not beings as beings, then it definitely seems that false speech really and truly arises from that kind of putting together of verbs and names. (263d)

To say that 'Theaetetus flies' is to say of Theaetetus who exists something that is different from and incompatible with one of the predicates (sits) that actually hold of him.

The final application of the method of division proceeds through concepts that cannot be understood without a proper account of negation and falsity. Having analysed these notions, the Visitor is able to arrive at the final, perspicuous definition of the sophist as one whose art belongs to "the imitative part of the dissembling part of the art of opinion which is part of the art of contradiction and belongs to the fantastical type of the image making art, which is not divine, but human" (265a–268d). This definition expresses knowledge, in so far as knowledge is possible in the sensible realm, of an identifiable and genuine kind; to arrive at it an understanding of the Forms was required to allow the definer to employ non-ideal concepts in a way that yielded conceptual clarity.

## Definition without Forms in the *Theaetetus*

The method of division in the *Sophist* seems a continuation and modification of Socratic *elenchus* in earlier dialogues whereas the call for a definition of *episteme* (knowledge) in the *Theaetetus* seems to be an attempt to do epistemology without having recourse to transcendent Forms. These topics are, however, closely related; to possess a perspicuous definition is to have knowledge of a real nature. If definition is possible without Forms, then knowledge, at least in some instances, must also be possible without Forms. The ontology of the *Theaetetus* is that of ordinary language. Socrates and Theaetetus discuss the nature of knowledge without ever explicitly invoking ideal objects. The relation between words and objects figures importantly in their efforts to define 'knowledge' by identifying it with other cognitive capacities— namely, perception, belief, and true belief. The first definition to be considered is: knowledge is perception. If one knows something, there must be something that is known. The act of knowing must be such that it is fully determined by the object. This makes perception a likely candidate.[13] The difficulty is that on some theories of

---

[13] For a general discussion of Plato's views about perception, see Modrak (2006).

perception that which is perceived need not be true. Such concerns ultimately lead Socrates to postulate a "secret doctrine" according to which the act of perceiving and the object perceived come into existence and go out of existence together. Indeed both are just aspects of a single event.

> Motions arise in the intervening space, sight from the side of the eye and whiteness from the side of that which cooperates in the production of colour. The eye is filled with sight; at that moment it sees, becomes not indeed sight, but a seeing eye; while its partner in the process of producing colour is filled with whiteness, and becomes not whiteness but white, a white stick or stone or whatever it is... (156e)

On this picture there is no possibility of error. Seeing white and being white just are two descriptions of the same occurrence; the first is a description of the state of the perceiver and the second, of the state of the object. This appears to be a promising account of perception, if the goal is to find a type of cognition that grasps its object as the object truly is. In the end, Socrates argues that this account, far from providing a knowable object, would eliminate the object and with it the act of perceiving/knowing.

> We were most anxious to prove that all things are in motion, in order to make the answer <knowledge is perception> come out correct; but what has really emerged is that if all things are in motion, every answer, on whatever subject, is equally correct... the proponents of this theory need to establish some other language, as it is, they have no words that are consistent with their hypothesis. (183a–b)

Not only does the theory eliminate knowable objects and with them perspicuous definitions; it also eliminates the possibility of linguistic definitions. This brings the reader, if not the participants in the dialogue, back to the need for stable objects to secure meaning even in the case of linguistic definition. In a world of constantly changing objects, language is not possible. The question remains, however, whether we need to posit unchanging, ideal objects to provide the necessary stability or whether ordinary objects that change over time but hold their characteristics temporarily will do.[14] The *Theaetetus* leaves this question unsettled, in contrast to the flat rejection of this possibility in the *Republic* and other middle dialogues.

Having examined the thesis that knowledge is perception under a series of initially plausible interpretations and found the thesis wanting under them all, Socrates and Theaetetus turn to belief. The dialogue concludes with a lengthy discussion of the thesis that knowledge is true belief with a *logos*. This, too, is examined under a number of interpretations. It is tempting to identify *logos* with explanation or justification. While there is some reason to do so, it should be noted that *logos* is one of the terms Plato uses for definition. Moreover, several of the interpretations given *logos* make more sense if the *logos* in question is a definition. Socrates begins by

---

[14] See Modrak (1981).

describing his dream that the primary elements are without an account and are immediately grasped by perception; the elements are combined to form a *logos*, which is knowable. He develops the picture further using the syllable and its component letters as a model; the syllable is analogous to the knowable *logos* and the letters, to the perceptible primary elements. Socrates goes on to argue that there is no way to make sense of this picture. If the elements are unknowable, because indefinable, then the syllable made up of them will also be unknowable; if the syllable is knowable, then its phonetic elements must also be knowable.

Socrates and Theaetetus then canvass three interpretations of *logos*. The first simply identifies *logos* with speech. This is rejected as being too broad. The second interpretation makes the knowledge in question be that of a wagon. The *logos* of a wagon is said to be a detailed, expert list of its proper parts and how they are put together. This is rejected on the grounds that one might know how a particular part fits into the whole in one instance but not in another. This, too, is illustrated with a syllable and its parts. A child learning to spell might know that Theaetetus' name begins with a theta but fail to know that Theodorus' name begins with a theta and believe falsely that it begins with a tau. *Logos* so defined would be consistent with a very specialized, narrow conception of knowledge, but this conception is not Plato's. The method of division as described in the *Sophist* seems designed to ensure that all the component concepts, theta in Socrates' example, are already embedded in a conceptual grid that would prevent such mistakes from occurring. The third formulation of the definition identifies the *logos* that makes true belief knowledge with grasping the distinguishing mark of the object. In the end, this definition of knowledge is rejected, because grasping a *logos* of it is identical to knowing the object. Interpreted thus, the third definition of knowledge is circular and uninformative. Note that the problem here is not that the definition is false but that it lacks explanatory adequacy. Even though it fails as a definition of knowledge, interpreting *logos* as an account of the distinguishing feature(s) of the object is consistent with the account of perspicuous definition from Socratic dialogues to the *Sophist*; however, in the *Theaetetus*, limiting ontology to the world as conceptualized in ordinary language and linguistic definition has resulted in a failure to explicate the nature of knowledge.

## Conclusion

From the Socratic dialogues through the *Sophist*, we find Plato deeply engaged by questions about meaning and the implications of various views about meaning for ontology and epistemology and by extension to other areas of philosophy such as ethics. As presented in the early dialogues, elenchus as practised by Socrates treats as self-evident and hence in no need of statement or defence a number of assumptions about what is required of an account in order for it to constitute a proper definition of the characteristic in question. An adequate definition must apply to all and only instances of the definiendum, must not contain vacuous notions, must be non-circular and explanatory. These criteria are still present in the middle dialogues and (at least in part) motivate the postulation of Forms as the foundational realities, the natures of which are expressible in definitions that meet the Socratic requirements for definition. The theory of division that Plato develops later in order to establish that a definition has a transparent, properly ordered conceptual content also embraces the Socratic requirements. If the philosopher is guided by an understanding of the relations obtaining among Forms, she will be able to employ the method of division in a way that yields perspicuous definitions. Socrates' and Plato's desire to arrive at definitions that embody knowledge of the object defined has culminated in a method of conceptual analysis and an ontology that *ex hypothesi* is adequate to the task.

Plato's abiding interest in definition is an interest not so much in definition for its own sake but in definition as a method for clarifying meaning. To be useful as a vehicle for knowledge, a meaning must, Plato believes, express a real nature. The primary value of language is to serve as a tool for understanding the world as it is. If the world is sufficiently unstable, as in the *Theaetetus*' Secret Doctrine or the *Cratylus*, language loses its value as a tool. A language that reflects instability will be unstable and undermine understanding and language. The *Cratylus* ends with the suggestion that an extra-linguistic grasp of reality is required in order to assign meanings. The same intuition drives the arguments in the *Republic* and *Symposium* for a cognitive ascent through understanding more and more abstract exemplars of a linguistically based concept to an object that when grasped provides an understanding of the concept that transcends its linguistic base. This understanding transforms the linguistic concept into an epistemically adequate concept. Such concepts are required for knowledge.

Modern philosophers have largely abandoned one feature of Plato's approach to meaning and truth—namely, the project of finding definitions that precisely express essences of real, extra-linguistic objects. Their indifference is in part motivated by a loss of confidence in the mind's capacity to get behind linguistic representation. The object of definition is not less a linguistic construction that the definition that expresses its character. It is worth noting, however, that Plato's Forms, despite being mind-independent realities, were denoted by names borrowed from ordinary language. The definitions that express real natures are more precise and more clearly delineated than are ordinary linguistic definitions, but they originate in ordinary linguistic meanings. Words often have multiple meanings, which may, but need not, overlap. Like Plato, modern philosophers often seek greater conceptual clarity than is initially provided by linguistic definition. The modern solution is to stipulate meanings and then in the light of the stipulated meaning determine the reference of the term. We differ from Plato not in rejecting certain normative criteria for definition but in our understanding of the ontological implications of the requirement that philosophical reasoning start from clear and distinct concepts.

Plato's interest in words throughout is not about categorizing linguistic items as names or predicates or *syncategoremata*; rather it is about the relation between the word and its object(s) and about the role the meaning of the word plays in mediating that relation. Broadly speaking, he treats all meaningful terms as names (*onomata*). In practice, he distinguishes between two types of definition, the ones that enable the members of a linguistic community to use the word in (roughly) the same way and the ones that express real natures of objects. The latter are required for philosophy and more generally for understanding. Since, in the case of many concepts, the sensible objects to which the word refers seem to provide an inadequate basis for a unique and stable meaning, Plato posits ideal exemplars that just are the nature in question—for instance, Beauty. Ideal exemplars (Forms) provide the metaphysical grounding for meaning and perspicuous definition. The perspicuous definition articulates the nature of the (idealized) object. The linguistic token, nevertheless, retains its linguistic referent. The meaning of the name mediates the relation between the word and its ordinary referents.

## References

Brown, L. (2010). 'Definition and Division in Plato's *Sophist*', in D. Charles (ed.), *Definition in Greek Philosophy*. Oxford: Oxford University Press.

Cohen, S. M. (1971). 'Socrates on the Definition of Piety: *Euthyphro* 10A–11B', *Journal of the History of Philosophy*, 9.

Dancy, R. M. (2006). 'Platonic Definitions and Forms', in H. H. Benson (ed.), *A Companion to Plato*. Oxford: Blackwell.

Modrak, D. (1981). 'Perception and Judgement in the *Theaetetus*', *Phronesis*, 26.

Modrak, D. (2006). 'Plato: A Theory of Perception or a Nod to Sensation?', in H. H. Benson (ed.), *A Companion to Plato*. Oxford: Blackwell.

Robinson, R. (1971). 'Socratic Definition', in G. Vlastos (ed.), *Philosophy of Socrates*. Notre Dame: University of Notre Dame Press.

# 2
# Names, Verbs, and Sentences in Ancient Greek Philosophy

*Francesco Ademollo*

My purpose here is to investigate some ancient conceptions of the composition and structure of sentences, focusing on Plato and Aristotle, with short forays into other authors and ages. I shall concern myself mainly with two mutually connected issues. First, both Plato and Aristotle hold that a minimal simple sentence consists of two expressions of different kinds, which they call *onoma* and *rhema*; I shall try to make clear the nature and purport of this distinction, which is controversial. Secondly (but partly at the same time), I shall try to trace the emergence and early development, from Plato to the Stoics, of the idea that a simple declarative sentence has a signification of its own over and above the signification of its parts. Most individual details of what I am going to say are, I am afraid, not new; but perhaps the story as a whole deserves to be told.[1] As so often with stories about ancient matters, telling it will require some detailed discussion and a modicum of philological excavation.

## I

The main subject of Plato's *Cratylus*,[2] and the common thread across its various arguments, is what the dialogue's characters call 'the correctness of names'—i.e. the relation between a name and the thing it names. More precisely, the *Cratylus*

---

I thank Michele Alessandrelli, Sergio Bernini, Lesley Brown, Margaret Cameron, Paolo Fait, and Michael Forster for helpful criticism and advice. I owe a special debt of gratitude to Paolo Crivelli for many discussions about these topics over the years; during one of these conversations he brought to my attention the point that is made here in the opening paragraph of Section VII.
 Throughout the chapter I quote existing translations of various ancient works, modifying them where that seemed appropriate: *Cratylus* (Ademollo 2011), *Sophist* (Crivelli 2012), *De interpretatione* (Ackrill 1963).

[1] For partly comparable and very valuable surveys, from which I have learnt much, see Nuchelmans (1973: 13–44) and Barnes (1996).

[2] All of my remarks on the *Cratylus* in this chapter depend on my own work on the dialogue (Ademollo 2011). See especially Ademollo (2011: 262–7 on *rhema*, 293–6 on 424e–425a, 345–50 on 431bc).

confronts the question whether this relation is natural—i.e. is somehow grounded in the nature of the thing named—or rather conventional and arbitrary. The characters take a very generous view of what may count as a 'name' (*onoma*), in accordance with normal Greek usage: the term is usually applied not only to proper and common nouns but also to pronouns, adjectives, adverbs, and verbs in the participle and infinitive mood.[3] Indeed, one passage (385c) goes as far as to say that the *onoma* is the 'smallest' part of a sentence, thus suggesting that even verbs in finite moods may be reckoned among *onomata*.[4] In the light of this evidence we might be tempted to suppose that the term *onoma* should actually be translated as 'word' rather than 'name'. But that would be a mistake: the Greek *onoma* has a close etymological connection with the verb *onomazein*, 'to name', whereas 'word' has no parallel connection with any transitive verb. Thus it seems that an *onoma* is essentially an expression that *names* or refers to something, and it is reasonable to adopt the translation 'name'.

In the course of their enquiry the characters discuss various matters that are related to our topic. Two passages are especially relevant. The first is at 424e–425a, where Socrates is describing the hypothetical construction of a new language:

SO ... We too shall apply letters to the objects, both one to one, where it seems to be required, and many together, making what they call syllables, and then in turn combining syllables, of which *onomata* and *rhemata* are composed. And again from *onomata* and *rhemata* we shall finally construct something great and beautiful and whole: as in the former case the picture with the art of painting, so in this case the *logos* with onomastic[5] or rhetoric or whatever the art is. (424e4–425a5)

The language Socrates is envisaging is built up on the assumption that names should somehow imitate the nature of their referents by being made up of letters which resemble various elements of the referent's nature. This assumption explains some features of the passage, including the final comparison with painting pictures, but it does not affect what Socrates says about the linguistic units he mentions. He arranges these units in a scale of increasing complexity: letters constitute syllables; syllables constitute both *onomata* and *rhemata*; eventually, *onomata* and *rhemata* together constitute the *logos*. In the light of Socrates' description of the *logos* as 'something great and beautiful and whole' (for which cf. *Phaedrus* 264c), I suggest that we translate this term as 'speech', conceived of as something whose size may vary from a single sentence to something much larger and more complex.[6]

---

[3] Pronouns: *Tim.* 50a. Adjectives: *Crat.* 416a, 417c, *Soph.* 251ab. Adverbs: Demosthenes 19.187. Participles: *Crat.* 421c. Infinitives: *Crat.* 414ab, 424a, 426c.

[4] This suggestion is confirmed at *Soph.* 261d (see Section V) and Arist. *De int.* $16^b19$–20 (see Section VII). Cf. Arist. *Poet.* $21.1457^b10$, $22.1458^b20$–4.

[5] Unlike rhetoric, which is mentioned immediately afterwards, the 'onomastic art', or 'art of names', is not an already existing science or practice. Socrates is applying this term to whatever discipline may turn out to be responsible for constructing the *logos* out of *onomata* and *rhemata*.

[6] Like a whole poem: cf. Arist. *Poet.* 20. $1457^a28$–30, *An. post.* 2.9. $93^b35$–7, etc.

Now, this *logos* is said to be composed of *onomata* and *rhemata*. What are *rhemata* meant to be? This question has been the subject of lively debate, with regard not so much to our passage as to others, as we are going to see; but the debate has mostly been going on without being grounded in a thorough analysis of the evidence. In what follows I shall first open with a brief digression on the history of the word *rhema* and then turn to what our passage can teach us about it.

## II

The word *rhema* derives from an Indo-European root whose meaning has to do with the activity of *saying* something.[7] The same root lies behind the Latin *verbum* and the very English *word*; in Greek it is, for example, the basis for the noun *rhetor* ('speaker'), the verbal adjective *rhetos* ('sayable'), and the passive aorist *rhethenai* ('to get said'). The common denominator between these various manifestations of the same Greek root has been spelt out as the notion of 'consciously saying something important, in which both speaker and hearers are involved'.[8] As for the suffix *-ma*, here it presumably has one of its typical functions—i.e. that of conveying that the word in which it is included refers to the result of a certain activity. Thus *rhema* originally and literally means 'thing said'. More precisely, the evidence suggests that the term is applied to linguistic expressions which the speaker regards as efficacious or relevant in context. The size of such expressions may vary and appears to be irrelevant: a *rhema* may be a whole sentence (for example, a saying or maxim: Plato, *Protagoras* 343ab, *Republic* 336a, Isocrates 15.166); a phrase like 'aether, Zeus's bedchamber' or 'time's foot' (Aristophanes, *Frogs* 97–100), or also 'not large' (Pl. *Sophist* 257b); a single word like 'sheep' (Aristophanes, *Pax* 929–31) or 'this' (Pl. *Timaeus* 49e).[9]

Especially interesting for our purposes, because it brings together *onoma* and *rhema*, is a passage in the fourth-century BC orator Aeschines (3.72), who recalls a previous occasion on which his foe Demosthenes

said we must not (I even remember the *rhema* whereby he expressed himself, because of the unpleasantness of both the speaker and the *onoma*) 'break away the alliance from the peace'.

Here the *rhema* is the whole expression 'break away the alliance from the peace' (or perhaps 'we must not break away...', etc.), while the *onoma* is just 'break away', which in Greek is a single infinitive. So here *rhema* refers to a complex expression or phrase as opposed to the *onoma* as a single word.[10]

---

[7] The contents of this section, like the fuller presentation of the same material in Ademollo (2011: 262–7), are indebted to Conti (1977–8).

[8] Conti (1977–8: 21).

[9] Here I am citing evidence from Plato and authors whose language is generally similar (i.e. his contemporary Isocrates, an orator, and the comical poet Aristophanes, active in the final quarter of the fifth century BC); but the list could be extended to other authors and ages.

[10] See Riddell (1867: 36). The same contrast is operating also at Pl. *Symp.* 198b; see Ademollo (2011: 263–4) for a detailed argument.

Some such contrast between expressions and words is present in several passages of the *Cratylus* featuring the term *rhema*. These all belong to the long section of the dialogue in which Socrates purports to illustrate the naturalist conception of the name–object relation by advancing a number of etymologies which allegedly aim to show that names reflect the nature of their referents.

- At 399ac Socrates claims that in so far as the name *Diphilos* derives from *Dii philos* ('dear to Zeus'), and the name *anthropos* ('human') derives from *anathron ha opopen* ('he who examines what he has seen'), both have 'become an *onoma* from a *rhema*', or 'in place of a *rhema*'. In both places the idea is precisely that an expression has been contracted into a single word.
- At 421b the name *aletheia* ('truth') is derived from *ale theia* ('divine roaming') and is itself referred to as a *rhema*—presumably on account of the fact that in this case the original expression has coalesced into the name without any phonetic change at all.[11]
- At 421de Socrates wonders what would happen if someone first tried to identify those *rhemata* of which an *onoma* is composed, and then inquired into the etymology of those *rhemata* themselves, and so on.[12] Here the *rhemata* are the parts of which a name is composed. They are unlikely to be whole phrases: a name may derive from one phrase, as in the examples we have just seen, but it is unlikely to derive from a plurality of phrases. But the *rhemata* may still be expressions whose identity is left indefinite (and which as a matter of fact might well be just single words), called *rhemata* in so far as in this context they are contrasted with the *onoma*.

The interpretations I have just been setting forth are endorsed by some commentators,[13] but by no means by all. In particular, an alternative construal of the evidence is fairly widespread, according to which in these passages the *onoma*/*rhema* contrast has an essentially syntactic nature and the notion of a *rhema* is close to that of a *predicate*: 'literally *rhēma* means only a "thing said", and a name ... is contrasted with it as that of which things are said.'[14] But this interpretation goes against the evidence on several counts. (i) It ignores the normal usage of *rhema* as 'expression', which I documented above by citing some passages—and more could be cited—from Plato and other authors. (ii) It over-interprets the term's etymological reference to 'saying' as 'saying something *about* something other'. (iii) It cannot explain why at 421b Socrates should characterize the noun 'truth' as a predicate (a predicate of what,

---

[11] Indeed, in the *scriptio continua* of Plato's times the original phrase and the resulting name would have been written in the same way.

[12] Socrates' answer is that this kind of etymological analysis must stop when it reaches the 'primary names', which cannot be analysed into other names: see Section I.

[13] See, e.g., Riddell (1867: 36) and Cambiano (1981), who translates *rhema* as 'espressione' in all three passages.

[14] Guthrie (1969: 220–1); cf., e.g., Sedley (2003: 162).

anyway?)—also in the light of the fact that just a few lines below, at 421b7, he refers to the noun 'falsehood' as an *onoma*. (iv) It is also unable to explain what on earth Socrates could mean at 421de when he claims that a name is composed of *rhemata*, in the plural: a name from *several* predicates?

So I reject this alternative construal and shall henceforth stick to my earlier conclusions. This wraps up my digression on *rhema*; we must now pick up the thread of our main argument.

## III

Back to *Cratylus* 425a. At the end of Section I we left open the question of what *rhemata* could mean there. The passage gives us two important clues. (i) The term must refer to linguistic units that are at the same level of complexity as the *onomata*, being directly composed of syllables: that is to say, they are individual words. This clue, which has generally gone unnoticed,[15] rules out the possibility that here *rhemata* may—in accordance with the passages we examined in Section II—be phrases, i.e. linguistic units intermediate between names and speech.[16] (ii) These words must, in combination with the *onomata*, constitute the *logos*.

These things being so, I can think of only one kind of word that could be meaningfully mentioned here, i.e. verbs. Therefore it seems clear to me that here *rhemata* are meant to be, not phrases or generic expressions, let alone predicates, but verbs; that the initial, very generic use of the term *onoma* is now being implicitly restricted to make room for a distinction between names and verbs; and that 'names and verbs' is precisely how we should translate the phrase '*onomata* and *rhemata*' in this text—as in fact is often done.

There is, of course, nothing scandalous (in spite of what some commentators seem to think) about the fact that *rhema* may mean one thing in several passages and another thing here. But Plato clearly seems to presuppose that we are already familiar with the new meaning. So where did it come from? I suppose that once someone, at the dawn of the theoretical reflection on language, recognized verbs as a distinct kind of expression, it was quite natural to identify this new kind by recourse to a term that was already in use in Greek to refer to individual words, was different from the much more common *onoma*, and lacked special connotations. This process, whereby *rhema* acquired a specific meaning besides its old, generic one, might have a close parallel in the semantic development of the cognate Latin word *verbum* from 'word' to 'verb'. In Greek the process was especially easy if, as seems likely, '*onomata* and *rhemata*' already formed a standard pair meaning generically 'names and expressions'.[17]

---

[15] But see Barney (2001: 186).   [16] *Pace*, e.g., Denyer (1991: 149–50).
[17] It is so at *Symp.* 198b, and cf. Aeschines 3.72 quoted in Section II; see also Pl. *Apol.* 17bc, *Symp.* 199b, 221e, *Rep.* 601a, *Theaet.* 168bc.

Who was the discoverer of verbs? We do not really know. Remember, however, that the *Cratylus* passage is sketching the construction of a new language. The sketch starts at 424bc by referring to the need for a classification of sounds or letters like the one carried out by 'those who set to work on rhythms'. This suggests no less interesting a candidate than Democritus, who is credited by Diogenes Laertius (9.47–8 = 68A33 Diels/Kranz) with works entitled *Explanations about Sounds, On Rhythms and Harmony, On Euphonious and Cacophonous Letters*, and... *On rhemata*.

## IV

We can now turn to the second of the two passages of the *Cratylus* that are especially relevant for our enquiry, 431bc. There Socrates is arguing against Cratylus, who has endorsed the sophistic paradox that it is impossible to speak falsely (429ce). For strategic reasons, Socrates' refutation still proceeds on the assumption, which Cratylus accepts, that names imitate their referents and to that extent can be compared with pictures. At 430a–431b he argues, and gets Cratylus to acknowledge, that, just as it is possible to assign or apply to a given object either a picture that imitates it or a picture that fails to do so, likewise it must be possible to assign to a given object either a name that imitates it (in which case the assignment is 'correct' and 'true') or a name that does not imitate it (in which case the assignment is 'incorrect' and 'false'). Then Socrates rounds off his argument, and extends its conclusion, as follows:

SO ... We want to call one of these two situations 'speaking truly' and the other 'speaking falsely'. And, if this is so, and it is possible to distribute names incorrectly and not to assign to each thing the appropriate ones, but sometimes the inappropriate ones, then it should be possible to do this same thing to *rhemata* too. And if it is possible to consider *rhemata* and names in this way, necessarily it is possible to consider *logoi* in this way too. For it is to *logoi*, I suppose, that the combination of these elements amounts. (431b1–c2)

Socrates is not only insisting that names can be assigned to objects either correctly and truly or incorrectly and falsely; he is also arguing that the same holds of *rhemata* and *logoi*, which are a combination of names and *rhemata*. Clearly, here *logoi* are meant to be (declarative) sentences that can be either true or false. What about *rhemata*? In the light of the previous passage, which is obviously relevant to the present one, there is a natural presumption that here too *rhemata* should be verbs. This presumption is now confirmed by Socrates' claim that sentences are a combination (*sunthesis*) of names and *rhemata*, which strongly suggests that names and *rhemata* are heterogeneous kinds of expressions and that it takes at least one *onoma* and one *rhema* to make up a sentence. The claim would make little sense if *rhemata* were phrases, which normally contain names and hence cannot be meaningfully said to be 'combined' with them. Nor would it make much sense if *rhemata* were instead predicates, which may themselves be or contain names: 'names and predicates' looks like an odd and ill-assorted pair.[18] Note also that Socrates' argument has been centred on the possibility of assigning to a particular man either of two general terms, 'man' and 'woman'; if *rhemata* here were meant to be predicates rather than verbs, then in this context we might have expected Socrates to refer to 'man' and 'woman' as *rhemata* rather than *onomata*.

So far so good. Now let us add some complications. It has been rightly pointed out[19] that Socrates here seems to be gesturing towards a dubious account of the falsehood of sentences. It is all very well that he, in order to defend the possibility of speaking falsely, should first of all focus on what can be regarded as the basic case of falsehood—i.e. the case in which the wrong name is attributed to a given object.[20] It also makes sense that he should treat verbs on a par with names (though it is unclear whether he assumes that a verb too is assigned to a given object or to some activity of a given object). But the way in which Socrates expresses himself in this passage may suggest that he is also treating sentences on a par with names, as though a sentence were to be assessed as true or false *in relation to an independently given object*. This is not how sentences really work. If you want to claim that Callias is wise, it is not the case that you first have to identify Callias as a subject of discourse and then go on to utter the sentence 'Callias is wise'; it will be enough to utter the sentence. For what is distinctive of sentences is precisely that they, in virtue of containing different parts endowed with different tasks (roughly, a subject term and a predicate term), are by themselves able to perform the twofold function of referring to an object and saying something true or false about it.

So the *Cratylus* passage suggests that Plato may lack a clear and sound conception of the structure of sentences. Indeed, this suggestion is borne out by two other passages from the same dialogue, which for reasons of space I cannot discuss in any detail: 385bd, where Socrates argues that the names of which a sentence is composed are true or false like the whole sentence; and 432d–433b, an extremely difficult passage where Socrates contends that a false sentence about something, like a bad picture of something, is a sentence that contains enough appropriate names to preserve the thing's 'general character' (*tupos*), but not so many as to be true.[21] There is, I suspect, no way of making these passages offer a single, consistent account of what it is for a sentence to be false. They should rather be viewed as successive attempts to grapple with a difficult problem, all affected by various forms of the same misconception according to which sentences are essentially akin to names or noun phrases.

---

[18] Unless, of course, you are ready to back it up with a theory along the lines of Frege's 'On Concept and Object'. But I assume that nothing like that can be ascribed to Plato.

[19] See McDowell (1973: 236).    [20] See Kahn (1973: 161).

[21] For a detailed discussion of these passages, see Ademollo (2011: 49–72, on 385bd, and 369–79, on 432d–433b).

Ironically, that misconception lies also at the basis of at least some versions of the sophistic paradox which Plato here is out to solve. If you assume that a sentence is nothing more than a noun phrase or a string of names, then you are likely to go on to make the further assumption that making a statement is analogous to naming. And if you make that further assumption (which some of the sophistic arguments make[22] and Plato in the *Cratylus* is striving to eschew), you are likely to run into trouble. For there seems to be nothing that a false sentence, thus conceived, could successfully name; and if this is so, then the act of making a false statement will appear to be as unsuccessful, and impossible to carry out, as the act of naming something that is not there to be named.[23]

Now, if this is so, does the fact that Plato is not clear about subject/predicate structure in sentences conflict with our earlier conclusion that he is distinguishing between names and verbs? Not at all. Names and verbs are two distinct word classes; you may distinguish between them on the grounds of some differences (names have cases, verbs have persons; verbs have tenses, names do not: cf. Aristotle's *Poetics*, 20. 1457$^a$14–15) and yet fail to see other differences. You may even come to believe that any sentence must contain at least one name and one verb without yet realizing that names and verbs perform different syntactic functions within a sentence. Thus the syntactic confusion that I am ascribing to Plato in the *Cratylus* might actually consist in assimilating a sentence like 'Callias walks' to a structureless string of names and verbs like 'Callias, walks.'

# V

We now leave the *Cratylus*, to plunge into the midst of a manhunt: a pair of investigators, a philosopher and a talented young mathematician, are chasing that elusive scoundrel, the sophist, trying to pin him down with a definition. They are now considering a new proposal, according to which the sophist is a kind of imitator. But the notion of imitation carries with it those of falsehood and not-being, and the sophist is likely to seek refuge in the contention that those notions have nothing to do with sentences and beliefs—i.e. that there is no such thing as a false sentence or a false belief. Therefore the investigators now set to enquire into what a sentence and a belief are and how they can possibly be false.

The Eleatic Stranger starts off at *Sophist* 261d by getting Theaetetus to agree that among *onomata* some 'fit with one another' and some do not. He makes what he has in mind more explicit thus:

---

[22] *Euthyd.* 283e–284a and *Crat.* 429d can be interpreted along these lines; but the clearest occurrence is at *Euthyd.* 285d–286c (on which see Section VI).

[23] This criticism stems from Wittgenstein (see Russell 1956: 187–8). You could escape it if you accepted Frege's doctrine that all true sentences name the True and all false sentences name the False.

ES  You mean perhaps this, that those of them which, when spoken in succession, indicate something fit together, whereas those which signify nothing by their succession do not fit together. (*Soph.* 261d9–e2)

So the 'fit' between 'names' is a matter of their being capable of indicating or signifying[24] something when they are uttered in succession. On the most natural interpretation (already advanced by the fifth–sixth century AD commentator Ammonius in his work on Aristotle's *De interpretatione*),[25] this seems to mean that it is a matter of different names being able to constitute some sort of semantic unity in virtue of being uttered in succession. Yet Theaetetus is puzzled. To dissolve his puzzlement the Stranger makes a fresh start:

ES  ... We have, I suppose, a double kind of vocal means to indicate being.
TH. How so?
ES  One called *onomata*, the other *rhemata*.
TH. Tell me about both.
ES  The one which is a means to indicate applied to actions we call, I think, *rhema*.
TH. Yes.
ES  The other, the vocal sign imposed on those that perform them, we call *onoma*.
TH. Certainly. (261e4–262a8)

There are a number of interesting points to be made about these lines before we move on.

(i) When at 261e5 the Stranger introduces *onomata* and *rhemata* as vocal 'indicators of being', or 'means to indicate being', 'being' (*ousia*) is used as a collective noun which stands for anything that there is in a most general sense, any object whatsoever. The special Platonic sense in which 'being' is contrasted with 'becoming' as the world of changeless forms with the world of changing sensible particulars (as at *Rep.* 525b, c, 526e, 534a) is out of the question here. And this is just as well; for the *Sophist* seems to reject that contrast in favour of a generous ontology in which being includes 'all changeless things and all changing things' (249d).[26]

(ii) The definition of *rhema* as a sign for actions, inadequate as it may be,[27] suggests that *rhemata* are verbs. This harmonizes with our previous conclusions and will be further confirmed in what follows.

(iii) It now turns out that two uses of *onoma* are in play. Here we are encountering a specific use whereby *onomata* are contrasted with *rhemata*; but besides this

---

[24] Here there is clearly no difference in meaning between the two verbs 'to indicate' (*deloun*) and 'to signify' (*semainein*). This is so again at 261e–262a, where also the two corresponding nouns, 'indicator, means to indicate' (*deloma*) and 'sign' (*semeion*), appear to be equivalent to each other. Indeed, the same equivalence is tacitly assumed in other relevant texts: Pl. *Crat.* 394bc; Arist. *Cat.* 3$^b$10–13; Diogenes of Babylon as cited by Diogenes Laertius 7.58 = *Stoicorum Veterum Fragmenta* 3.22. See Ademollo (2011: 173 and n. 66).
[25] See *Commentaria in Aristotelem Graeca* IV.5, ed. A. Busse, 48.25–9, and Blank (1996) for a translation.
[26] Cf. Crivelli (2012: 95), who cites the relevant literature.
[27] To mitigate the inadequacy of this definition we may point out that the Greek *praxis* can sometimes mean 'state, condition' instead of 'action': see Herodotus 3.65.7 and Sophocles, *Ajax* 790, *Antigone* 1305.

there must also be a generic use according to which *onomata* instead include *rhemata*, as was (implicitly) the case at 261d, where *onoma* appeared to refer to any kind of word.

(iv) Theaetetus' initial failure to understand has suggested to many commentators that the Stranger's distinction is being put forward as a novelty. This, however, need not really be so. At 262a1–4 the Stranger claims that we have two kinds of expressions, 'one called *onomata*, the other *rhemata*', and that 'we call' *rhema* the sign for actions; he does not say 'I propose to call' or 'let us call'.[28] So it is at least possible that the emphasis on the distinction does not mean that it is completely new: conceivably, it might be a way of stressing its importance rather than its novelty. And this is just as well, if *rhemata* are verbs and I was right that names and verbs were already distinguished in the *Cratylus*.

Thus far it has not yet become clear what Socrates meant when, at 261de, he said that some 'names' (generic sense), but not others, indicate or signify something when spoken in succession. Let us read on.

ES Now, a sentence [*logos*] never consists of names alone spoken in succession, nor yet of *rhemata* spoken in succession without names.
TH. I didn't understand this.
ES [262b] Clearly you had something else in view when you agreed just now. For this is what I wanted to say, that these, spoken in succession in this way, are not a sentence.
TH. In what way?
ES For example, 'walks runs sleeps', and all the other verbs that signify actions, even if one speaks them all in a row, do not, for all that, produce a sentence.
TH. How could they?
ES Again, when 'lion stag horse' is spoken, and all the names that have been given to those who perform actions, [c] in virtue of this succession no sentence yet results, either. For neither in this way nor in that do the sounds uttered indicate any action or inaction or being of what is or of what is not, until one blends *rhemata* with names. Then they fit and the first interweaving immediately becomes a sentence, the first and smallest of sentences.
TH. What do you mean thereby?
ES When someone says 'Man understands', do you say that this is a shortest and first sentence?
TH. [d] I do.
ES For it, I suppose, already indicates something about the things that are or are coming to be or have come to be or shall come, and does not merely name but accomplishes something, by interweaving *rhemata* with names. For this reason we claim that it does not merely name but *says* something, and we gave the name 'sentence' to this interweaving.
TH. Rightly so.
ES Thus, as some objects turned out to fit with one another and others not to, so, also with vocal signs, some [e] do not fit, whereas those of them that fit produce a sentence.
TH. By all means. (262a9–e3)

---

[28] See Szaif (1998: 461 n. 157).

A string consisting just of *rhemata* (the examples are, tellingly, all verbs), or of names, is not yet enough to yield a complete declarative sentence (*logos*). It is only when you combine items from these two heterogeneous kinds of expressions that the resulting unity is a sentence: thus one name and one verb are enough to constitute the minimal form of sentence. Indeed, the Stranger appears to think that there is some sense in which a name or verb (or for that matter a string of names or verbs) alone is incomplete. This is revealed by his claim that a sentence, or the speaker who utters it, 'does not merely name' but 'accomplishes something' or 'brings something to completion' (*ti perainei*, 262d3–4).[29]

Another way in which the Stranger draws a distinction between complete sentences and their components is by claiming that a sentence, or someone who utters it, 'does not merely name... but *says* [*legein*] something' (262d4–5). Here the idea is that a sentence has a special semantic job of its own to carry out, different from that of its components and referred to by a pregnant use of the verb 'to say'[30] as equivalent, roughly, to 'to state'. But *what* exactly are the components whose function is being contrasted with that of the whole sentence? The Stranger's claim that the sentence/speaker 'does not merely name' reveals that he is at least contrasting sentences with names: names name, whereas sentences say or state. Now, it is often supposed that the function of the verb is, instead, especially relevant to that of the whole sentence and is precisely to say something about that which the name names. It is also sometimes supposed that this special role of the *rhema* is somehow reflected by the etymology of the word *rhema* as 'thing said' (see Section II).[31] The latter supposition seems dubious: although we happen to use the single verb 'to say' in connection with both terms, in fact the noun *rhema* and the verb *legein* derive from two completely different roots; moreover, *rhema* was not a new word, but was commonly used to mean 'expression,' as we saw in Section II, and this would have made it difficult for it to be invested with this special etymological significance.[32] As for the former, more generic supposition, I suspect that it is ultimately unwarranted:

---

[29] It is unclear, and controversial, whether the subject of 'indicates,' 'names', and 'accomplishes' at 262d2–4, and then the referent of the demonstrative 'he' (αὐτόν) at d5, is 'someone' (c9) or 'the sentence' (which can be easily supplied from the same line). The participle 'interweaving' (d4) may seem to tell in favour of the former construal (cf. c4–5); on the other hand, at c4 the subject of 'to indicate' is 'the sounds uttered' (cf. *Crat.* 393a, 394bc, 433e), and at 263b4–9 the subject of 'says' is unambiguously a sentence. Henceforth I shall proceed on the assumption that the text is intended to admit of both construals and that in any case the claim that speakers, by uttering a kind of expression *E*, perform speech act *A* is intended to be equivalent to the claim that *A* is the function of *E*: e.g. the claim that with names speakers name things is intended as equivalent to the claim that names name things.

[30] There is an obvious etymological connection, which gets lost in my translation, between *logos* ('sentence') and *legein* ('to say'). To mirror it we could render *logos* as 'saying' as suggested by Barnes (2007: 2 n. 3, 180): cf. n. 32.

[31] See, e.g., Ackrill (1963: 118), Frede (1992: 413–14), and cf. Crivelli (2012: 228–9).

[32] As an analogy, suppose we decided to render *rhema*—both in its common broad use as 'expression' and in its narrow use as 'verb'—with the (now obsolete) English noun 'speak', *legein* as 'to say', and *logos* as 'saying'. If we then claimed that a saying says something by being composed of a name and a 'speak', such a

verbs are, after all, reckoned among *onomata* in the generic sense of this term (261d), and it is presumably true by definition that whatever is a name names something. Indeed, later on we shall encounter a further reason for questioning the former supposition: see Section VI.

So, absent other evidence, we should suppose that in a minimal sentence both name and verb name something—respectively an agent and an action—and that only the sentence as a whole 'says' something. This may strike some as a philosophically unfortunate outcome, because it threatens, after all, to reduce a sentence to a mere list of names.[33] In mitigation we should compare Frege's view that 'Callias walks' consists of two referring expressions or names: a singular term, 'Callias', which refers to an object, and a concept-word, 'walks', which refers to a function or concept. It has to be said, however, that Frege strongly emphasizes the difference between object and concept, and in particular what he calls 'the predicative nature of the concept',[34] in a way that has no parallel in Plato.[35]

So far I have been ascribing to the Stranger a concern with 'minimal' sentences, without explaining what these are exactly meant to be. We must now be more precise on this issue. The Stranger calls a sentence of the 'name + verb' form both 'first', or 'primary', and 'smallest' (262c6–7). The former term means 'elementary' or 'simple' and conveys the suggestion that more complex sentences are composed of 'first' ones, while the latter term refers to the fact that even among simple sentences some are larger than others. This is because, if *rhemata* are verbs, not all simple sentences consist of just one name and one verb like 'Callias walks': some comprise more elements, like 'Callias is wise' or 'Callias loves Coriscus'. The Stranger is probably hinting at copula sentences at 262c2–5, where he implies that a sentence indicates an '*action or inaction or being of what is or of what is not*'—which I regard as a compendious and somewhat loose formulation intended to cover also such sentences as 'Callias is wise' and 'Callias is not wise' among others. The Stranger does not say how he would parse such sentences, but in the light of the evidence we have been examining so far it seems that he should regard 'Callias is wise' as consisting of two names, 'Callias' and 'wise', and one verb, 'is'.

These lines are interesting also in that they seem to lend some content to the claim, made by the Stranger at 261de and still unexplained, that only some 'names', but not others, signify something in virtue of being spoken in succession.[36] What is said here

---

claim would not necessarily have to be understood as conveying that the function of 'speaks' is especially relevant to that of sayings.

[33] See Denyer (1991: 164–7).

[34] See especially 'Über Begriff und Gegenstand' (1892), in Frege (1967: 167–78) = 'On Concept and Object', in Beaney (1997: 181–93).

[35] It also has to be said that it is unclear whether Frege really believes that the relation between a singular term and its referent is *the same* as the relation between a concept-word and its referent. See Furth (1968).

[36] At 262d8–e2 ('Thus, as...produce a sentence') the Stranger concludes the passage with a back-reference to that initial claim, apparently taking himself to have, at last, provided a satisfactory explanation.

suggests that a sentence indicates an 'action or inaction or being of what is or of what is not':[37] thus 'Callias walks' indicates the walk or walking of Callias.[38] This is consistent with what Socrates will say later on—namely that, as he puts forward an example of a minimal sentence, he is 'combining an object and an action by means of a name and a verb' (262e13-14). In the Greek text the participle 'combining' (*suntheis*) has a close etymological relation to one of the terms used to refer to the 'combination' of name and verb (*sunthesis*, 263d3: we encountered the same term at *Crat.* 431c2). This suggests that there is some correspondence between the combination of name and verb and the combination of object and action. But how far should this correspondence be pressed? Does Plato believe that, as the former combination constitutes a new linguistic unity which is the sentence, so the latter combination constitutes some sort of new unity, a compound entity which is signified by the whole sentence?

The Stranger says nothing on this score, and Plato is unlikely to be willing to push the correspondence to such an extreme; for that would land him in philosophical trouble. First, it would then become impossible for him to account for the difference between the sentence 'Callias walks' and the noun phrase 'Callias' walk'. Secondly,[39] a sentence like 'Callias walks', if it were false, would have to signify a *nonexistent* object-action complex; and this is precisely the sort of situation that the *Sophist*'s investigation of not-being has come to regard as extremely problematic (see 258d-259b).[40]

So the Stranger's explanation is not much of an explanation after all; we still have to read on to find out what he really means. But, before doing that, there is one more remark I wish to advance about this passage. It is about the claim that a sentence (or a speaker who utters it), besides 'bringing something to completion' and 'saying' something, also 'indicates something about the things that are or are coming to be or have come to be or shall come' (262d2-3). This must involve a recognition of the fact that sentences have present, past, or future *tense*. More precisely, it is tempting to suppose that when the Stranger speaks of indicating something 'about the things that are' he is thinking of those present-tense sentences that we might want to consider as timeless (e.g. 'Cats are felids', '2 + 2 = 4'), whereas when he speaks of indicating something 'about the things that...are coming to be or have come to be or shall come' he is thinking of sentences respectively about the present, past, or future time.

---

[37] I cannot accept Crivelli's contention (2012: 227, cf. 229-30) that here the Stranger 'might be implying that only within sentences do verbs and names signify, respectively, actions and objects'. Names and verbs have been introduced as expressions whose signification is independent of their being included in a sentence: see especially 262b5-6, b10-c1.

[38] Cf. Hoekstra and Scheppers (2003: 70-1).     [39] See Crivelli (2012: 249-51).

[40] Plato would be able to avoid these difficulties, while holding that a sentence signifies a compound entity, if he identified such a compound entity as a *proposition*, whose existence did not entail its truth. But Plato does not seem to take any serious theoretical notice of such items.

## VI

At 262e4–10 the Stranger gets Theaetetus to agree that any sentence has two further features: it must be 'of something' (*tinos*) and it must be 'of a certain quality' (*poios tis*). As becomes evident in what follows, 'of something' means 'about something', and the former feature amounts to the fact that the sentence must have a subject matter, whereas 'of a certain quality' means 'either true or false'.

At 262e11–263d5 the Stranger and Theaetetus consider two minimal sentences, 'Theaetetus sits' and 'Theaetetus flies', both composed of a name and a verb, both 'of' and 'about' (*peri*) Theaetetus, but one true and the other false. These two sentences bring out, just in virtue of their being juxtaposed and without the Stranger stating it explicitly, that the name which they have in common is responsible for the fact that they are both about Theaetetus, whereas the two different verbs are responsible for the fact that they are one true and one false. Thus it comes to light that, besides the lexical distinction between name and verb, there is also a syntactic distinction, between subject and predicate, to be drawn. The two distinctions coincide in minimal sentences, in which the name is the subject and the verb is the predicate; but they do not coincide in general, and it is possible to draw one without the other, as we saw with regard to the *Cratylus* in Section IV.[41] This is actually a further, weighty reason for being suspicious of the interpretation, which I discussed in Section V, according to which the *rhema* is meant to be the 'saying' part of a sentence: it would be inconsistent of Plato to think so, if he recognizes that this is not the function of the *rhema* in some relevant kinds of sentence.

The Stranger's claim that any sentence is 'of' something, and that his two sample sentences are 'of' Theaetetus no less than 'about' Theaetetus, confirms that the subject–predicate distinction is the central point of these lines. For this apparently peculiar formulation probably alludes to a kind of argument that we can read at *Euthyd.* 285d–286c.[42] According to this argument, it is impossible for two speakers to contradict each other (and hence for either of them to speak falsely), because one of three alternatives must obtain: (*a*) both say 'the *logos* of the same object' and hence say the same thing, (*b*) neither says 'the *logos* of the object' and hence neither so much as mentions the object, (*c*) one says 'the *logos* of the object' whereas the other says the *logos* 'of something other' and hence does not speak of the object at all. This argument can be regarded as running together the notion of a *logos* as a sentence *about* something and the notion of a *logos* as a description *of* something. And it seems fairly clear that Plato in the

---

[41] On the two distinctions, cf. Szaif (1998: 459–62).
[42] And which might have something to do with the philosopher Antisthenes: cf. Arist. *Metaph. Δ* 29.1024$^b$32–4.

*Sophist* is appropriating the talk of a *logos* 'of' something precisely in order to stress that he is countering this sort of argument.⁴³

At 263b4–d5 Plato has the Stranger set forth his famous analysis of the truth and falsehood conditions of sentences.⁴⁴ According to this analysis, the true sample sentence 'Theaetetus sits'

says of the things which are that they are about you [λέγει... τὰ ὄντα ὡς ἔστιν περὶ σοῦ],

that is, ascribes to something, saying that they hold of it, things which actually hold of it. The false sentence 'Theaetetus flies', instead, says

of things different from the things which are [ἕτερα τῶν ὄντων] (sc. that they are about you),

that is, it

says the things which are not as things which are [τὰ μὴ ὄντα... ὡς ὄντα λέγει].

In yet other words, the false sentence says

things which are different from things which are about you [ὄντων... ὄντα ἕτερα περὶ σοῦ].

That is to say, the false sentence ascribes to something, *X*, saying that they hold of *X*, things which, while perfectly real in themselves, are actually different from everything which holds of *X*. Generally speaking, the 'things' ascribed to the subject will be properties; in the case of a minimal sentence like 'Callias walks', they will more specifically be what the Stranger called 'actions'.

For our present purposes these definitions are important in two respects. First, they continue to stress the distinction between what a sentence is about and what the sentence says about it. Secondly, they contain, I think, the final answer to our questions about a sentence's signification. Let us make the straightforward hypothesis that there is a close connection between what a sentence 'says' and what it signifies or indicates. Then it follows that a minimal sentence like 'Callias walks' 'combines an object and an action', and signifies 'an action or inaction or being of what is or of what is not', not by bearing a simple relation of signification to an action–object complex, but rather by bearing a complex relation of signification to *two* entities, an action and an object—i.e. by signifying an action *as* the action of some object (remember 263b9: the false sentence 'says the things [i.e. the properties] which are not *as* things which are'). So, when we say that 'Callias walks' signifies the walk of Callias, what this really means is that 'Callias walks' signifies the walk as Callias', as holding of Callias.⁴⁵

---

⁴³ See Frede (1992: 414–16).

⁴⁴ This is a controversial passage; I am assuming the correctness of the text and interpretation that I find most convincing (for an excellent discussion, see Crivelli 2012: 233–59). The gist of what I am going to say, however, is compatible also with other possibilities.

⁴⁵ This suggestion bears some resemblance to the account of judgement and belief advanced by Russell (1912: ch. XII).

## VII

There is progress in philosophy. When it is Aristotle's turn to address the issues that Plato had dealt with in the *Cratylus* and the *Sophist*, the possibility of falsehood has ceased to be a live philosophical issue: Plato has laid it to rest once and for all.

The main place where Aristotle concerns himself with matters of sentence structure is the treatise *De interpretatione*, which in chapters 2–3 gives an account of *onoma* and *rhema* before moving on to consider more complex linguistic units—i.e. the *logos* and especially its declarative variety, which is the subject of the remaining chapters. Chapter 2 is about the *onoma*, which is defined thus:

A name is a spoken sound significant by convention, not involving time, none of whose parts is significant in separation. (*De int.* 2. 16$^a$19–21)

The remainder of the chapter is devoted to elucidating various aspects of this initial definition and adding some qualifications. Two points are important for our present purposes: (i) Aristotle gives proper and common nouns as examples of names; (ii) although Aristotle is not explicit about this here, he seems to believe that another distinctive feature of a name is that it can serve as subject term in a sentence. This is his reason for regarding nouns in cases other than the nominative not as 'names' proper but as 'inflexions of names':

'Philo's', 'to-Philo', and the like are not names but inflexions of names. The same account holds for them as for names, except that an inflexion when combined with 'is', 'was', or 'will be' is not true or false, whereas a name always is. Take, for example, 'Philo's is' or 'Philo's is not': so far there is nothing either true or false. (*De int.* 2.16$^a$32–$^b$5)

Then, in chapter 3, Aristotle turns to the *rhema*. Here is his famous definition:

A *rhema* is what additionally signifies time, no part of which is significant separately; and it is always a sign of the things said of something other. It additionally signifies time: e.g. 'recovery' is a name, but 'recovers' is a verb, because it additionally signifies the thing's holding now. And it is always a sign of the things which are said of something other, i.e. are said of a subject or in a subject. (*De int.* 3. 16$^b$6–10)[46]

Here Aristotle is, first of all, implicitly claiming that a *rhema* has the normal features of a name: as he puts it later on (16$^b$19–20), 'When spoken just by themselves, *rhemata* are names and signify something'—i.e. *rhemata* are names

---

[46] I am translating and citing the passage's text as reported by the majority of witnesses and edited by Waitz (1844) and Montanari (1984, 1988). The text of the standard Oxford edition (Minio-Paluello 1949) is different at various points, but none of these differences is very relevant to our present concerns. Weidemann's new edition (2014) was published too late for me to be able to consult it.

This and the ensuing paragraphs, down to the end of Section VI, recur almost identically in Ademollo (in preparation), where, however, among other things I add a discussion of the variant readings in *De int.* 16$^b$10–11.

in the generic sense, as in Plato. But he is also claiming that the *rhema* has another additional feature: it signifies time (cf. *Poet.* 20. 1457ᵃ14–15) by locating, as it were, in time⁴⁷ the item it signifies. Thus 'recovers' signifies something—indeed, presumably the very same item as the name 'recovery' does, as Aristotle's example suggests; but it also signifies that there is some recovery now, that recovery holds of someone now.

Aristotle here states also an explicit connection between *rhemata* and predication: a *rhema* always signifies something that is predicated of something other (ἔστιν ἀεὶ τῶν καθ' ἑτέρου λεγομένων σημεῖον, 16b7). Part of what this means is that a *rhema* signifies a predicate in the ontological sense—an attribute or property, like recovery in the example (cf. e.g. *An. pr.* 1.27. 43ᵃ25–43). Thus Aristotle's claim concerns (also) the ontological status of the referents of *rhemata*.

But while this is undoubtedly part of the point here, there is more to it, as Aristotle's use of the adverb 'always' suggests:⁴⁸ Aristotle means also that a verb always, i.e. in every context of use, signifies an item which gets predicated of (i.e., predicatively ascribed to) something in that context. In other words, a verb always occurs in predicate position in a sentence. This is a genuinely distinctive characteristic of the verb, which distinguishes it, in particular, from general terms, which do signify predicates in the previous, ontological sense, and do occur in contexts in which they signify an item that gets predicated of something ('Some animals are *cats*'), but which also occur in contexts in which they signify something of which an item gets predicated ('Some *cats* are grey').

Indeed, it is reasonable to suppose that Aristotle takes a *rhema* to signify also *that* such an item is getting predicated of something other—i.e. to signify not just a predicate, but also predication itself.⁴⁹ This further notion is already presupposed when Aristotle says of 'recovers' that it 'additionally signifies the thing's holding now' (προσσημαίνει ... τὸ νῦν ὑπάρχειν, 16ᵇ9). Though, in context, the emphasis of this lies on 'now', it conveys also an implicit commitment to the view that the *rhema* additionally signifies a predicate's now *holding*.

At the end of the passage Aristotle explains what he means by 'things which are said of something other'. He does so with a phrase that is transmitted by almost all witnesses as 'i.e. those which are said of a subject or in a subject' (οἷον τῶν καθ' ὑποκειμένου ἢ ἐν ὑποκειμένῳ, 16ᵇ10–11). This must refer to the well-known distinction advanced in *Categories* 2 between items which 'are said of a subject' and items which 'are in a subject'. It is a thorny distinction, but this much seems to be clear: if *X* 'is said of a subject', then *X* is an essential attribute of something, whereas if *X* 'is

---

⁴⁷ I am drawing the phrase 'locating...in time' from Frede (unpublished).
⁴⁸ This is clearly seen by Ammonius in his commentary (see n. 25), 48.10–13, 49.7–14. Cf. Stephanus (*Commentaria in Aristotelem Graeca* XVIII.3, ed. Hayduck), 14.16–20.
⁴⁹ Frede (unpublished). Cf. Ackrill (1963: 118–19) and Whitaker (1996: 58).

in a subject', then $X$ is a non-essential attribute of something. Therefore in *De interpretatione* 3 the phrase means that verbs are always signs of something that gets predicated *either essentially or non-essentially* of something.

## VIII

Unlike the *Sophist*, the *De interpretatione* pays explicit attention to copula sentences of the form '$S$ is $P$'. Indeed, such sentences are especially important for Aristotle in view of their role in his syllogistic. Aristotle, however, omits to make explicit how they are to be parsed and how the distinction between *onomata* and *rhemata* is relevant to them. Here are some considerations.

(i) Aristotle recognizes that 'There is no difference between saying that a human being walks and saying that a human being is an item that walks', as he puts it at *De int.* 12. 21$^b$9–10 (cf. *An. pr.* 51$^b$13–16, *Metaph.* 1017$^a$22–30). That is to say, the phrase 'is $P$' in a sentence of the form '$S$ is $P$' plays a role analogous to the role played by the verb '$Ps$' in a sentence of the form '$S$ $Ps$'. Nevertheless, 'is $P$' cannot constitute a *rhema*; for Aristotle plainly takes *rhemata* to be individual words, and 'is $P$' fails to satisfy one of the conditions stated in the definition of *rhema*: it is not an expression 'no part of which is significant separately'.

(ii) Aristotle regards the copula as a *rhema*. This is very clear in chapter 10, where he says that

Without a *rhema* there will be no affirmation or denial. For 'is', 'will be', 'was', 'becomes', and the like are *rhemata* according to what was laid down, since they additionally signify time. (*De int.* 10. 19$^b$12–14)

Granted, the immediate subject matter of these lines is 'to be' in its complete use, equivalent to 'to exist'; thus Aristotle immediately goes on to say 'So a first affirmation and denial are: "A human being is", "A human being is not"' (19$^b$14–16). But a few lines below we do come to 'is' as a copula, without the slightest indication that this is an essentially different 'is' or that what has been said before does not hold here:

But when 'is' is predicated additionally as a third element, there are two ways of expressing opposition. (I mean, e.g., 'a human being is just': here I say that 'is' is a third component, name or *rhema*, in the affirmation.) (*De int.* 10. 19$^b$19–22)

In fact Aristotle's claim that the copula 'is a third component, name or *rhema*, in the affirmation', or 'is a component in the affirmation as a third name or *rhema*' (τρίτον ... συγκεῖσθαι ὄνομα ἢ ῥῆμα ἐν τῇ καταφάσει), is almost invariably[50] interpreted as expressing either uncertainty or indifference towards the question whether

---

[50] Even by Barnes (2009: 31–2, within a thorough discussion of the Aristotelian copula).

the copula should be reckoned a name or a *rhema*. I for one do not see how Aristotle could be uncertain or indifferent. He has just said that 'is' is a *rhema* on the grounds that it signifies time; now he is adding that 'is' 'is predicated additionally' in a sentence, i.e. that 'is' and '*P*' in '*S* is *P*' are joined together in being predicated of '*S*'—which is exactly what we should expect in the light of (i) above.[51] Therefore Aristotle is actually implying that the copula is a *rhema* and giving us two good reasons for doing so, the first of which also rules out the possibility that it may be a name. (It may be unclear whether the copula has any basic signification, and we would wish that Aristotle told us more on this; but in fact that unclarity is, if anything, first of all a further argument against interpreting the copula as a name.) The claim that the copula 'is a component in the affirmation as a third name or *rhema*' need mean no more than this: that the copula is the third element among names and *rhemata* counted together—i.e. the third *word*.[52]

(iii) Aristotle cannot regard the subject complement '*P*' in '*S* is *P*' as a *rhema*. In fact there is an ancient and influential interpretation—advanced already by Ammonius in his commentary[53]—according to which this is what Aristotle does. But that interpretation cannot, I think, be right. To be sure, '*P*' refers to the extra-linguistic item that gets predicated in '*S* is *P*'; indeed, the *Analytics* would call it precisely the predicate *term* (*An. pr.* 1.1. 24$^b$16–18). But '*P*' lacks both of the distinctive features of a *rhema* according to Aristotle's own definition in chapter 3: it does not signify time and does not *always* signify a predicate, because it can also signify a subject of predication ('Every *S* is *P*' converts to 'Some *P* is *S*').

Ammonius' interpretation has been thought to receive some support from three passages (*De int.* 1. 16$^a$13–15; 10. 20$^a$31–3, $^b$1–2) where Aristotle makes a claim that is meant to apply to both *onomata* and *rhemata* alike, but then exemplifies it only with names and adjectives—as though adjectives could count as instances of *rhemata*. Just by way of example, here is the third of these passages:

---

[51] Both expressions and the items they signify can be said by Aristotle to be predicated in a sentence.

[52] A kindred but unnecessarily strained suggestion ('name-or-*rhema*' used as a generic term for 'word') is advanced by Montanari (1996: 354–6).

A passage often cited in connection with the copula is *De int.* 3. 16$^b$23–5, where Aristotle, immediately after stressing the distinction between isolated verbs and complete sentences, says of 'to be' or 'not to be' that 'by itself it is nothing, but it additionally signifies some combination, which cannot be thought of without the components'. This is usually interpreted as meaning that the copula lacks any basic signification and is a mere link between the subject and the predicate term. I cannot properly discuss the passage here, but I doubt that this standard interpretation is correct; for there is no reason why Aristotle should suddenly refer to the copula in this context. I rather incline to the view (for which see (*b*) in Ackrill 1963: 123) that Aristotle is speaking of the existential 'to be', which has been repeatedly mentioned in the previous chapters; that 'by itself it is nothing' in the emphatic sense that it does not constitute a complete sentence; and that 'it additionally signifies some combination' in the sense that, as Ackrill puts it, 'it calls for the addition of a subject-term'.

[53] Ammonius (see n. 25), 28.5–9, 52.32–53.8. Cf. Weidemann (2002: 155).

If names and *rhemata* are transposed they still signify the same thing, e.g. 'a human being is white' and 'white is a human being'.

Here Aristotle has been taken to be thinking of the sentence 'A human being is white' and regarding 'white' as the *rhema* in such a sentence, in so far as 'white' is the predicate term in it. Now, this construal is attractively economical, as long as we focus on these three passages alone. But once you have the larger picture in view and are aware that general terms cannot satisfy the definition of *rhema*, what is really economical is rather to suppose that in this and in the two other passages Aristotle is misleadingly offering two examples of *onoma* and none of *rhema*.[54]

So, to sum up, the *De interpretatione*'s distinction between *onoma* and *rhema* is, as in Plato, essentially a lexical distinction between name (including proper and common nouns as well as adjectives) and verb. Thereby the *De interpretatione* turns out to be consistent with Aristotle's brief remarks in the *Poetics*, 20.1457$^a$10–18 (which clearly include the adjective in the *onoma* and distinguish it from the *rhema*), and with later grammatical wisdom.[55] Aristotle's distinction, however, takes fully into account, more explicitly and deeply than even Plato's *Sophist* does, the syntactic function of both word classes.

# IX

There is one final issue I wish to broach. A recurring theme of our discussion of the *Sophist* passage has been that the Stranger there suggested that the right sort of combination between names and verbs should succeed in signifying something not signified by names or verbs alone (see Sections V–VI). I should now like to say something about how that idea is developed by Aristotle.[56]

*Metaphysics Δ* 29, a chapter devoted to charting the various uses of the term 'false', opens up by identifying the notion of a false *pragma*, 'object.' One variety of false *pragma* is false

> by not being combined or by its being impossible for it to be composed. This is how we speak of the diagonal's being commensurable or your being seated; for one of these is false always, the other sometimes; for these things are non-beings in this way. (*Metaph. Δ* 29.1024$^b$18–21)

What sort of 'objects' could Aristotle be talking about here? He refers to them by means of *infinitive* clauses (τὸ τὴν διάμετρον εἶναι σύμμετρον and τὸ σὲ καθῆσθαι), which can be translated respectively as 'that the diagonal is commensurable', or 'the

---

[54] See Montanari (1988: 69–70); Whitaker (1996: 53–4).

[55] See the *Art of Grammar* ascribed to Dionysius Thrax, §§12–13. Frede (unpublished) comments that 'there is something deeply unsatisfactory' about the fact that Aristotle is working with a basic distinction between names and verbs as two word classes instead of a more appropriate distinction between noun phrase and verb phrase or between subject and predicate. Frede also plausibly suggests that Aristotle's emphasis on word classes is due to the influence of the *Sophist*.

[56] On the following remarks on Aristotelian *pragmata* see Crivelli (2004: 46–62).

diagonal's being commensurable', and 'that you are seated', or 'your being seated'. This suggests that the 'objects' at issue are items of a propositional nature, like propositions or states of affairs. These items, Aristotle says here, can be said to be false, or 'non-beings', in virtue of their not being combined—i.e. in virtue of the fact that the (extra-linguistic) subject and predicate of the corresponding sentence are not combined in reality: in fact the diagonal is not commensurable (sc. with the side of the square) and you are not seated.

Aristotle seems to be talking about the same *pragmata* in other places. One is the beginning of *Metaph.* Θ 10, 1051$^a$34–$^b$9, a very difficult passage where he mentions a sense of 'being' and 'not being', and of 'true' and 'false', which holds 'in the case of the *pragmata*' and consists in their being 'combined or divided'. Indeed, according to one possible construal of that passage, Aristotle might even be claiming that the 'being' or 'not being' of these *pragmata* constitutes the strictest sense of being true or false, in that *pragmata* are the primary bearers of truth and falsehood.

Aristotle's conception of *pragmata* as states of affairs is no fully-fledged theory; it is rather something we can reconstruct on the basis of a few passages. But its aftermath might have been momentous. After Aristotle, Stoic semantics and logic centred on the notion of a (complete) *lekton*, 'sayable', conceived of as the *pragma* said and signified by a (complete) sentence, and even more specifically on the notion of those *lekta* that were called *axiomata*, or propositions, and regarded as the primary bearers of truth and falsehood (see Diog. Laert. 7.57–65, Sext. Emp. *Adv. Math.* 8.11–12). Thus Aristotle's *pragmata* seem to have been forerunners of the Stoic ones and might even have played some role in their genesis. But the Stoic theory is another story.

# References

Ackrill, J. L. (1963). *Aristotle: Categories and De interpretatione.* Oxford: Clarendon Press.
Ademollo, F. (2011). *The Cratylus of Plato: A Commentary.* Cambridge: Cambridge University Press.
Ademollo, F. (in preparation). 'Pseudo-Plato on Language'.
Barnes, J. (1996). 'Grammar on Aristotle's Terms', in M. Frede and G. Striker (eds), *Rationality in Greek Thought.* Oxford: Oxford University Press, 175–202; repr. in Barnes (2012: 147–71).
Barnes, J. (2007). *Truth, etc. Six Lectures on Ancient Logic.* Oxford: Oxford University Press.
Barnes, J. (2009). 'Notes on the Copula', *Dianoia,* 14: 27–62.
Barnes, J. (2012). *Logical Matters: Essays in Ancient Philosophy II.* Oxford: Oxford University Press.
Barney, R. (2001). *Names and Nature in Plato's Cratylus.* New York and London: Routledge.
Beaney, M. (1997) (ed.). *The Frege Reader.* Malden, MA, Oxford, and Carlton: Blackwell.
Blank, D. (1996). *Ammonius: On Interpretation 1–8.* London: Duckworth.
Cambiano, G. (1981). *Platone: Dialoghi filosofici,* vol. 2. Turin: Unione Tipografico-Editrice Torinese.
Conti, C. (1977–8). 'Storia di una parola greca: ῥῆμα'. Unpublished thesis, University of Florence.

Crivelli, P. (2004). *Aristotle on Truth*. Cambridge: Cambridge University Press.
Crivelli, P. (2012). *Plato's Account of Falsehood: A Study of the* Sophist. Cambridge: Cambridge University Press.
Denyer, N. (1991). *Language, Thought and Falsehood in Ancient Greek Philosophy*. London: Routledge.
Frede, M. (1992). 'Plato's *Sophist* on False Statements', in R. Kraut (ed.), *The Cambridge Companion to Plato*. Cambridge: Cambridge University Press, 397–424.
Frede, M. (unpublished). 'Aristotle on Nouns and Verbs in De Interpretatione'. Paper presented at the 13th Symposium Aristotelicum (Pontignano, 1993).
Frege, G. (1967). *Kleine Schriften*, ed. I. Angelelli. Hildesheim: Olms.
Furth, M. (1968). 'Two Types of Denotation', in *Studies in Logical Theory*. American Philosophical Quarterly Monograph Series, 2. Oxford: Blackwell, 9–45.
Guthrie, W. K. C. (1969). *A History of Greek Philosophy*, vol. 3. Cambridge: Cambridge University Press.
Hoekstra, M., and Scheppers, Fr. (2003). 'Ὄνομα, ῥῆμα et λόγος dans le *Cratyle* et le *Sophiste* de Platon: Analyse du lexique et analyse du discours', *L'Antiquité Classique*, 72: 55–73.
Kahn, C. H. (1973). 'Language and Ontology in the *Cratylus*', in E. N. Lee, A. P. D. Mourelatos, and R. M. Rorty (eds), *Exegesis and Argument: Studies in Greek Philosophy Presented to Gregory Vlastos*. Assen: Van Gorcum, 152–76.
McDowell, J. (1973). *Plato: Theaetetus*. Oxford: Clarendon Press.
Minio-Paluello, L. (1949). *Aristotelis Categoriae et Liber De Interpretatione*. Oxford: Oxford University Press.
Montanari, E. (1984). *La sezione linguistica del* Peri hermeneias *di Aristotele. Volume primo: il testo*. Florence: Università degli Studi di Firenze, Dipartimento di Scienze dell'Antichità 'Giorgio Pasquali'.
Montanari, E. (1988). *La sezione linguistica del* Peri hermeneias *di Aristotele. Volume secondo: Il commento*. Florence: Università degli Studi di Firenze, Dipartimento di Scienze dell'Antichità 'Giorgio Pasquali'.
Montanari, E. (1996). 'ONOMA H PHMA nel X capitolo del «Peri hermeneias» aristotelico', in M. S. Funghi (ed.), *ΟΔΟΙ ΔΙΖΗΣΙΟΣ—Le vie della ricerca. Studi in onore di Francesco Adorno*. Florence: Leo S. Olschki Editore, 345–56.
Nuchelmans, G. (1973). *Theories of the Proposition: Ancient and Medieval Conceptions of the Bearers of Truth and Falsity*. Amsterdam and London: North-Holland.
Riddell, J. (1867). *The Apology of Plato*. Oxford: Oxford University Press.
Russell, B. (1912). *The Problems of Philosophy*. London: Williams and Norgate; New York: Henry Holt and Company.
Russell, B. (1956). 'The Philosophy of Logical Atomism', in R. C. Marsh (ed.), *Logic and Knowledge*. London: Routledge, 57–281.
Sedley, D. (2003). *Plato's Cratylus*. Cambridge: Cambridge University Press.
Szaif, J. (1998). *Platons Begriff der Wahrheit*. 2nd edn. Freiburg and Munich: Karl Alber.
Waitz, Th. (1844). *Aristoteles: Organon graece. Pars prior*. Leipzig: Hahn; repr. Aalen 1965.
Weidemann, H. (2002). *Aristoteles: Peri hermeneias*. 2nd edn. Berlin: Akademie Verlag.
Weidemann, H. (2014). *Aristoteles: De interpretatione*. Berlin and New York: De Gruyter.
Whitaker, C. W. A. (1996). *Aristotle's* De interpretatione: *Contradiction and Dialectic*. Oxford: Oxford University Press.

# 3

# On What is Said: The Stoics and Peter Abelard

*Margaret Cameron*

A novel kind of meaning shows up, apparently independently, in the philosophy of the Stoics and of Peter Abelard (1079–1142). For the Stoics it is the *lekton*, or 'sayable' (or, more precisely, the *axioma*, or 'assertible', which is one type of *lekton*), and for Abelard it is the *dictum*. The extent of similarity between their doctrines is surprising, especially because there is no evidence of a historical connection between them: as far as we know, Abelard did not have access to any Stoic writings, or reports of Stoic views, on the topic of linguistic content.[1] The similarity is more surprising still, given that Abelard was working within the context of Aristotle's logic, which contains no comparable doctrine.

Historians of philosophy have noticed this similarity.[2] When the comparison is drawn it is with reference to the fact of their shared recognition of this new type of content—propositional content. But there are other remarkable points of similarity in their views. First, both seem to have been motivated, at least in part, by the need to disambiguate the notion of 'predication' in the ancient philosophical tradition. Second, both the Stoics (at least beginning with Chrysippus, the third head of the school) and Abelard were driven by a commitment to anti-realism, and by the need to present an anti-realist, or at least deflationary, metaphysics. After a brief outline of each of their doctrines, I will compare their views on the points mentioned here.

---

[1] While Augustine's *De dialectica* contains some version of the Stoic doctrine, his treatise does not appear to have circulated until the thirteenth century. Another possible source might have been Cicero, but I know of no evidence to support such a transmission.

[2] Martin (2004), who cites Nuchelmans (1973) and Schenkeveld (1984). See also Jacobi (1983) and Lenz (2005). But see Nuchelmans (1973: 152): 'it is hardly necessary to add that the Abelardian term *dictum* has nothing to do with the Stoic term *lekton*.'

## The Stoics

Unlike the situation with Abelard's philosophy, much of which has been preserved and transmitted to us in lengthy writings, the historical record preserving the Stoic doctrine of the *lekton* is patchy and piecemeal. Stoic views on this topic, as with most others in their philosophy, are drawn from scattered reports, many of which were written by philosophers who either were not themselves Stoics or were hostile to their views. Consequently, the doctrine has had to be reconstructed, and there remains a fair amount of guesswork involved.[3]

The Stoics introduced a new type of linguistic content called the *lekton*, which we will translate as 'sayable'. There is a variety of ways to translate *lekton* into English. Some say it is the state of affairs or the 'fact' signified by an expression. But it is misleading to translate it this way, not least because *lekta* can be, as we will see, either true or false. 'Sayable' is best, and, in fact, there is historical precedent for a translation that emphasizes the modal character of the *lekta*: 'Now that which the mind, not the ears, perceives from the word [*verbum*] and which is held within the mind itself is called a "sayable" [*dicibile*].'[4]

The idea is this: there are some things we are able to talk about on the basis of our experiences in the world. That which can be talked about, that which can be said, is the sayable. The *lekta* are discovered, so to speak, by means of what the Stoics called 'rational impressions'. A rational impression is a thought (*noêsis*), 'one in which the content <of that thought> can be exhibited in language'.[5] *Lekta* are said to supervene upon those impressions.[6] To better understand *lekta*, let us first look at their ontological character;[7] then we will examine the types of *lekta* and their features. Finally, some speculation as to the Stoics' motivation for devising the *lekta* will help better characterize what the sayables are.

The *lekton* had a particular status in Stoic philosophy. Famously, the Stoics were materialists, or corporealists, and held that everything that exists is a body. Their view was that only bodies have the capacity to act or to be acted upon, and that only

---

[3] I am particularly indebted here to the reconstructions by Frede (1994), Bobzien (1999, 2003), and Caston (1999). See also Nuchelmans (1973).

[4] Augustine (1975: 89). For comparison of Stoic theory with Augustine's, see Markus (1972) and Long (2005).

[5] Long and Sedley (1987: 33C). On Stoic concepts and concept acquisition, see Hankinson (2003) and Brittain (2005).

[6] The verb is *to paryphistamenon*, which is best understood as 'parasitic upon', or 'supervenes upon'; see Atherton (1993): based on Sextus Empiricus, *Adversus Mathematicos* 8, 11–12: 'That which signifies is speech ("Dion"), what is signified is the specific state of affairs [*auto to pragma*] indicated by the spoken word and which we grasp as co-existent with [*paryphistamenon*] our thought but which the barbarians do not understand although they hear the sound.'

[7] It might appear odd to ask about the metaphysical underpinnings of *lekta* since, famously, the Stoics eschewed metaphysics in favour of physics, which they considered to be First Philosophy. Still, the question is appropriate and the answer will involve some of the very reasons why the Stoics aimed to be anti-metaphysicians at all.

things with these capacities can properly be said to exist. The *lekta* cannot, properly speaking, either act or be acted upon, and, accordingly, they are not bodies. In what sense are *lekta* not bodies? When a speaker and a hearer communicate, the air that comes out of the speaker's mouth is made up of bodies, and this air acts upon the hearer's ears, which are also bodies. But what is *said by* the speaker is not a body: it is the *lekton*, the sayable. The Stoics recognized that *lekta*, as they put it, 'subsist', along with three other non-bodies in the universe (time, void, and space); precisely what it is to subsist is not wholly clear, but it suffices to say that *lekta*, while not being bodies and so not part of the Stoic physical universe, could still be recognized to play a part in it. When we take up the question of the Stoics' motivation for their doctrine, the reasons for this queer metaphysical status should become clearer.

The initial division of *lekta* is this: some are complete, others incomplete. *Lekta* are distinguished on these lines by what we can call the 'suspense criterion'—that is, by whether the utterance of a *lekton* leaves a hearer with a complete or incomplete understanding of what is said. For example, when someone utters the single predicate 'writes', the hearer is prompted to ask, 'Who?' Whether this is meant to be a psychological test for completeness, or is indeed a *criterion* for completeness, is unclear. What is clear is that incomplete *lekta* contain only the predicate of a subject–predicate construction, and these are verbs or verb phrases, and so 'writes' or 'is wise' (as compared to, say, 'writing' or 'wisdom', taken as verbal nouns).[8] These incomplete *lekta* were considered to be defective and 'must be joined onto a nominative case to yield a judgement'.[9]

A complete *lekton* satisfies the suspense criterion. The Stoics recognized a variety of complete *lekta*. Most common are: propositions (*axiomata*), syllogisms (*sullogismoi*), questions (*erotemata*), and what they called 'enquiries' (*pusmata*).[10] Questions were distinguished from enquiries since the former could admit 'yes/no' answers ('Do you like pudding?'), whereas the latter must be answered with further words ('Why do you like pudding?'). Although it might at first seem as if the Stoics recognized varieties of speech acts by recognizing different types of sayables, it is somewhat misleading to assimilate the types of complete *lekta* to modern-day speech acts. It is true that an *axioma*, or proposition, is a type of *lekton* characterized by the fact that, when one expresses it, one at the same time states it: 'it is that by saying which we make a statement.'[11] The Stoic proposition is, thus, a *stateable*, or an *assertible*. Similarly, it would seem, the Stoic question is a *questionable*; or it is the type of *lekton* with questionability. And so on for the others. However, note that the content, or what is said by a *lekton*, does not remain fixed, since the force or attitude

---

[8] See Seneca *Ep.* 117, 11–12. Contrast this with Aristotle's view that predicates can be either verbs or verbal nouns.
[9] Diogenes Laertius VII 63.
[10] Diogenes Laertius VII 63–6; Sextus Empiricus *M* VIII, 71 ff.; Long and Sedley (1987: 33F).
[11] Diogenes Laertius VII 66.

is actually *part of* each type of content itself. Instead of countenancing different speech acts, then, the Stoic distinction between types of *lekta* is in terms of the mood of what is said. The assertibility or stateability of the proposition is the mood of that particular sayable, just as the questionability of a question is the mood of another.

The Stoics were primarily concerned with *axiomata*, or propositional contents, because of their importance to logic.[12] While *lekta* do not preserve their content across different types of *lekta* (that is, there is not one type of content that is now questioned, now asserted), the contents of Stoic propositions *can* be preserved when embedded in different contexts. These contexts are not, however, types of speech acts, but are different logical contexts—for example, negations, conditionalizations, and so on. Consider this passage:

When they [the Stoic dialecticians] say that the proposition 'It is day' is at present true but 'It is night' false, and 'Not: it is day' false, but 'Not: it is night' true, one will wonder how a negative which is one and the same, by being joined to truths makes them false, and by being joined to falsehood makes them true.[13]

Three interesting observations can be made regarding this little passage. First, *axiomata* can change truth-value. Each *axioma* is indexed to its time of utterance. As such, the change in truth-value can occur owing to the presence of parts of speech such as indexicals and demonstratives in propositions, depending on the time of their utterance. The Stoics called these *metapiptonta*, since they are truth-sensitive to changes in time. Second, when the proposition is negated, as in 'Not: it is night', it is the whole proposition, and not just some part of it (such as the predicate term, as in, 'It is not-night'), that is negated. To this extent, Stoic propositions have a kind of constituent structure and can be embedded in negations and other logical contexts.[14] Third, it appears that the Stoics held that 'It is day' is the same proposition asserted both without and within the negation operator. As S. Bobzien has clearly shown, at least in the case of assertibles with a definite subject: 'the Stoics regarded these as two assertibles of the same assertible.'[15] Consequently, types of *axiomata* with definite subjects can be tokened by being uttered on different occasions.[16]

To sum up so far, Stoic *lekta* are a special type of linguistic content. They are what can be said by expressions. Complete *lekta* are distinguished by mood (assertibility, questionability, and so on). One type of *lekton*, the proposition, seems to have a constituent structure such that it can be uttered in, or embedded in, multiple contexts.

---

[12] See especially Bobzien (2003) on the assertible. I am grateful for Bobzien's clear and stimulating work on this topic.
[13] Sextus Empiricus *M* 8.103; see Long and Sedley (1987: 34F).
[14] See Bobzien (1999: 101–3).    [15] Bobzien (1999: 99).
[16] For example, a definite assertible would be 'This one is walking' asserted when the speaker points to an actual person. Bobzien (1999) explains how *axiomata* with indefinite subjects (e.g., 'someone') can also be tokened in so far as there is a way deictically to refer to a definite subject.

They can change truth-value on different occasions of utterance. But why did the Stoics introduce this new type of content? No explicit explanation has been found in the literature, but a number of reasons can be deduced from the fragmentary surviving documentation.

According to one reconstruction of the *lekton* doctrine, *lekta* emerged or evolved from being metaphysical entities to being logical ones. To explain this development, it is necessary to recognize and explain a particular feature common to much of ancient philosophy, which is that predicables (*kategoremata*) were considered in an equivocal way. That is, 'predicate' seemed to do double duty for both the predicate term, considered linguistically, and the thing signified by that predicate term. The equivocation is especially present in Aristotle's philosophy. Aristotle, in his work on language and logic (see particularly *Categories* and *On Interpretation*) was primarily interested in the signification of the principal parts of speech required to construct a complete sentence, or assertion. These are names and verbs, which according to him have a complete meaning in themselves and are not dependent on other words (as syncategorematic expressions such as conjunctions are) for their signification. Nouns and verbs are what came to be called 'kategorematic' expressions. Aristotle's interpreters pointed out that the first work in the Aristotelian Organon, the *Categories*, dealt primarily with these expressions. But the presentation in that treatise of these types of expressions seemed to introduce into the discussion of signification a confusion or conflation, since predicates are introduced both as (i) things that are said and (ii) things that are (or exist). For example,

Whenever one thing is predicated of another as of a subject, all things said of what is predicated will be said of the subject too. For example, man is predicated of the individual man, and animal of man; so animal will be predicated of the individual man also—for the individual man is both a man and an animal.[17]

More is at stake here than a simple failure to employ a device such as inverted commas to distinguish between the use and mention of an expression. At issue is what appears to be at least an inconsistency in the understanding of what predicates are (either attributes and properties of things or the expressions signifying those attributes), and at worst a failure to recognize this problem of equivocity at all. Indeed, the *Categories* provoked a long history of debate over just what these so-called predicates are (that is, the problem of universals).

In this context, it is easy to appreciate how the introduction of the *lekton* was warranted. According to a reconstruction of the evolution of the doctrine by M. Frede, philosophers after Aristotle began to make a distinction between qualities or attributes and predicates, but there was some debate over the issue:

---

[17] Aristotle (1963a: $1^b 10$–15).

They distinguished between wisdom, the quality, and being wise, the predicate. Seneca not only tells us that the Peripatetics rejected the distinction, but also attributes the origin of the distinction to the 'Old Dialecticians' from whom, he says, the Stoics inherited it.[18]

The Peripatetics, who were followers of Aristotle, rejected the distinction. For the 'Old Dialecticians', who are presumably early or proto-Stoics, the predicate is still a metaphysical item: it is the condition or state of being wise, as contrasted with the quality of wisdom itself. Frede, following an illustration of the distinction given by Seneca, explains:

> the field which a farmer has is one thing, namely something corporeal; but it is not to be identified with having the field, which is something incorporeal; similarly wisdom is one thing, namely on the Stoic view a quality and hence a body; having wisdom or being wise is something altogether different, namely something incorporeal. The point which is made here is clearly a metaphysical point: in addition to Socrates and to wisdom, both of which are bodies, there is also such an item as Socrates' being wise, which is not a body but something incorporeal.[19]

According to Frede, at some point the Stoics cut the metaphysical tie and recast *lekta* as logical entities, and an attribute became 'something that is or can be expressed'.[20] Accordingly, *lekta* are the linguistic counterparts of rational impressions, which just are those impressions we have that can be put into words. If I see, for example, a dog barking, I see a body, but I also have a thought, a rational impression, that can be verbally articulated: 'The dog is barking.' What is said is not a body, but a *lekton*.

The thought that I have when I see the dog barking is a cognition upon which the *lekton*, what can be said, supervenes. It is easy enough to surmise that, at some point, there was a debate regarding whether this new type of content was the same as a cognitive content, such as a concept. Here we can see a second motivation—related and compatible with the first—for the development of the *lekton* as a linguistic, not cognitive, content. According to a reconstruction of the Stoics' changing views about concepts (*ennoiai*) by V. Caston, the *lekton* eventually came to replace concepts in Stoic epistemology.[21] Earlier Stoics acknowledged a role for concepts, since they enabled a hierarchicalization of genera and species, which were required for Stoic logic and rational investigation.[22] But, at some point, probably with the work of Chrysippus, the Stoics stopped all reference to concepts and replaced them with reference to 'conventions involving names'.[23] As eliminativists about *ante-rem* (that is, Platonic) Forms, the *lekton* was the right tool for their anti-realist position.

---

[18] Frede (1994: 114), citing Seneca *Ep.* 117, 11–12.  [19] Frede (1994: 114).
[20] This is their view at least after Cleanthes: see Clem. *Strom.* 8.9.26.4; this is discussed in Caston (1999: 206).
[21] Caston (1999). The point was first mentioned without elaboration by Frede (1994).
[22] Diogenes Laertius VII 60–1; Caston (1999: 159) claims that, while early Stoics seemed to speak about Forms as if they were concepts (*ennoêmata*), this way of thinking was stopped. See Stobaeus I.136, 21–137, 6.
[23] Caston (1999: 149), based on Syrianus, *In met.* 105, 22–3. According to this report, some Stoics thought that Plato's Forms 'were originally introduced for the "use of conventions involving names"'.

It seems that later Stoics, then, beginning with Chrysippus, recognized that what is said by propositions could play a better explanatory role in Stoic logic than concepts do. Chrysippus, whose work in Stoic logic continues to be regarded as monumental in the history of Stoicism and the history of logic, was wary of the generic character of concepts. He advocated instead an analysis of propositions containing generic terms—for example, 'Man is a rational, mortal animal'—into universal generalizations—for example, 'If something is a man, then that thing is a rational, mortal animal.'[24] As Caston explains, changed accordingly, the statements are hypothetical, the term in the subject position has been changed to the predicate position, and the subjects in the antecedent and consequent are indefinite pronouns linked anaphorically.[25] Universal generalizations are different from definitions only in syntax and thereby signify *the same proposition*, as Chrysippus noted, but they thereby remove any reference to a generic object. The expression concerns only individuals, not kinds or concepts, which is consistent with and provides logical support for the Stoic commitment to non-realism (that is, the view that only individuals exist).

Chrysippus recognized that, without involving concepts, these sorts of statements are merely *lekta*, or sayables, and are nothing more ontologically robust. This deflationary move is characteristic of Stoic philosophy, and seems to have been brought about at least in part as a further reaction against the robust, hypostasized Forms of Plato's ontology. What is said by an expression—for example, 'If it is a man, it is a rational mortal animal'—is just 'what subsists <versus exists> in virtue of an articulable state of being appeared to'.[26] *Lekta* do not cause mental states (whereas sensible objects acting on the sense organs, both of which are bodies, do). They merely subsist and supervene on mental states. As a result, they are metaphysically very lean.

## Peter Abelard

Much more can be said about the Stoic theory, but we will now turn to Abelard for a brief overview of his new type of linguistic content, after which the Stoics' and Abelard's views on this topic can be directly compared.

In order to appreciate Abelard's advances in the philosophy of language, we need to set his views in the broader context of Aristotelian theory. Abelard was working at the very start of the twelfth century during the first major wave of logical study after hundreds of years in the Latin west. Abelard's main source for his views on logic and

---

[24] Sextus Empiricus *M* 11.8.   [25] Caston (1999).
[26] Sextus Empiricus *M* 8.70; Diogenes Laertius VII 63. See Caston (1999: 206–7), who suggests that 'the Stoics seem to have realized that [the *lekton* theory] could easily be applied to the problems that gave rise to Plato's theory of Forms; and if so, then there would no longer be any special need for a theory of concepts, even when speaking about conceptions (*ennoiai*) and preconceptions (*prolepsis*)—all of this can be handled much more simply and elegantly by appealing to expressibles alone'.

language is Aristotle's logical writings, especially the *Categories* and *On Interpretation*, as well as the ancient Roman commentator Boethius' commentaries on them.[27]

The key is to explain what Abelard meant by 'to signify' (*significare*), which was a technical term used by Latin logicians. Abelard accepted that words that are significant had been imposed or instituted by some name-giver in order to give rise to an understanding of what is signified. These words stand in a triadic relationship with the thoughts or concepts to which they give rise and that which is signified by those concepts. This relationship is described by Aristotle at the start of *On Interpretation*.[28] 'That which is signified', in Aristotle's vocabulary, are *pragmata*: while no theoretically neutral translation of this Greek term is available, Abelard had inherited from Boethius' Latin translation *res*, which is translated into English as 'things' (and could perhaps be translated more blandly by 'stuff'). Aristotle's lesson about the semantic triad was this: spoken utterances directly signify, or give rise to, understandings or thoughts, and thereby indirectly signify the things that those spoken utterances name.[29] The technical term *significare* accordingly came to mean 'to give rise to an understanding', since what is primarily or directly signified is what is understood by speakers and hearers.

Abelard cast Aristotle's doctrine in terms of a theory of double signification: nouns and verbs have both a signification of things (*significatio rerum*) as well as a signification of understandings/concepts (*significatio intellectum*). These need to be kept sharply distinct, especially because, as Abelard realized, some utterances are able to give rise to understandings even when the things signified by those utterances no longer exist. Consider, for example, a case in which a speaker claims 'A rose is a flower' in a world where, as it turns out, flowers no longer exist. In a move comparable to Chrysippus' described above, the listener is not directed to understand something about a particular rose (which does not exist) or roses in general (ditto). Instead, the logical form of what the listener understands is this: '*If* something is a rose, then it is a flower—even if there are no roses currently in existence.'[30] Signification is possible even when the objects signified no longer exist because of this special feature of double signification, and because the logic of what is understood does not require the existence of what is signified. The distinction between the two types of signification (of things, of understandings) reflects Abelard's awareness of the need to disambiguate what Aristotle meant by 'predicate' and 'predication'. Abelard was very specific

---

[27] Abelard also commented on Porphyry's *Isagoge*, taken to be an introduction to Aristotle's logic, as well as a number of logical treatises by Boethius. On Boethius' logical writings, see Magee and Marenbon (2009: 303–10).

[28] Aristotle (1963b: $16^a3$–9).

[29] Aristotle also mentions written expressions, which are in some sense likenesses of spoken utterances. But, in the ancient and medieval traditions, nearly all discussion in philosophy of language concerns language that is spoken.

[30] Abelard (2010: Prooemium $19^{69}$–$20^{89}$ [§§8–10]).

about this move, and he was well aware of the confusion in his ancient sources over the issue. But Abelard is unequivocal: predicates are significant words, not things (attributes, qualities, and so on) themselves.

Abelard introduced into this modified Aristotelian framework a new type of linguistic content, the *dictum* (or *dicta*, plural). According to him, *dicta* are what are said by propositions. Abelard had inherited from Boethius a definition of the proposition: a proposition 'is an utterance signifying what is true or false', or 'is a complete utterance containing what is true or false'.[31] However, Abelard modifies this definition in an important way. He says,

> in the definition of the proposition, 'to signify what is true or false' should not be taken according to the understanding, but according to the *dictum propositionis* (the 'what is said' of the proposition), that is, to propose by stating that which is in reality or that which is not in reality.[32]

A few things need to be explained to make sense of Abelard's point here. The first is what he means by saying that signifying what is true or false 'should not be taken according to the understanding'. The second is what is the '*dictum propositionis*', and the third is what it is 'to propose by stating'. These will be taken up in turn.

Recall that, on Aristotle's view, signifying is a matter of giving rise to an understanding. But, for Abelard, whatever thoughts or understandings are generated by what is said are not relevant to whether the proposition has signified what is true or false. According to him:

> Just as names and verbs have a double signification, namely of things and of concepts, so also I concede the proposition to be double: the concept composed of the parts of concepts and their *dicta*, which are sort of the 'thing' of the proposition (*quae sunt quasi res propositionis*), although they are not existing things (*essentiae*).[33]

We will address the point made at the end of this quotation about the ontological status of *dicta* in a moment. At issue here is the addition of *dicta* to the theory of double signification. Unlike the double signification of single words such as 'cat', which signifies both the four-footed furry thing in reality and a corresponding concept, the double signification of a proposition does not include real-world, actually existing items. Rather, a proposition such as '(A) man is human' signifies a concept, by which Abelard means that it gives rise to an understanding of some mental items (that is, 'the concept composed of the parts of concepts', here being 'man' plus 'human'). And it also signifies, or gives rise to, a *dictum*—that is, what is said by the proposition. *Dicta*, then, are sharply distinguished from cognitive contents, or understandings.

---

[31] Boethius (1990: 1174B, 1177C); Boethius (1877: 42). As Nuchelmans (1973: 134) points out, Boethius uses a variety of broadly similar verbs when characterizing the proposition, for example, to signify, to designate, to demonstrate, to show, to say, to propose, and so on.

[32] Abelard (2010: I, $55^{706-715}$ [§100]).     [33] Abelard (2010: IV, $135^{155-159}$ [§26]).

Abelard offers a proof of the distinction between thoughts or understandings and *dicta*, which also shows that a proposition's signifying what is true or false has to do with *dicta* alone. Quite sensibly, Abelard notices that we can have a false understanding that is generated by what is in fact a true proposition. What matters is what the *dictum propositionis* says:

If indeed we call a proposition 'true' insofar as it asserts what is true, that is, it states it just as it is in reality, it seems a true proposition *can* generate a false understanding, just as can statements regarding the future and the past. For, when Socrates is sitting, I hear, 'Socrates stood', or 'Socrates will stand', it is indeed true what is said, but the mental concept seems false.[34]

To appreciate Abelard's point, picture him in front of a sitting Socrates when he hears these propositions spoken. Seeing the sitting Socrates generates a corresponding thought of that reality. What, then, is in Abelard's mind when he see Socrates seated and at the same time hears the propositions about Socrates' past and future actions?

For I join <in my mind> *the sitting Socrates* with *the standing Socrates* in past or future time, attending to it in the present, and since *the standing itself* is not now, nor was at this time (which I also attend to at the same time), the mental conception which I now presently have does not agree with the *status* of the thing itself.[35]

By 'attending to', or focusing his mind's attention on, *the sitting Socrates* plus *Socrates' standing in future (or past)*, clearly Abelard has a false mental conception.[36] It does not correspond to what he calls the *status* of the thing, which is Socrates' present way of being. This is perhaps an overly complicated way of making his point, but what Abelard wants to convey is that the way we understand something can be completely at odds with the content of a proposition, and so it cannot be our understanding in virtue of which the proposition is true or false. What is said by a proposition, the *dictum propositionis*, thereby is not (or is not necessarily) what is understood by that proposition, and is accordingly independent of any (private) concepts generated upon hearing or speaking it.[37] What makes the *dictum propositionis* true or false is explained next.

---

[34] Abelard (2010: I, 56$^{735-739}$ [§105]).   [35] Abelard (2010: I, 56$^{740}$–57$^{743}$ [§105]).
[36] On Abelard's theory of *attentio*, see Rosier-Catach (2004), Cameron (2007), and Martin (2009).
[37] Jacobi et al. (1996) charted out an evolution in Abelard's thinking according to which understandings (*intellectus*) that are true or false are eventually replaced by the *dictum propositionis*. However, they then puzzled over why, after hitting upon the *dictum* theory, Abelard continued to make reference to true and false understandings, since that theory on their view is now considered otiose. Marenbon (2004) argues that their developmental account relies on a tendentious chronology of Abelard's writings (which Marenbon rejects). But, by rejecting the developmental account, Marenbon finds it difficult to accept that Abelard's *dictum* theory was a mature and corrective one. My interpretation entails that the Jacobi et al. interpretation is mistaken, and that it is possible to have true or false understandings that are entirely independent of the *dictum propositionis*, according to Abelard.

The second aspect of Abelard's theory to be explained is the *dictum propositionis* itself. *Dicta* are what are said by propositions. Propositions are, unlike individual names and verbs, truth-evaluable. What makes a proposition true or false, as we have just seen, are not the concepts or understandings generated in the hearer's or speaker's mind. But neither are the things signified by each of the words taken individually in that proposition, whether they actually exist in reality or not, responsible for the proposition's truth or falsity. Rather, *dicta* are true or false according to the way things are by nature (that is, in accordance with the natural order of kinds as created by God), which Abelard called their *status*.[38] Take the following example as illustration. Keep in mind that Abelard follows Aristotle's *Categories* as a means by which to distinguish substances from their accidents (that is, their qualities, quantities, relations, and so on for Aristotle's nine categories of accident). The *Categories*, by distinguishing between primary substances, which are individuals, and secondary substances, which are species and genera, also provides a basis for a taxonomy of substances organized by genus and species relations.

Here is the example:

'Socrates and Plato agree in being human.'

The example is motivated by a major debate in Abelard's day, the debate over what genera and species, which are called 'universals', actually *are*. Abelard was an anti-realist about universals. He accordingly devised many arguments against those who in any way reified or hypostasized certain features as universals.[39] Additionally, as mentioned above, he was well known to have advanced a semantic or linguistic approach to the problem of universals, and to have insisted that predicates—*pace* the confusion in Aristotle's texts—are significant words, not properties or qualities of things in the world. As such, if Abelard is to succeed in accounting for the meaning and truth conditions of the proposition 'Socrates and Plato agree in being human', without appealing to anything such as a real universal (for example, Socrates' and Plato's Humanity Itself), then the truth-maker of the proposition must abide by and/or support his non-realism.

Socrates and Plato agree in being human, Abelard explains, because *being human* (*esse hominem*) is what Abelard calls a '*status*'—that is, a way of being. The range of ways of being is constrained by the way things are by nature or, as Abelard would see it, by the way God made things.[40] So, there is no *status*, or way of being, for *living dead men*, since nature could not allow for such a thing. There is nothing, therefore,

---

[38] Abelard called the *status* also the 'common conception' and the 'cause of the imposition of names'. See Abelard (1919: 20$^{1-17}$).
[39] See especially Abelard's commentaries on *Isagoge*.
[40] Abelard (1919: 223$^{1-4}$) (trans. Spade 1994): 'Now this common conception <i.e., *status*> is rightly attributed to God, not to man. For those works—the general or specific *status* in a nature—are God's work, not a builder's. For instance *man, soul, stone* are God's work, but a house or a sword are man's.' The point here is that Abelard is concerned only with natural kinds and natural kind terms.

that makes 'The living man is dead' or 'A dead man is alive' true propositions. But being human *is* a way of being, and it is because of this *status*—that is, *being human*—that the proposition 'Socrates and Plato agree in being human' is true. If it happened that, say, all humans were wiped from existence, the *status* of *being human* would not be, on Abelard's view, affected. It would simply be the case that what is said by any proposition about the human species at that time would be true or false in virtue of the *status* of *being human*.

We now need to address the third item raised, which is what Abelard means by saying that propositions 'propose by stating' what is true or false. On this issue there has been some scholarly debate.[41] To answer the question, note that Abelard, like the Stoics, distinguished between complete (or perfect) and incomplete (or imperfect) expressions. Unlike the Stoics, however, and unlike Abelard's main ancient resource Boethius, the difference between a complete and an incomplete expression is not merely psychological—that is, it is not merely the suspense criterion according to which an incomplete utterance leaves the listener waiting for more.[42] In addition, Abelard appeals to both a grammatical criterion, according to which a complete expression must contain a finite verb, as well as a logical criterion—namely, that the expression signifies a predication. Incomplete expressions can generate *either* a complete *or* an incomplete understanding on his view. For example, 'Man runs' (*Homo currit*) and 'Running man' (*Homo currens*) both generate a complete thought—that running inheres in man—although the latter is an incomplete expression in so far as it does not contain a finite verb. In other words, even though one expression—'running man'—is grammatically defective, it generates the same understanding as 'man runs'.

But, even though 'man runs' and 'running man' share the same signification, the latter does not properly *predicate* running of man. In order for a predication to be effected, something more is needed, and this is the crucial point of Abelard's theory. According to Abelard, a finite substantive verb[43] is needed in order to *say* or *state* that the predicate (for example, running) inheres in the subject (for example, man). In his words, 'it is not enough to signify the inherence. It has to be *said* or *stated*.'[44] The propositional attitude or force of asserting or stating is needed in order to perfect the sense of what is otherwise an incomplete expression.

Without question, then, Abelard recognized that, with regard to propositions, something other than the content is needed in order to effectuate what is said, and this is the force of stating or saying. For Abelard, the content of the proposition has a constituent structure that can be embedded in, or asserted in, different contexts.

---

[41] See Jacobi et al. (1996), Marenbon (2004), and Lenz (2005).

[42] Although this point had been recognized by previous scholars, I owe the particular point of this observation to Lenz (2005).

[43] The substantive verb is 'to be'. According to Abelard (1919: $16^{39}$–$17^6$), Aristotle took 'man walks' and 'man is walking' to be equivalent. Only the latter explicitly contains the substantive verb.

[44] Abelard (1970: 149). See Jacobi et al. (1996: 19) and Lenz (2005: 381–2).

Abelard's way of marking this point was to use a particular logical construction: it takes the form of an accusative plus an infinite verb. This logical construction is equivalent to a *that* phrase in English. For example, 'It is true that *Socrates is sitting*' and 'It is possible that *Socrates is sitting*' share the same content—namely, that *Socrates is sitting*—and each is prefaced by a different type of force. In Abelard's Latin, that *Socrates is sitting* takes the form of *Socratem sedere* = accusative + infinite verb, to which can be prefaced any number of forces. This construction, which becomes commonplace in medieval logic, preserves the sameness of content of the proposition in various contexts of assertion, modality, and so on. On its own the content *Socratem sedere* is an incomplete expression, not a predication, and it needs to be perfected or completed by a finite substantive verb, which is supplied by the force or attitude with which it is expressed: 'Verum est: *Socratem sedere*' = 'It is true that *Socrates is sitting*', or 'Possibile est: *Socratem sedere*' = 'It is possible that *Socrates is sitting*'.[45]

A final important point needs to be made about Abelard's *dicta* in this brief overview of his theory. It is that, if *dicta* are true, then they are, it would seem, timelessly true. As for the Stoics (following Chrysippus), for Abelard every categorical proposition, such as 'Man is a rational animal', is in fact a disguised hypothetical claim, 'If it is man, it is animal'. What makes this proposition true is the *status*, which is *man's being rational and animal*. Although some scholars have complained that Abelard's commitment to the timeless truth of such propositions seems to contravene his nominalism about universals,[46] this is not the right way to see what is going on. Nominalism for Abelard is not the same kind of nominalism found in, say, the philosophy of John Locke, according to whom our epistemological scepticism about our grasp of real essences entails a recognition of merely nominal essences (or kinds). For Abelard, God's universe is made up of natural kinds, which are the subject of study for the natural sciences, and there is no hint of worry or scepticism about our capacity to grasp these kinds by our natural abilities nor any worry about whether the universe is so carved. What Abelard's nominalism, or (better) non-realism, charged was that there are no real things (*res*), such as *The Animal* or *The Human*, corresponding in the world to our claims about animals and humans, which would thereby make our propositions about animals and humans true.[47] Rather, what makes propositions true are the *status*, in this case, *human being animal*. So propositions about humans, if true, are timelessly true, whether or not the referents of the terms 'human' or 'animal' happen to be instantiated at a given time.

---

[45] For a different interpretation, see Marenbon (2004: esp. 65–7).
[46] See especially Marenbon (1997).
[47] See Boethius (1906) for a list of suggestions for what a real universal could be. Abelard's contemporaries put forward different theories to support realism about universals, such as William of Champeaux's material essence realism. On Abelard's semantic solutions to the problem of universals, see King (forthcoming).

What about the timeless truth of contingent or non-universal true propositions? For example, in what way are 'This man is in Athens' or 'Socrates is sitting' timelessly true? Abelard engages in a twofold analysis of the verb 'to be' used in subject–predicate constructions, and he recognizes that sometimes 'to be' is used timelessly, as in the proposition 'Man is animal' (or, 'If it is man, it is animal'). But there is also a use of 'to be' that is time-indexed, such that the expression 'Socrates is sitting' is to be construed as 'Socrates is (here and now) sitting', or 'It is presently the case that *Socrates is sitting*'. Later nominalists in the twelfth century upheld the following maxim: 'If something is true now it is always true' (*Semel est verum semper est verum*). While Abelard's theory of the *dictum* cannot be tied directly to this maxim, the principle behind it remains at work. Abelard explained that the *dictum* corresponding to the expression uttered now, 'Socrates is sitting', is the state of affairs in which Socrates is sitting. Suppose Socrates is indeed sitting right now. Any future reference to this state of affairs—that is, any future expression that states or asserts the *dictum*—must adjust its time-index—for example, 'Socrates was sitting then'—but the *dictum*, what is said by the expression, remains the same—for example, 'It **was** the case that *Socrates is sitting*'.[48]

In sum, like the Stoics, Abelard recognized a new type of linguistic content, the *dictum*. The *dictum* is distinguished from what is understood when a proposition is spoken or heard, since it is possible to have false thoughts generated by true *dicta* and vice versa. It seems to follow, therefore, that *dicta* are mind-independent. *Dicta* are what make propositions true or false, and this is due to their correspondence with *status*, which are ways that the world can be. Accordingly, the *dictum* 'The dead man is alive' is false in virtue of the fact that there is no way of being for dead men—that is, there is no corresponding *status*. Propositional contents, for Abelard, need to be asserted or stated: for example, 'It is true that *Socrates is sitting*'; otherwise they are incomplete. The same content can be embedded in various contexts, such as questioning, wishing, as well as modal contexts (for example, 'It is possible that *Socrates is sitting*'). This suggests that propositional contents are types of contents that are tokened on the various occasions of their use. Finally, if true, propositional contents are timelessly true. This is not a contravention of Abelard's non-realism, and he is careful to explain how *dicta*, which he took to be non-existents (recall from the quotation already given: '*dicta*, which are sort of the "thing" of the proposition [*quae sunt quasi res propositionis*], although they are not existing things [*essentiae*]'), could be the cause of the truth or falsity of propositions. Abelard's non-realism compelled him to be as deflationary as possible about *dicta*. In fact, he seemed to have been explicitly questioned about this very issue, and confronts head-on the complaint that a non-thing—what is said by a proposition—can bring about, or be the cause of, true

---

[48] According to Lewis (1987) (re: Abelard 1970: 213): 'Abelard seems rather to be saying that the same *dictum* is expressed by differently tensed statements uttered at different times (an idea which he would use in connection with prophecy and faith...)'.

propositions. In other words, how can that, which altogether is not and cannot exist, be thought of or called a *cause*?[49] Abelard lists a number of comparisons to make his case. Something can be a cause and yet be nothing (or, a not-thing) in the following ways: just as a victory is a cause of war; just as not-eating is the cause of a man's death; just as being caught is the cause of a thief's hanging; just as not doing good is the cause of being damned. These comparisons are meant to show how *dicta* can be metaphysically thin but explanatorily robust.

## Comparison of the views of the Stoics and Peter Abelard

We can quickly summarize the obvious common features of the Stoics' and Abelard's theory. Properly speaking, it is only the Stoic theory of *axiomata*, or assertibles, that is to be compared with Abelard's *dicta*, since these are both propositional contents. For both, the sayable is to be distinguished from any type of cognitive content, such as concepts, thoughts, or understandings. Both the *lekton* and *dictum* have queer metaphysical status in their philosophical systems. The *lekton* is what the Stoics classify as a not-something, or a non-existing, non-corporeal item that nonetheless can be said to have some attenuated status as subsisting. Abelard's *dictum* is what he called the 'quasi-thing of the proposition', and cannot be located among actually existing things. Whereas, for the Stoics, as a non-body the *lekton* would seem to have no causal power of its own, for Abelard the *dictum* can be considered the cause of the truth or falsity of propositions, but only in the attenuated way that, say, not-eating is a cause of death. One might compare their views in the following way: by allowing for *lekta*, and especially *axiomata*, to be recognized as (subsisting) features of the Stoic universe, and for *dicta* to be non-existent but 'quasi-things', both the Stoics and Abelard recognized the explanatory need for this new type of linguistic content, while nonetheless insisting on its metaphysical thinness.

Both the Stoics and Abelard seem to have been similarly motivated to develop their theories of propositional content. Both in their own way had to contend with the ambiguity that had plagued the notion of predication in ancient philosophy. The *lekton* (or *axioma*) and the *dictum* introduce a logical sense of predication, which permits both to distinguish between the metaphysical (or physical) sense of predicates as attributes or properties in the world and the logical sense of predicates as what can be said about those attributes. Both also seemed motivated to put forward this means to disambiguate predication in order to support a non-realist, or deflationary, account of what exists.

There are some less obvious similarities between their views, ones that at first sight might appear to be differences. Most striking is that there is nothing in Stoic

---

[49] Abelard (2010: IV 138$^{230-242}$ [§36]).

philosophy of language and logic that can be explicitly compared to the role played by *status* in Abelard's philosophy of language. However, it needs to be emphasized that the Stoics took the universe to be (as did Abelard) wholly rational in its construction. This is a major topic that cannot be examined here, but it is crucial to note: for the Stoics, the universe is a unity and is utterly coherent. It is governed by an all-encompassing divine reason: 'reason (*nous*) pervades (*dihêkontos*) every part of it, just as does the soul in us.'[50] The same fundamental rationality and divine order permeate both the Stoic and Abelardian universe, and thereby play the same logical role in constraining the truth-value of what is said.

There is, however, an important difference between their views, one that has to do with the role of cognitive content. For the Stoics, at least according to current developmental reconstructions of their view, *lekta* eventually took the place of concepts in a deliberately deflationary attempt to rid their philosophy of unwanted realist commitments (such as thinking of concepts as playing a role akin to Platonic Forms). But for Abelard, such deflationism about cognitive content was not so extreme. He continued to recognize that the cognitive content, or the understanding that is generated by hearing or speaking a significant expression, is present. It ceases to play the main role in predication, which is what is at issue regarding determination of the truth or falsity of what is said. But cognitive content did continue to play the key role in Abelard's theory of signification:

> The signification of things, obviously, is transitory, but the signification of understandings is permanent. For when the subject of the things is destroyed, if one utters the name 'rose' or 'lily', although the signification of the *things* which they name no longer hold, the signification of the *understandings* is not empty, because whether the things exist or whether they don't, understandings are always constituted.[51]

The permanence of the signification of understandings (*significatio intellectus*) allows for names to retain their meaningfulness even if the things they name no longer exist. Thus, when using names in predications, such as 'Roses are flowers', even in a situation in which all roses have been destroyed, these names ('roses', 'flowers') continue to be meaningful; as a result, the truth or falsity of the predication can be determined. (Here the predication is true even if there are no actual roses, since the predication is logically equivalent to 'If it is a rose, it is a flower', which is true because it corresponds to the *status* of roses—namely, to their *being flowers*.)[52]

---

[50] Diogenes Laertius VII 138, quoting Chrysippus from *On Providence* and Posidonius from *On the Gods*.
[51] Abelard (2010: Prooemium 20[80–84] [§9]).
[52] Another difference concerns how words come to be, and continue to be, significant. Most striking is that the Stoics, unlike Abelard, have been strongly associated with having an interest in the practice of etymology, which seems to suggest that the Stoics took there to be a natural relationship between significant words and what they name, at least in the first place when named by a name-giver. There is ample evidence to support the reputation that the Stoics had for etymologizing, although there is little explanation of what they hoped to achieve by means of the exercise. Abelard did not show a sincere interest in the practice of etymologizing and, given that he was operating within the confines of Aristotle's theory of

## Conclusion

In conclusion, what happens to this new type of linguistic content after Abelard? Theories of propositional content emerge, disappear, and re-emerge throughout the medieval and scholastic periods. The interest is preserved in the continuation of the logical tradition, still rooted in Aristotelian logic, beginning in the twelfth century. Some theorists seemed to have been entirely unconcerned with the ontological implications and underpinnings of these sorts of linguistic content. For example, the author(s) of a thirteenth-century logical textbook called the *Ars Burana* explain(s) that it is best considered to be an extrapredicamental thing (that is, not countenanced in what exists in an Aristotelian ontology of substances and accidents):

> Note that whether it is called a *dictum propositionis* or the *significatum propositionis* or the *enuntiabile*, it is the same. The enuntiable is that which is signified by the proposition... If you inquire what kind of thing it is, whether it is a substance or an accident, it must be said regarding the enuntiable, just as regarding the predicable, that it is neither a substance nor an accident nor is it of any other category. For it has its own *per se* mode of existing. And it is called 'extrapredicamental', not for the reason that it does not belong to any category, but because it does not belong to any of the ten categories that Aristotle distinguished. It is therefore of a certain category which can be called the 'enuntiable category'.[53]

Later, some philosophers attempted to defend a view that took the opposite tack—that is, to defend a view of propositional realism, only to encounter some of the same sorts of anti-realist challenges.[54]

## References

Aristotle (1963a). *Categories*, trans. J. L. Ackrill, in *Aristotle's Categories and De interpretatione*. Oxford: Clarendon Press, 3–42.
Aristotle (1963b). *On Interpretation*, trans. J. L. Ackrill, in *Aristotle's Categories and De interpretatione*. Oxford: Clarendon Press, 43–68.
*Ars Burana* (1967). Anon., *Ars Burana*, in L. M. de Rijk (ed.), *Logica modernorum: A Contribution to the History of Terminist Logic*. Assen: Van Gorcum, 175–213.
Atherton, C. (1993). *The Stoics on Ambiguity*. Cambridge: Cambridge University Press.
Augustine (1975). *De dialectica*, trans. B. D. Jackson. Dordrecht, Holland: D. Reidel.
Bobzien, S. (1999). 'III. The Stoics', in K. Algra, J. Barnes, J. Mansfeld, and M. Schofield (eds), *The Cambridge History of Hellenistic Philosophy*. Cambridge: Cambridge University Press, 92–157.
Bobzien, S. (2003). 'Logic', in B. Inwood (ed.), *The Cambridge Companion to Stoic Philosophy*. Cambridge: Cambridge University Press, 85–123.

---

meaning, was committed to the conventionality of significant words. Although the details cannot be explored here, this difference in their views may also turn out to be only apparent.

[53] *Ars Burana* (1967: 208). See De Libera (1981); Martin (2004).
[54] The best study of this topic is Cesalli (2007).

Boethius (1877). *Commentarii in librum Aristotelis Peri Hermeneias pars prior*, ed. C. Meiser. Leipzig: Teubner.
Boethius (1880). *Commentarii in librum Aristotelis Peri Hermeneias pars posterior*, ed. C. Meiser. Leipzig: Teubner.
Boethius (1906). *In Isagogen Porphyrii commenta*, ed. S. Brandt. Leipzig: Tempsky & Freitag.
Boethius (1990). *De topicis differentiis*, ed. D. Z. Nikitas, in *Corpus Philosophorum medii aevi, Philosophi Byzantini* 5. Paris: J. Vrin.
Brittain, C. (2005). 'Common Sense: Concepts, Definition and Meaning in and out of the Stoa', in B. Inwood and D. Frede (eds), *Language and Learning: Philosophy of Language in the Hellenistic Age*. Cambridge: Cambridge University Press, 164–209.
Cameron, M. (2007). 'Abelard (and Heloise?) on Intentions', *American Catholic Philosophical Quarterly*, 81/2: 323–39.
Caston, V. (1999). 'Something and Nothing: The Stoics on Concepts and Universals', *Oxford Studies in Ancient Philosophy*, 17: 145–214.
Cesalli, L. (2007). *Le Réalisme propositionnel: Sémantique et ontologie des propositions chez Jean Duns Scot, Gauthier Burley, Richard Brinkley, et Jean Wyclif*. Paris: J. Vrin.
De Libera, A. (1981). 'Abélard et le dictisme', *Cahiers de la revue de théologie et de philosophie*, 6: 59–92.
Diogenes Laertius (1925). *Lives of Eminent Philosophers*, ii, trans. R. D. Hicks. Cambridge, MA: Harvard University Press.
Frede, M. (1994). 'The Stoic Notion of a *lekton*', in S. Everson (ed.), *Companions to Ancient Thought 3: Language*. Cambridge: Cambridge University Press, 109–28.
Geyer, B. (1919–27; 1933). *Peter Abaelards philosophische Schriften*. Beiträge zur Geschichte der Philosophie und Theologie des Mittelalters, vol. XXI. 1–3. Münster, Aschendorff.
Hankinson, R. J. (2003). 'Stoic Epistemology', in B. Inwood (ed.), *Cambridge Companion to the Stoics*. Cambridge: Cambridge University Press, 59–84.
Jacobi, K. (1983). 'Abelard and Frege: The Semantics of Words and Propositions', in *Atti del convegno internazionale di storia della logica*, ed. V. M. Abrusci (San Gimignano: CLUEB), 81–96.
Jacobi, K., King, P., and Strub, C. (1996). 'From intellectus verus/falsus to the dictum propositionis: The Semantics of Peter Abelard and his Circle', *Vivarium*, 34: 15–40.
King, P. (forthcoming). 'Abelard's Answers to Porphyry', *Documenti e studi sulla tradizione filosofica medievale*.
Lenz, M. (2005). 'Peculiar Perfection: Peter Abelard on Propositional Attitudes', *Journal of the History of Philosophy*, 43/4: 377–86.
Lewis, N. (1987). 'Determinate Truth in Abelard', *Vivarium*, 25: 81–109.
Long, A. (2005). 'Stoic Linguistics, Plato's *Cratylus*, and Augustine's *De dialectica*', in B. Inwood and D. Frede (eds), *Language and Learning: Philosophy of Language in the Hellenistic Age*. Cambridge: Cambridge University Press, 36–55.
Long, A., and Sedley, D. (1987). *The Hellenistic Philosophers. Volume 1 Translations of the Principal Sources, with Philosophical Commentary*. Cambridge: Cambridge University Press.
Magee, J., and Marenbon, J. (2009). 'Appendix: Boethius' works', in *The Cambridge Companion to Boethius*. Cambridge: Cambridge University Press, 303–10.
Marenbon, J. (1997). *The Philosophy of Peter Abelard*. Cambridge: Cambridge University Press.

Marenbon, J. (2004). '*Dicta*, Assertion and Speech Acts: Abelard and Some Modern Interpreters', in A. Maierù and L. Valente (eds), *Medieval Theories on Assertive and Non-Assertive Language*. Florence: Olschki, 59–80.

Markus, R. A. (1972). 'St Augustine on Signs', in R. A. Markus (ed.), *Augustine: A Collection of Critical Essays*. New York: Anchor Books, 61–91.

Martin, C. (2004). 'Propositionality and Logic in the *Ars Meliduna*', in A. Maierù and L. Valente (eds), *Medieval Theories on Assertive and Non-Assertive Language*. Florence: Olschki, 111–28.

Martin, C. (2009). 'Imposition and Essence: What's New in Abelard's Theory of Meaning', in T. Shimizu and C. Burnett (eds), *The Word in Medieval Logic, Theology and Psychology*. Turnhout: Brepols, 173–214.

Nuchelmans, G. (1973). *Theories of the Proposition: Ancient and Medieval Conceptions of the Bearers of Truth and Falsity*. Dordrecht: North-Holland.

Peter Abelard (1919). *Glossae super Porphyrium*, ed. B. Geyer, vol. i of Geyer, 1919–27; 1933.

Peter Abelard (1970). *Dialectica*, ed. L. M. de Rijk. 2nd edn. Assen: Van Gorcum.

Peter Abelard (2010). *Glossae super Periermeneias Aristotelis*, ed. K. Jacobi and C. Strub, in *Corpus Christianorum continuatio medievalis*. Turnhout: Brepols.

Rosier-Catach, I. (2004). 'Les Discussions sur la signifié des propositions chez Abélard et ses contemporains', in A. Maierù and L. Valente (eds), *Medieval Theories on Assertive and Non-Assertive Language*. Florence: Olschki, 1–34.

Schenkeveld, D. M. (1984). 'Stoic and Peripatetic Kinds of Speech Act and the Distinction of Grammatical Moods', *Mnemosyne*, 37: 291–351.

Seneca *Ep.* = Seneca (1965). *L. Annaei Senecae Ad Lucilium Epistulae Morales*, ed. L. D. Reynolds. Oxford: Oxford University Press.

Sextus Empiricus *M* = Sextus Empiricus (1998). *Sextus Empiricus: Against the Grammarians* (Adversus Mathematicos I), ed. and trans. D. L. Blank. Oxford: Oxford University Press.

Spade, P. V. (1994). *Five Texts on the Mediaeval Problem of Universals*. Indianapolis: Hackett.

# 4

# Philosophy of Language in the Medieval Arabic Tradition

*Peter Adamson and Alexander Key*

In the Arabic-speaking intellectual world from the seventh century onwards, Hellenic analyses of linguistic content found fertile ground. But the tripartite theory of meaning consisting of sounds, thoughts, and things (*phônai, noêmata*, and *pragmata*) based on Aristotle's *De interpretatione* was not universally welcomed. An autochthonous and pre-existing Arabic bipartite theory of meaning, consisting solely of vocal form (*lafẓ*) and mental content (*maʿnā*), provided an alternative. This Arabic pairing was the predominant model used to relate mental content to linguistic content, and it was in play across all available genres, from poetry to exegetical hermeneutics and legal theory. When Hellenic knowledge arrived on the scene in the eighth century, the bipartite Arabic model swiftly became part of the vocabulary for philosophy as well.

Despite this agreement on elementary terminology, there was no sense of shared endeavour among the scholars who worked in Arabic on linguistic content across Hellenic philosophy, on the one hand, and grammar, poetics, and legal theory, on the other. Instead, there was an often bitter division between those who followed the *Organon* and those who stayed within the autochthonous disciplines of Arabic scholarship. In this chapter, we will analyse a notorious debate between two scholars of this period, a logician and a grammarian, who represented the philhellenic and phil-Arabic approaches to the philosophy of language.

Our analysis will show that the distinction between Hellenic philosophy and the autochthonous Arabic disciplines was not the result of any prima facie incompatibility between the two epistemologies. In fact, once the sensitivities of politics and culture had died down, the tripartite and bipartite theories of meaning that each tradition brought to the table proved perfectly compatible and mutually productive. But, before that point was reached in the eleventh century, the two sides in our debate needed to work through their political and cultural differences. The polemical context drove them to make exaggerated claims for their respective disciplines: either logic was the only way to think, or it was grammar.

The self-evidently false nature of that dichotomy contributed to its abandonment, but not before casting a long shadow on the philosophy of language in the medieval Arabic tradition. Our chapter will, through its analysis of the debate, provide a clarification of the autochthonous Arabic position, which has received less attention than the philhellenic discourse. There was a pre-existing theory of meaning in Arabic before Hellenic philosophy appeared, and we will show how that bipartite Arabic theory of meaning, consisting solely of vocal form and mental content, provided the terminology and epistemological architecture for a whole series of ideas about how the mental content could, and should, be turned into linguistic content.

We begin with a brief exercise in historical scene-setting. Philosophers working in the medieval Arabic tradition had good reason to be interested in language. The opportunity to read Hellenic philosophy depended on works that had to be translated from Greek into Arabic.[1] At the same time, the Arabic cultural context was literary. It was dominated by a poetic and oratorical tradition that stretched back before Islam, penetrated almost all scholarly disciplines, and gave rise to a pronounced sensitivity towards semantic concerns.[2]

Practitioners of Hellenic philosophy engaged closely with Arabic versions of Aristotle and other Hellenic thinkers throughout the ninth, tenth, and eleventh centuries AD.[3] This naturally led them to reflect on, and sometimes boldly assert, the possibility of rendering Greek philosophical ideas in the Arabic language. These early thinkers were especially engaged with the Aristotelian logical corpus, or *Organon*. And the issues of polysemy and naming raised by the *Categories* and *On Interpretation* had already appeared in the Arabic grammatical and exegetical traditions that sprang up around both the pre-Islamic poetic corpus and the new divine text of the Quran in the seventh and eighth centuries. As Arabic intellectual civilization developed, so these debates about language, using the bipartite theory of vocal forms that interact with mental content, became more complex.

Three primary drivers for discussion about the philosophy of language in the Middle East from the seventh century onwards were therefore the philhellenic analyses of Aristotle's logical works in Arabic, the dominance of poetry and oratory in the Arabic cultural context, and hermeneutical responses to that newest of monotheistic revelations, the Arabic Quran. These three streams flowed into the debate over the relative merits of logic and grammar. One side of this debate looked to ancient Greece for its inspiration, while the other gave precedence to the desert Bedouin environment and the Arabic language chosen by God for the Quranic

---

[1] Often with Syriac as an intermediary, and increasingly as the centuries progressed directly from the Greek. On this translation movement, see Gutas (1998, 2010), in addition to Endress (1987).
[2] For a review of the literary tradition, see Heinrichs (1987, 2012). An invaluable resource for the ideas and people of the literary tradition is Meisami and Starkey (1998). For further reading, see Key (2013).
[3] For an introduction to Arabic philosophy, see Adamson and Taylor (2005) and McGinnis and Reisman (2007). And for the Greek texts that became available, see Gutas (2010) and D'Ancona (2013).

revelation. The contrast is well exemplified by the choice of al-Khuwārizmī, the scholar in whose works algebra first appears, to divide his survey of the ninth-century intellectual landscape into two halves: "Arabic and Islamic", and "Greek and foreign".[4]

In the year 937 or 938 the vizier Ibn al-Furāt,[5] sitting in his Baghdad court, called for a grammarian to contest logic's claim to possess a tool without which the truth could not be known. The logician and philosopher Abū Bishr Mattā was asked to defend his subject against the criticism of the grammarian and polymath Abū Saʿīd al-Sīrāfī. Mattā was a founding member of the "Baghdad school" of Aristotelian philosophers, which included the somewhat more famous Yaḥyā Ibn ʿAdī and the much more famous al-Fārābī.[6] Mattā, like Ibn ʿAdī, was a Christian of Syriac extraction, a fact that provides al-Sīrāfī with opportunities for sarcasm during the debate (he points out that expertise in logic apparently does not prevent one from thinking that the same thing can be both one and three).

We have only one account of this debate, and it comes from the literary, political, and sociological anthology of the *littérateur* and philosopher Abū Ḥayyān al-Tawḥīdī, who was writing somewhat less than a century later.[7] Abū Ḥayyān was comfortable with Hellenic philosophy, as witnessed by his intellectual love affair with Abū Sulaymān al-Sijistānī "the Logician", a pupil of Yaḥyā Ibn ʿAdī.[8] However, as an Arabic *littérateur* given a choice between a famous Arab polymath and a Syriac-speaking logician who was happily professing ignorance of the culturally totemic subject of Arabic grammar, Abū Ḥayyān supported al-Sīrāfī.[9] Abū Ḥayyān had also heard brief anecdotes about the debate from al-Sīrāfī himself, while more detail had been provided by the Muʿtazilī grammarian al-Rummānī, Abū Ḥayyān's beloved teacher and a pupil alongside al-Sīrafī of the commentator on Sībawayh's grammar, Ibn al-Sarrāj.[10] Abū Ḥayyān's unsurprisingly partisan reportage of the debate also

---

[4] Abū Jaʿfar Muḥammad al-Khuwārizmī (fl. c.830) wrote that he was dividing his survey of the disciplinary landscape into "the disciplines of the [Islamic] revelation and those Arabic disciplines associated with it" and "the foreign disciplines from the Greeks and other nations" (al-Ḥuwārizmī 1895). On the culture clash, see *inter alia*, Zimmerman (1981) and Key (2012). For the matter of algebra, see Brentjes (2012).

[5] Abū al-Fatḥ al-Faḍl b. Jaʿfar Ibn al-Furāt (Ibn Ḥinzāba), d. 938. Appointed to the vizierate by the caliph al-Muqtadir (reg. 908–32) in 932 and for a second time by the caliph al-Rāḍī (reg. 934–40) in 937. For the history of this period, see Kennedy (2004). And for its historiography, El-Hibri (1999).

[6] Abū Bishr Mattā b. Yūnus, d. 940. Abū Saʿīd al-Ḥasan al-Sīrāfī, d. 979. Yaḥyā Ibn ʿAdī, d. 974. Abū Naṣr Muḥammad al-Fārābī, d. 950.

[7] Abū Ḥayyān, d. 1032. On the debate, see Mahdi (1970), Endress (1977, 1986), Elamrani-Jamal (1983), and Kühn (1986). For English translation, see Margoliouth (1905). Margoliouth, however, did not have access to a critical edition of the Arabic text, which subsequently became available through the publication of Abū Ḥayyān's original anthology (al-Tawḥīdī 1965: i. 104–5, 107).

[8] On Abū Sulaymān (d. c.991) and these philosophical/literary circles more generally, see Kraemer (1986a, b).

[9] On the other hand, Joseph E. Lowry has profitably suggested, in personal communication, that Abū Ḥayyān's report of the debate can be read as an ironic presentation of al-Sīrāfī as a sophist, using as he does all the classic rhetorical tools of sophistry, from deliberate misunderstanding to *reductio ad absurdum* via homonymy.

[10] Abū al-Ḥasan ʿAlī al-Rummānī, d. 994. Abū Bakr Muḥammad Ibn al-Sarrāj, d. 929. For an accessible review of Sībawayh's work and importance, see Carter (2004).

mirrors the original context in which it was held: Ibn al-Furāt's exact request to the court had been for someone to "break down Mattā's position" that truth could be found only through logic and Aristotle.[11]

Despite the partiality of the reportage, we gain insight into Mattā's philosophy of language, and a careful reading shows that he and al-Sīrāfī share a surprising amount of common ground. Both subscribe to a fundamental bipartite distinction between language and the thoughts or meanings that language expresses. They even employ the same terminology for articulating this distinction: the linguistic entity is referred to as a *lafẓ* (vocal utterance or form), while the mental content the word expresses is called a *maʿnā* (meaning, idea, content).[12] A workable analogue for this Arabic pairing is the distinction that Ferdinand de Saussure made between two bands of wavy lines representing sound and thought.[13] But, whereas Saussure's theory of meaning used a third element, the linguistic sign, to explain how people said and meant things, the Arabic theory of meaning uses only vocal form, mental content, and the connections made between them by each act of language use.

Both al-Sīrāfī and Mattā describe mental contents as objects of the mind or intellect; all are objects of reason (*maʿqūlāt*). They are universal; Mattā explicitly says that intelligible mental content is common to people of different nations—he gives the example of grasping that $4 + 4 = 8$—yet different nations express that same mental content with completely different vocal forms.[14] Al-Sīrāfī is even more explicit about the stark differences between mental content and its corresponding vocal form. The former endures through time, whereas the latter is composite and fleeting, disappearing even as it is spoken. In a strikingly Platonist remark, he explains this by saying that the vocal form, being "natural" or "physical" (*ṭabīʿī*), is subject to constant disappearance, whereas mental content endures because it involves no matter and belongs to the intellect, which is divine.[15]

Mattā and al-Sīrāfī disagree, however, about the lesson to be drawn from this basic distinction. Mattā is given little to say in the debate as reported, yet his position appears in clearer focus than that of al-Sīrāfī. At its heart is a claim about the subject matter of logic and the indispensability of Hellenic logic for thought.

---

[11] Margoliouth (1905); al-Tawḥīdī (1965: i. 108).

[12] The plural form of *lafẓ* is *alfāẓ*, and the plural form of *maʿnā* is *maʿānī*. They will be rendered in this chapter by "vocal form" and "mental content" respectively. On the terms *lafẓ* and *maʿnā*, see Frank (1981), Heinrichs (1998), and Key (2010).

[13] Saussure (1949: 156) has a diagram showing these two bands, the *plan indéfini des idées confuses* and the [*plan*] *non moins indéterminé des sons* ("[p]lane of vague, amorphous thought" and "equally featureless plane of sound"). See also Saussure (2005: 110–11).

[14] Margoliouth (1905: 113); al-Tawḥīdī (1965: i. 111).

[15] Margoliouth (1905: 117); al-Tawḥīdī (1965: i. 115). Al-Sīrāfī also explicitly agrees that mental content is not different for speakers of different languages: Margoliouth (1905: 118); al-Tawḥīdī (1965: i. 116).

By "logic" I mean one of the tools of speech by which one knows its correct usage from its incorrect usage, and by which one knows unsound mental content from sound mental content. It is like a balance, with which I know which side goes up and which side goes down.[16]

Subsequently, when asked to explain the different aspects of mental content that the Arabic particle *wāw* (a conjunction that usually but not exclusively means "and") engenders in the discipline of logic, Mattā says:

This is grammar, which I have not investigated. For the logician does not need grammar, whereas the grammarian does need logic, because logic examines mental content whereas grammar examines vocal form. If a logician passes by a vocal form, he does so accidentally, and if the grammarian stumbles upon mental content, this is also accidental. Mental content is more noble than vocal form.[17]

Notice that the second passage introduces a substantial caveat to the first. He has claimed that logic is a way of determining true from false *speech*, but now it becomes clear that the relation of logic to speech is an indirect, "accidental" one. This is because logic properly deals only with the relationships between ideas in the mind.[18] Furthermore, both grammarians and logicians need to understand mental content, so logic is essential for both undertakings despite its neglect by grammarians. Language is not similarly essential; it is the central focus of grammar but only an accidental aspect of logic.

Mental content on Mattā's view is not an inward rehearsal of a natural language. But it is (at least sometimes) propositional. This is clear not only from the example he gives (4+4=8) but also from the association of logic with mental content: logic allows us to combine (propositional) mental content into valid syllogisms. Unsurprisingly, the position he is defending comes from Aristotle's *Organon*, which was of intense interest to the Baghdad school.[19] It can be traced ultimately to a passage at the beginning of *On Interpretation*:

Now spoken sounds are symbols of affections in the soul, and written marks symbols of spoken sounds. And just as written marks are not the same for all men, neither are spoken sounds. But what these are in the first place signs of—affections of the soul—are the same for all.[20]

Here in *On Interpretation* thoughts are called by Aristotle affections of the soul, but in the commentary tradition they are sometimes called "objects of the mind" (*noêmata*,

---

[16] Margoliouth (1905: 112); al-Tawḥīdī (1965: i. 109). In a not insubstantial irony of which Abū Ḥayyān was most likely aware, Mattā is speaking in the faultless parallel cadences of an Arab *littérateur*—because his speech is being reported second hand by one such expert.

[17] Margoliouth (1905: 116); al-Tawḥīdī (1965: i. 114).

[18] See Margoliouth (1905: 113); al-Tawḥīdī (1965: i. 111).

[19] Mattā himself translated the *Poetics*, which was considered a part of the *Organon* (on this see Black 1990; Aristotle 2012).

[20] 16ᵃ3–7 (Ackrill trans.): Ἔστι μὲν οὖν τὰ ἐν τῇ φωνῇ τῶν ἐν τῇ ψυχῇ παθημάτων σύμβολα, καὶ τὰ γραφόμενα τῶν ἐν τῇ φωνῇ. καὶ ὥσπερ οὐδὲ γράμματα πᾶσι τὰ αὐτά, οὐδὲ φωναὶ αἱ αὐταί· ὧν μέντοι ταῦτα σημεῖα πρώτων, ταὐτὰ πᾶσι παθήματα τῆς ψυχῆς.

which corresponds to the Arabic "reasoned or intellected things", *ma'qūlāt*).[21] This gives us the tripartite theory, according to which vocal form refers to things, but only through the intermediary of mental content.[22] Mattā accepts this and, in his debate with al-Sīrāfī, insists that logic operates at the level of the mental content. Grammar studies only the external vocal forms of this mental content, and, since it is at the level of thought that knowledge and truth primarily reside, grammar is not really very important.

Al-Sīrāfī's first response to Mattā's claim that logic is the balance with which mental content can be weighed is to keep "logic" tightly circumscribed as the practice pursued by Mattā and his fellow enthusiasts of a foreign *falsafa*. For al-Sīrāfī, logic is a tool of the logicians, whereas everyone else simply uses human reason (*al-'aql*) to decide what is what. This is more a cultural and terminological than a substantive critique; Mattā might say (but does not) that logic is precisely the way that reason works. But al-Sīrāfī quotes the second hemistich of a line from a wine poem by the famous poet Abū Nuwās to the effect that anyone who claims to be a philosopher has only a partial apprehension of the problem at hand.[23]

Al-Sīrāfī then objects that logic lacks the universality claimed for it by Mattā. It is, rather, a Greek phenomenon (indeed the invention of only one Greek, namely Aristotle) and therefore subject to the conventions of the Greek language.[24] Neither, therefore, can it be a universal tool for distinguishing truth from falsity, nor can it hope to resolve all disagreements or advance the cause of human understanding: "the world after Aristotle's logic remained the same as it had been before his logic."[25] Certainly Mattā's position would be undermined if it were true that Aristotelian logic were still wedded to the linguistic and conceptual particularities of Greek and the Greeks. But al-Sīrāfī does not pursue this potentially lethal point. Instead, he switches to a line of attack that admits the universal potential of logic, saying that logic does manage to abstract away from the particularities of natural language: "grammar is a logic drawn out from Arabic, and logic is a grammar understood through language."[26] With this somewhat Delphic statement al-Sīrāfī claims grammar as a synonym for logic, and implies that, while (presumably Arabic) grammar has to be extracted from the Arabic language, logic can be universal. Yet, while logic can be a universal tool for structuring mental content, it can only ever be understood through a language. The intentions about which we reason and the mental content

---

[21] See, e.g., Simplicius *in Cat.* 10.
[22] On the possible origins of this theory with Boethus of Sidon, see Griffin (2012).
[23] Abū Nuwās (al-Ḥasan al-Ḥakamī, d. c.814): [say to anyone who claims to know *falsafa*/] 'you have learnt a little and missed a lot'. al-Tawḥīdī (1965: i. 110 (n. 6)); Abū Nuwās (1958–2006: iii. 4).
[24] Margoliouth (1905: 113); al-Tawḥīdī (1965: i. 110).
[25] Margoliouth (1905: 115); al-Tawḥīdī (1965: i. 113). This comes in response to Mattā's statement that the Greeks, alone among all other nations, devoted themselves to the intellectual pursuit of wisdom (*ḥikma*) and this makes them worthy teachers. Margoliouth (1905: 114); al-Tawḥīdī (1965: i. 112).
[26] Margoliouth (1905: 117); al-Tawḥīdī (1965: i. 115).

that we know "can only be accessed by a language made up of nouns, verbs, and particles".[27]

If grammar has no pretentions to universality, then its importance must come from the fact that the mental tool of logic is useless without mastery of vocal form. Such mastery enables us to avoid logical errors that could happen to a speaker of any language as well as those errors that are specific to the language one is speaking. Al-Sīrāfī catches out Mattā for thinking two Arabic constructions are equivalent when they are not: "Zayd is one of the brothers" and "Zayd is one of his brothers" (a mistake, since no one can be his own brother). Al-Sīrāfī describes this as "a question that has more to do with reasoned mental content than with the appearance of words".[28] Because Mattā lacks grammatical expertise, he falls into mistakes that are relevant to the level of thought. In this way, al-Sīrāfī gives grammar at least some of the responsibility for shielding us from what Mattā would consider to be "logical" errors.

An even more powerful point made by al-Sīrāfī is that the logician must put his thoughts into language if he is to communicate:

> Why do you claim that grammarians only investigate vocal form to the exclusion of mental content, and logicians the reverse? That would only be true if the logician was silent, circulating his ideas only on the level of mental content, and organizing whatever he wanted with imaginative intimations, passing thoughts, and sudden guesses. However, when this logician wants to justify to a student or interlocutor that which upon consideration and careful reflection seems correct to him, he must use the vocal form that encompasses his intention, fits his aim, and corresponds with his goal.[29]

For al-Sīrāfī, thought and language are inextricably bound up in each other, and their mutual relationship is not as simple as Mattā assumes:

> If that which is sought by reason and that which is mentioned in vocal form could be taken back through their different branches and variant paths to that clear level on which four plus four equals eight, then our argument would be over and we would agree. But that is not the case.[30]

Because language is no mere mirror of mental content, putting thoughts into language can hardly be the trivial afterthought that Mattā makes it out to be.

One example of the differences between language and thought is that language is limited to a smaller scope than the mental level:

> It is now clear that composite vocal forms do not encompass the extent of human reason, that mental content is reasoned, and that they are both intensely connected and expansively spread.

---

[27] Margoliouth (1905: 113); al-Tawḥīdī (1965: i. 111).
[28] Margoliouth (1905: 121–2); al-Tawḥīdī (1965: i. 118–19).
[29] Margoliouth (1905: 121); al-Tawḥīdī (1965: i. 119).
[30] Margoliouth (1905: 113); al-Tawḥīdī (1965: i. 111).

The vocal form, in whatever language, has the power neither to command nor to contain that expanse.³¹

This idea did not originate with al-Sīrāfī. A century before our debate, one of the most renowned Arabic theorists, al-Jāḥiẓ, wrote that mental content (*maʿānī*) is different from the linguistic names given to it (*asmāʾ al-maʿānī*) "because mental content is spread out without end, and stretched out infinitely, whereas its names are curtailed and numbered, collectable and limited".³² The inevitable consequence, albeit one al-Sīrāfī does not spell out as clearly as some later authors would do, was polysemy. A limited corpus of vocal forms has to do the work of expressing an infinity of mental content. Some vocal forms therefore had to mean more than one thing (homonymy). Conversely, some mental content could be expressed with a multiplicity of vocal forms (synonymy). In the debate this is first revealed in the examples that al-Sīrāfī uses to get from Mattā's position that grammar only accidentally addresses mental content to his own statement that grammar is in fact a logic drawn out from the Arabic language.³³ Al-Sīrāfī gives a long stream of synonyms that can be used to refer to language, from "speech" and "conversation" to "presentation" and "demand", before demonstrating that, while these vocal forms are different, their meanings are "in the same space when it comes to resemblance and similarity". One cannot, therefore, say that "Zayd spoke the truth but did not talk truthfully": it would be an error that "used the vocal form contrary to the reason of both the speaker and the listener".³⁴

A command of polysemy, or more simply of the various ways that vocal form can interact with mental content, is therefore a prerequisite for any intellectual exercise. It "was the way the truth was determined before logic was devised and it remains the way the truth is determined".³⁵ This orientation produces a particular sort of intellectual endeavour: one in which language takes centre stage and the potential for semantic breadth is exploited. As al-Sīrāfī says, "make your mental content clear through eloquence!"³⁶ When a good scholar makes the audience think, they appreciate their apprehension of that scholar's intention all the more, and yet the scholar should also, at the same time, provide explanations and commentary sufficient to ensure complete understanding.³⁷ The manipulation of homonyms and synonyms,

---

³¹ Margoliouth (1905: 127); al-Tawḥīdī (1965: i. 126). Cf. Hume's denial of the infinity of the mind as quoted by Griffin (2012: 72 n. 14): "The capacity of the mind is not infinite... no idea of extension or duration consists of an infinite number of parts or inferior ideas, but of a finite number, and these simple and indivisible" (*Treatise* 1.2.4).
³² al-Jāḥiẓ (1960: i. 76). This passage in al-Jāḥiẓ (d. 869) supports our reading of *b-s-ṭ* in the debate passage as "spread out" rather than "simple", *pace* Margoliouth's translation, Mahdi (1970: 83), and Kühn (1986: 358).
³³ Both statements already translated; see nn. 17 and 26.
³⁴ Because "speak" and "talk" are synonymous verbs. Margoliouth (1905: 116–77); al-Tawḥīdī (1965: i. 114–15).
³⁵ Margoliouth (1905: 127); al-Tawḥīdī (1965: i. 126).
³⁶ Margoliouth (1905: 125–6); al-Tawḥīdī (1965: i. 125).
³⁷ Margoliouth (1905: 126); al-Tawḥīdī (1965: i. 125).

for instance through metaphor, is indispensable for effective language use, and analysis of these manipulations is the only way to determine the truth.

As this might suggest, for al-Sīrāfī poetics is a central case of language use.[38] This is why the literary nature of the Arabic culture into which Greek philosophy was translated was so important. Opinions like al-Sīrāfī's were culturally, politically, and professionally dominant and they explain why Mattā's claim that words are too superficial to matter would tend to fall on deaf ears. But al-Sīrāfī's claim was more than just persuasive rhetoric or an attempt to save the art of poetry. He sees understanding of language as the route to truth, and thus claims for grammar what Mattā claimed for logic. He offers this illustrative challenge to Mattā:

> Here is a problem that has caused disagreement, so solve it with your logic. Someone says 'so-and-so owns from the wall to the wall'. What is the correct legal ruling? How much land should be approportioned to so-and-so?[39]

This is a matter of law (*fiqh*), which like grammar was a discipline of paramount importance in the centuries immediately before and after our debate. So it counts as another point in al-Sīrāfī's favour if grammar, and not the supposedly universal tool that is logic, can be used to reach correct legal decisions. The solution to the problem of the walls is, as with al-Sīrāfī's other examples, to be found in a lexical analysis of word meanings and their usages in context. For al-Sīrāfī, Mattā is handicapped in his ability to deal with reality by his failure adequately to consider the clouding effect that language has on logic.

Mattā lost the debate before Ibn al-Furāt, and his embarrassment stung other members of the Baghdad school into a response. The question of how logic relates to grammar received particular attention from two members of the school: the Muslim al-Fārābī and his Christian student Yaḥyā Ibn ʿAdī. The latter wrote a combative treatise *On the Difference between Logic and Grammar*, to which we shall return.[40] As for al-Fārābī, he addresses the question throughout his writings, often defining logic in part by way of contrast to grammar. A good example appears in his *Introductory Epistle on Logic*:

> [Logic's] role in relation to the intellect is the same as the art of grammar in relation to language. Just as grammar rectifies language among the people for whose language the grammar has been made, so logic rectifies the intellect in order that when there is the possibility of error it intellects only what is right. Thus the relation of the science of grammar to language and vocal form is like that of the science of logic to the intellect and the intelligibles (*maʿqūlāt*).[41]

---

[38] Cf. Kühn (1986: 344–5).   [39] Margoliouth (1905: 126–7); al-Tawḥīdī (1965: i. 125–6).
[40] Yaḥyā b. ʿAdī (1988: 414–24). French translation: Elamrani-Jamal (1982). German translation: Endress (1986).
[41] Dunlop's translation (1956: §1, 225.5–9), modified.

Here al-Fārābī seems to take over Mattā's position more or less unaltered. Logic operates at the level of the intelligibles, grammar at the level of vocal form.[42] Logic and grammar are complementary, and each discipline is equally indispensable in its own sphere.[43]

Later in the epistle, however, we find a passage that complicates matters. Here al-Fārābī ponders the etymological connection between the words for "reason" or "speech" and "logic", a connection present in both Greek (*logos, logikê*) and Arabic (*nuṭq, manṭiq*).

> Logic is the only route to certainty of truth with regard to anything that we desire to know. And the name 'logic' is derived from 'discourse'. According to the ancients, the expression 'logic' indicates three things: [first,] the faculty with which man intellects the intelligibles, acquires disciplines of knowledge and arts, and distinguishes between admirable and repugnant actions; second, the intelligibles obtained in the soul of man through comprehension, which are called interior discourse (*al-nuṭq al-dākhil*); third, the expression by language of what is in the mind, which is called exterior discourse (*al-nuṭq al-khārij*). This art of logic is called 'logic' because it provides the rational faculty with rules for the interior discourse that is the intelligibles, because it provides all languages with shared rules for the exterior discourse that is the vocal forms, because it guides the rational faculty towards what is correct in both discourses, and because it protects the rational faculty from error in both discourses. Grammar is similar in some respects and yet also different because it only provides rules for the vocal forms that are specific to whichever nation and the people who speak its language. Logic, on the other hand, provides rules for the vocal forms that are common to all languages.[44]

This passage provides a detail that was lacking in the presentation of Mattā's position in the debate—namely, that the intelligibles or mental content take the form of "interior discourse". Of course this goes back to Plato (*Theaetetus* 189e–190a). We need to be careful, though: when al-Fārābī uses the word *nuṭq* for the phenomenon internal to the mind, he does *not* mean language (*lisān*).[45] Language comes under the third heading of "exterior discourse". It is hard to find a good translation of *nuṭq* here (just as it would be difficult to translate the Greek *logos* in analogous contexts). We have chosen "discourse" for its relative neutrality, but even this goes too far in a linguistic direction. In fact al-Fārābī must mean something similar to what we ascribed to Mattā: mental content that has a propositional character, but is not in any particular language.[46]

---

[42] Al-Fārābī makes the same statement in his *Catalogue of the Sciences*, and subsequently notes that, just as a grammarian would insist that the rules of grammar must be known before poetry and oratory can be memorized or used, so a logician would make a parallel claim that logic must be known in order for thoughts and beliefs to be known as true or false. al-Fārābī (1949: 54, 58–9; 1953: 28–31, cf. 20 (Arabic text)).

[43] al-Fārābī (1949: 59).

[44] Dunlop (1956: §4, 227.23–228.10); Gutas (1998: 272). Cf. Avicenna (2007a: i. 20) on the same matter.

[45] *Pace* Dunlop (1956), who translates *nuṭq* here as "speech".

[46] Gutas (1998: 172) chooses "articulation".

However, al-Fārābī adds a new qualification to the Mattā view: logic also operates at the level of vocal form, in so far as it deals with aspects of exterior discourse common to all languages. The restriction of grammar to the level of vocal form is retained, but logic is given a wider remit, spanning the divide between mental content and vocal form. One can readily see why al-Fārābī wants logic to apply to vocal forms. After all, Aristotle's *organon* is the canonical group of texts on logic, and these texts do concern themselves with language. The Baghdad school accordingly characterizes logic as dealing with vocal form. For instance, the last member of the school, Abū l-Faraj Ibn al-Ṭayyib (d. 1044), says in his commentary on Porphyry's *Isagoge* that "the subject-matter of the art of logic is the simple vocal forms that refer to common ideas [*al-ṣuwar al-ʿāmma*]".[47] Ibn ʿAdī likewise says that both logic and grammar have "vocal forms" as their subject matter.[48] He stresses, however, that logic deals with vocal forms in so far as these are *referring*, unlike grammar, which deals only with their more superficial linguistic form (for example, vocalization to show case).[49] Al-Fārābī and Ibn al-Ṭayyib make the same point.[50] But there still seems a tension, if not an outright contradiction, with Mattā's claim that logic deals with mental content and *not* vocal form.

Al-Fārābī has not just one, but two, ways of resolving this tension. First, as we have seen, he allows logic to deal with universal features of language. We can find examples in his commentary on *On Interpretation*: the tenses of the verb, and even a certain range of uses for the definite article, are said to occur in all languages.[51] Second, al-Fārābī explains that, although logic does deal properly with mental content and not vocal form, Aristotle nonetheless writes as if language were at stake because "mental content is difficult to grasp".[52] Actually, though, language is being used only as a convenient substitute for mental content: it is easier to work with the sentence "Socrates is mortal" than the thought that Socrates is mortal. This habit of Aristotle's might suggest that thoughts and bits of language combine in exactly the same ways.[53] But in fact language sometimes fails to capture mental content adequately. One can be led into error by linguistic features that do not reflect what is happening at the level of thought.

Al-Fārābī is happy to exploit this point for polemical purposes, as we can see from another passage in the *On Interpretation* commentary. Here al-Fārābī is considering the phenomenon of tense, which had long played an important role in Aristotelian logic. In *On Interpretation*, chapter 3, Aristotle distinguishes nouns from verbs in

---

[47] Ibn al-Ṭayyib (1975: §173; 1979: §85).   [48] Yaḥyā b. ʿAdī (1988: 416.7, 421.9).
[49] Yaḥyā b. ʿAdī (1988: 421.10).
[50] Zimmermann (1981: 10); al-Fārābī (1986: 24). Ferrari notes that the issue already arises in the Greek commentators (Ferrari 2006: 24.8–9106–7).
[51] Dunlop (1959: §9); Zimmermann (1981: 38, 63); al-Fārābī (1986: 46, 69).
[52] Zimmermann (1981: 14); al-Fārābī (1986: 25).
[53] Zimmermann (1981: 13–14); al-Fārābī (1986: 25–6).

part by their lack of tense.⁵⁴ He then adds that past and future tense are only an inflexion (*ptôsis*) of a basic verb; the basic verb "additionally indicates the present", whereas past and future verbs indicate what is "around" the present.⁵⁵ In commenting on this passage, al-Fārābī considers a view denying that there are in fact present-tense verbs. The view is bound up with a standard sceptical worry about time itself—namely, that nothing can happen at the present time, but only over an extended period of time. But it is not philosophers of time who are particularly prone to the misconception: it is scholars of grammar. Some Arabic grammarians have, says al-Fārābī, proposed that, in the absence of a proper present-tense verb, derived nouns should instead be taken as expressing the present tense. Al-Fārābī traces this unfortunate proposal to a feature of Arabic—namely, its (supposed) lack of present-tense verbs.⁵⁶

Whatever we make of al-Fārābī's analysis of this particular point,⁵⁷ the broader implication is clear. Anyone who confines her attention to the level of vocal form is liable to make mistakes, being misled by features of the particular vocal forms she is considering. Grammarians are particularly, perhaps uniquely, likely to commit such errors. Notice that the same point need not apply to logic in so far as it deals with language. For, on al-Fārābī's account, it considers only *universal* aspects of language—that is, features that appear in every language.⁵⁸ Nowhere does he suggest that such features might be misleading in the way that Arabic's handling of the present tense is misleading. Rather he seems to presume that universal features of exterior discourse correspond to features of interior discourse and, ultimately, the world. Indeed, al-Fārābī's confidence that every language does share these features is obviously not empirically grounded in a representative anthropological survey.⁵⁹ So he must assert it on the strength of a tacit assumption, along the following lines: any language that lacked these features would be unfit for purpose, and would therefore never arise.

Al-Fārābī thus has the resources both to attack grammar, which studies the frequently parochial features of specific languages, and to defend logic, which has

---

⁵⁴ On the late ancient reception of this in Boethius, see Suto (2012). It is interesting to note that Boethius also endorses the notion of an "inner discourse" that is not in any particular language, and explores the contrast between logic and grammar: Suto (2012: 82, 119).

⁵⁵ *De int* 16ᵇ16–18: τὸ ὑγίανεν ἢ τὸ ὑγιανεῖ οὐ ῥῆμα, ἀλλὰ πτῶσις ῥήματος· διαφέρει δὲ τοῦ ῥήματος, ὅτι τὸ μὲν τὸν παρόντα προσσημαίνει χρόνον, τὰ δὲ τὸν πέριξ.

⁵⁶ Zimmermann (1981: 30–3); al-Fārābī (1986: 40–2). The passage is paralleled in an introduction to logic by al-Fārābī, which, however, complains about mistakes made by certain ancients, rather than contemporary grammarians. Dunlop (1955: §5).

⁵⁷ For critical remarks, see: Zimmermann (1981: pp. cxxxi–v).

⁵⁸ In this respect Zimmermann (1981: p. cxxvii) is right to call logic a "universal grammar", though this leaves out its (in fact more important) role in studying thought. A "grammar of thought" would be a contradiction in terms, because grammar is by definition the study of language and thought is for al-Fārābī not linguistic.

⁵⁹ Al-Fārābī does, however, appear to have attempted some limited form of survey, as can be seen from his Arabic/Persian/Greek comparison at al-Fārābī (1969: 61–2).

emerged as the indispensible study of both thought and the universal aspects of language. This substantiates the Greek commentators' claim that "philosophy uses logic to show, in the theoretical domain, what is true and what false, and in the practical domain what is good and what is bad".[60] Ibn ʿAdī fills out the picture further. For him logic is the instrument that allows us to extend our knowledge from immediate truths—first principles of the intellect and the deliverances of sensation—to demonstrated conclusions.[61] This is why, in his treatise *On the Difference between Logic and Grammar,* Ibn ʿAdī can say that "the subject-matter for the art of logic is vocal forms that refer to universal things".[62] Logic's purpose is after all the discovery of syllogistic demonstrations whose conclusions are necessary, certain, and universal.[63] Logic's exalted aims are again in stark contrast to the purpose of grammar. Grammar seeks nothing more than correct vocalization, correctness being measured against culturally specific custom.[64]

Another work by Ibn ʿAdī, *On the Existence of Common Things,* sets the Baghdad school's theory of logic within a broader metaphysical context, by considering the universal thought in the soul as one of three types of common (*ʿāmm*) thing.[65] *Human,* for instance, can exist as a particular, material thing (like Zayd or ʾAmr), or as a form in the soul. Ibn ʿAdī calls these two ways that *human* can exist "physical" and "logical" respectively, and says that the vocal form "human" signifies the latter.[66] This indicates his allegiance to the tripartite theory of words ("vocal forms"), mental content ("logical" commonality), and things ("physical" object instantiating a commonality). But, following the Neoplatonic commentary tradition, he also recognizes a more fundamental way that the commonality might exist: not in individual bodily things nor as an idea in the soul, but as "divine" and "essential". It is this sort of commonality that is the real target of a definition like "rational mortal animal".[67] Bringing this together with his other remarks about logic, we can say that for Ibn ʿAdī logic is the instrument by which the soul arrives at demonstrative knowledge that conforms the soul, in so far as is possible, to that which is "divine".

We take this to be a particularly vivid instance of a more general phenomenon. The philosophers of the Baghdad school, in part because of their enthusiasm for logic and in part because of their rivalry with the grammarians, present logic (and by extension philosophy) as an art that transcends language. The diversity of human languages is an inevitable consequence of the fact that vocal forms are only conventional

---

[60] Westerink (1961: 134, ll. 23–4). Notice the similarity to Abū Bishr's opening characterization of logic in his debate with Abū Saʿīd.

[61] He sets out this view in a short work called *The Four Scientific Questions Regarding the Art of Logic.* For translation and discussion, see Shehadi and Rescher (1964); Adamson (2011).

[62] Yaḥyā b. ʿAdī (1988: 422.9).    [63] See further Adamson (2007).

[64] "[Grammar] is an art that concerns itself with vocal forms, in order to give rise to motions and rests in the way that Arabs do" (Yaḥyā b. ʿAdī 1988: 421.3).

[65] Edited at Yaḥyā b. ʿAdī (1988: 148–59). On the treatise, see Adamson (2007), and more importantly (including a French translation) Rashed (2004).

[66] Yaḥyā b. ʿAdī (1988: 148.12–16).    [67] Yaḥyā b. ʿAdī (1988: 154.17–20).

signs for mental content. The features of a given language are no more revelatory of reality than a given convention regarding table manners is revelatory of the moral law. By contrast, mental content relates to its objects naturally and is therefore the same for anyone who has an understanding of reality.[68] This means that the human intellect is adequately related to reality, including divine reality (for instance Ibn ʿAdī's "divine" commonalities, and one could extend the point to the ability of metaphysics to discern the nature of God). None of this can be said for language.

We saw that al-Sīrāfī's defence of grammar appealed to practice, and in particular to the role of language in legal disputes, as with the example of the boundary dispute and the wall. Some further investigation of legal practice will be useful for our chapter, an illuminating complement for al-Sīrāfī's ideas, just as the broader Baghdad school complements Mattā's position.

The claim of the Baghdad school that language is inadequate to deal with reality while logic shows both what is true and false in the theoretical domain and what is good and bad in the practical[69] was met with a demonstration of how theory could rest on poetics and how practice could rely on semantics. We have already seen that, a century before the debate, Arabic scholars had developed a model of finite vocal forms interacting with the infinite potential of mental content. This remained one of the central ways in which the art of poetics was understood. However, the results of the analysis of poetry would never constitute a sufficiently practical science to combat the claims of certainty put forward by the logicians. Jurisprudence offered itself as a practical discipline that sat alongside grammar on the "Arabic" side of the cultural divide.

From the very beginning, Arabic legal scholars had faced the problem of an Arabic-language revelation, a new religion, a literary culture, and the socio-political imperative to create order and certainty. The first major scholar that we know of to put forward a comprehensive theoretical framework to deal with these interlocking problems was the legal scholar al-Shāfiʿī (d. 820).[70] In the following passage he sets out the relationship between God, Arabic, and law:

God addressed the Arabs with his book in their language. He did so because the Arabs knew the mental content behind their language. They knew that the language had semantic breadth, and that it was in God's nature to address them in the Quran with explicit language of general application while intending that language to be indeed explicit, unrestricted, and independent of the words around it, or alternatively intending the explicit and unrestricted language to contain specificity that rested on the surrounding words, or intending the explicit and

---

[68] Zimmermann (1981: 12); al-Fārābī (1986: 27). [69] Shehadi and Rescher (1964: 574).
[70] Al-Shāfiʿī has been the subject of substantial recent scholarship in English: Lowry (2007); al-Šāfiʿī (2013). Also the relevant sections of Vishanoff (2011). For a readable translation (with historical introduction) of a twentieth-century manual of Islamic law that represents the continuity of the tradition after al-Shāfiʿī, see aṣ-Ṣadr (2003; repr. 2005).

unrestricted language to be in fact specific, or intending explicit language to be non-explicit, this being known from its context. The Arabs begin their speech with vocal forms that clarify what follows, and they begin speech with vocal forms that need to be clarified by what follows. The Arabs say something and they make the mental content behind it understood without this being manifest in the vocal form. This is comparable to the way that they indicate something with a physical gesture. They consider this way of speaking to be the most elevated, because only those who know it can do it and those who are ignorant of it cannot. The Arabs call a single thing many names, and they call many ideas with a single name.[71]

Furthermore, Arabic has a privileged position among languages as "the most vast in scope".[72] Within it, both God and Arabs use words like "man" to mean either all men, or a single specific man.[73] Both also use words that make no sense on their own, but rather require context. Homonymy and synonymy likewise feature in both divine and human language. The confessional (and political) message is that Islam is a religion for which God chose the Arabic language. Philosophically, the message is that allusion and intimation are part of clear and effective communication, and consequently that semantic and linguistic analysis is central to determining both what is theoretically true and false, and what is practically good and bad—precisely the function claimed by the philosophers for logic.[74]

The reliance of law upon language led to (and was fed by) a sustained commitment to both grammar and lexicography. Grammar made it possible to understand rigorously how sentences fit together, allowing scholars to determine exactly what God had told people in the Quran, or exactly what commitments arose from legally binding declarations. But this presupposed the possibility of discerning the meaning of individual words in the relevant speech acts.[75] For that purpose, lexicographers drew on ethnic and literary sources, predominantly histories of language use among the Bedouin Arabs and the poetic corpus that lay at the heart of Arabic culture.

Scholars such as al-Shāfiʿī and al-Sīrāfī thus had their own model of how language and reality interacted. It assumed polyvalency and was underpinned by an enumeration of lexical and grammatical rules and precedents. They could use linguistic analysis to make sense of the world, making claims of epistemic certainty regarding practical matters of human action and theoretical matters of divine creation and command. The Arabic set of hermeneutical and analytical tools that was being developed was capable of dealing with hermeneutics, poetics, semantics, and law. It

---

[71] al-Shāfiʿī (1938: 51–2 (§§173–6)).This passage is translated and analysed by Montgomery (2006), Lowry (2007), El Shamsy (2009), and Vishanoff (2011), and we have profited from their efforts.

[72] Lowry's translation. Lowry (2007: 253, 251–4); see also aš-Shāfiʿī (1938: 42 (§138)).

[73] See the discussions of this problem in Schöck (2006, 2007).

[74] Al-Shāfiʿī's belief in the "idiosyncratic...irreducible semantic and structural vastness and complexity" of the Arabic language has been read as a response to incipient legal formalism in Iraq at his time. The central thrust of that legal formalism was that "language and its rules and structures yield meanings in predictable ways" (Lowry 2007: 251–2; see also Jackson 2002).

[75] For example, in the lexicographical sub-genre of aḍdād works, Arabic words with two opposite meanings were enumerated and analysed. See Bettini (2010); Key (2012: 221–3).

was also steadily accumulating cultural capital. In this context it is scarcely suprising that a scholar like al-Sīrāfī felt no need for another *organon*, especially one that appeared to claim that it alone could carve reality at the joints.[76]

We can now see how much was at stake in the tenth-century debate over the relative merits of logic and grammar. A fundamental disagreement about the path to truth, in both practical and theoretical contexts, ran parallel to a cultural and political divide. The success or failure of our two debaters at the court of Ibn Furāt ultimately depended more on the prejudices of their audience than on the substance of their arguments; al-Sīrāfī, Abū Ḥayyān (and earlier al-Shāfiʿī) felt strongly about the privileged position of Arabic literary culture. As for the beleaguered party at Ibn Furāt's court, scholars such as Mattā and al-Fārābī could console themselves with the thought that, however much the currency of grammar might outstrip that of logic in the culture of their day, the superiority of thinkers like Aristotle was timeless.

This divide may seem insurmountable, yet a coming-together was inevitable, especially once intellectual life began to be systematically institutionalized in the *madrasa* from the eleventh century onwards. As in so many other fields, the pivotal figure who synthesized what had come before and set the stage for later developments was Avicenna (d. 1037).[77] His logical writings proved immensely influential in the subsequent centuries. In particular, the *Pointers and Reminders* (*al-Ishārāt wa-l-Tanbīhāt*), a popular object of commentary in the centuries after Avicenna's death, presented logic in a way that did not raise the hackles of scholars in the way Mattā had alienated al-Sīrāfī.

Take, for example, the section on the relationship of vocal form and mental content in *Pointers and Reminders*:

There is a certain relationship between the vocal form and the mental content. And the patterns of the vocal form may affect the patterns of the mental content.[78]

One of the most influential commentators on *Pointers and Reminders*, Naṣīr al-Dīn al-Ṭūsī (d. 1274), used this statement to distinguish between the existence of something in the mind, its existence in speech (and writing), and its existence in external physical reality (the Aristotelian tripartite division). He then made a further distinction

---

[76] For a discussion of this phrase, originating in Plato's *Phaedrus* (265e), see Griffin (2012: 69 n. 3, 87, 92).

[77] Abū ʿAlī al-Ḥusayn Ibn Sīnā (Avicenna), on whom see Gutas (1998); Wisnovsky (2003); Street (2008). Honourable mention must also be made at this point of another bold synthesizer, albeit one whose theories did not have as much impact as Avicenna's. In Islamic Spain the legal theorist Ibn Ḥazm of Cordoba (Abū Muḥammad ʿAlī, d. 1064) developed an account of law, theology, and language that has unfairly been characterized as simply literalist. In fact, it included a thoroughgoing account of Aristotelian logic, and rested on a commitment never to exceed the meaning contained in one's premisses. "A proposition", he wrote in a statement that applies to both logic and law, "cannot give you anything more than itself" (Vishanoff 2011: 95, 88–9; see also Ibn Ḥazm 2003).

[78] Avicenna and al-Ṭūsī (1983–94: i. 131).

between the natural and unchanging connection between things in the mind and their counterparts outside it, and the non-natural connection between things in the mind and their vocal forms. The indicative connection that links mental content and vocal form (the Arabic bipartite division) changes according to circumstance. Because the mind may well think with its own internal language ("mental vocal forms"), the problems that affect language may come to affect thought. Homonymy is one of those linguistic problems, and it therefore becomes a problem for logic.[79]

Al-Ṭūsī has taken the linguistic stick that al-Sīrāfī used to beat Mattā (that his logic failed to account for polysemy) and fitted it back into what was now fast becoming (an) Arabic logic,[80] rather than just an iteration of Aristotle's *Organon*. We say "fitted back" because polysemy had, of course, been present in the *Categories* and *On Interpretation* at the outset. But the post-Porphyrean position that logic is only about vocal forms in so far as they signify (universal) mental content had, in the heated climate of debate with an established discipline of grammar, led Arabic logicians away from the kind of analysis of linguistic ambiguity that was championed by al-Sīrāfī. The Baghdad school sought to insulate both logic and mental content from the polysemy of natural languages. As we saw, al-Fārābī saw logic as dealing with only the universal aspects of these languages, and with the unambiguous sphere of mental content.

In *The Cure*, Avicenna also takes up this question of the extent to which the logician must concern himself with the features of language:

> An investigation of vocal form is a matter of necessity, and yet vocal forms are not something that the logician *qua* logician should concern himself with, unless [he is simply using them] in conversation or discussion with others. If it were possible to study logic through pure thought with only the mental contents themselves observed, then that would be enough. If the logician were to be able to apprise his interlocutor of that which is in his soul through some contrivance, then he would be able to dispense with vocal forms.[81]

This passage is taken from the *Eisagoge*, with which *The Cure* begins. Subsequently, at the start of his discussion of the *Categories*,[82] Avicenna writes that logic is not concerned with the totality of language, but rather only with certain combinations of words: the syllogism, the definition, and the description. As for the question of whether a given mental content deserves the vocal form used for it, this is no part of logic, but rather the concern of the lexicographers.[83]

---

[79] Avicenna and al-Ṭūsī (1983–94: i. 131).

[80] On the subsequent development of which, see Wisnovsky (2004); El-Rouayheb (2010).

[81] Avicenna (2007a: 22–3). See also Sabra (1980).

[82] Avicenna was highly critical of the late antique position, discussed above, that Aristotle's *Categories* had a linguistic aspect. See Avicenna (2007b: 1–8, esp. 8.4–9).

[83] Avicenna (2007b: 5, ll. 10–11).

To return to the same passage in *Pointers and Reminders*:

[AVICENNA] The patterns of the vocal form may affect the patterns of the mental content. For this reason, the logician must take heed of absolute vocal forms, inasmuch as they are unrestricted by any specific language.

[AL-ṬŪSĪ] This means that Avicenna's investigation of mental content is his primary goal, while the investigation of vocal form is his secondary goal. His investigation of vocal forms, inasmuch as they are unrestricted by any specific language, is knowledge of their single, combined, homonymous, or ambiguous state, and indeed any of the other patterns that affect the way in which they refer, such as the effect of a negative on a necessarily negative copula, its necessary conversion to metathesis,[84] the effect of these two on a mode, and the effect of a mode on them both.[85]

Avicenna has enabled al-Ṭūsī to combine classical logical analysis—extolled by Mattā and dismissed by al-Sīrāfī—with the polysemic analyses of linguistic ambiguity, regarding which Mattā was ignorant and al-Sīrāfī an expert. Mattā had been led to downplay the role of language in logic, but al-Ṭūsī felt no such pressure. Avicenna rehabilitates the traditional ground-clearing exercise of considering polysemy, presenting the study of "the patterns of the vocal form" as a necessity (even if a regrettable one) for the logician, rather than a mere source of confusion and error.

In *Pointers and Reminders*, Avicenna furthermore reclassifies the ways that vocal form refers to mental content, and vice versa. He writes that vocal form indicates mental content in one of three ways. First, congruence (*muṭābaqah*), where each vocal form directly connects to its mental content. An example would be the relationship between the vocal form "triangle" and the idea of a three-sided shape. Second, implication (*taḍammun*) between a vocal form and a mental content, such as the word "shape" and the idea of a triangle. Third, concomitance (*al-istitbā' wa-l-iltizām*), in which one idea requires that another follow it. An example is the relationship between the word "ceiling" and the idea of a wall supporting it.[86] This third type allows the sort of connections between mental content and vocal form that tended to concern literary non-philosophers. What is a metaphor, if not an expression that calls to mind an idea that is not directly connected to it? (We are not concerned here with the Arabic reception of Aristotle's own work on poetics and metaphor in the *Poetics* and *Rhetoric*. Commentaries on these texts were substantially

---

[84] Metathesis: reversion of the order. See Zimmermann (1981: pp. lxiii, 98 n. 1).
[85] Avicenna and al-Ṭūsī (1983–94: i. 131).
[86] Avicenna (Ibn Sīnā) and al-Ṭūsī (1983–94: i. 139).

disconnected from Arabic literary theory,[87] despite their use of the poetic syllogism as a way to analyse metaphor.[88])

Another example of Avicenna's attention to the relation between verbal form and mental content can be found in his discussion of the indefinite nouns in Aristotle's *On Interpretation* (16$^a$20f). Here he compares the way that nouns like "human" signify to the way that definitions signify:

> The composition can be... composed of two mental contents... for which a single vocal form can be substituted. For example "Zayd is a rational, mortal, animal". The part of this phrase "rational, mortal, animal" is a composition that acts in this way, and a single vocal form like "human" can be substituted for it.[89]

Here we have a case where a composite at the level of thought can be represented by either a composite vocal form or a single word. Elsewhere, a composition at the linguistic level tracks a composition at the level of mental content. When explaining Aristotle's inclusion of composite negative nouns such as "not human" or "not seeing" alongside simple nouns like "human", Avicenna remarks: "the vocal form 'not' and the vocal form 'seeing' both indicate a mental content, and the combination of their two mental contents is the mental content of the 'not seeing' whole."[90] Of course Avicenna's model is constructed to meet a very different need from that of the literary tradition. He seeks to establish the types of words that can be used to construct syllogisms, and to establish the relationships between words' single or composite natures. Linguistic scholars instead want to give both a hermeneutical account of linguistic ambiguity and a poetic account of metaphor and imagery. Nevertheless, the results of the two processes were analogous. Both models used the pairing of vocal form and mental content to represent the interaction of language

---

[87] The rhetoric and poetics of Hellenic philosophy were dealt with at length by practitioners of *falsafa* such as al-Fārābī and Avicenna. Their relative lack of impact outside *falsafa* was due to the prior existence of a functional theory for reading and thinking about poetry, an indigenous theory untroubled by puzzling references to Greek tragedy, or other persistent difficulties of cross-cultural literary translation. The definitive study of that transmission is Vagelpohl (2008). There was, for example, no dialogue between Aristotle's statement at *Rhetoric* 1404$^b$–1405$^a$ that homonymy was primarily used by sophists to mislead and the very different role that al-Sīrāfī, as we have seen, accorded to homonymy. This must have been in part due to the difficulties (detailed by Vagelpohl) experienced by the translator of the *Rhetoric*. For the homonymy in the *Rhetoric*'s discussion of metaphor he used the same Arabic (*ittifāq al-ism*) as had been used for the very different homonymy of the *Categories*. Wansborough (1984); Aristotle (1948: i. 1; 1982: i. 176.19–20, ii. 106). Abu Deeb (1979: 303–22, esp. 310–11) shows the scale of the disconnect between Aristotle's *Poetics* and *Rhetoric* and Arabic literary theory, with a discussion of Avicenna's commentary on the *Poetics* and *Rhetoric* and the work of al-Jurjānī. An illustrative excerpt of Avicenna's analysis of poetry is translated in van Gelder and Hammond (2008: 26–8). See also Black (1990).

[88] Both al-Fārābī and Avicenna sought to address poetry's dominance of their cultural context in part by analysing it in terms of syllogisms that rested on imagination. For referenced analysis of this logic of poetics, see Heinrichs (2008: 3–10).

[89] Avicenna (2007c: 32–3). See also Black (1991: 67).

[90] *On Interpretation*, 16$^a$30. Avicenna (2007c: 12). Cf. Black (1991: 67).

and mind, and both models emphasized the possibility that a single vocal form can denote multiple mental contents.

As we have already discussed, al-Sīrāfī's advocacy for his linguistic analysis of polysemy presented a challenge to the discipline of logic. Mental content was infinite and its vocal form finite, so only a technique that came to terms with the linguistic ambiguity of homonymy could suffice. Avicenna's remarks imply an answer to this challenge: logic can handle the idea that finite forms capture the more expansive mental content that lies behind them, because single words and compound vocal forms can both indicate combination of several thoughts. Avicenna takes one of the dominant modes of analysis in Arabic intellectual culture and integrates it into the *Organon*, a typically syncretic step that was bound to be more culturally successful than the aggressive claims of supremacy on behalf of logic made by the Baghdad school. Nevertheless, as the commentators on *Pointers and Reminders* make clear,[91] the relationships with which Avicenna was concerned were between mental contents more than they were between mental content and vocal form. Language comes into the logical picture only as an accident, by accident. To understand the relation between "human" and "not-human" is to understand the implications of one piece of mental content for another piece of mental content, not one bit of language for another bit of language.

Nevertheless, Avicenna's focus on the relationships between the mental content behind a vocal form may have enabled Arabic literary theory to progress beyond the binary of vocal forms and mental content to a recognition of the mental processes that could be prompted by encountering a literary expression. For al-Sīrāfī, vocal forms were simply mapped onto a range of individual static mental contents. Now Avicenna had applied this traditional terminology of vocal form and mental content to understand how mental contents (internal language) interact. The resulting analysis of dynamic thought processes had potential for poetics.

That potential was heightened by the work of such figures as ʿAbd al-Qāhir al-Jurjānī, the dominant figure in the analyses of secular and profane language from the eleventh century onwards.[92] Al-Jurjānī was the first literary theorist to investigate the mental processes that take place when a line of poetry, or a Quranic verse, is heard or read.[93] He wrote that:

---

[91] See Avicenna and al-Ṭūsī (1983–94: i. 139).
[92] For more on al-Jurjānī, see Abu Deeb (1979); Larkin (1995); van Gelder and Hammond (2008: 29–69). Van Gelder and Hammond's translation includes a section in which al-Jurjānī addresses the relationships of poetry and logic to truth (van Gelder and Hammond 2008: 30–8).
[93] Some previous steps had been taken in this direction by al-Rāghib al-Iṣfahānī (fl. in or before 1018), who described complex poetic metaphors in terms of the connection between target and the source not being mentioned in any vocal expression, but instead being left to be reasoned by the audience. Key (2010: 58; 2012: 232–3); Abū al-Qāsim al-Ḥusayn b. Muḥammad Ragib al-Iṣfahānī, '[Ragib on the New Style] Afānīn al-Balāġah', MS 165 in Landberg Collection, Yale University, Beinecke Rare Book and Manuscript Library, New Haven, fo. 12b.

Language is divided into two types. In one, you grasp the intended aim with the indication of the vocal form alone, for example if you intended to inform [someone] about Zayd's literal departure, you would say 'Zayd left'. In the other type of language you do not grasp the intended aim with the indication of the vocal form alone. Instead, the vocal form indicates its mental content to you through a process that is constrained by the vocal form's lexical position. You then find that mental content to contain a second indication that leads you to the intended aim. This type of language relies on allusion ... and analogy.[94]

Language is either simple indication, or complex reference. For al-Jurjānī, complex reference is defined by the second level of mental effort on the part of the audience that goes into deciphering it. He was aware of the theoretical originality of this claim:

If you have understood all of the above, then here is an abbreviated way to express it. You can just say 'the mental content and 'the mental content's mental content'. By 'the mental content' you will mean that content directly understood from the vocal form itself without an intermediary. By 'the mental content's mental content' you will mean that you reason mental content from the vocal form and then that mental content leads you to further mental content ...[95]

We do not know that al-Jurjānī had indeed read the work of Avicenna or other logicians, but we can see that their two models had the potential for productive interaction. No longer was logic claimed to have universal domination over all thought and language, as in Mattā and to a lesser extent in al-Fārābī. Avicenna limited the scope of logic to the syllogism, the definition, and the description. In doing so he enabled logic to take what would be an increasingly central place in the Islamic *madrasa* in the coming centuries, even as he left room for the autochthonous linguistic sciences of Arabic grammar, lexicography, and literary theory. Al-Jurjānī did not solve, or indeed address, the problems of logic. Nor did Avicenna answer the questions of Arabic literary theory. But the poisonous atmosphere of the debate between Mattā and al-Sīrāfī had dissipated; the war between grammar and logic was over.[96]

# References

Abu Deeb, Kamal (1979). *Al-Jurjānī's Theory of Poetic Imagery*. Warminster: Aris & Phillips.
Abū Nuwās, al-Ḥasan b. Hānī (1958–2006). *Der Diwān des Abū Nuwās*, ed. Ewald Wagner. Bibliotheca Islamica. 7 vols. Wiesbaden: Franz Steiner; Berlin: Klaus Schwarz.
Adamson, Peter (2007). 'Knowledge of Universals and Particulars in the Baghdad School', *Documenti e studi sulla tradizione filosofica medievale*, 18: 141–64.

---

[94] al-Jurǧānī (1978: 202; 1992: 262); Key (2012: 233). Also translated and edited by Larkin (1995: 74, 184–5).
[95] al-Jurǧānī (1978: 203; 1992: 263); Key (2012: 233). Also translated by Abu Deeb (1979: 75–6).
[96] Other cultural, political, and intellectual debates of course continued to rage, perhaps most notably the philosophical argument about the status of Hellenic *falsafa*, in which al-Ghazālī wrote philosophy that attacked *falsafa*. For al-Ghazālī, see Griffel (2009).

Adamson, Peter (2011). 'The Last Philosophers of Late Antiquity in the Arabic Tradition', in U. Rudolph and R. Goulet (eds), *Entre Orient et Occident: La Philosophie et la science gréco-romaines*. Vandoeuvres: Fondation Hardt, 1–43.

Adamson, Peter, and Taylor, Richard C. (2005). *The Cambridge Companion to Arabic Philosophy*. Cambridge: Cambridge University Press.

Aristotle (1948). *Organon Aristotelis in versione Arabica antiqua / Manṭiq Arisṭū*. ed. ʿAbd ar-Raḥmān Badawī. 3 vols. Cairo: Dār al-Kutub al-Miṣrīyah.

Aristotle (1982). *Aristotle's Ars Rhetorica. The Arabic Version*, ed. M. C. Lyons. 2 vols. Cambridge: Pembroke Arabic Texts.

Aristotle (2012). *Aristotle Poetics: Editio maior of the Greek Text With Historical Introductions and Philological Commentaries*, ed. Leonardo Tarán and Dimitri Gutas. Leiden: Brill.

Avicenna (Ibn Sīnā, Abū ʿAlī al-Ḥusayn) (2007a). 'al-Shifāʾ: al-Manṭiq I (al-Madḫal)', in *al-Šifāʾ*, ed. Ibrāhīm Madkūr. Cairo: Wizārat al-Maʿārif al-ʿUmūmīyah, 1952; repr. Qum: Ẓovī el-Qurbā.

Avicenna (Ibn Sīnā, Abū ʿAlī al-Ḥusayn) (2007b). 'al-Shifāʾ: al-Manṭiq II (al-Maqūlāt)', in *al-Šifāʾ*, ed. Ibrāhīm Madkūr. Cairo: Wizārat aṭ-Ṯaqāfah wa-l-Iršād al-Qawmī, 1959; repr. Qum: Ẓovī el-Qurbā.

Avicenna (Ibn Sīnā, Abū ʿAlī al-Ḥusayn) (2007c). 'al-Shifāʾ: al-Manṭiq III (al-ʿIbārah)', in *al-Shifāʾ*, ed. Ibrāhīm Madkūr. Cairo: Dār al-Kātib al-ʿArabī, 1970; repr. Qum: Ẓovī el-Qurbā.

Avicenna (Ibn Sīnā, Abū ʿAlī al-Ḥusayn), and Naṣīr al-Dīn aṭ-Ṭūsī (1983–1994). *al-Išārāt wa-l-Tanbīhāṭ*, ed. Sulaymān Dunyā. 3rd edn. 4 vols. Cairo: Dār al-Maʿārif.

Bettini, Lidia (2010). 'Ḍidd', in Kees Versteegh, Lutz Edzard, and Rudolf de Jong (eds), *Encyclopedia of Arabic Language and Linguistics Online Edition*. Brill Online: Brill.

Black, Deborah L. (1990). *Logic and Aristotle's Rhetoric and Poetics in Medieval Arabic Philosophy*. Leiden: Brill.

Black, Deborah L. (1991). 'Aristotle's "Peri hermeneias" in Medieval Latin and Arabic Philosophy: Logic and the Linguistic Arts', *Canadian Journal of Philosophy: Supplementary Volume* 17: 25–83.

Brentjes, Sonja (2012). 'Algebra', in Gudrun Krämer, Denis Matringe, John Nawas, and Everett Rowson (eds), *Encyclopaedia of Islam, THREE*. Brill Online: Brill.

Carter, M. G. (2004). *Sibawayhi*. London: I. B. Tauris.

D'Ancona, Cristina (2013). 'Greek Sources in Arabic and Islamic Philosophy', in Edward N. Zalta (ed.), *The Stanford Encyclopedia of Philosophy* (Winter 2013 edn), <http://plato.stanford.edu/archives/win2013/entries/arabic-islamic-greek/> (accessed 11 August 2014).

Dunlop, D. M. (1955). 'Al-Fārābī's Introductory Sections on Logic [I]', *Islamic Quarterly*, 2: 264–82.

Dunlop, D. M. (1956). 'Al-Fārābī's Introductory Sections on Logic [II]', *Islamic Quarterly*, 3: 224–35.

Dunlop, D. M. (1959). 'Al-Fārābī's Paraphrase of the Categories of Aristotle', *Islamic Quarterly*, 5: 21–54.

Elamrani-Jamal, A. (1982). 'Grammaire et logique d'après le philosophe arabe chrétien Yaḥyā b. ʿAdī (280–364 H/893–974)', *Arabica*, 29: 1–15.

Elamrani-Jamal, A. (1983). *Logique Aristotélienne et grammaire arabe: Étude et documents*. Paris: J. Vrin.

El-Hibri, Tayeb (1999). *Reinterpreting Islamic Historiography: Hārūn al-Rashīd and the Narrative of the 'Abbasid Caliphate*. Cambridge: Cambridge University Press.
El-Rouayheb, Khaled (2010). *Relational Syllogisms and the History of Arabic Logic, 900–1900* (Leiden: Brill).
El Shamsy, Ahmed (2009). 'From Tradition to Law: The Origins and Early Development of the Shāfiʿī School of Law in Ninth-Century Egypt', Ph.D. thesis, Harvard University.
Endress, Gerhard (1977). 'La Controverse entre la logique philosophique et la grammaire arabe au temps des khalifs', *Journal for the History of Arabic Science*, 1: 339–51.
Endress, Gerhard (1986). 'Grammatik und Logik: Arabische Philologie und griechische Philosophie im Widerstreit', in B. Mojsisch (ed.), *Sprachphilosophie in Antike und Mittelalter*. Amsterdam: Grüner, 163–299.
Endress, Gerhard (1987). 'Die wissenschaftliche Literatur', in Helmut Gätje (ed.), *Grundriss der Arabischen Philologie II*. Wiesbaden: Dr Ludwig Reichert, 24–61.
al-Fārābī, Abū Naṣr Muḥammad (1949). *Iḥṣāʾ al-ʿUlūm*. ʿUṯmān Amīn. Cairo: Dār al-Fikr al-ʿArabī.
al-Fārābī, Abū Naṣr Muḥammad (1953). *Catálogo de las Ciencias [Iḥṣāʾ al-ʿUlūm]*, trans. A. Gonzalez Palencia, ed. A. Gonzalez Palencia. Madrid: Dār al-Fikr al-ʿArabī.
al-Fārābī, Abū Naṣr Muḥammad (1969). *Kitāb al-Ḥurūf*, ed. Muhsin Mahdi. Beirut: Dār al-Mašriq.
al-Fārābī, Abū Naṣr Muḥammad (1986). *Šarḥ al-Fārābī li-Kitāb Arisṭūṭālīs fī-l-ʿIbārah*, ed. Wilhelm Kutsch and Stanley Marrow. Beirut: Dār al-Mašriq.
Ferrari, C. (2006). *Die Kategorienkommentar von Abū l-Farāj ʿAbdallāh ibn aṭ-Ṭayyib*. Leiden: Brill.
Frank, Richard M. (1981). 'Meanings are Spoken of in Many Ways: The Earlier Arab Grammarians', *Le Museon*, 94/3–4: 259–319.
al-Ǧāḥiẓ, Abū ʿUṯmān ʿAmr b. Baḥr (1960). *al-Bayān wa-l-Tabyīn*, ed. ʿAbd al-Salām Muḥammad Hārūn. 4 vols. Cairo: Maktabat al-Ḫānǧī.
Griffel, Frank (2009). *Al-Ghazālī's Philosophical Theology*. Oxford: Oxford University Press.
Griffin, Michael J. (2012). 'What Does Aristotle Categorize? Semantics and the Early Peripatetic Reading of the Categories', *Bulletin of the Institute of Classical Studies (The Peripatetic School through Alexander of Aphrodisias (Issue in Honour of R. W. Sharples))*, ed. Peter Adamson, 69–108.
Gutas, Dimitri (1998). *Avicenna and the Aristotelian Tradition: Introduction to Reading Avicenna's Philosophical Works*. Leiden: Brill.
Gutas, Dimitri (2010). 'Greek Philosophical Works Translated into Arabic', in Robert Pasnau and Christina van Dyke (eds), *The Cambridge History of Medieval Philosophy*. Cambridge: Cambridge University Press, ii. 801–14.
Heinrichs, Wolfhart (1987). 'Poetik, Rhetorik, Literaturkritik, Metrik und Reimlehre', in Helmut Gätje (ed.), *Grundriss der Arabischen Philologie II*. Wiesbaden: Dr. Ludwig Reichert, 177–207.
Heinrichs, Wolfhart (1998). 'Lafẓ and maʿnā', in Julie Scott Meisami and Paul Starkey (eds), *Encyclopedia of Arabic Literature*. London and New York: Routledge, 461–2.
Heinrichs, Wolfhart (2008). 'Taḫyīl: Make-Believe and Image Creation in Arabic Literary Theory', in G. J. H. van Gelder and Marlé Hammond (eds), *Taḫyīl: The Imaginary in Classical Arabic Poetics*. Cambridge: Gibb Memorial Trust, 1–14.

Heinrichs, Wolfhart (2012). 'Takhyīl', in P. Bearman, Th. Bianquis, C. E. Bosworth, E. van Donzel, and W. P. Heinrichs (eds), *Encyclopaedia of Islam*, 2nd edn. Brill Online.

al-Ḫuwārizmī, Abū ʿAbdallāh Muḥammad b. Aḥmad b. Yusūf (1895). *Mafātīḥ al-ʿUlūm*, ed. G. Van Vloten. Leiden: Brill. Facsimile edition, ed. Muḥammad Ḥusayn ʿAbd al-ʿAzīz. Cairo: al-Hayʾah al-ʿĀmmah li-Quṣūr al-Ṯaqāfah, 2004.

Ibn al-Ṭayyib, Abū al-Farağ ʿAbdallāh (1975). *Ibn al-Ṭayyib's Commentary on Porphyry's Eisagoge [Arabic text]*, ed. Kwame Gyekye. Beirut: Dār al-Mašriq.

Ibn al-Ṭayyib, Abū al-Farağ ʿAbdallāh (1979). *Arabic Logic: Ibn al-Ṭayyib's Commentary on Porphyry's Eisagoge [English translation]*, ed. Kwame Gyekye. Albany: State University of New York Press.

Ibn Ḥazm, Abū Muḥammad ʿAlī b. Aḥmad (2003). *al-Taqrīb li-Ḥadd al-Manṭiq wa-l-Madḫal ilayhi bi-l-Alfāẓ al-ʿĀmīyah wa-l-Amṯilah al-Fiqhīyah wa-yalīhi Miḥakk an-Naẓr fī-l-Manṭ iq taʾlīf Abī Ḥāmid Muḥammad al-Ġazālī*, ed. Aḥmad Farīd al-Mazīdī. Beirut: Dār al-Kutub al-ʿIlmīyah.

Jackson, Sherman (2002). 'Fiction and Formalism: Toward a Functional Analysis of *uṣūl al-fiqh*', in Bernard G. Weiss (ed.), *Studies in Islamic Legal Theory*. Leiden: Brill, 177–201, 406–11.

al-Jurğānī, ʿAbd al-Qāhir b. ʿAbd al-Raḥmān (1978). *Dalāʾil al-Iʿğāz*, ed. Muḥammad Maḥmūd al-Šinqīṭī. Beirut: Dār al-Maʿrifah; repr. 1987.

al-Jurğānī, ʿAbd al-Qāhir b. ʿAbd al-Raḥmān (1992). *Dalāʾil al-Iʿğāz*, ed. Maḥmūd Muḥammad Šākir. Cairo: Dār al-Madanī; repr. 1987.

Kennedy, Hugh (2004). *The Prophet and the Age of the Caliphates: The Islamic Near East from the Sixth to the Eleventh Century*. 2nd edn. Harlow: Pearson.

Key, Alexander (2010). 'Language and Literature in al-Rāġib al-Iṣfahānī', in *Reflections on Language and Knowledge in Middle Eastern Societies*. Cambridge: Cambridge Scholars Publishing, 32–62.

Key, Alexander (2012). 'A Linguistic Frame of Mind: al-Rāġib al-Iṣfahānī and what it Meant to be Ambiguous'. Ph.D. thesis, Harvard University.

Key, Alexander (2013). 'English-Language Resources for Arabic Poetics', Stanford University Division of Literatures, Cultures, and Languages <http://arcade.stanford.edu/english-lan guage-resources-arabic-poetics> (accessed 11 August 2014).

Kraemer, Joel L. (1986a). *Philosophy in the Renaissance of Islam: Abū Sulaymān Al-Sijistānī and his Circle*. Brill: Leiden.

Kraemer, Joel L. (1986b). *Humanism in the Renaissance of Islam*. Studies in Islamic Culture and History Series. Brill: Leiden.

Kühn, Wilfried (1986). 'Die Rehabilitierung der Sprache durch den Arabischen Philologen al-Sirafi', in B. Mojsisch (ed.), *Sprachphilosophie in Antike und Mittelalter*. Amsterdam: Grüner, 301–402.

Larkin, Margaret (1995). *The Theology of Meaning: ʿAbd al-Qāhir al-Jurjānī's Theory of Discourse*. New Haven: American Oriental Society.

Lowry, Joseph E. (2007). *Early Islamic Legal Theory: The Risāla of Muḥammad ibn Idrīs al-Shāfiʿī*. Leiden: Brill.

McGinnis, Jon, and Reisman, David C. (2007). *Classical Arabic Philosophy: An anthology of sources translated from the Arabic*. Indianapolis: Hackett.

Mahdi, Muhsin (1970). 'Language and Logic in Classical Islam', in Gustave E. von Grunebaum (ed.), *Logic in Classical Islamic Culture*. Wiesbaden: O. Harrassowitz, 51–83.

Margoliouth, D. S. (1905). 'The Discussion between Abū Bishr Mattā and Abū Saʿīd al-Sīrāfī on the Merits of Logic and Grammar', *Journal of the Royal Asiatic Society of Great Britain and Ireland*, 79–129.

Meisami, Julie Scott, and Starkey, Paul (1998). *Encyclopedia of Arabic Literature*. London and New York: Routledge.

Montgomery, James E. (2006). 'Al-Jāḥiẓ's Kitāb al-Bayān wa al-Tabyīn', in Julia Bray (ed.), *Writing and Representation in Medieval Islam: Muslim Horizons*. New York: Routledge, 91–152.

Ragib, Abū al-Qāsim al-Ḥusayn b. Muḥammad al-Iṣfahānī (n.d.). '[Ragib on the New Style] Afānīn al-Balāġah'. MS 165 in Landberg Collection, Yale University, Beinecke Rare Book and Manuscript Library, New Haven.

Rashed, M. (2004). 'Ibn ʿAdi et Avicenne: Sur les types d'existants', in V. Celluprica and C. D'Ancona (eds), *Aristotele e i suoi esegeti Neoplatonici*. Naples: Bibliopolis, 109–71.

Sabra, A. I. (1980). 'Avicenna on the Subject Matter of Logic', *Journal of Philosophy*, 77/11: 746–64.

aṣ-Ṣadr, Muḥammad Bāqir (2003). *Lessons in Islamic Jurisprudence*, trans. Roy Mottahedeh. Oxford: Oneworld; repr. 2005.

al-Šāfiʿī, Muḥammad Idrīs (1938). *al-Risālah*, ed. Aḥmad Muḥammad Šākir. Cairo: Muṣṭafā al-Bābī al-Ḥalabī.

al-Šāfiʿī, Muḥammad Idrīs (2013). *The Epistle on Legal Theory*, trans. Joseph E. Lowry. New York: New York University Press.

Saussure, Ferdinand de (1949). *Cours de linguistique générale*, ed. Charles Bally, Albert Sechehaye, and Albert Riedlinger. Paris: Payot.

Saussure, Ferdinand de (1983/2005). *Course in General Linguistics*, trans. Roy Harris. London: Duckworth.

Schöck, Cornelia (2006). *Koranexegese, Grammatik und Logik*. Leiden: Brill.

Schöck, Cornelia (2007). 'Discussions on Conditional Sentences from the Year AH 17/AD 638 to Avicenna (d. AH 428/ AD 1037)', in Peter Adamson (ed.), *Classical Arabic Philosophy: Sources and Reception*. Warburg Institute Colloquia. London: Warburg Institute, 55–73.

Shehadi, N., and Rescher, F. (1964). 'Yaḥyā Ibn ʿAdī's Treatise on the Four Scientific Questions Regarding the Art of Logic', *Journal of the History of Ideas*, 25: 572–8.

Street, Tony (2008). 'Arabic and Islamic Philosophy of Language and Logic', in Edward N. Zalta (ed.), *The Stanford Encyclopedia of Philosophy* <http://plato.stanford.edu/>. Stanford: The Metaphysics Research Lab, Stanford University.

Suto, T. (2012). *Boethius on Mind, Grammar and Logic: A Study of Boethius' Commentary on Peri Hermeneias*. Leiden: Brill.

al-Tawḥīdī, Abū Ḥayyān (1965). *Kitāb al-Imtāʿ wa-l-Muʾānasah*, ed. Aḥmad Amīn and Aḥmad al-Zayn. 3 in 1 vols. Beirut: Dār Maktabat al-Ḥayāh.

Vagelpohl, Uwe (2008). *Aristotle's Rhetoric in the East: The Syriac and Arabic Translation and Commentary Tradition*. Leiden: Brill.

van Gelder, Geert Jan, and Hammond, Marlé (2008). *Takhyīl: The Imaginary in Classical Arabic Poetics*. Cambridge: Gibb Memorial Trust.

Vishanoff, David R. (2011). *The Formation of Islamic Hermeneutics: How Sunni Legal Theorists Imagined a Revealed Law*. American Oriental Series, vol. 93. New Haven: American Oriental Society.

Wansborough, John (1984). 'Review of Aristotle's *Ars Rhetorica*: The Arabic Version. A New Edition with Commentary and Glossary by M. C. Lyons', *Bulletin of the School of Oriental and African Studies*, 47/3: 550–1.

Westerink, L. G. (1961). 'Elias on the Prior Analytics', *Mnemosyne*, 14: 126–39.

Wisnovsky, Robert (2003). *Avicenna's Metaphysics in Context*. London: Duckworth.

Wisnovsky, Robert (2004). 'One Aspect of the Avicennian Turn in Sunni Theology', *Arabic Science and Philosophy*, 14: 65–100.

Yaḥyā b. ʿAdī (1988). *Maqālāt Yaḥyā b. ʿAdī al-Falsafīyah*, ed. Saḥbān Ḫulayfāt. Amman: Manšūrāt al-Ǧāmiʿah al-Urdunīyah.

Zimmermann, F. W. (1981). *Al-Farabi's Commentary and Short Treatise on Aristotle's De Interpretatione*. Oxford: Oxford University Press for the British Academy.

# 5

# Those 'Funny Words'
## Medieval Theories of Syncategorematic Terms

*Joke Spruyt and Catarina Dutilh Novaes*

What does it mean to say that words have meaning? Perhaps the most immediate answer to this question would be to point out that words have the property of *standing for things* so that we can talk about the latter by using the former. This is why the Lilliputians in *Gulliver's Travels* thought they could do away with language by carrying around large collections of objects, so that (for the purpose of communication) the objects themselves could be demonstrated rather than being designated by means of words.

One immediate problem with the Lilliputian conception of word meaning is that there are all kinds of words that we regularly use, but that do not obviously designate 'things', properly speaking. This is true even of some kinds of nouns (say, in the case of abstract nouns such as 'solitude' or 'justice'), adjectives, and verbs—that is, the kinds of words that would typically mean objects. But the issue becomes more acute with respect to a large number of words that are regularly used in discourse and yet do not signify things, not even abstract things, in any obvious way. Some examples are, 'every', 'some', 'not', 'if', 'and', 'or', and many others. If the Lilliputians are right, these words do not make any significant contribution to the overall meaning of a piece of discourse; their existence would perhaps be for mere adornment. But, of course, the Lilliputians are wrong: such words typically perform crucial functions for the meaningfulness of complex expressions, and therefore their semantic import must be accounted for by any encompassing theory of linguistic meaning.

Some of the philosophical questions pertaining to such words are: Do they have meaning at all? If yes, what is the nature of their meaning? What is the ontological status of whatever it is that they signify? Do they have meaning when taken in isolation, or are they meaningful only in conjunction with other words that themselves do signify 'things'? What do they contribute to the meaning of the complex expressions where they occur, and how do they do so?

As it happens, the Latin thirteenth and fourteenth centuries constituted a period of intense philosophical interest in this class of words. The medieval authors conceptualized the distinction between terms that (usually) signify things on their own (which are typically the subjects or predicates of propositions)[1] and these other 'funny words'[2] by means of the opposition between *categorematic* and *syncategorematic* terms. To be sure, the distinction as such (if not the terminology) dates back to Aristotle and the sixth-century grammarian Priscian (see Section 1.1); but in the thirteenth century, for the first time, a large number of treatises focusing specifically on such terms and bearing the title *Syncategoremata* were composed. In the fourteenth century, discussions on *syncategoremata* were absorbed into general logical treatises, and this later period represents the maturation and consolidation of this tradition. These authors offered various answers to questions pertaining to the meaning of *syncategoremata* (such as the ones listed in the previous paragraph), giving rise to a wealth of interesting discussions on the nature and meaning of such terms.

One of the important features of this collection of texts is that authors were interested in the behaviour of such terms from a distinctively *logical* point of view, thus departing from the earlier grammatical focus. Because this tradition adopts a logical perspective to discuss these words that do not obviously stand for things, the range of expressions that were dealt with tended to correspond to terms specifically contributing to the inferential and truth-conditional properties of propositions, such as quantifying terms ('every' (*omnis*), 'something' (*aliquid*), and so on) and propositional connectives ('or' (*vel*), 'if' (*si*), 'and' (*et*), etc.). So these medieval authors did not discuss extensively words that are now of interest to the modern linguist (such as prepositions, particles, auxiliaries, and so on), but that arguably do not have a significant impact for the inferential properties and truth-conditions of propositions.

Given this distinctively logical focus, it is not surprising that the medieval tradition on *syncategoremata* has received ample attention predominantly from historians and philosophers of logic. Nevertheless, these discussions represent an example of the fluidity with which philosophical issues pertaining to logic and to language were treated in the Latin medieval period.

Some contemporary authors, such as MacFarlane (2009), have suggested that the concept of *syncategoremata* is to be seen as the medieval counterpart of the modern notion of *logical constants*. There are, however, important conceptual dissimilarities going beyond the mere differences in historical context; to begin with, the extension of the class of syncategorematic terms was typically considered to be much wider than what is now typically considered to be the extension of the class of logical constants. Now, reflecting on the differences and commonalities between medieval discussions on syncategorematic terms and modern discussions on logical constants

---

[1] In what follows, we will use 'proposition' in the medieval sense of *propositio*, which roughly means a declarative sentence.
[2] A very apt expression used by Sten Ebbesen (1995: 180) to refer to *syncategoremata*.

offers a fruitful vantage point to discuss significant philosophical implications on both sides of the story. In particular, the contrast with medieval discussions on *syncategoremata* allows for a critical evaluation of some of the presuppositions underpinning current debates on logical constants.

The goal of this chapter is thus to present a survey of the *syncategoremata* literature in the Latin thirteenth and fourteenth centuries. The emphasis will be on the different answers given to the question of the nature of *syncategoremata* and their meaningfulness. The first part offers a historical overview of the medieval discussions on *syncategoremata*, focusing in particular on thirteenth-century treatises and their analyses of the nature of these terms, as well as some of their semantic and metaphysical implications. It ends with a brief account of later developments in the fourteenth century. Overall, it may be said that the main concern of medieval authors in their analyses of syncategorematic terms is to investigate the contribution of these terms to the meaning (and truth-conditions) of the propositions in which they occurred. Such discussions were integrated in the broader context of the medieval focus on issues of linguistic interpretation in general—in particular, but not exclusively, *textual* interpretation. Indeed, the generation of the possible meaning(s) of complex expressions such as propositions is a key component of Latin medieval logic and semantics (Dutilh Novaes 2008).

The second part presents a systematic comparison between the medieval concept of *syncategoremata* and the modern concept of logical constants—a salient comparison, given that medieval authors conceptualized the meaning of such terms mostly in terms of their inferential and truth-conditional (logical) properties. One important commonality between the two frameworks is the issue of whether *syncategoremata*/logical constants have meaning at all, and if they do, what is the nature of their meaning. The main difference, by contrast, seems to be that medieval authors did not in any way view the enterprise of demarcating the class of *syncategoremata* as related to the broader issue of the scope of logic. Relatedly, while some medieval authors did conceptualize the notion of the *form* of an argument or proposition in terms of *syncategoremata*, most of them recognized that the demarcation between categorematic and syncategorematic terms (which would correspond to the matter and the form of an argument or proposition, respectively) need not (or cannot) be a sharp one.

All in all, the chapter presents an overview of a textual tradition where the issue of the meaning of words that do not obviously stand for things is extensively discussed, and where different answers are given. The comparison with modern debates on logical constants serves to illustrate the systematic interest of this historical analysis for an important issue in current philosophy of logic and language. However, the relevance of these medieval discussions for contemporary questions on linguistic meaning in general most likely goes well beyond the specific debate on logical constants, and concerns more generally the issue of the nature of these 'funny words', which represent a serious challenge to the Lilliputian conception of linguistic meaning.

## 1. *Syncategoremata* in the Medieval Context

In order to make sense of medieval analyses of the properties of terms[3] in general, including those of syncategorematic words, we need to be aware of their starting point. As is well known, logic in the Middle Ages was listed alongside rhetoric and grammar as composing the *trivium* curriculum, to be pursued (alongside the *quadrivium*) by students before they embarked on a specific academic curriculum (theology, law, medicine). Indeed, logic was thought to provide the methodological foundations for students in their further academic pursuits; in particular, skills of (*textual*) *interpretation* were highly relevant.

Discussions of *syncategoremata* are found in a variety of treatises. From the way in which linguistic expressions like *syncategoremata* were dealt with, especially in the thirteenth century and later on, we can see that the authors attempted to find a way to solve specific problems, in particular with respect to propositions that pose interpretational difficulties (known as *sophismata*).[4]

In the recent literature, it has been suggested that *syncategoremata* should be viewed exclusively as logical operators or constants. For example, in her comprehensive study on the *Syncategoremata* of William of Sherwood, Kirchhoff emphasizes the logical import of syncategorematic words. Focusing on this particular aspect of *syncategoremata* leads her to make a distinction between syncategorematic words in a broad and a strict sense. It is, she thinks, only words that fall in the latter category that are to be qualified as *syncategoremata* proper—that is, words that carry out a specific (logical) function in a proposition. Specifically, she seems to identify syncategorematic words with expressions whose function can give rise to ambiguities of scope, and thus have a potential to lead to fallacious inferences. Hence her claim that many of the expressions studied in the *syncategoremata* treatises of the thirteenth century are not really syncategorematic words at all, by which she obviously means to say that the expression *syncategorema* for such expressions is a misnomer (Kirchhoff 2008: 162).

However, the history of *syncategoremata* itself reveals that, for quite a long time, the division between categorematic and syncategorematic words was not based on any unified system of linguistic or logical analysis. Even though many authors presented similar-sounding definitions of *syncategoremata*, none of the earlier treatises actually provided a clear-cut criterion to distinguish them from other linguistic

---

[3] 'Term' is the translation of *terminus*, an expression that was used for the subject and predicate in a proposition. But when the medievals spoke about 'properties of terms', they meant the features of words relevant for deciding on the truth or falsity of a proposition where they occurred. See Read (2011).

[4] A *sophisma* is a proposition that is something of a puzzle, or of which the truth-value is difficult to determine because it can be understood in different ways. Well-known examples of *sophismata* are 'Only one is', 'Infinitely many are finitely many', 'Nothing is nothing', 'Nothing and a chimaera are brothers', 'No one running you are an ass'. For a list of *sophismata* discussed in the *Syncategoremata* treatises, see Kirchhoff (2008: 173–7); for a detailed explanation of *sophismata* and a discussion of examples, see Pironet and Spruyt (2011).

expressions. It is not surprising then that different authors of *Syncategoremata* treatises were not in agreement about which expressions counted as *syncategoremata*, and thus which were to be dealt with in those works. After the thirteenth century, the descriptions and explanations of syncategorematic words became more refined, but, even so, there was still no decisive way to differentiate these expressions from others.

Moreover, the nature of *syncategoremata* is not always explained in the same way. Some authors focused on semantic aspects of such terms taken in isolation, by considering the peculiar kind of (con)signification of syncategorematic words, while others highlighted the role of syncategorematic expressions within the context of a proposition as a bearer of truth and falsity.

## 1.1. Early Sources and Medieval Treatises on Syncategoremata

It would be beyond the scope of this chapter to go through the entire, very long history leading up to the development of *syncategorema* treatises,[5] so let us confine ourselves to a few important landmarks leading up to the distinction between categorematic and syncategorematic terms in the Middle Ages. One of the origins of the medievals' interest can be traced back to Aristotle's *De interpretatione*, specifically the passage in *De interpretatione* 3, 16$^a$19–25, in which he distinguishes between noun and verb, and the expression 'to be'.[6] Aristotle explains that nouns and verbs are tied up with some *res*, whereas the expression 'is' taken by itself has no such connection. This distinction is based on the notion that there are words that have a complete meaning of their own—that is, they allow the intellect to come to rest by presenting a concept to it. The expression 'to be', however, acquires its meaning only by being adjoined to other expressions.

The medievals' interest in *syncategoremata* was also inspired by Priscian's *Grammar*, which presents a division of linguistic expressions into different classes. Priscian mentions the 'dialecticians' (presumably the *Peripatetici*, following Aristotle), who considered nouns and verbs as having a signification of their own, whereas other kinds of expression, the *syncategoremata*, were claimed to 'consignify' only (*Inst. gramm.* II, 15, 54$^{5-7}$). The notion of consignification also came to the fore in another important source for the medieval classification into two separate types of expression—that is, the work of Boethius. He drew a distinction between true parts of speech—that is, nouns and verbs—and other linguistic expressions, on the grounds that only the former can function as the subject or predicate of a proposition; others, such as 'is' (*est*) and 'is not' (*non est*), the expressions 'every' (*omnis*), 'no' (*nullus*), and 'some' (*aliquis*)—that is, the signs of quantity (*signa quanititatis*),

---

[5] More details can be found in Braakhuis (1979: pt I, ch. 1) and (Kirchhoff 2008: pt I). A shorter but informative account can be found in Kretzmann (1982).

[6] From the Aristotelian perspective, and within the tradition of the thirteenth-century *Syncategorema* treatises, it is not correct to identify the verb 'is' (*est*) as the copula. For an in-depth discussion of the Aristotelian background of medieval analyses of the verb 'to be', see de Rijk (2002: 75–80).

expressions we now know as quantifiers—merely indicate the quality and quantity respectively of the propositions they occur in—for example, 'Every man is an animal' (*omnis homo est animal*). The semantic function of such signs of quality and quantity, according to Boethius, is to consignify (cf. Boethius, *In periherm.* II, 14$^9$–15$^7$; *De syll. cat.*, 706C–797A).

*Syncategoremata* came to be a separate domain of enquiry only in the thirteenth century, with the emergence of treatises devoted exclusively to this class of terms. This period is interesting for our purposes, because of the growing importance of studying linguistic expressions in general from the perspective of their being a vehicle of truth.[7] From this period, there are three kinds of tracts on syncategorematic words—namely, *Distinctiones* treatises, *Sophistaria*, and *Syncategoremata*. All these treatises present, analyse, and discuss syncategorematic terms, albeit from slightly different starting points,[8] and all of them deal with the analysis of propositions that require close scrutiny in virtue of the syncategorematic words occurring in them.

From the outset, the nature of syncategorematic words was usually established along two main lines—namely, in semantic or in grammatical terms.[9] The first type of explanation is based on the meaning of these linguistic expressions: unlike categorematic terms, syncategorematic ones do not have a (complete) signification of their own, but only if they are combined with an expression of the former kind. The grammatical approach to *syncategoremata* is based on the idea that certain words can function as subjects or predicates (which were called the 'extremes') of a proposition, whereas *syncategoremata* by themselves cannot; instead, if a syncategorematic word is combined with a subject or a predicate, it will modify that term in a certain way.

Besides these characterizations, authors had other ways to single out *syncategoremata* from other kinds of terms in the texts. For example, the famous medieval logician Peter of Spain (one of the most widely read logicians in the Middle Ages)[10] claims that the expressions 'is' (*est*) and 'not' (*non*) are the two basic *syncategoremata*, and that all others are such that they can be substituted by expressions with the addition of 'is'.[11] Throughout his exposé we can see traces of the different perspectives—that is, grammar and (Aristotelian–Boethian) logic from which the interest in *syncategoremata* had started to grow. But, although these perspectives are still alive in the thirteenth century, more attention is devoted to the analysis of complex expressions in which the syncategorematic terms occur.

---

[7] See Goubier (2003) for a discussion of this development.
[8] For a more elaborate discussion of the different perspectives on syncategorematic expressions, see Braakhuis (1979: pt I, 16–21).
[9] In fact, Kirchhoff (2008: 47) identifies four different ways in which authors distinguished between categorematic and syncategorematic expressions.
[10] See Spruyt (1989, 2012).
[11] For example, the *syncategorema* 'alone' (*solus*) signifies 'not with another' (*non cum alio*); see Peter of Spain, *Syncategoreumata*, III, ch. 6).

## 1.2. Explaining the Nature of Syncategoremata

Most authors of *syncategoremata* treatises in the thirteenth century simply mention the meaning of syncategorematic words as one of the properties of terms in general, apparently taking for granted that syncategorematic terms do have a meaning/ signification. One exception is Nicholas of Paris: he raises the question whether syncategorematic words have signification at all, and mentions a number of arguments pro and contra the suggestion that syncategorematic words do signify something, somehow. The arguments contra are all related to the suggestion that signification is tied up with a 'thing' (*res*) of some kind—that is, a substance or a quality, and, since syncategorematic words do not fulfil that requirement, they do not have a signification. The arguments in favour of the claim pertain to the idea that the combination of a syncategorematic word with a categorematic expression affects the signification of the resulting expression, and therefore a *syncategorema* must have a signification in its own right as well.

In order to settle the dispute, Nicholas refers to the well-known distinction between 'general signification' (*significatio generalis*) and 'specific signification' (*significatio specialis*) (cf. Nicholas of Paris, Syncategoreumata, $4^{5-9}$; the distinction also features in *modistae* treatises). To give an example, the noun 'man' has a twofold signification: the general signification is to signify substance with a quality, and the special signification of 'man' is a substance under the (specific) quality of humanity. While the general signification tells us which type of word we are dealing with (for instance, whether a word is a noun, or a verb, and so on)—something we need to know in order to produce a well-formed locution[12]—the special signification forms the basis of a locution in so far as it signifies something that is true or false.

This distinction is then used to explain the nature of *syncategoremata*. Some words, like indeclinables (that is, adverbs that modify the expressions they are conjoined with, such as 'now', 'not', 'when', 'possibly'; *syncategoremata* are reckoned among them), do have a distinctive characteristic that identifies them as being an expression of a certain type (like a *syncategorema*), but they are different from nouns and verbs, because they can have a complete signification only if they are conjoined with a categorematic word.[13]

For some authors, for example, Peter of Spain, all syncategorematic words can ultimately be reduced to the verb 'is' (*est*) and to the negative particle 'not' (*non*). These expressions have a general signification. To be sure, *syncategoremata* do not

---

[12] This is to say that there are rules about which kinds of words can be combined with one another. So a verb can be combined with a noun (i.e., any nominalized expression, including nominalized verbs and adjectives) and vice versa, but one cannot produce a meaningful phrase by just placing two verbs after one another.

[13] Nicholas of Paris, *Syncategoreumata* (= Braakhuis 1979: pt II), $6^{8-9}$: "Unde significatio generalis eorum [sc. syncateg.] est quidam modus significandi incomplete per se, quod modus terminatur ad adiunctum."

signify some 'thing' (*res*), but they indicate a disposition, which is a kind of 'quality' that pertains to the subject or predicate—not in the sense of their being some 'thing', but in their function of being the subject or predicate of a proposition. To give an example of this distinction, in the expression 'A white man runs well', the adverb 'well' and the adjective 'white' are (expressions of) dispositions of the things underlying the predicate and subject respectively (that is, the adverb 'well' expresses a disposition of the act of running and the adjective 'white' expresses a disposition of the substance man), whereas *syncategoremata* do not signify things or dispositions of things, but instead they signify dispositions of a subject in its function of being a subject and/or of a predicate in its function of being a predicate.[14] So the expression 'not' in the proposition 'A man is not running' expresses a disposition of the predicate in its function of being the predicate of the proposition, which is to say it is not some quality of the act of running, but rather some 'quality' of the predicate in relation to the subject.

Thus, for Peter of Spain, the notions of composition and negation (as expressed by the terms 'is' and 'not', respectively) form the basis for all *syncategoremata*. The concept of 'composition' used here derives from the traditional way of explaining the signification of nouns and verbs. As already mentioned, a noun is said to signify a composition of a quality with a substance, and a verb (a conjugated verb, that is, like 'runs') a composition of an act with a substance. The starting point for the analysis of the verb 'is' is an account of the verb in general. This is because every verb contains 'is' as a basic element.[15] Every verb, Peter says, signifies a composition of an act with a substance: the composition involved is based upon an inclination—that is, the natural inclination of an act towards a substance.[16] But a verb also (con)signifies a second kind of inclination—namely—one of the *intellect*: the intellect has a natural inclination to unite the act (or being acted upon) signified by the verb with a substance, and so the intellect carries out that composition.[17] For instance, the verb 'runs' signifies a specific something (which the medievals called a *res verbi*)—that is, the act of running—but to be meaningful this verb also requires an underlying substance—that is, the thing that is carrying out the act of running. So this (second) composition of the act of running with a substance comes about only as a result of an

---

[14] The expression 'every' (*omnis*) is explained in a similar way (*Tractatus* XII, p. 211$^{2-4}$).

[15] This is explained by analysing a verb; e.g. the verb 'runs' (*currit*) is identical to 'is running' (*est currens*), i.e. a combination of the verb 'is' plus the participle corresponding to the verb.

[16] Traditionally, the noun was said to signify a quality with a substance without 'distance', i.e., the substance and quality are understood as being completely united; for example, in the noun 'man' the quality of manhood and the entity that posesses it are understood as completely one. The verb, on the other hand, signifies an act with a substance, but with 'distance', i.e., the act is not considered as being completely united with the substance, but as being 'inclined' towards a substance; so the verb 'runs' obviously gives to understand a something that is doing the running, but the act is understood separately from any particular kind of substance (anything can be doing the running).

[17] For details, see Spruyt (1989: 134–7).

activity of the intellect: the intellect realizes that the running must be executed by a substance.

Interestingly, the way in which Peter makes use of the notion 'as carried out' in this connection is ambiguous. His explanation of the basic *syncategorema* 'is' as (con) signifying a composition 'as carried out' contains two elements: the carrying-out of the composition applies both to the function of the verb itself, that is, the verb 'is' itself combines a substance with an act, but it also indicates the underlying activity of the intellect, which has the inclination to unite an act with substance. This would mean that the signification of the expression 'is' is ultimately based upon a mental activity of combining. The intellect is affected by some relationship between two 'things' (that is, a substance and some act or being acted upon), and then proceeds to unite them. To put it differently, the intellect understands the act expressed by the verb as being inclined towards a substance, and is affected by that inclination, whereupon it proceeds to unite that act with a substance.[18]

The second basic notion underlying the signification of all *syncategoremata* is that of the negation expressed by the particle 'not', which is discussed in depth by Peter of Spain and others.[19] The way in which this particle expresses negation, however, is not the same as that of the noun 'negation'. While the noun signifies negation 'as signified' (*ut significatus*), that is to say it indicates a kind of something, a concept, the particle signifies negation 'as carried out' (*ut exercita*).[20]

The *syncategorema* 'not' is predominantly explained in terms of its function, which is to remove a composition. Besides explaining consignification of the particle in these general terms, Peter also analyses the kinds of composition the particle can remove, when it is added to a noun (as in 'not-man', the particle removes the composition of some substance with the quality of humanity), or a verb (for example, 'not runs', or 'is not running', in which case the particle removes the act of running from some substance), or a complex expression, containing a noun and a verb (for example, 'Socrates is not running', in which case the whole composition that Socrates is running is denied). The discussion in this section also focuses on issues pertaining to scope.

Another *Syncategoremata* author, Robert Bacon (early thirteenth century), also speaks of *syncategoremata* in terms of "affects of the intellect" (Braakhuis 1979: pt. I, 109). This mental counterpart of syncategorematic expressions plays a vital role in his way of explaining the syncategorematic word 'if' (*si*). Bacon says that the expression

---

[18] The noun and verb are different in that respect: unlike the noun, the *significatio* of the verb only indirectly includes the substance it belongs to, and so it requires the detour of 'predication' to be united with its substance; see Spruyt (1989: 124–5).

[19] For an overview, see Kirchhoff (2008: 133).

[20] For a linguistic expression to signify something *ut conceptus* means that it gives to understand a something (a concrete or abstract 'entity' of some sort), whereas to signify something *ut exercita* is to signify it as a function. A negation is a kind of something, you could say, but a negation can also be understood as something that is carried out, or performed. For further details on this feature of *syncategoremata*, see Spruyt (1989: 144–5).

'if' consignifies a "continuation" of the prior (that is, that which precedes the expression 'if' in the sentence) to the posterior (that is, what comes after 'if'), as in 'If Socrates is running, he is moving'. However, it does not signify this continuation in the manner of a concept, but instead in the manner of an affect: the intellect is affected, so to speak, by a particular ordering between two complex states of being—for example, that Socrates is running and that he is moving—to the extent that the two states are related to each other in such a way that one complex state, that Socrates is moving, follows from the other, that Socrates is running. So the intellect conceives two coherent complexes and is affected by the ordering between them—that is to say, it is "disposed" by the ordering. And the sign of this ordering actually affecting the intellect is the word 'if'.[21]

From this very short survey of some *Syncategoremata* authors and their views as to what a *syncategorema* is, we can see that the accounts are quite diverse.[22] Moreover, their discussions are not always in line with what they explicitly present to us as *syncategoremata* in their treatises. The lists of *syncategoremata* they discuss are not always the same either.[23] Finally, it is not always clear how to distinguish between a *syncategorema* and other expressions. Most authors recognized that certain expressions, such as 'infinite' (*infinitus*), can be used in two different ways: some make a distinction between 'infinite' as a something (*res*) or a mode (*modus*).[24] Another way of putting it is to say that 'infinite' can be used either categorematically—in which case it indicates a something, that is, a particular number, which is infinite—or syncategorematically—in which case it indicates a 'mode', as they say: 'infinite' in this way is taken to be equivalent to something like 'more than whichever number you choose'. These two ways of understanding 'infinite' are then used as a means to analyse the sophisma[25] *Infinita sunt finita*, somewhat inappropriately translated as 'Infinitely many are finitely many'.[26]

## 1.3. Syncategoremata *and the Meaning of Complex Expressions*

The authors of *Syncategoremata* treatises are also deeply concerned with how syncategorematic expressions occurring in a proposition can affect its meaning as a whole. The presence of these words is a decisive factor to establish the truth-value of an expression. In the words of Peter of Spain, "it is because a state of affairs is or is not

---

[21] Robert Bacon, *Syncategoreumata*, in Braakhuis (1979: pt I, 153): "hec coniunctio 'si' significat continuationem prioris ad posterius. Verbi gratia: 'si Sortes currit, Sortes movetur'. Notandum tamen quod non significat continuationem tamquam conceptum sed tamquam affectum. Hoc est dictu quod anima concipit duo complexa coherentia, et ita afficitur ordine eorum; cuius ordinem actualiter afficientis anima nota est hec dictio 'si' ".

[22] The diverse approaches are highlighted in Goubier (2003: 96-7) and Kirchhoff (2008: 163).

[23] For an overview of all the expressions included among the *syncategoremata* in the thirteenth century, see Kirchhoff (2008: 133-4).

[24] See, e.g., Henry of Ghent, *Syncategoremata*, $13^{331-335}$.

[25] For an explanation of *sophisma*, see n. 3.

[26] See, e.g., William of Sherwood, *Syncategoremata*, $30^{11-23}$.

the case that a proposition is true or false. Now the truth or falsity in an expression is caused by [sic] the syncategorematic words, such as 'only', 'alone', 'unless', 'but' and the like" (Peter of Spain, *Syncategoreumata*, Introduction, ch. 1). Propositions then are explained as signifying a kind of 'composition' between extremes. For instance, the proposition 'John is running' is said to signify the composition of the substance *John* with the act of running. Accordingly, some authors (following Peter of Spain) take the notion of 'composition'[27] as the starting point of their discussion on syncategorematic words (cf., e.g., Nicholas of Paris, *Syncategoremata*, 9–11).

In order to understand a complex expression (*enuntiatio*), we need to understand its principal parts—that is, the noun and verb—and the secondary parts, which include (a) the parts that determine what exactly the primary parts signify—that is, adjectives and conjunctives—and (b) the parts that determine the primary parts as subjects or predicates of a proposition—that is, the *syncategoremata* (William of Sherwood, *Syncategoremata*, $3^{1-18}$). Sometimes the specific logical contribution of such terms is made explicit, by listing their functional properties—that is, distribution, exclusion, negation, and so on (Henry of Ghent, *Syncategoremata*, $4^{1-3}$).

Thus, the thirteenth-century treatises share one very important premiss: they all recognize that it is of paramount importance to understand how a *syncategorema* operates in a proposition. All the treatises on syncategorematic terms show a keen interest in problems related to the correct understanding of the propositions in which they occur. Goubier has duly noted this particular thirteenth-century perspective on *syncategoremata*, a development he sees as connected to a "list of problems analysed within a *formal* semantics of natural language" (Goubier 2003: 85; emphasis added). However, it remains to be seen whether it is indeed specifically a formal semantics of natural language that the authors are after.

### 1.4. Syncategoremata *and Metaphysical Issues*

It is worth noticing that, in discussions about the basic syncategorematic terms, authors actually delve quite deeply into metaphysical problems. Thus, questions are asked along the lines of "What kind of being is a composition?", "What exactly is the nature of the composition that is removed by the negation?" These questions are addressed by looking at specific problematic propositions containing 'is' and 'not'. How should we interpret propositions like 'A chimera is a non-being'? What is the subject matter of the denial involved? Similar problems are addressed when the authors discuss the expressions 'necessarily' (*necessario*) and 'contingently' (*contingenter*), two syncategorematic terms.[28]

---

[27] For a more detailed explanation of 'composition', see Section 1.4.
[28] For a survey of thirteenth-century accounts of the *syncategoremata* 'necessario' and 'contingenter', see Spruyt (1994). (Everyone agreed that 'necessarily' and 'contingently' are *syncategoremata*.)

To be sure, the topics just mentioned enter the logical treatises mainly because of the authors' engagement in argumentation.[29] But, by doing so, the authors' underlying metaphysical interests clearly come to the surface. From the different solutions in their treatments of syncategorematic words, we can see that they have distinct views regarding the truth-value of the expressions where they occur. The diverse approaches to syncategorematic words reveal different stances with regard to ontological questions, as some examples will show.

Let us start with the expression 'is'; for Peter of Spain, it is apparent that it does not necessarily have ontological import. The author reveals his position by addressing the question of whether the composition expressed by the verb 'is' (that is, in a locution of the form of 'A is B' expressing the composition *that A is B*) is a being or not. He answers in the affirmative, claiming that every composition expressed by the verb 'is' is indeed a being of some kind, but not necessarily a being of a real kind. One should distinguish between 'being *simpliciter*', as expressed in statements like 'man is an animal' (*homo est animal*) and 'Socrates is running' (*Sortes est currens*, on the assumption, of course, that Socrates exists and is in fact running), and what he calls 'being in certain sense' (or 'being in a qualified sense'), as expressed by 'a chimera is opinable' (*chimaera est opinabile*; 'opinable' means that it can be thought of, or thought about). This distinction is also explained in terms of the inferential force of the three different expressions: from 'Socrates is running' it follows 'Socrates is' (*Sortes est*, in which case 'is' amounts to 'exists'), whereas from 'man is an animal' it does not follow '(a) man is' (*homo est*, in which case too 'is' amounts to 'exists') and from 'a chimera is opinable' it does not follow 'a chimera is'.[30]

Similar considerations are found in Peter's analysis of the expressions containing the *syncategorema* 'necessarily' (*necessario*). The issue is brought forward by considering the question whether or not the modal adverb 'necessarily' has ampliative force—that is, whether the application range of the subject term of the proposition in question includes (in medieval parlance, 'ampliates to') past, present, future, and even possible instances of the relevant entities. According to Peter of Spain, it does. For example, the proposition 'every man is necessarily an animal' (*omnis homo necessario est animal*) is true whether or not any man actually exists: the modifier 'necessarily' ampliates the application range of the expression 'man' to include past, present, future, and possible instances of men. The truth of this proposition is based upon the subject matter at hand: the proposition is about the necessity involved in being a man, which includes his being an animal. Thus what is referred to in this proposition is man as such (that is, the species man), not individual men.

Other *Syncategoremata* authors, like Henry of Ghent—who, incidentally, presents an elaborate account of the notion of necessity in general—disagree with this approach.

---

[29] Ebbesen (2011: 101) rightly remarks that what thirteenth-century logicians were interested in was "detecting flaws in argumentation".
[30] For details, see Spruyt (1989: 138–42).

His view emerges in his analysis of the inference 'every man is of necessity an animal; therefore Socrates is of necessity an animal' (*omnis homo de necessitate est animal; ergo Sortes de necessitate est animal*). Peter of Spain says that the inference is invalid, on account of his perspective on the kind of being spoken of in the first proposition; Henry of Ghent, on the other hand, denies that 'necessarily' (or 'of necessity') has ampliative force, claiming that the necessity here applies to the relationship between the subject and the predicate only. Considering the fact that every man is necessarily an animal, and given that Socrates is a man, then of course Socrates is of necessity an animal.[31]

Another example of a *syncategorema* inviting reflection on ontological issues is 'only' (*tantum*), particularly bought up in connection with the sophisma 'only one is' (*tantum unum est*).[32] Even in some relatively short expositions, the ontological problems underlying the discussion are apparent.

In Peter of Spain's work the sophisma 'only one is' comes up when he introduces two rules that govern the use of 'only': the first rule roughly runs "If you use an exclusive word (e.g. in 'Only men are white') the very thing you are excluding (in the example, 'whiteness') should be asserted in that (i.e., in 'men') from which all other things are excluded" (*Syncategoreumata*, III, 9, 108–9); the second says that "Every true exclusive proposition (e.g. 'Only men are white'), leaves the truth of the basic proposition intact" (*Syncategoreumata*, III, 10, 110–11). The proof of the sophisma runs: One is, and there is nothing that is not one; therefore only one is. The disproof runs: Many things are; therefore not only one is (*Syncategoreumata*, III, 11, 110–11). Peter concludes that the sophisma 'Only one is' is ambiguous, because the term 'one' is equivocal: it can indicate either an essential or an accidental (that is, a numerical) unity. Taken in the first sense, the proposition is true, but, taken in the second sense, it is false (*Syncategoreumata*, III, 12–13, 110–13).

In the *Sophistaria* treatise by Matthew of Orléans, the sophisma 'only one is' features in a discussion about one particular distinction between the kinds of exclusion 'only' is said to perform—namely, an exclusion owing to form (*gratia forme*) or owing to matter (*gratia materie*).[33] Such a distinction applies only when an exclusive word like 'only' is adjoined to an 'accidental' term (that is, a term indicating an 'accidental' property, like 'white'). Matthew says then that the sophisma 'only one is' can indeed be interpreted in two ways, depending on whether we take it as an exclusion owing to form or owing to matter. In the first way, the exclusion applies to

---

[31] For a more detailed discussion of the difference between Peter of Spain's and Henry of Ghent's analyses, see Spruyt (2011: 102–7).

[32] This *sophisma* features briefly in Peter of Spain's and Henry of Ghent's treatises, among others and is discussed at length in the treatise of Ribert Kilwardby. For a detailed commentary on an elaborate discussion of the *sophisma* in the thirteenth century, see Braakhuis (1999). For the vicissitudes of this thesis in the thirteenth century, see Ebbesen (1995).

[33] For more information about the distinction between syncategorematic functions (such as exclusion and exception) *gratia forme–gratia materie*, see Spruyt (2003).

a substantial form, as is given to be understood in the expression 'that which is', whereas, in the second way, it applies to an accidental form, as is given to be understood in the expression 'unity'. In the first sense the proposition is true, in which case it means 'Only that which is, is', and thus non-beings are excluded. In the second sense it means 'Only a unity is', in which case multitudes are excluded, and in that case it is false (Matthew of Orléans, *Sophistaria*, II, chs 14–15, 149$^{16}$–150$^4$).

In sum, analyses of some particular *sophismata* led medieval authors to delve into metaphysical issues in connection with syncategorematic terms. Conversely, the authors' particular perspectives on such issues also affected the way in which they interpreted specific linguistic expressions containing syncategorematic words.

## 1.5. Later Developments

After the thirteenth century, *syncategoremata* were no longer discussed in separate treatises, but became incorporated in general logical textbooks. Authors now tended to dwell less on their *significatio* than had been done previously. Instead, the expressions were increasingly dealt with from the viewpoint of their functions in propositions, and the role they play in argumentation.

However, we still find interesting explanations of what kinds of terms they are. John Buridan (*c*.1300–*c*.1358/9, one of the most influential fourteenth-century logicians), for example, distinguishes between *three* different kinds of words. Some words are purely syncategorematic, some are categorematic, and others are of a mixed, intermediate variety. The purely syncategorematic words, such as 'not', 'and', 'or', 'therefore', 'every', and so on, he defines as words that "signify nothing besides the concepts they immediately signify, except, perhaps, the things that the terms to which they are attached signify" (Buridan 2001: 232). This description of purely syncategorematic words is based on the traditional, semantic account of *syncategoremata*.

However, if this were the only criterion to separate categorematic words from syncategorematic ones, many other interesting expressions that do have syncategorematic features would fall off the radar screen (Kirchhoff 2008: 688). Buridan, therefore, introduces a new class of words, which is located between categorematic and purely syncategorematic words. The idea of a third class of terms, between categorematic and syncategorematic terms, is both novel and philosophically important (see Section 2).

The intermediate or mixed ones, however, are so called either because besides the concepts that they immediately signify they also signify the things conceived by these concepts, but cannot be subjects or predicates in themselves, or because they imply categorematic and syncategorematic terms as well, e.g., 'today' (*hodie*), 'somewhere' (*alicubi*), 'no one' (*nemo*), 'nothing' (*nihil*), 'with itself' (*secum*), and many others. (Buridan 2001: 233)

Another significant fourteenth-century development is the emergence of the concept of mental language (Panaccio 1999). While the notion of some form of 'interior discourse' had been available for centuries, fourteenth-century authors such as Ockham (active in the 1320s and 1330s) and Buridan took thought to be a kind of language, not fundamentally different from spoken or written language. With respect to *syncategoremata* in particular, this led to an account of the signification of such terms, which exploited even more systematically the idea that *syncategoremata* correspond to the *mental acts* modifying the signification of categorematic mental terms (concepts). We have seen that precursors of this general idea can already been found in Peter of Spain and other thirteenth-century authors, but it receives a different twist in terms of the notion of a fully fledged mental language. There is, in fact, a growing tendency in the fourteenth century (culminating in, for example, Peter of Ailly) of increased emphasis on the role of the agent and her (mental) acts as providing the foundations for semantic phenomena; in this context it is very natural to account for the meaning of *syncategoremata* in terms of mental acts and operations, as Buridan (2001: 234) does:

the copulas 'is' and 'is not' signify different ways of combining mental terms in order to form mental propositions, and these different ways [of combining] are in their turn complexive concepts... And so also the words 'and', 'or', 'if', 'therefore', and the like designate complexive concepts that combine several propositions or terms at once in the intellect, but nothing further outside the intellect. These words are called purely syncategorematic, because they signify nothing outside the intellect, except along with others, in the sense that the whole complex consisting of categorematic and syncategorematic words does signify the things conceived outside the intellect, but this is on account of the categorematic words.[34]

Finally, a noteworthy fourteenth-century novelty is the explicit association of syncategorematic terms to the concept of the *form* of a proposition or argument. The idea that the form of an argument would correspond to a subset of its constituent parts emerged from the complex history of logical hylomorphism in the later Middle Ages (Dutilh Novaes 2012a, 2012b). It then became tacitly assumed by fourteenth-century authors, but not often explicitly formulated. In his treatise on consequence, however, Buridan (1976: 30) explicitly draws this connection:

In the present context, the way in which we here speak of matter and form, we understand by the "matter" of the proposition or *argument* the purely categorematic terms, i.e. subjects and predicates, omitting the syncategorematic terms that enclose them and through which they are conjoined or negated or distributed or forced to a certain mode of supposition. All the rest, we say, pertains to the form.[35]

---

[34] Similar statements can be found in other fourteenth-century authors such as Albert of Saxony, Peter of Ailly, and Thomas of Cleves. See Klima (2006) further details.

[35] "Et dico quod in proposito, prout de materia et forma hic loquimur, per 'materiam' propositionis aut consequentiae intelligimus terminos pure categorematicos, scilicet subiecta et praedicata, circumscriptis syncategorematicis sibi appositis, per quae ipsa coniunguntur aut negantur aut distribuuntur uel ad certum modum suppositionis trahuntur; sed ad formam pertinere dicimus totum residuum." Translation Dutilh Novaes.

It may be tempting to conclude that Buridan is indeed saying that *syncategoremata signify* the form of an argument or proposition, but his formulation is vaguer than this: he simply says that the terms that are not categorematic terms ('the rest') *pertain* to the form of a proposition or argument. (Notice also that this passage is from a different text— namely, his treatise on consequences—whereas the previously quoted passages are from his treatise on supposition.)

While the fourteenth-century analyses often present a more precise focus on the semantics of syncategorematic terms if compared with the thirteenth-century analyses, this is still very far from saying that their approaches became more 'formal' or that their endeavours were aimed at a formal semantics of natural language. The distinctions drawn by Buridan help us understand the different kinds of functions words can play in a proposition, in such a way that we may be able to interpret propositions that contain syncategorematic words more accurately. They continued to be the set of 'funny words' that were important to discuss because of the underlying interpretative and semantic issues.

## 2. Medieval *Syncategoremata* and Modern Logical Constants

As we have seen, the terms that are now typically described as 'logical constants' were among those that were treated under the heading of *syncategoremata* in the Middle Ages. But we have also seen that the class of *syncategoremata*—which in any case varied slightly from author to author, and was often thought not to have sharp borders—is strictly larger than the modern class of logical constants.

Now, the possibility of a sharp, precise demarcation of the class of logical constants remains an open question (MacFarlane 2009). It is true that many contemporary authors maintain that it is pointless to search for such a demarcation (and MacFarlane refers to them as the 'debunkers'), but numerous others believe that it is possible to demarcate this class, and moreover that such a demarcation is the best and perhaps the only route towards a proper philosophical understanding of the nature of logic as such. In other words, the general attitude of medieval logicians towards *syncategoremata* contrasts sharply with some modern widespread views on logical constants. In this section, we offer a systematic comparison between the two.

### 2.1. A Commonality

One salient similarity between medieval and modern discussions on *syncategoremata*/logical constants is the focus on the issue of their *significatio*/meaning. As we have seen, medieval authors often took as their starting point the idea that *syncategoremata* did not have the same kind of signification as categorematic terms, which typically (though not always) signify 'real things', substances, or qualities. The question was thus whether, besides modifying the signification of *categoremata*, *syncategoremata* had a signification of their own, and, if they did, what kind of special signification it was. Medieval authors offered distinct answers to this general question, and (as we have seen) a recurring theme is the idea that *syncategoremata* signify entities belonging to the mental realm, such as the mental acts of composition and division. These theories in many senses anticipate Kant's account of judgement as the mental act of composition (or division) (Klima 2006). In the early twentieth century, the issue of the meaningfulness of logical constants was a central point of disagreement between Russell and Wittgenstein. Russell held that logical constants were indeed meaningful, and parting with this belief was viewed by Wittgenstein himself as the crucial turning point in which he began to develop his own account of logic (Potter 2009: §5.7). He thus famously writes in the *Tractatus* (4.0312): "My fundamental thought is that the 'logical constants' do not represent. That the *logic* of the facts cannot be represented."

To this day, the debate on the meaning of logical constants remains a lively one. The main contenders are inferentialist accounts (the meaning of logical constants is determined by the inferential relations between the propositions in which they occur and others), inspired in particular by the work of Dummett (1991); and truth-theoretical accounts (according to which the meaning of logical constants is determined by their contribution to the truth-conditions of propositions) such as Davidson's (1984). While it would be rather anachronistic to attempt to map these two positions onto medieval discussions, what this commonality shows is the continued interest in the issue of the meaning/signification of expressions that do not obviously signify 'things', and in particular those that influence the inferential/truth-conditional properties of the propositions where they occur.

## 2.2. Dissimilarities

Nevertheless, for the purposes of philosophical analysis, it is arguably more illuminating to reflect on the *dissimilarities* rather than on the similarities between medieval discussions on *syncategoremata* and modern discussions on logical constants. Examining the differences between the two frameworks allows us to evaluate some of the assumptions and tacit theoretical commitments underlying current discussions on logical constants.

A widespread (though not unanimously endorsed) position among current philosophers of logic is that the boundaries of logic as a discipline can be determined by a demarcation of the class of logical constants (Bonnay 2008; Sher 2008). In fact, some seem to claim that demarcating the class of logical constants is the *only* way to attain "a proper understanding of the scope and nature of logic" (MacFarlane 2009: Introduction).

The rationale for this position seems to be captured by three main theses, which together might be described as the 'textbook' account of the nature of logic (Dutilh Novaes 2012a):

1. The subject of logic par excellence is the validity of arguments.
2. Arguments are valid in virtue of their (logical) forms.
3. The form of an argument, in turn, is (at least partially) determined by the logical constants occurring in it.

If one endorses these theses, it may seem natural to view the boundaries of logic as defined by the concept of logical constants. By the same token, on this picture, logic is *formal* in virtue of dealing with the *forms* of arguments. However, all three points rest on substantive theoretical assumptions, and yet are typically treated as uncontroversial, almost trivial, claims (Dutilh Novaes 2012a). Now, while different versions of these claims can be found in some medieval authors, none of them was taken to be self-evident truths. An examination of some medieval positions on these issues reveals a very different conception of logic, so let us examine them in turn.

1. It is fair to say that, for medieval authors, the scope of logic went well beyond where we now typically draw the borders of the discipline, including much of what we would now consider to belong to the fields of philosophy of language, semantics, and epistemology (see Ebbesen 2011). To be sure, the theory of syllogisms and arguments in general occupied a central position in the medieval conception of logic, but syllogistic was not in any way thought to *exhaust* the scope of logic. Perhaps most importantly, the very concern with sharply demarcating logic as a discipline is not to be found in the Latin medieval authors.

As we have seen in the previous section, much of the writings of medieval logicians pertains to issues of interpretation and meaning, and this holds in particular of their analyses of *syncategoremata*. While it is true that *syncategoremata* analyses did contribute to the emergence of medieval theories of consequence—that is, theories about the logical relations between propositions (Green-Pedersen 1984; Dutilh Novaes 2012c)—the focus of these analyses is clearly not reduced to the issue of the validity of arguments.

2. While some authors, in particular Abelard (twelfth century), did claim that at least *some* arguments (which he referred to as *perfect inferences*) are valid in virtue of their structure or construction alone (Martin 2004),[36] several other authors rejected the idea that the grounds for the validity of arguments pertain to a sub-set of their vocabulary. Buridan, who in fact even developed a sophisticated concept of *formal* consequence, evidently viewed the validity of arguments as pertaining to the impossibility of the antecedents being the case while the consequent is not (Dutilh Novaes 2005). Even Abelard, who distinguished between perfect and imperfect inferences, did view imperfect inferences as perfectly *valid*, even though they were not valid in virtue of their structure. So the prevailing view on the validity of arguments was that

---

[36] Abelard did not use the hylomorphic terminology in his discussion on validity in the *Dialectica*, so he does not use the term 'form' to refer to what he calls the *complexio* of a proposition.

validity is not strictly related to a special sub-set of the terminology—namely the logical or 'syncategorematic' terminology (Dutilh Novaes 2012c).

3. The notion of the 'form' of an argument has a long and complex history, going from the ancient commentators to Arabic and Latin medieval logicians (Dutilh Novaes 2012b). It came to be associated to the division between categorematic and syncategorematic terms only at a fairly late stage, and Buridan is one of the few authors to have formulated this association explicitly (as we have seen). On this view, one might be tempted to think that categorematic terms signify the matter of an argument/proposition, while syncategorematic terms signify its form, but Buridan continues to view the signification of *syncategoremata* as connected to mental operations.

Now, if the form of an argument (as determined by its syncategorematic terms) were to be that in virtue of which a valid argument is valid, then presumably a sharp demarcation between form and matter, and thus between categorematic and syncategorematic terms, should exist. But, as we have seen, some authors, including Buridan himself, did not take the separation between *categoremata* and *syncategoremata* to be a clear-cut, sharp one. Again, this is not surprising, given that the concept of *syncategoremata* emerged within traditions of grammatical and semantic analyses, not from discussions on the validity of arguments. It was only at a later stage that the two debates somewhat crossed paths.

Thus, the main dissimilarity between the medieval distinction between categorematic and syncategorematic terms and the modern distinction between logical constants and extra-logical terms seems to be that medieval authors did not in any way view their distinction as somehow related to the scope of logic or specifically to the validity of arguments. The distinction played no broader demarcating role whatsoever; instead, investigations on *syncategoremata* constituted just one of the sub-fields within logical analysis, and pertained in particular to issues of interpretation of propositions containing those 'funny words'.

Philosophically, the discrepancies between the medieval and the modern distinctions suggest that our own conception of logical constants as a means to demarcate the scope of logic may be contentious. The fluidity with which medieval authors studied *syncategoremata*—that is, not searching for the exact borders of the class—may serve as inspiration for an open-ended conception of logical constants: one in which it *is* of logical interest to study the systematic behaviour of certain terms, but where they are not expected to perform a demarcational function for logic as a discipline.

# References

Bonnay, D. (2008). 'Logicality and Invariance', *Bulletin of Symbolic Logic*, 14/1: 29–68.
Braakhuis, H. A. G. (1979). 'De 13de Eeuwse Tractaten over Syncategorematische Termen. Deel I: Inleidende Studie. Deel II: Uitgave van Nicolaas van Parijs' *Syncategoreumata*. Nijmegen (diss.).

Braakhuis, H. A. G. (1999). 'Convertibility of Being and One in a Sophism Attributed to Robert Kilwardby', in Sten Ebbesen and Russell Friedman (eds), *Medieval Analyses in Language and Cognition: Acts of the Symposium, the Copenhagen School of Medieval Philosophy, 10–13 January 1996.* Historisk-filosofske Meddeleser 77. Copenhagen: Royal Danish Academy of Sciences and C. A. Reitzels Vorlag, 117–38.

Davidson, D. (1984). *Inquiries into Truth and Interpretation.* Oxford: Oxford University Press.

Dummett, M. (1991). *Logical Basis of Metaphysics.* London: Duckworth.

Dutilh Novaes, C. (2005). 'Buridan's *consequentia*: Consequence and Inference within a Token-Based Semantics', *History and Philosophy of Logic,* 26/4: 277–97.

Dutilh Novaes, C. (2008). 'An Intensional Interpretation of Ockham's Theory of Supposition', *Journal of the History of Philosophy,* 46/3: 365–93.

Dutilh Novaes, C. (2012a). 'Reassessing Logical Hylomorphism and the Demarcation of Logical Constants', *Synthese,* 185: 387–410.

Dutilh Novaes, C. (2012b). 'Form and Matter in Later Latin Medieval Logic: The Cases of *supposition* and *consequentia*', *Journal of the History of Philosophy,* 50/3: 339–64.

Dutilh Novaes, C. (2012c). 'Medieval Theories of Consequence', in E. Zalta (ed.), *The Stanford Encyclopedia of Philosophy (Summer 2012 Edition).* <http://plato.stanford.edu/archives/sum2012/entries/consequence-medieval/> (accessed 15 September 2013).

Ebbesen, S. (1995). 'Tantum Unum Est: 13th-Century Sophismatic Discussions around the Parmenidean Thesis', *Modern Schoolman,* 72: 175–89.

Ebbesen, S. (2011). 'What Counted as Logic in the Thirteenth Century?', in M. Cameron and J. Marenbon (eds), *Methods and Methodologies.* Investigating Medieval Philosophy 2. Leiden: Brill, 93–107.

Goubier, F. (2003). 'Les Syncatégorèmes au xiiie siècle', *Histoire Épistémologie Langage,* 25/2: 85–113.

Green-Pedersen, N. J. (1984). *The Tradition of the Topics in the Middle Ages.* Munich: Philosophia Verlag.

Henry of Ghent (2010). *Syncategoremata Henrico de Gandavo adscripta,* ed. H. A. G. Braakhuis, Girard Etzkorn, and Gordon A. Wilson, with an Introduction by H. A. G. Braakhuis. Leuven: University Press.

John Buridan (1976). *Tractatus de Consequentiis,* ed. Hubert Hubien. Louvain: Publications Universitaires.

John Buridan (1989). *Johannes Buridanus, Summulae De Suppositionibus,* ed. Ria van der Lecq (= *Artistarium* 10-4). Nijmegen: Ingenium.

John Buridan (2001). *Summulae de Dialectica,* trans. G. Klima. New Haven: Yale University Press.

Kirchhoff, R. (2008). *Die Syncategoremata des Wilhelm von Sherwood. Kommentierung und Historische Einordnung.* Leiden: Brill.

Klima, G. (2006). 'Syncategoremata', in *Elsevier's Encyclopedia of Language and Linguistics,* ed. Keith Brown. 2nd edn. Oxford: Elsevier, xii. 353–6.

Kretzmann, N. (1982). 'Syncategoremata, exponibilia, sophismata', in N. Kretzmann, A. Kenny, and J. Pinborg (eds), *The Cambridge History of Later Medieval Philosophy.* Cambridge: Cambridge University Press, 211–45.

MacFarlane, J. (2009). 'Logical Constants', in E. Zalta (ed.), *Stanford Encyclopedia of Philosophy* <http://plato.stanford.edu/entries/logical-constants/> (accessed 15 September 2013).

Martin, C. (2004). 'Logic', in J. Brower and K. Gilfoy (eds), *The Cambridge Companion to Abelard*. Cambridge: Cambridge University Press, 158–99.

Matthew of Orléans (2001). *Matthew of Orléans (Mattheus Aurelianensis) Sophistaria sive Distinctiones sophismatum*. First critical edition with introduction, notes and indices by Joke Spruyt. Leiden, Cologne, and New York: Brill.

Panaccio, C. (1999). *Le Discours Intérieur: De Platon à Guillaume d'Ockham*. Paris: Éditions de Seuil.

Peter of Spain (1972). *Petrus Hispanus Tractatus Called afterwards Summule Logicales*. First Critical Edition from the Manuscripts with an Introduction by L. M. de Rijk. Assen: Kluwer.

Peter of Spain (1992). *Petrus Hispanus Syncategoreumata*. First critical edition with introduction, notes and indices by L. M. de Rijk. With an English translation by Joke Spruyt. Leiden, Cologne, and New York: Brill.

Pironet, F., and Spruyt, J. (2011). '*Sophismata*', in E. Zalta (ed.), *The Stanford Encyclopedia of Philosophy (Winter 2011 Edition)* <http://plato.stanford.edu/archives/win2011/entries/sophismata/> (accessed 15 September 2013).

Potter, M. (2009). *Wittgenstein's Notes on Logic*. Oxford: Oxford University Press.

Read, S. (2011). 'Medieval Theories of Properties of Terms', in E. Zalta (ed.), *The Stanford Encyclopedia of Philosophy (Winter 2011 Edition)* <http://plato.stanford.edu/entries/medieval-terms/> (accessed 15 September 2013).

Rijk, L. M. de (2002). *Aristotle: Semantics and Ontology*, i. *General Introduction. The Works on Logic*, ii. *The Metaphysics. Semantics in Aristotle's Strategy of Argument*. Leiden: Brill.

Sher, G. (2008). 'Tarski's Thesis', in D. Patterson (ed.), *New Essays on Tarski and Philosophy*. Oxford: Oxford University Press, 300–39.

Spruyt, J. (1989). *Peter of Spain on Composition and Negation: Text. Translation. Commentary*. Nijmegen: Ingenium.

Spruyt, J. (1994). 'Thirteenth-Century Discussion on Modal Terms', *Vivarium*, 32: 196–226.

Spruyt, J. (2003). 'The Forma–Materia Device in Thirteenth-Century Logic and Semantics', *Vivarium*, 41: 1–46.

Spruyt, J. (2011). 'The "Realism" of Peter of Spain', *Medioevo: Rivista di storia della filosofia medievale*, 37: 89–111.

Spruyt, J. (2012). 'Peter of Spain', in E. Zalta (ed.), *The Stanford Encyclopedia of Philosophy (Winter 2012 Edition)* <http://plato.stanford.edu/archives/win2012/entries/peter-spain/>. (accessed 15 September 2013).

William of Sherwood (2012). *William of Sherwood, Syncategoremata*. Textkritisch herausgeben, übersetzt, eingeleitet und mit Anmerkungen versehen von Christoph Kann und Raina Kirchhoff. Hamburg: Felix Meiner Verlag.

# 6

# Semantic Content in Aquinas and Ockham

*Gyula Klima*

## Introduction: Externalism, Brains-in-a-Vat, and Related Asininities

Talking about semantic content in a contemporary philosophical context will inevitably include some reference to Hilary Putnam's famous slogan (2000: 422) "meanings just ain't in the head" and his "Twin Earth Experiment" to argue for what is usually called "linguistic externalism", which of course we need to distinguish from other, though not unrelated, forms of externalism, such as "mental content externalism" and "epistemic externalism", distinguished as such in an important recent paper by Claude Panaccio (2014). Nevertheless, in the present chapter I will be concerned not so much with Putnam as with Panaccio, and his reconstruction of the externalist nominalist semantics of William Ockham, to provide a sharp contrast to the position I call here "the 'hyper-externalism' of Thomas Aquinas"; although I would argue that this position, at least implicitly, was the paradigmatic conception of nearly all philosophizing before the emergence of late-medieval nominalism that first allowed the theoretical possibility of "Demon-scepticism" made famous by Descartes in his *Meditations*.

After this plethora of allusions to philosophers from different historical periods and traditions, hints at various subtly defined positions, and gestures towards arguments for them, I guess I have a lot of explaining to do. I will do so in the following order. I will first introduce Panaccio's description of linguistic externalism and the way he identifies it in Ockham's semantic theory, and I will indicate how it relates to contemporary considerations concerning the issue, in particular, to Putnam's "Twin Earth" argument. Second, I will point out the theoretical as well as the historical significance of the issue, by relating Ockham's position as reconstructed by Panaccio to the emergence of the theoretical possibility of "Demon Scepticism". In the third place, I will present an argument against Ockham's position, inspired by Putnam's "brains-in-a-vat" (BIV) scenario, widely popularized by the movie trilogy

*The Matrix*. Next, I will argue that the problem raised for Ockham is shared by anyone committed to the logical possibility of (an extreme form of) the BIV-scenario, indeed, both externalists and internalists, as long as they share a key post-late-medieval nominalist assumption concerning concept-identity, which is precisely the assumption not shared by the position I call "the hyper-externalism of Aquinas". The key assumption in question, as we shall see, is that our concepts—that is, our naturally representative mental acts (for this is how I shall use the term 'concept' in this chapter)—are merely contingently related to their objects, in the sense that I can have the exact same mental concept, say, the concept of donkeys, regardless of whether it actually represents donkeys or something else, say, merely virtual donkeys in the virtual reality of *The Matrix*. Finally, I will return to the issue of how these considerations concerning *mental content* relate to both medieval and contemporary notions of *semantic content*. But to get to that issue, let us see in the first place Panaccio's distinctions of some varieties of externalism, and how he discovers them in the philosophy of William Ockham.

## Panaccio on Ockham's Externalism

Claude Panaccio describes the forms of externalism he identifies in Ockham in the following way:

- *Linguistic externalism* is the thesis that the meaning of the words a speaker utters depends not solely on the internal state of the speaker at the moment of their utterance, but on certain external factors as well.
- *Mental content externalism* is the thesis that the very content of what an agent thinks depends not solely on the internal states of the agent, but on certain external factors as well.
- *Epistemic externalism* is the thesis that what an agent believes or knows depends not solely on the internal states of the agent, but on certain specific external factors as well.

As I have said, in this chapter I will focus on linguistic externalism, but what I will have to say will have obvious consequences concerning the other varieties described here, too. Also, even within the scope of the issue of linguistic externalism, I will deal only with the meaning of what are commonly called "natural kind terms", such as 'man', 'donkey', or 'monkey', but, again, with obvious provisos, what I will say can easily be generalized to other linguistic categories as well.

So, how does Ockham characterize the meaning of such a common term? And how and why is that characterization externalist? To answer these questions, we should know in the first place that for Ockham, in line with the medieval Aristotelian tradition in general, a term in itself is just an articulate sound, an utterance, or the corresponding written marks or any other easily producible and reproducible entity (say, gestures, and so on) that can acquire meaning through linguistic convention, or, as the medievals would have it, by *imposition* (Klima 2012). An act of imposition is any socio-linguistic mechanism ranging from ceremonial baptisms to unceremonious slips of tongue or typos (as happened with 'Google', according to one plausible urban legend) that establishes a connection between an utterance and a naturally representative mental act, a human concept. But no matter *how* this connection is established, once it *is* established, the utterance in question becomes a meaningful or significative utterance subordinated to the concept, inheriting, as a result of this conventional imposition, the natural semantic or representative features of this concept. Thus, linguistic meaning is conventional simply because imposition and the resulting subordination of utterances to concepts are conventional. But the conventionally acquired meaning or semantic content of the utterance is nothing but the natural representational content of the concept to which it is conventionally subordinated.

Looking at the picture so far, it might seem that, if this is indeed the general medieval Aristotelian doctrine, then this entire tradition must be inherently *internalist*: after all, the linguistic meaning of a term seems to be entirely determined by the representational content of the concept to which the term is subordinated, which in turn is nothing but a mental act or mental state of language-users; *ergo*, linguistic meaning is entirely determined by internal mental states, which is precisely the definition of linguistic internalism. So, how can Ockham possibly be claimed to be an externalist, once he shares the assumptions of this tradition?

According to Panaccio's intriguing interpretation of Ockham's semantics and cognitive psychology, the representational content of the concepts in question is twofold: one has to distinguish (1) their *objective content*, which I will call their *semantic content*, from (2) their built-in *sensory recognition schemes*, which I will call their *phenomenal content*. As Panaccio convincingly argues, these two types of representational content are merely contingently related according to Ockham: the semantic content of a concept is nothing but the first object of a certain natural kind (in particular, a *species specialissima*, a *most specific species*) that the cognitive subject first encounters, and all present, past, future, and merely possible co-specific individuals represented indifferently by the same mental act. By contrast, the *phenomenal content*, or, as Panaccio calls it, the *sensory recognition schema*, of such a concept is the collection of characteristic sensible features of such an object as perceived by the cognitive subject (one may even say, it is the collection of sensory *qualia* that this sort of object is naturally apt to evoke in the cognitive subject), helping the cognitive subject to recognize individuals as falling under the concept.

The reason for the divergence of these two types of content is that, while the first is determined by the causal laws of nature concerning the natural kind of the object and the cognitive subject, the second is determined merely by whatever the subject happens to perceive in the first object it encounters, or, at any rate, the necessarily finite sample of objects it has observed, as opposed to the potential infinity of the objects of the same natural kind. For, on Ockham's account of concept acquisition, the first sensory encounter with the first instance of a natural kind naturally gives rise to an intuitive singular sensory cognition, as well as a singular, intuitive intellectual cognition of the same object. But what accounts for the singularity of these intuitive acts of cognition is not their distinctive content: on the contrary, the content of these acts indifferently represents any other sufficiently similar objects; in the case of the intellectual cognition, any essentially similar objects—that is, any other objects of the same natural kind. As Ockham (1991: 65–6) writes:

> it does not seem that an intuitive cognition is a proper cognition, since any given intuitive cognition is equally a likeness of one singular thing and of another exactly similar thing, and it equally represents both the one and the other. Therefore, it does not seem to be more a cognition of the one than a cognition of the other...I reply that an intuitive cognition is a proper cognition of a singular thing not because of its greater likeness to the one thing than to the other, but because it is naturally caused by the one thing and not by the other, and it is not able to be caused by the other...You might object that it can be caused by God [acting] alone. This is true, but such a vision is always apt by nature to be caused by the one created object and not by the other; and if it is caused naturally, then it is caused by the one and not by the other, and is not able to be caused by the other. Hence, it is not because of a likeness that an intuitive cognition, rather than a first abstractive cognition, is called a proper cognition of a singular thing. Rather, it is only because of causality; nor can any other reason be given.

Thus, the singularity of the first intuitive act is merely due to its actual causal contact with the singular object in question. Therefore, removing the object, or severing the actual causal connection in any other way, immediately renders the remaining intellectual act an abstractive act of cognition, a common concept, indifferently representing all co-specific individuals of the same kind, which will then constitute its objective, semantic content.

By contrast, the phenomenal content of the same act is whatever the subject typically perceives of objects of this kind. For the semantic content of a concept, determined solely by the natural causality of its objects and the natural receptivity of the mind, does not give the cognitive subject any clues as to whether the next thing it meets in its perceptual environment does or does not fall under this concept. What provides these clues is the concept's perceptual recognition schema or phenomenal content (Ockham 1970: 276; 1991: 390) This is what provides for concepts, to use Normore's happy phrase (2003), "a hook out to perception", however, not without the possibility of error. Since the perceivable qualities of the objects of these concepts are their accidental qualities, these qualities may vary widely among different individuals (or even in the same individual over time); therefore, de facto co-specific individuals may not appear to belong to the same species (think of species with morphologically very different sexes, for instance), while there may be very similar individuals apparently belonging to the same species, but in fact belonging to different ones (think of cases of near-perfect mimicry, and so on). In short, phenomenal content *does not* determine semantic content (Panaccio 2004: ch. 7).

Note also that in the previously quoted passage Ockham ties the identity of a concept to its co-specific objects—that is, its semantic content—only by natural necessity, but with logical contingency: *the same concept* could be caused supernaturally directly by God, who can do anything that does not involve a logical contradiction, without its natural cause, its naturally represented first object, and all those co-specific with it. Thus, the same concept, the same act with the same phenomenal content, may be produced in the same mind supernaturally without any actual relation to its actual, natural objects. But this immediately establishes the connection between Putnam's "Twin Earth Experiment" and Ockham's conception. For, just as on Putnam's account the rigidly designating terms '$H_2O$' and 'XYZ' would have to have necessarily disjoint extensions, even if the transparent liquid that is $H_2O$ on this earth would be phenomenally indistinguishable from the similar liquid on Twin Earth, whence the inhabitants of each planet would be inclined to call both liquids 'water' in their miraculously matching English, so too, on Ockham's conception, rigidly designating natural kind terms designating distinct species would have to have disjoint extensions, still, on account of their phenomenal similarity, competent speakers of Latin may mistake members of one species for another, even systematically, on account of some similar miracle. Indeed, as Ockham and his ilk clearly realized in their speculations concerning the possibility of perfect divine deception, the occasional, naturally occurring, and naturally detectable misjudgements might supernaturally be turned systematic, and in principle undetectable, which is precisely the core idea of the Demon-scenario (Lagerlund 2010).

## Ockham and the Demon

But then, this is precisely how Ockham's semantic externalism opens up the apparent *possibility* of an *extreme version* of "Demon-scepticism", which, however, as I have argued elsewhere and will argue soon here, is in fact *not* a genuine possibility.[1] But to get to this point, let us first see exactly what this *extreme version* of "Demon-scepticism" involves.

In *The Matrix*, the celebrated movie premissed on a BIV-scenario, there is an interesting conversation among "the rebels"—that is, persons living in the devastated physical world of the twenty-second century, who originally acquired their concepts in the virtual reality of "the Matrix", a computer program feeding artificially generated humans, nurtured in complete sensory isolation from physical reality, the virtual experiences of twenty-first-century America as *we* know it. The conversation concerns what the artificial peptide goo served for dinner tastes like. The suggestions range from runny egg to Tasty Wheat to snot. But it soon turns out that the main concern *is not* that one of the interlocutors makes an *error in judgement* in the sense

---

[1] See my exchange with Claude Panaccio on this issue (Klima and Hall 2011: 83–128). In fact, part of what follows is drawn from that discussion.

that what he deems, say, Tasty Wheat taste is really oatmeal, or chicken, or tuna taste. Rather, the concern is that the interlocutors literally have *no idea* of Tasty Wheat taste or chicken taste or tuna taste, or of genuine chicken or real tuna, for that matter. Having acquired their concept of, say, chickens in the virtual reality of the Matrix, in complete cognitive isolation from a real world that at least used to be populated by real chickens, this concept can represent only the virtual objects of this virtual reality, whatever those are, but *not* the real objects of physical reality. Let me call the kind of concept acquired in virtual reality that completely fails to engage reality in this way a *non-veridical concept*.

Semantically speaking, we may clarify the idea of a non-veridical concept's failure to engage reality by saying that in a formal semantics categorematic terms expressing non-veridical concepts and those expressing veridical ones would take their semantic values from two disjoint sets (serving as "the universe of discourse"), even if, perhaps, phenomenally, from the perspective of the minds that form these concepts, they may be indistinguishable. Thus, for instance, if I have the concept of chickens formed in physical reality upon encountering genuine chickens, then the concept I express by the word 'chicken' represents genuine chickens, and so I can use the word to stand for genuine chickens (as in 'Chickens are birds'). On the other hand, if I was raised in the Matrix, what I can express by the word 'chicken' is at best a concept that represents virtual chickens, whatever those are, but definitely not chickens as we understand them, and so in that scenario I can at best use the word to stand for virtual chickens, but not for real chickens (thus, in the sentence 'Chickens are birds' uttered by me in this scenario, the word 'chickens' cannot stand for actual chickens). Still, the claim of the Demon argument is that I can have phenomenally the exact same mental contents whether I acquire my concepts in genuine or in virtual reality. So, the concept acquired in the Matrix would appear to me to represent the same things in the same way as the concept acquired in genuine physical reality, despite the fact that only the latter represents chickens, and the former does not. It is *this* idea of a non-veridical concept that I would briefly describe as one that appears to represent something that it does not represent. But with *this* understanding of the idea of a non-veridical concept we can easily see that Ockham's externalism is committed to the possibility of the Demon-scenario, despite the fact that it is not a genuine possibility.

## Exorcizing the Demon

But first let us see why Ockham is in fact committed to this possibility. Given the way he describes how we acquire our concepts of natural kinds, Ockham has to admit that these concepts have their semantic contents independently from one another, and that their semantic content is merely contingently related to their phenomenal content—that is, one can have the exact same concepts with the same phenomenal contents, even if they may, perhaps supernaturally, have wildly different semantic contents from what they actually have, which is precisely the gist of Ockham's externalism as Panaccio describes it: phenomenal content (which some might even call *intension*) does not determine semantic content (which again some may call *extension*). In fact, in Ockham's theory of concepts, the same observations would apply to all simple categorematic concepts. But then, this means that Ockham is committed to the claim that any of our simple categorematic concepts may possibly be non-veridical (that is, they may be phenomenally the same whether they are acquired in actual physical reality or in the Matrix), and since, given their simplicity, they can be so independently of one another, it is at least logically possible that they are *all* non-veridical at the same time. But this is precisely how I would *define* a BIV, a brain-in-a-vat, to allude to Putnam's scenario, but I might as well call it the Cartesian solipsistic self, to allude to Descartes's scenario: *a BIV is a cognitive subject that has no simple veridical concepts*. As we can see, under this definition, Ockham's conception is committed to the claim that it is at least supernaturally possible that there is a cognitive subject, say, $s$, such that $s$ is a BIV.

Now, since $s$ has phenomenally the same simple concepts as we do, and complex thoughts and judgements are semantically composed of these simple concepts, $s$ and you and I are capable of thinking the same thoughts, in particular, the thought that $s$ is a BIV. Now let us assume that a mad scientist, or better yet, God, has made it to be the actual state of affairs that $s$ is a BIV. So the judgement that $s$ is a BIV is true. But an affirmative, contingent judgement, whoever forms it, can be true (in the strong sense of expressing some actual, real state of affairs) only if it is made up from veridical concepts (for otherwise it simply cannot express any real state of affairs containing genuine real items of actual reality, given that its categorematic concepts simply cannot pick out any real items in actual reality, as we could see earlier). Therefore, since by our assumption $s$ is a BIV, $s$ has no veridical concepts; thus, his judgement that $s$ is a BIV cannot be true. However, his judgement, being made up from the same concepts by Ockham's criteria of concept-identity, is the same as ours or anybody else's. So our judgement that $s$ is a BIV, which is true, is the same as $s$'s judgement, which, however, is not true. Therefore, we have to conclude that the same judgement that $s$ is a BIV is both true and not true, which is an explicit contradiction. However, since we have derived this contradiction from the assumption that $s$ is a BIV with the help of other self-evident premisses, the assumption cannot be true. But it is a consequence of Ockham's position that this assumption can be true; therefore, by *modus tollens*, Ockham's position cannot be true.

In fact, by virtue of this reasoning, no position concerning concept-identity, whether it is "internalist" or "externalist", which allows the possibility of the Demon-scenario *as defined here* can be true. Historically, I would say this is true of most of late-medieval and modern philosophy, the prominent representatives of which all worked under the same unquestioned assumptions we have just identified in Ockham. But, without even trying to justify here this sweeping historical claim, I would rather contrast it with an earlier conception, which simply does not allow the possibility of the

Demon-scenario, and which is often referred to as Aquinas's doctrine of *the formal identity of knower and the known*, but which, for the sake of better contrast, I would rather refer to as "the 'hyper-externalism' of Aquinas".

## The "Hyper-Externalism" of Aquinas and the Pervasiveness of Forms

As we have seen, Demon-scepticism in the sense defined here is possible only if our simple cognitive acts are merely contingently veridical, leaving open the possibility that perhaps *all* our simple, non-introspective cognitive acts, including our simple intellectual concepts, are non-veridical. However, if a certain conception of the identity conditions of these cognitive acts demands that at least some of our simple non-introspective cognitive acts are essentially veridical—that is, their veridicality is part and parcel of their conditions of identity—then this conception directly excludes the possibility of Demon-scepticism *without* any appeal to the introspective certainty of a solipsistic Cartesian self. The necessary veridicality of simple cognitive acts with regard to their proper objects is a consequence of the Aristotelian idea that the cognitive act is nothing but the form of the object in the cognitive subject in a different mode of existence.[2]

One way of demystifying this apparently obscure idea is by appealing to the nowadays common ideas of encoding, transcoding, and decoding—that is, the process of transferring *the same information* through different media in a way that allows it to be reproducible in a numerically different copy. For instance, the recording and playback of a song provide an obvious case of this process. The song played back is a copy of the song originally played, where the reproduction of the song is possible by virtue of the preservation of the same information in the record, which, in this sense, is but the form of the song originally played (the modulation of airwaves in the studio over a period of time) in a different mode of existence, say, existing in the form of the pattern of tiny pits on the surface of a music CD encoding the modulation of airwaves.

Without arguing for it, let us just assume for the time being that this "demystification" correctly captures the original Aristotelian idea (originally illustrated by the example of a signet ring pressed into wax).[3] However, even granting this perhaps dubious proposal, one may still have doubts whether it would yield the idea of the necessary veridicality of some simple cognitive acts with regard to their proper objects. After all, just as the pattern of pits on the surface of the CD could in principle be produced by something other than the recording apparatus without the original song actually played in the studio, so the same cognitive act could be produced in the

---

[2] For more on this issue, see my unpublished exchange with Robert Pasnau available online (Klima 1996; Pasnau 1996).

[3] *De anima* II. 12, 424$^a$17–24.

subject without a "matching" object, rendering the act non-veridical, just as the Demon-scenario would suggest. So, apparently, the suggested "demystification" of the Aristotelian idea supports precisely the contingency of the veridicality of cognitive acts and thus the possibility of Demon-scepticism, contrary to what it was devised to illustrate.

However, to proceed from the better known to the lesser known, let us take a closer look at the case of sound recording. The pattern of tiny pits on the surface of the CD is certainly producible by means other than the recording apparatus. After all, the same kind of laser beam with the same kind of modulation would produce the same pattern if the modulation of the laser beam were not driven by the modulation of electronic signals driven in turn by the modulation of airwaves hitting the microphones in the recording studio, but, say, by a computer producing the same modulation without any sound whatsoever. (Of course, this is the same sort of scenario as Putnam's ant producing what looks like a sketch of Churchill by crawling in the sand (Putnam 1981: 1).) However, and this is the important point, in that case the pattern of pits on the surface would *not* be a *record* of any sound whatsoever: it may be an ornament, it may be a surface feature, and so on, but *not a record of some sound*. For the pattern of pits to qualify *as the record of a song*, it has to be part of the system of encoding and preserving information about the actual modulation of air vibrations constituting the song. Indeed, that for the *record of a song* as such it is *essential* to encode information about the song, whereas it is *accidental* that it is this pattern of pits in this system of encoding, is further confirmed by the fact that if I "rip" the track from the CD onto my computer's hard drive, then I get *the same song* onto my hard drive, but now recorded in a different medium, this time encoded in the pattern of different magnetic polarities on the surface of the disk.

Describing this process in the language of Aristotelian hylomorphism, we can say that the form of the song that first informed the air in *esse reale*, existing as the modulation of airwaves, first was received in the matter of the CD in *esse intentionale*, without the matter it originally informed, merely coinciding with the pattern of pits informing the CD in *esse reale*; then again, it was received in the matter of the hard disk, in another instance of *esse intentionale*, again, without the matter of the original, this time coinciding with the pattern of polarities informing the disk in *esse reale*.
Thus, in the whole process, what qualifies any real feature of any medium *as the record* or *encoding* of the original form is "the formal unity" of these real features in the sense that the system of encoding secures transferring and preserving *the same information* about the original form throughout the process. If the chain of transferring and preserving the same information is broken, and a merely accidentally similar pattern is produced by some other means, then it may be "misinterpreted" by the next decoder as a recording of some original, but it will never be *the same*, precisely because it does not fit into the chain in the same way, which is essential for the identity of any encoded bit of information. Thus, to switch to another example, even if a recorded TV programme could not be distinguished from the live feed of the

same by just looking at the screen, the two are *not the same*, and their difference *is* detectable precisely by looking at the process of the transfer of information producing the *exact same looking*, but *essentially different*, images on the screen.

However, if on the strength of these examples we are willing to interpret the idea of formal unity between a cognizer and some cognized thing in the sense of the preservation of information, so that this is essential for the identity of the cognitive act in so far as it is an encoding of the form of the object, then it is not hard to see that those simple cognitive acts that are identified precisely in terms of receiving, storing, and further processing information about their proper objects will have to be *essentially veridical*. For then these simple cognitive acts, regardless of what firing patterns of neurons in the brain or what spiritual qualities of an immaterial mind realize them, will count as the cognitive acts encoding information about their proper objects only if they do in fact represent those objects that they appear to represent to the cognitive subject, for they present or represent to the subject precisely the information they encode about their proper object. In fact, Aquinas very clearly realized this consequence in his repeated insistence on the claim that "no cognitive power is deceived about its proper object" (Aquinas 2000–13: SCG lb. 3, c. 108, n. 4; ST1 q. 17, a. 3).

Thus, on this conception, the veridical acts of perception, memory, and intellectual apprehension (as opposed to the non-veridical or contingently veridical acts of hallucination, imagination, misremembering, judging, believing, and so on) are essentially, and not merely contingently, veridical. But then, within this conception, the idea of "Demon scepticism" as described earlier is *ab ovo* excluded. Things *are* as they appear in our veridical acts of cognition, but sometimes, on account of the similarity of a veridical act of cognition to a non-veridical act or to a veridical act of cognizing something else, we may rashly judge things to be the way they appear to be through the non-veridical act, or to be that other thing. But, since the veridical act is essentially veridical, and so it cannot be the same as a non-veridical act or the veridical cognition of something else, we can correct our mistake, by detecting the difference, as when we say, "Oh, I thought the bed was on fire, but it was just a dream" or "Oh, I thought I saw water on the road, but it was just a mirage".

But similar observations apply in more elaborate cases. For instance, in the scenario of *The Matrix*, the characters eating the peptide goo in physical reality have to realize that when they say it tastes like chicken, they have no genuine conception of chickens, as the only experiences they have about "chickens" are about the virtual "chickens" of the Matrix. They could say they had a conception of chickens through those virtual experiences only if they could look at those virtual experiences as somehow carrying genuine information about genuine chickens, say, if they could verify that whoever created the program had modelled the virtual chickens after real chickens and presented them as representations of real chickens, in the way a nature video provides us with genuine information about genuine animals in remote lands. However if the virtual, quasi-experiences these people had in the Matrix are merely similar to genuine experiences, but *are not* genuine experiences (whether through direct perception or through "mediated perception" as through a documentary), then the concepts abstracted from those quasi-experiences *are not* the concepts of genuine things that would produce similar, but *never the same*, experiences. Thus, again, when it comes to the identity conditions of *intellectual concepts*, which on the Aristotelian account would carry just further processed, abstracted information about the genuine objects of genuine experiences, it is clear that on this conception they also have to be essentially veridical.

So, how is this conception related to the issue of semantic externalism? As we could see, the way this conception identifies concepts has practically nothing to do with their internal or phenomenal properties: we talk about the same concept as long as it is a carrier of the same information whatever realizes it, and what determines this information is precisely the type of external object that the concept carries information about. Thus, from the perspective of this conception, whatever internal properties the concept has (say, whether it is a neural firing pattern of a certain type, and so on) is irrelevant, since the same concept, carrying the same information, can be realized in just any other type of "medium". Therefore, not only do the internal properties of the concept not fully determine its content; they have basically nothing to do with it; on this conception the content of the concept is fully externally determined, and so this conception can justifiably be dubbed "hyper-externalism". In any case, whatever we name it, it is clear that this conception does not allow the apparent possibility of the Demon-scenario. On this conception, God might create a quality in my mind entirely similar in its internal properties to the one whereby I presently conceive of human nature without that quality actually representing human nature, but that quality, not being the encoding of human nature in my mind would not be a concept of humans, just as a pattern of tiny pits on a CD resembling a recording of a song would not be a recording of the song if it were not the encoding of information about that song. But the same information may certainly be encoded or recorded in different media, yielding again *the same* representation, realized, however, in entities with radically different internal properties.

So, on this "hyper-externalist" conception, the formal unity of concept and object, interpreted as the sameness of information encoded in the concept and constituting the object, determines the identity of the concept quite independently from its internal or "phenomenal" properties. Thus, this "formal unity" does not have to amount to any qualitative similarity between concept and object (or even between my mental act and yours), so of course Aquinas is perfectly justified in insisting in some passages on the *qualitative dissimilarity* of concept and object. As he often remarks, what I have in mind when I think of a stone is not the stone, but the species of the stone, and not in the way in which it is in the stone, informing mineral matter, but differently, informing my mind *about* the form informing that matter.[4] So, the

---

[4] "Between the cognizer and the cognized thing is not required a similarity by concordance in nature, but by representation only: for it is clear that the form of the stone within the soul is of an entirely different

passages critics of this interpretation quote from Aquinas do not speak against *this* understanding of Aquinas as a "conformalist"—that is, someone who insists on the formal unity of a concept and its formal object (that is, the form or nature of its individual, ultimate objects considered in abstraction from its individuating conditions in these objects) (Klima 2008a: §§7–8).

Indeed, for Aquinas, forms pervade both the entire sensible and intelligible creation, as each creature seeking its perfection is striving to live up to the standard set by its Divine Idea. And I would say that it is basically this idea of the "pervasiveness of Forms" that unites the pre-nominalist ("moderate realist") paradigm, and separates it from all post-nominalist, and especially post-Cartesian, modern thought.

Forms, then, on this conception, being the determinations of the modes of being of all natural kinds, the different ways in which these kinds of things are, can be the determinations not only of the ways of being, but also of the ways of cognizing (including re-cognizing and pre-cognizing), which is nothing but for the form of the object to be present in (and to) a cognitive subject, naturally representing the object on account of their formal unity. Thus, for Aquinas, there is no difference between phenomenal and semantic content: the semantic content of my concept of, say, donkeys, is the form, nature, essence, or quiddity of really existing donkeys,[5] although considered in abstraction from its individuating conditions. Accordingly, Aquinas's "hyper-externalist" semantics is a "WYSIWYG-semantics": you can have a donkey concept, the mental act the semantic properties of which are inherited by the term 'donkey', only if your mind is informed by genuine donkey-nature *in esse intentionale*; so, on this conception, if a BIV were possible (which it is not), then a BIV's fake/virtual donkey-concepts would not be donkey-concepts at all, and so the word 'donkey' as used by this BIV would not and could not refer to donkeys at all.

## Nominalist (Extensionalist) and Realist (Intensionalist) Conceptions of Semantic Content

This last remark directly takes us back from considerations of mental content to the issue of semantic content properly speaking, even if, as we could see, in line with the Aristotelian conception of the "semantic triangle", the conventional semantic properties of our words are basically inherited by them from the natural semantic properties of our mental acts, our concepts. However, as we could also see, this relationship is somewhat more complicated.

---

nature than the form of the stone in the matter, but insofar as the form of the stone in the soul represents the form of the stone, the former is the principle leading to the cognition of the latter" (Aquinas 2000–13: De Veritate, q. 8, a. 11, ad 3).

[5] For Aquinas's own explanation of the relationships among the meanings of these different terms referring to the same thing, see Aquinas (2000–13: *De Ente*, c. 1).

After all, on Ockham's externalist conception our words do not inherit *all* representational features of our concepts: our words properly express or signify only the *semantic content* of our concepts, although they may regularly evoke the same sorts of phenomenal contents in the minds of the users of the same words with the same understanding. However, that pertains not to the semantics, but to the psychology and epistemology of concepts. Strictly speaking, our simple universal categorematic terms signify only the things naturally signified by the concepts to which they are subordinated, and those are only the individual things indifferently conceived (or co-conceived in the case of connotative concepts) by these concepts. Thus, the signification or semantic content of such a simple categorematic term is simply the multitude of individuals indifferently conceived (or co-conceived) by these concepts (best representable in a modern formal reconstruction as *sets* of individuals or sets of ordered *n*-tuples thereof) (Klima 2008b). In this sense, then, the nominalist semantics of Ockham and his followers, in keeping with their parsimonious ontology, is a "coarse-grained", extensionalist semantics. Since the descriptive, phenomenal content of our categorematic concepts has no role in determining their signification, it has no role in their logic either. For whether an individual is naturally signified by such a concept is not determined by whether the individual satisfies the descriptive criteria of its phenomenal content (say, whether it is red or spherical, and so on), but exclusively by its objective co-specificity with the individual that originally gave rise to this concept. The only reason why this individual is represented by this concept is that the concept generated by the original instance of the same species was already indifferently represented by the concept with regard to any member of the same species. But this indifference for Ockham is just a brute fact about the causality of co-specific individuals and the receptivity of our minds, not to be explained in terms of anything like shared properties or common natures. Thus, *phenomenal content*, which would be the best candidate to be called the *intension* of a concept and of the corresponding term, does not determine their *semantic content* or *extension* in Ockham's externalist psychology and logic. However, precisely because of their divergence and logically contingent relationship, Ockham's conception allows the possibility of the extreme version of a Demon-scenario, which, as I have already argued, cannot be a genuine possibility.

By contrast, Aquinas's "hyper-externalism" does not allow this divergence between  phenomenal and semantic content: the semantic content of a concept and of the corresponding term is but the nature of the thing encoded in the concept of the mind, which in this encoded form *informs the mind about* the thing in its *intentional* being, just as in its un-encoded form it *informs the thing* in its *real* being (Klima 2008a: §7). This information, then, which is the best candidate to be called the *intension* of the concept and of the corresponding term, does determine the *extension* of the term— that is, the range of things that can be referred to by this term in the context of a proposition. And yet, although by Putnam's lights this feature would define *semantic internalism*, Aquinas's conception does deserve to be called "hyper-externalism", rather than internalism. The reason is that linguistic or semantic content and "internal", mental content for Aquinas are one and the same, tied by *logical necessity* to the *external*, essential nature of the things that constitute the extension this intension determines, whether or not any particular language-user is actually aware of the particular criteria whereby *they* could determine this extension. The kind of internalism Putnam had in mind (exemplified by Locke's theory of meaning, for example) when he contrasted it with his own externalism presupposes precisely the same idea that Ockham's externalism does—namely, the logical contingency of the relationship between internal, phenomenal content and external, objective semantic content. However, for Aquinas, this contingency is excluded by his idea of the formal unity or sameness of both.

# References

Aquinas (2000–13). *Corpus Thomisticum, S. Thomae De Aquino Opera Omnia* <http://www.corpusthomisticum.org/iopera.html; recognovit ac instruxit Enrique Alarcón automato electronico Pompaelone ad Universitatis Studiorum Navarrensis aedes a MM A.D.> (accessed 4 August 21014).

Klima, G. (1996). 'Nulla virtus cognoscitiva circa proprium obiectum decipitur—Critical Comments on "Robert Pasnau: The Identity of Knower and Known"' <http://faculty.fordham.edu/klima/APA.htm> (accessed 4 August 2014).

Klima, G. (2008a). 'The Medieval Problem of Universals', in *The Stanford Encyclopedia of Philosophy* (Winter Edition), ed. Edward N. Zalta <http://plato.stanford.edu/archives/win2008/entries/universals-medieval/> (accessed 4 August 2014).

Klima, G. (2008b). 'The Nominalist Semantics of Ockham and Buridan: A Rational Reconstruction', in D. Gabbay and J. Woods (eds), *Handbook of the History of Logic*. Amsterdam: North Holland, 389–431.

Klima, G. (2012). 'Medieval Philosophy of Language', in Gillian Russell and Delia Graff Fara, *Routledge Companion to Philosophy of Language*. New York and Abingdon: Routledge, 827–40.

Klima, G., and Hall, A. (2011) (eds). *The Demonic Temptations of Medieval Nominalism*. Proceedings of the Society for Medieval Logic and Metaphysics, vol. 9. Newcastle upon Tyne: Cambridge Scholars Publishers.

Lagerlund, H. (2010) (ed.). *Rethinking the History of Skepticism: The Missing Medieval Background*. Leiden and Boston: Brill.

Normore, C. (2003). 'Burge, Descartes, and Us', in M. Hahn and B. Ramberg (eds), *Reflections and Replies: Essays on the Philosophy of Tyler Burge*. Cambridge, MA: MIT Press, 1–14.

Ockham, W. (1970). *Opera Theologica*, ii, ed. S. Brown and G. Gál. St Bonaventure, NY: Franciscan Institute.

Ockham, W. (1991). *Quodlibetal Questions*, vols i and ii, trans. A. J. Freddoso and F. E. Kelly. New Haven: Yale University Press.

Panaccio, C. (2004). *Ockham on Concepts*. Aldershot: Ashgate.

Panaccio, C. (2014). 'Ockham's Externalism', in G. Klima (ed.), *Intentionality, Cognition and Mental Representation in Medieval Philosophy*. New York, Fordham University Press.

Pasnau, R. (1996). *The Identity of Knower and Known* <http://faculty.fordham.edu/klima/APAPasnau.htm> (accessed 4 August 2014).
Putnam, H. (1981). *Reason, Truth, and History*. Cambridge: Cambridge University Press.
Putnam, H. (2000). 'Meaning and Reference', in E. D. Klemke and Heimir Geirsson, (eds), *Contemporary Analytic and Linguistic Philosophies*. 2nd edn. Amherst, NY: Prometheus Books.

# 7

# Meaning and Linguistic Usage in Renaissance Humanism: The Case of Lorenzo Valla

*Lodi Nauta*

## 1. Renaissance Humanism and the Philosophy of Language

In the history of the philosophy of language Renaissance humanism does not play a prominent role, and it is not difficult to see why. While in medieval times the scholastics had developed interesting theories about all aspects of language, humanists were generally not interested in theoretical issues. Arising in late-medieval Italy, the humanist movement spread across the rest of Europe by the end of the fifteenth century. Humanists studied classical Latin and (to a lesser extent) Greek and their literatures, advocating a return to a classical style in writing and speaking. Education was reformed and based on the *studia humanitatis*, a programme consisting in the study of grammar, rhetoric, history, poetry, and moral philosophy. This programme of study then had a distinctly pragmatic and practical character. Humanists wanted to write and speak as the ancients had done, not only because they thought classical Latin was a semantically rich and rhetorically elegant language but also because they found the Latin as used in the schools and universities of their day barbarous, ungrammatical, and less than a shade of classical Latin. Hence their programme was one of rediscovery and reappropriation of the riches of antiquity. This meant immersing oneself in the texts in order to understand what this or that word meant, and how and when it was appropriate to use this or that grammatical construction. Their studies included ancient rhetorical texts, from which they learned how to argue, how to structure a text, which arguments should be used when and where, and which style should be used on which occasion, and so on. Naturally, the

---

I am grateful to the editors for their valuable comments on an earlier draft of this chapter. For a more extensive treatment of the issues treated here, see Nauta (2009).

humanists often encountered problems of a nature that we regard as philosophical, and at times they did not shrink back from offering some reflections on general questions about meaning, but their whole programme was imbued with a pragmatic spirit, and at first sight it does not seem to offer much to the historian of the philosophy of language.

For this reason, it is even more tricky than usual to adopt the language of modern philosophy to categorize and analyse the ideas and work of the humanists. In the case of Scholastic theories about supposition, it has already proved notoriously difficult to categorize them in terms of modern distinctions such as sense/reference or signification/meaning, but at least the type of problems the Scholastics were addressing are familiar to the modern philosopher. Because of the apparent absence of such theoretical concerns among the humanists, it seems even more anachronistic to apply modern distinctions and terminology to their work, which were principally of a philological, grammatical, rhetorical, and literary kind. In the language of this book, we do not see much explicit reflection on linguistic content and on its metaphysical grounding. We do find the humanists paying a lot of attention to the meaning of particular words, but we do not find them offering theories of linguistic content—that is, semantic theories. Of course, they distinguished between the several parts of speech such as nouns, adjectives, and verbs, and they dutifully repeated traditional distinctions such as categorematic and syncategorematic words ("all", "some", "not", etc.), but in general they simply took for granted that words have meaning. For them language can be studied only in context—that is, in the way people actually use language. To abstract from this context and start theorizing about meaning in general was precisely what the scholastic philosophers had done, with all the detrimental effects for the study of grammar, reasoning, argumentation, and language in general.

And yet it would be wrong to see the humanist project as wholly devoid of theoretical interest, and only of interest to the student of the classical tradition, literature, or culture history. There is a good reason to include a chapter on Renaissance humanism in a book on the history of ideas on linguistic content. Some scholars have regarded the humanists' study of meaning in context—that is, in the way people actually used this or that word or grammatical construction—as an important *theoretical* insight, associating it with the Wittgensteinian idea that meaning is use. Rather than being a mysterious entity that a word *has* and that refers to something else (for example, a thing in the outer world or a concept), meaning is an activity, the kind of work the word "does". To determine the meaning of a word is to map the rules that govern its use, not finding an entity somehow owned by the word that ties the word to a thing in some mysterious way. It also meant, at least for these modern interpreters, that questions of meaning can be settled only by looking at the normal, ordinary way in which people talk and write. The humanist rejection of the technical jargon of the Scholastics was more than the expression of an aesthetic preference. Their convictions might be compared—according to such a line of interpretation—to that of J. L. Austin, an ordinary language philosopher, who complained that "philosophers often seem to think that they can just 'assign' any meaning whatever to any word", while forgetting that "our common stock of words embodies all the distinctions men have found worth drawing" (Austin 1962: 62; 1979: 182).

It is a moot point in the scholarly literature whether we can ascribe such innovative ideas to the humanists. Most scholars continue to see the humanist movement as essentially a literary and rhetorical movement that did not radically change the linguistic paradigm. This chapter aims to show that the truth lies somewhere in the middle. Humanists had interesting ideas about linguistic content and language in general, but we should not exaggerate the innovative nature of these ideas nor their anticipation of contemporary views. The best way to show this is to examine the work of one of the most important humanists, Lorenzo Valla (c.1406–57), because the modern debate on the possible philosophical contributions of Renaissance humanism has centred on him. Valla is indeed a central figure. He wrote the first advanced handbook of the Latin language, the *Elegantiae Linguae Latinae* ("The Fine Points of the Latin Language"), which was immensely influential. He criticized scholastic thought from a linguistic point of view in his *Dialectical Disputations*. In his hands, philology became a critical tool for sifting spurious from authentic works and forgeries from real documents, and hence a weapon for attacking established philosophical and theological dogmas and practices. It is the *Dialectical Disputations*, on which Valla worked his entire, itinerant life, that show him at his most polemical but also, willy-nilly perhaps, at his most philosophical. We will look at three issues: the assimilation of words and things, his notion of linguistic usage as the principal criterion for settling questions of meaning, and his grammatical approach to language and argumentation that must show that many philosophical problems are rooted in a misunderstanding of language. We will discuss the question to what extent his ideas resemble those of modern philosophers. (For a more extensive treatment, see Nauta (2009), on which this contribution is largely based, though sometimes with a different focus.) Our discussion will show a common pattern— namely, that Valla is not such a radical reconceiver of language as has sometimes been claimed, yet that his insistence on common usage as the prime parameter is an important idea, something that leads him to conclude that philosophers cannot just invent their own language or assign new meanings to old words. His scholarly contributions aside, his recognition of the varieties of meaning and their grounding in convention and common usage is an important contribution to thinking on the historical and social-cultural embeddedness of language.

## 2. Word and Thing

One of the basic distinctions in humanist thought was that between things and words (*res* and *verba*). Cicero and other ancient rhetoricians had placed the distinction at the heart of rhetoric: "thing" is, of course, a wide and amorphous category that included anything that could be the subject of linguistic expression: historical events, the subject matter of one's speech, one's ideas, or whatever one had to put into words. The distinction fostered the idea that speech is an instrument of thought, the clothing of a body, or the translator of the mind. (Cf. Nauta 2011, 2012.) The metaphorical nature of such pictures was hardly recognized: it was taken as a matter of fact that language was an instrument of thought, the verbal expression of what went on inside the mind. But the same rhetorical tradition also stressed the close connection between words and things. Powerful speech that convinces the reader or listener brings the subject to light, and the best orator uses words in such a way that one feels almost physically present at the events described. "Bringing to light" or "before one's eyes" was indeed a common way of referring to this power of speech. The intimate connection between words and things was also underscored in another way: clear thinking was a sine qua non for clear speech: confused thinking leads to unclear speech, as everybody agreed.

But now a question arises: if things can be grasped and brought to light and understood only if we use the right language, does this not imply that our view of the world is somehow shaped by language? Such an intimate connection between words and things may render it difficult to distinguish between the two categories. Indeed, the claim has been made that Valla equates them. As one scholar has put it:

Being and meaning, the thing and the word, are in the world of human beings not to be separated... Valla pushes against the limits of the representational power of language, for here is the place where he can no longer maintain linguistically, and therefore logically, the separation of word and not-word and also of thing and not-thing. For the sign and the signified are on both occasions *res*, that is, word and not-word are likewise *res*. (Gerl 1974: 223, 221; quoted Waswo 1987: 108–9; cf. Camporeale 1986: 227: "un tutto inscindibile", an inseparable whole.)

The consequences are radical: "language and the people who use it do not 'represent' a reality but constitute it", leading to a denial of "the correspondence theory of truth and the referential theory of meaning, which is no longer to be sought in objects, but rather in words that name and categorize them" (Waswo 1987: 110, 109).

Is Valla indeed such a radical "reconceiver of language"? The passage on which this interpretation is based comes from the first book of the *Dialectical Disputations*. In this passage Valla presents a metaphysical grounding of meaning by looking at how words get meaning: words are sounds to which we human beings have assigned a particular meaning (Valla 2012: i. 219):

For humans invented the vocal sounds [*voces*] that they adapted to things once they had recognized them, consequently calling them "signs", and the first of those people was Adam when God created him. And they taught them along with their significations [*significationibus*] to their descendants, so that sounds [*soni*] indeed come from nature, but vocal sounds [*voces*] or signs and significations come from a maker... Hence, it follows that the ear perceives sounds, the mind perceives significations and both perceive vocal sounds.

A sound (*sonus*) can thus become meaningful when it is assigned a particular signification (*significatio*); it then becomes an "articulated" vocable sound, that is a *vox*. The vocable sound is "like [*quasi*] an image of its signification", by which Valla seems to suggest no more than that meaning is conventional: "human vocal sound is natural, but what it signifies is conventional." These signs *with their significations* were taught to later generations, and here Valla starts saying something about meaning rather than giving a grounding of it. Meaning involves the understanding, for, though he does not mention concepts here, his account presupposes the presence of a mental understanding of the thing, and we find him using words such as *sensus*, *intellectus*, and *significatio* almost interchangeably (Nauta 2009: 311 n. 48). This seems to be in line with the medieval notion of *significare*, a notion that goes back to Boethius' translation of Aristotle's *De interpretatione* 16$^b$19. *Significare* means "to make known", "to reveal", "to manifest", "to express", "to bring something to mind", "to establish an understanding of it"—all expressions that do not exactly correspond to the modern concepts of reference and meaning. According to Paul Vincent Spade, signification is therefore a species of a causal relation: "The psychological overtones of 'to signify' are similar to those of the modern 'to mean'. Nevertheless, signification is not meaning. A term signifies that of which it makes a person think, so that, unlike meaning, signification is a species of the causal relation" (Spade 1982: 188). This makes signification perhaps too much dependent on the mental process in the speaker's or hearer's mind, and other scholars have argued for a different interpretation of the term (see Pinborg 1976; Henry 1999: 143-4; Ashworth, Chapter 8, this volume). In Valla's account signification turns out to be a complex notion that involves our understanding of a word, and what we understand by a word is derived from or connected to the thing it names.

This last aspect—of meaning being the name (*nomen*) of the thing—leads to an important problem for Valla: words signify things, or, as he puts it: "'wood' is the name [*nomen*] of wood," "knowledge" of knowledge, and so on. But what about the word "thing"? It does not seem to signify in the same way as "tree" signifies a tree. We need a little bit of background in order to understand Valla's discussion. Very briefly, one of Valla's aims in the *Dialectical Disputations* is to criticize the metaphysical foundations of what he sees as the Aristotelian–Scholastic edifice: the ten Aristotelian categories of substance, quality, quantity, relation, time, place, and so on; the six so-called transcendental terms such as "being", "good", "one", "true" that transcend the categories (that is, they can be said of each category); traditional distinctions such as form/matter and act/potency, and so on (Mack 1993; Nauta 2009). He wants to defend a common-sense picture of the world in which concrete things take centre stage rather than what he thinks is an abstract ontology of bare substances, essences, quiddities, beings (*entia*), transcendals, and so on. If we want to be philosophical, we can analyse a thing in terms of substance, quality, and action, but for most purposes we can just speak about "things", which is a much simpler term than the scholastic notion of "being" (*ens*). He thus wants to reduce the transcendental terms as distinguished by the Scholastics to just one—namely "thing" (*res*), which has the advantage of being a perfectly normal Latin word. He also thinks that the traditional classification as visualized in the Tree of Porphyry does not make sense: thing rather than substance should be placed at the top of the tree; bare substance does not exist: a thing is always substance plus qualities and actions.

But, because everything can be called a thing, the question thus arises: what does "thing" signify? It seems a different kind of term than "tree" that signifies trees or "knowledge" that signifies knowledge. Valla's answer is that "thing" is a word that "embraces the significations of all other words": it embraces, for example, the signification of "tree", because tree is a thing and can be called a thing. But, because "thing" is just one word out of many, is "word" not a more general word? No, says Valla: "word" refers solely to words (a sub-class of things), while "thing" refers to all things (including the sub-class of words, which as sounds are physical things after all). He explains the special status of "thing" in a typically grammatical way: it does not matter whether we ask "What is man?" or "What does the word 'man' signify?" To both questions the answer will be the same—namely a definition of man. But with "thing" this is different (Valla 2012: i. 221):

> But about *thing* nothing can be asked in this way by "what is thing" and "what does 'thing' signify" because "what" is analyzed into "what thing". Therefore, those who say "what" of "thing" say something foolish. But if I should ask "which vocal sound is 'thing'", your correct reply will be "it is the vocal sound that signifies the meaning or sense [*intellectum sive sensum*] of all other vocal sounds.

What Valla in effect is saying is that it is a category mistake to treat the word "thing" as signifying things in the same way as "wood" signifies wood. There is no separate class of things signified by the sign or word "thing" besides stones, trees, and other objects; these are all things, and hence we can apply the sign "thing" to all of them. Since "what" (*quid*) simply means "what thing" (*que res*), it does not make sense to ask "what is thing?" (*quid est res*) or "what does the word 'thing' signify?" In the last paragraph Valla once again differentiates between things and meanings. A thing such as man is in space and time, while the signification of the word "man" is not such a thing but enters as a conventional sign in our language and categorizations ("man is an animal").

What our discussion thus suggests is that Valla is not so radical to assimilate words and things or—to use rather grand terminology—meaning and being, or language and reality. Since he wants to assign a privileged position to the word "thing" as the only transcendental term that he accepts, he has to discuss words and things, but he takes care to distinguish between word-things (parcels of air) and non-word-things (tree, stone), and between words as conventional signs or tokens (*nota*) and the things they signify: "'thing' signifies a thing; the latter is signified, the former is the sign or token of the latter; the one is not a vocal sound, the other is a vocal sound" (Valla 2012: i. 221). There is no collapse between words and things, even though Valla is not always consistent, for elsewhere he also calls significations qualities (*qualitates*), which in Valla's ontology are real things (*res*) (Valla 2012: i. 223-5).

Nevertheless, the general drift of his argument is clearly to distinguish between the conventional sign and the thing it "names", that is signifies (Monfasani 1989; Nauta 2009). This does not mean that there is nothing interesting going on here. It might not be too far-fetched to say that Valla grapples with the categories of things and words, which are ingredients of any semantic theory, and, while it seems unproblematic—and wholly traditional as well—to say that the one signifies the other, the relationship is not as straightforward as it might seem. Indeed, people tend to say that the meaning of the word "x" *is* x (or, alternatively, the concept of x), and some of Valla's statements too suggest this, even though he is also at pains to distinguish words with their meanings from things. (Cf. Mack 1993: 55–6.) This grappling might be inspired by an awareness of the centrality of meanings by which the world of things get mentioned, picked out, talked about, and perhaps observed and categorized. In later humanist texts the things to be talked about are not always easy to distinguish from the words. Discussing Erasmus' famous text *De copia* (1512), Terence Cave (1979: 21), for example, has argued: "*Res* are neither prior to words as their 'origin,' nor are they a productive residue which remains after the words cease. *Res* and *verba* slide together to become 'word-things'; the notion of a single domain (language) having a double aspect replaces that of two distinct domains, language and thought." Though not the only source for this development—as already mentioned, it was part and parcel of the rhetorical tradition—Valla's emphasis on the centrality of words and their impact on how we categorize things was not lost on later humanists such as Erasmus.

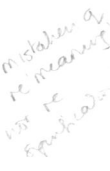

## 3. Latin and the Scope of "Common Usage"

This brings us to a second theme, closely connected to the previous one, where we find the same pattern of an overly radical interpretation versus a more moderate reading of Valla's semantic ideas. As we have seen, Valla stressed the conventional nature of language. This in itself was a wholly traditional idea: virtually all Scholastics would agree with that, following Aristotle's account according to which words are conventional while concepts are common and natural. But that meanings are established in society was not something the Scholastics were greatly interested in, while for Valla this was of huge importance. It is here that Valla offered the humanists a model of how to explore the meaning of words by studying closely how words and grammatical constructions were actually used by classical authors. Unlike most medieval grammarians and logicians, who—at least according to the humanist critique—constructed abstract rules first and then assessed the correctness and validity of expressions on the basis of them, Valla stressed that linguistic usage (*loquendi consuetudo*) should sanction the rules of grammar and determine the meaning of words, an opinion that was also developed by other humanists, based, of course, on ancient authorities such as Cicero and Quintilian. While not putting it in these terms, Valla assigns to custom a grounding role for meaning. He repeatedly states that we should follow the "common language", "popular custom" (*consuetudo popularis*), or "spoken usage" (*usus loquendi*).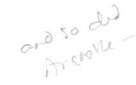

But what exactly does Valla mean by these expressions? For some scholars Valla must be regarded as an ordinary language philosopher *avant la lettre*, someone who is interested in how language works by studying the ordinary use of words. Other scholars think that common use for Valla always meant what the learned, the orators and literates, say—that is, the literary practice of the best authors rather than ordinary people's parlance. Here too the truth lies somewhere in the middle. In this section we will first study what "common" means for Valla, and how he treats Latin, which is obviously the language he is concerned with; in the next section we will look in more detail at the way in which common usage is put to use by Valla in his analysis of meaning in some concrete examples.

Classical Latin is certainly the main theme of Valla's widely read handbook, the *Elegantiae Linguae Latinae* ("The Fine Points of the Latin Language"), in which he elucidates a great variety of Latin's morphological, syntactical, and semantic features. Behind the mass of detail, a clear programme can be discerned: the replacement of a philosophical approach to the study of language by a grammatical and philological one, grounded on the premiss that only a close study of the usage of ancient authors can teach us how to use Latin correctly and most effectively. By right use Valla means grammatically correct and rhetorically effective, *elegantia* standing for semantic precision and refinement rather than for stylishness. Throughout the *Elegantiae*, Valla's main concern is classical Latin, and his observations often presuppose a distinction between Latin as a literate language and the vulgar tongues spoken by the common people (*vulgus, populus*).

This does not automatically entail an elitist privileging of Latin, however. As the language of the Roman Empire, Latin spread far and wide, becoming the language of "virtually the entire human race", and hence the rule and norm of our speaking and writing (Valla 1982: 386; Nauta 2009: 277–8). While in the *Elegantiae* he speaks of Latin in terms of an *ars*—an invented language that existed alongside but independent from the vernacular languages (to which it added lustre rather than destroying them)—in his *Dialectical Disputations* he occasionally treats Latin on a par with other (vernacular) languages such as Greek, Hebrew, "Punic", "Dalmatian" (Valla 2012: ii. 84). At its initial stage, Latin was very close to the language of the *vulgus*: in fact it was "practically one and the same" language, "sometimes called 'Roman' [*romana*], sometimes 'Latin' [*latina*]" (Valla 2012: i. 9). This is also why in antiquity it was much easier to master the learned Latin than it is now (in the fifteenth century), even though—as Valla stressed in a protracted debate with his archenemy Poggio Bracciolini (1380–1459)—this does not mean that a Roman child did not need instruction and teaching at all: the learned Latin was close to but not the same as the mother tongue learned at home from parents and instructors. (On this debate in which many humanists took part, see Tavoni 1984; Rizzo 2002.) Nevertheless, Latin-speakers in antiquity belonged to one and the same linguistic community. In later times Latin and the vernacular developed as separate varieties of one and the same language, and both underwent corruption: Latin of the Scholastics as well as the Roman *volgare* of modern times are depraved forms of learned Latin, on the one hand, and the vernacular form of ancient Latin, on the other hand.

Why does Valla link the *sermo popularis* and the *sermo eruditorum* so closely? A probable answer is patriotism. For the Roman Valla, it was in Rome that Latin developed and from whence it had spread. Latin was Rome's gift to the world. It was, therefore, vital for him to argue that "Latin" was the common denominator of both varieties of speech. The vernacular spoken by the masses was Latin too, and, though the learned spoke Latin "more ornately" or "more eloquently", one cannot say that they were "more Latinate" (Tavoni 1984: 266). Denying the existence of a Roman vernacular linguistically independent from Latin was also important for Valla; he insisted that the Roman *volgare* of his own day was a form of Latin, though of a highly degenerate sort. If he had accepted the existence of an independent Roman vernacular vis-à-vis literate Latin, this would have threatened the cultural–linguistic continuum that Latin had established through the ages. It would also have led to a competition between the contemporary Roman vernacular and its Florentine counterpart—a contest that Rome would surely lose (Cesarini Martinelli 1980). For Valla, then, spoken Latin (*latine loqui*) not only referred to the refined Latin of the great authors but also defined Latin more generally—and rather tautologically—as the language of the Latins (both then and now), just as the Gallic language was the language spoken by the Gauls (Camporeale 1972: 522; Tavoni 1984: 263).

The picture is therefore somewhat complicated: we have "Latin" as the language of the arts and sciences (which may have derived from the Latin spoken in antiquity), and we have depraved forms of "Latin" (the Roman vernacular and medieval-Scholastic Latin). What complicates matters even more is that Valla uses the word "natural" in different ways. He sometimes applies it to the vernacular as being the language spoken "at home or in one's city" (Florence, Naples, and so on), but he also uses the term to denote a common way of speaking opposed to the artificial language of the Scholastics (who speak "against nature" (Valla 2012: ii. 231; see also Tavoni 1986: 208–12; Nauta 2009: 277–9)). It is, therefore, not surprising that Valla frequently mentions "the common as well as the learned speech" in one breath (*popularis sermo atque eruditorum* (Valla 2012: i. 106)). His aim may be to contrast both of these categories with the "distorted", technical language of the scholastics. When, for instance, he admonishes us to speak "in a natural way and by popular custom [the way of the people]" (*naturaliter atque hominum more* (Valla 1982: i. 485)) or when he uses expressions such as "speech that is natural, speech commonly used by educated people" (*ad naturalem et a doctis tritum sermonem* (Valla 2012: ii. 208)) or "natural meaning and ordinary usage" (*ad naturalem sensum usumque commune* (Valla 2012: i. 232)), the term "natural" refers not to "vernacular" as opposed to "Latin", but to our common way of speaking and writing Latin, regarded as a natural language, as opposed to the technical and distorted language of the

Scholastics. In his discussion of the various forms of syllogism, for instance, he supports his rejection of the third form of syllogism by appealing "to learned authors as well as the simple, unlearned people, that is, those who speak naturally" (*imperitorum idest naturaliter loquentium* (Valla 1982: i. 548)).

Dependent on the context, then, Valla seems to apply "natural" for the vernacular, the users of elementary Latin, and classical Latin. But, in his fight against Scholastic language—which forms a major theme of the *Dialectical Disputations*—"natural" does not serve to distinguish the language we speak at home from the refined Latin of the learned; it refers instead to our "normal", "common", "usual" way of saying things, as opposed to the non-natural, "distorted" language of the Scholastics. Since Valla positions both classical Latin and our common way of speaking in contrast to Scholastic language, it was a short step for him to blur the distinction between learned Latin and the language of the common people, particularly when such an elision aided in his fight against that Scholastic language. Thus, at many places in the *Dialectical Disputations* his appeal to common, natural language does not serve foremost to make a grammatical point about classical Latin (though he does employ classical Latin, of course), but a broader goal: to establish what "we usually say" (*dicere solemus* (Valla 1982: i. 434; 2012: i. 234, 254, 264).

We must conclude then that Valla's view of the sources of meaning—that is, where linguistic facts come from—is diverse: local speakers of one of the many vernacular languages in the past and now, the Latin of the elite as well as the lower classes in classical antiquity, the Latin of the educated people of his own day (to be based as closely as possible on classical Latin), and Scholastic usage that does not manage to alter the semantic facts—that is, cannot assign meanings at its own will. Classical Latin was for him, as for all other humanists, of course normative, but it was normative because it was considered to be a common language, a language used far and wide and for a very long time. Linguistic custom was thus used by him in a broader sense than what the great Latin authors had written, as we can see when he pressed the *sermo popularis* and the *sermo eruditorum* into a coalition as the occasion arose (and the polemic required). Would this legitimatize calling Valla a kind of ordinary language philosopher, after all, or at least someone who defines meaning in terms of use, or what we ordinarily would say in such and such a situation? As before, the truth lies somewhere in the middle: it is not too far-fetched to see some agreements—at a suitably general level—in basic convictions about the central importance of common usage, which philosophers often misuse or disregard, and that this neglect creates confusions in philosophy. But a closer look will also show important differences, which will be the subject of the last section of this chapter.

## 4. Meaning and Linguistic Usage

Valla's appeal to "common language", to what we normally would say in such and such a situation, is a recurrent feature of his work. He believed that words and arguments should not be taken out of context, since this will easily change their normal, common meaning and, consequently, will give rise to philosophical problems where none previously existed. And this is precisely what the philosopher does, he thinks. Philosophical speculation—with its technically abstruse, vague, and esoteric vocabulary, with its tendency to disregard the grammatical rules and conventions of the Latin language—soon takes on a life of its own. Leaving the world of common experience far behind, the philosopher employs terminology that can just be handled and understood only by other philosophers. Against this, Valla champions the ordinary conception of the world and of the way it is reflected in Latin. He thus takes issue with what he considers the philosophers' *ficta*, their abstractions and theories, which take terms out of their 'ordinary' semantic network or reduce the richness of language to simplistic models. It is therefore not surprising that P. O. Kristeller, who was hardly an enthusiast for anachronistic readings of past thinkers, conceded that, in the case of Valla, "one is reminded of present-day attempts to base philosophy and especially logic on ordinary language" (Kristeller 1964: 34). Kristeller does not cite modern authors, but one can think of the ordinary language philosopher J. L. Austin, who expressed a view that Valla would have shared (Austin 1979: 182):

our common stock of words embodies all the distinctions men have found worth drawing... they surely are likely to be more numerous, more sound, since they have stood up to the long test of the survival of the fittest, and more subtle, at least in all ordinary and reasonably practical matters, than any that you or I are likely to think up in our armchairs of an afternoon—the most favored alternative method.

Austin (1962: 62) therefore complained that "philosophers often seem to think that they can just 'assign' any meaning whatever to any word". Without first exploring the richness of common language, philosophers abandon too easily and too quickly this powerful and subtle tool and advance theories and ideas that take terms out of their normal context. As Austin writes on a particular philosophical doctrine (the theory of sense-data): "it is a typically *scholastic* view, attributable, first to an obsession with a few particular words, the uses of which are over-simplified, not really understood or carefully studied or correctly described...". Austin even identifies "Scholastic" with "philosophical": "over-simplification, schematization, and constant obsessive repetition of the same small range of jejune 'examples' are not only not peculiar to this case [the doctrine of sense-data], but far too common to be dismissed as an occasional weakness of philosophers." As his close colleague and literary executor, J. O. Urmson (1998: i. 571), summarizes Austin's convictions: "Ordinary language... contains all the distinctions about the world that people have found it necessary to make" and "a much more powerful and subtle tool of thought than philosophers had traditionally recognized"; "philosophers consistently misused and abused ordinary language, blurring and perverting the distinctions it made. When they abandoned ordinary language in favor of a technical vocabulary of their own, it was usually confused and imprecise, creating confusion and darkness rather than shedding light."

If we substitute "Latin" for "ordinary language" and "Scholastics" for "modern philosophers", we can easily understand why scholars have associated Valla with ordinary language philosophy. Let me give some examples. Valla denounces Aristotle's account of number. Aristotle had said that one is not a number but the principle of number. Valla appeals to common usage to argue that this is ridiculous. In everyday practice one is counted as the first uneven number, and Valla provocatively adduces the example of "mere women" dividing eggs and taking one as the first (uneven) number, "so mere women sometimes have a better sense about understanding of words than mighty philosophers" (Valla 2012: i. 32; see also Rizzo 2002: 112): the former employ words for a purpose (*ad usum*), the latter just for a game (*ad lusum*). We find the same contrast between two ways of speaking (*loquendi formulam*)—that of the ordinary people (*populus*) and that of the philosophers—in Valla's discussion of place (Valla 2012: i. 264). The first is the most proper and correct one, says Valla, for they have "the choice and norm of speaking" (*arbitrium et normam loquendi*) on their side. We say, for instance, that a jar is empty when it lacks liquid and that the market is empty when there are no people, while philosophers deny that a jar or a market can ever be empty, since they are full of air. However, we never call something "full" when it contains nothing but air, except when the air performs a clear function: sails full of wind or a ball full of air. (The example may have been borrowed from Cicero's *De fato* 11.24.) Valla thus objects to an arbitrary restriction on the meaning of words, as if philosophers can assign, by stipulation, a meaning it normally does not have.

Philosophers do not only restrict the meaning of individual words; they also arbitrarily restrict the range of relevant words in their logical studies. They only admit "all", "some", and "no one" to express the quantity of a proposition, and only "not" to express quality (negation versus affirmation). To express modality they usually treat only six terms: "possible", "impossible", "true", "false", "necessary", and "contingent". Valla's criticism of such restrictions is that (*a*) the Scholastics often do not understand the working of these words in Latin, and (*b*) they forget that Latin is much more resourceful in expressing quantity, quality, and modality of propositions. The validity of such criticisms aside, Valla's explorations of the use and function of such words, including negation in all its variety, is an impressive achievement.

But philosophers not only arbitrarily restrict the meaning of words or range of words; they also assign new meanings to words—that is, use these words in contexts in which, Valla claims, they are not at home. "Matter" (*materia*), for instance, is erroneously applied to God. Indeed, to speak of God as an Unmoved Mover, as Aristotle and his followers had done, is to apply concepts of rest and movement outside their normal field. God does not move or rest, nor does the soul move (except in a metaphorical sense). In the same vein, final causes should not be applied to inanimate objects, as if a stone has a purpose in falling down; inanimate things lack a "purpose of mind". And to apply the term *pati*, being acted upon or to suffer, to the senses is also an abuse of terms, as if the eyes suffer when they see an object. We should apply this word to the senses only when they really suffer—for example, in a case of too loud a noise or too bright a light. In all such cases, philosophers have "no regard for usage and custom in speaking" (*usum consuetudinemque loquendi* (Valla 2012: i. 88)). In his chapter on the virtues he makes the point that Aristotle goes against linguistic usage (*loquendi consuetudo*) when he says that—Valla cites the Greek—"happiness is an activity", since, according to Valla (2012: i. 172), "good action is not happiness or enjoyment but one gets to happiness through good action and, above all, through teaching and knowledge, part of which is prudence." In this case linguistic usage does not even refer to Latin, which shows that, for Valla, it does not always refer to the literary practice of the best authors.

The appeal to linguistic usage also recurs in Valla's long chapter on the Aristotelian categories (substance, quality, action, quantity, relation, place, time, and so on). As we have already seen, Valla wanted to defend a common-sense picture of the world that consists of things that we can analyse as substances qualified by qualities and actions: we can describe a thing as a substance having certain qualities and doing or undergoing some things. From a grammatical point of view, however, "two metres long" can be considered a quality just as "white" or "father". Hence we do not need separate categories of quantity, relation, and so on: "Linguistic usage itself confirms this. For when some someone asks 'what kind of field did you buy', you answer, 'oblong at the start, then wider, two furrows long and of varying width'" (Valla 2012: i. 245). Valla uses linguistic usage also to criticize a number of other Scholastic notions and distinctions such as the six transcendental terms (true, one, good, and so on), the distinction between abstract and concrete terms (fatherhood/father, whiteness/white), virtue as a mean between two extremes.

This reduction of the categories to substance, quality, and action shows another feature of Valla's approach—a feature that also concerns meaning but at a different level. Ancient and medieval grammarians distinguished word-classes such as nouns, verbs, adjectives, pronouns, and so on, trying to relate these word-classes to aspects of reality. Verbs were generally said to signify actions, nouns substance plus quality, pronouns substance without quality, and so on. Because Valla thinks reality exists of only substances that we come to know by their qualities and actions, he tries to relate words to these three categories. In this case the search is not for a particular meaning of a (Latin) word but for the meaning (*significatio*) of a type of word. Valla finds that verbs, for instance, often "indicate" (*indicare*) a quality even though they seem to signify an action—for example, "he writes well" indicates the quality of being a fine writer rather than the action of writing. Some verbs always signify a quality: "to be cold" signifies "I am cold", "to redden" signifies "I am red", and so on. This is also the case with verbs such as "feeling happy", "hoping", and "loving". In some cases the signification may change from action into quality, as when an oration, which is an action when spoken, becomes a quality when read (Valla 2012: i. 232–4). In other cases, verbs seem to refer to the absence of action, such as "to sleep", "to lie", "to stand", "to feel sorrow", or "to rest", but this does not make sleeping, lying, and so forth less of an action (Valla 2012: i. 234–6). Such an analysis also enables Valla to reject a separate Aristotelian category of passion of which Aristotle had given the examples "being-cut" and "being-burned" (*Categories* 2ª3). Valla warns us that the passive mood of a verb does not mean that it signifies passive things. Being-affected is nothing else than to feel a passion, that is, *to act* in a certain way: "because feeling an affect is an action" (for example, understanding a danger), "or else it will be just that affect that is now a quality" (Valla 2012: i. 277). In all these cases Valla is exploring not so much the meaning of this or that (Latin) word but the meaning of words in terms of a particular state of the world: does the word signify an action, a substance plus quality, or the quality only? Consequently, it is not so much linguistic usage that is at stake here but rather the way in which our grammatical categories map onto the world. This grammatical categorization thus pertains to meaning at a different level from that of the individual (Latin) word.

With these examples we are now in a better position to see why Valla's semantic–grammatical approach has been associated with ordinary language philosophy. Like ordinary language philosophers Valla's insists on common usage as prime parameter in questions of meaning. Because language is essentially a social phenomenon, meaning can be established only by examining the multiple ways in which words are actually used. To us it might seem strange to launch a programme of study and use of language based on a dead language, classical Latin, but this was of course not the point of view of a humanist such as Valla, who was in daily contact with users of Latin. He also looks like a modern ordinary language philosopher when he criticizes the Scholastics for assigning their own meaning to existing words, for creating a jargon that often raises more problems than it solves, because it invites us to postulate abstract entities as referents of these technical words.

Hence, scholars have seen—though on a much weaker textual basis than offered in the preceding paragraphs—"strong parallels between Valla and Wittgenstein's sense of 'usage'", and between "Wittgenstein's aphorism 'Philosophy leaves everything as it is'" and "Valla's meticulous authentication of usage" (Struever 1992: 110 n. 23, 119). Valla's effort is said to be "comparable to that of the most radical reconceiver of language in our time, the later Wittgenstein", whose *Philosophical Investigations* offered "a virtual summary of Valla's main theses and attitudes" (Waswo 1979: 268) or at least "not dissimilar to the way in which Wittgenstein talks about 'the grammar of the word'" (Camporeale 1986: 233). But agreements can be deceptive, and in the last section I will indeed suggest, once again, that the truth lies somewhere in the middle. The examples I have adduced demonstrate Valla's impressive sensitivity to semantic nuances and to the way language works—but we should not forget that his grammatical approach also had ancient roots, something that makes a close association with ordinary language philosophy problematic.

## 5. Valla and Ordinary Language Philosophy

Ordinary language philosophy was, of course, not a monolithic movement, and it is probably incorrect to group Wittgenstein under this label at all. This type of philosophizing was strong in the 1950s and 1960s, often called "Oxford philosophy", and the most famous proponents were J. L. Austin and Gilbert Ryle (Hacker 1996). For many reasons, it fell into decline, and today not many philosophers would present themselves as such. Yet the type of analysis that we find in their works is still of value (and to some even more than that). For all their differences, what such philosophers have in common is the conviction that the analysis of concepts should start with a careful mapping of the ways in which these concepts are used in ordinary contexts. Ryle (1949: 10) called this mapping the "logical geography of our concepts":

To determine the logical geography of concepts is to reveal the logic of the propositions in which they are wielded, that is to say, to show with what other propositions they are consistent and inconsistent, what propositions follow from them and from what propositions they follow. The logical type or category to which a concept belongs is the set of ways in which it is logically legitimate to operate with it.

Ryle argued, for instance, that many of our mental concepts are treated as if they are a kind of physiological or physical process that can be clocked and measured. Much of his work thus aimed at putting concepts back in their proper category, correcting what he famously called "category mistakes": concepts such as enjoying and disliking do not belong to the same category as having pain (they are not sensations or feelings); seeing does not belong to the same category as pain or knee jerk (it is not an activity, a process, or a state); mental concepts such as intelligent, careful, inventive, and so on, do not refer to mysterious or occult episodes as causes of which observable actions and utterances are the effects; the doctrine of fatalism can arise because logical necessity is applied to events, and so on (Ryle 1949, 1954).

In this Ryle was inspired by Wittgenstein, who also tried to explicate and delineate the boundaries of concepts by closely examining the ways in which they are used in language. Wittgenstein famously called such enquiries "grammatical". Among these concepts studied by him were knowledge, belief, pain, perception, thought, certainty, doubt, evidence, the "I", cause and effect, intuition, meaning, promising, pretending, acting, colour, and many more. Wittgensteinian grammar tries to evoke the rules that govern our concepts by closely paying attention to the many ways in which we ordinarily use these concepts in language and in forms of life (Hacker 1996; McGinn 1997: 14). Thus, if we want to understand the concept of knowledge, we need to consider how and when we speak of knowledge, when we use phrases such as "I know $p$", and consider (imaginary) contexts in which the phrase can and cannot properly be used; other, related concepts (for example, doubt, certainty), must be taken into account as well: "When philosophers use a word—'knowledge', 'being', 'object', 'I', 'proposition', 'name'—and try to grasp the *essence* of the thing, one must always ask oneself: is the word ever actually used in this way in the language-game which is its original home" (Wittgenstein 2009: 53$^e$, §116).

With this all too brief indication of the type of conceptual analysis that these philosophers pursued, we can now see the differences between them and Valla's grammatical–semantic method. For a start, Valla does not show much interest in the type of conceptual analysis these modern philosophers practise. He is mainly interested in the Latin language, and, even though he treats it often as a common language—opposite to the esoteric, technical language of the Scholastics—he does not use this common language to philosophize about concepts such as truth, meaning, knowledge, virtue, emotion, doubt, evidence, belief, pain, and so on. Indeed, in much of what Valla says about general philosophical themes, he does not examine the concepts in any great detail. In his discussion of virtue, for instance, he simply equates virtues with emotions (affects), and the virtue fortitude with a whole range of terms such as love, charity, happiness, and beatitude. When he speaks about the soul Valla does not embark on a Wittgensteinian analysis of how and when we speak of the soul, but states—conventionally enough, of course—that it is an incorporeal substance. In his brief discussion on time he states that time is a kind of action—a type of claim that an ordinary language philosopher would characterize as highly problematic. The same is true for many other statements such as that truth is, among other things, a quality of the mind. On many such topics Valla, while often critical of particular theories, follows well-established traditions (for example, the Augustinian tradition on soul and perception), without aiming to map the "logical geography of our concepts".

To illustrate this let us take a brief look at some examples. Ryle's discussion of emotion is aimed at showing that emotions are not the sort of thing to which we have, in some mysterious way, private access: they are not "the sorts of things which could be among the direct intimations of consciousness, or among the objects of introspection, as these factitious forms or Privileged Access are ordinarily described" (Ryle 1949: 115). Such a category mistake arises because we are often associating emotions with moods and inclinations. The details of Ryle's analysis are not important here, but it is clear that Valla's claim about emotions as virtues (for reasons we do not need to go into either) is of a wholly different kind; from a Rylean point of view Valla's statement is no less a category mistake than saying that emotions are "direct intimations of consciousness". Another example comes from Wittgenstein (2009: 26e, §47):

Asking 'Is this object composite?' *outside* a particular game is like what a boy once did when he had to say whether the verbs in certain sentences were in the active or passive voice, and who racked his brains over the question whether the verb 'to sleep', for example, meant something active or passive.

Valla turns out to be such a boy. As we have seen, it was this very question about verbs in the passive and verbs seemingly indicating a lack of action such as "sleeping" that he asked, standing as he did in an age-old grammatical tradition. This background makes all the difference, as we can see when we compare Valla's question about verbs such as "sleeping" with Ryle's analysis of a particular kind of verbs that he called "achievement verbs" such as "seeing", which are "not process words, experience words, or activity words", even though they are often treated as such. "They do not stand for perplexingly undetectable actions or reactions, any more than 'win' stands for a perplexingly undetectable bit of running" (Ryle 1949: 145–6). Without going into detail, his analysis might look a bit similar to Valla's question about the category to which "sleeping" belongs: both Valla and Ryle seem to point to the possibly misleading surface grammar of certain verbs—"seeing" looks to stand for a process (Ryle), "sleeping" seems to signify an absence of action (Valla)—but the context is wholly different. Valla asks the typically grammarian's question: "Does this (type of) word refers to substance or quality or action?" He wants to have language refer to reality—that is, to his three categories: substance, quality, or action (all called "things", *res*). Ryle's investigation is of a wholly different kind and comes to a wholly different conclusion (cf. also Ryle 1954: 93–110). As said, he wants to map the logic of the concept of perception by showing that a psychological or physiological account of it puts us on the wrong track. "Seeing" is not like running: it does not stand for a bodily or psychological process. It does not refer to a process at all or to a state of being; the whole idea of looking indiscriminately for a referent "out there" is wrong. It is precisely to look for a referent "out there" that characterizes Valla's grammatical approach.

In spite of the label "ordinary language philosophy"—a label never used by the philosophers in question themselves—ordinary language is not considered sacrosanct, and this brings us to another way of seeing the differences. As Austin famously wrote: ordinary language must be the "first word" but it "has no claim to be the last word" (Austin 1979: 185), and he himself said at one point that "modern scientists have been able...to reveal its [i.e. of ordinary speech] inadequacy at numerous points" (Austin 1979: 203); hence "we may wish to tidy the situation up a bit, revise the map here and there, draw the boundaries and distinctions rather differently" (Austin 1962: 63). Similarly, Ryle also thinks that the surface grammar may lead us astray; indeed, expressions in the common language may be "systematically misleading," as the title of his famous paper from 1931 has it. Hence, a philosopher is engaging in "rectifying the logic of mental-conduct terms" (Ryle 1949: 17). Wittgenstein, too, thought that language embodies "pictures" that may mislead us into thinking, for instance, that the mind is a kind of stuff, that meanings are things in the head, or that perceiving is a bodily state. He famously spoke of the "bewitchment of our understanding by the resources of our language" (Wittgenstein 2009: 52$^e$, §109). Valla would have been greatly puzzled by these statements. For him the language that he considers as the "ordinary", common language—the *sermo eruditorum* closely associated with the *sermo popularis*—is not "bewitching" at all. He is not treating what modern philosophers call "the surface grammar" as misleading or bewitching. It is the contorted, ungrammatical, and unnatural language of the scholastics that is misleading, something that can be cured only by having restored Latin to its former beauty and expressiveness. Valla is not using classical Latin as the common language to see—to quote Ryle again—what the logical geography of concepts is in order to rectify the map. What he is doing is something else: Valla's categories—substance, quality, and action—are real aspects of reality, so that, when he attempts to relate words to one of these three categories, he is doing something entirely different from what Ryle describes as bringing concepts in their categories or "logical types"—that is "the set of ways in which it is logically legitimate to operate with it" (Ryle 1949: 10). Valla would perhaps agree with the idea that we ought to struggle "against the bewitchment of our understanding by our resources of language", but he would not share Wittgenstein's notion (2009: $7^e$, §5) that it is also the common language—and not only the technical jargon of "scientific" philosophers—that bewitches us and becomes a "fog" obscuring from view how our concepts are used and misused.

Valla's originality, therefore, is not that he anticipated the kind of analysis propagated by modern philosophers. He did not come up with revolutionary ideas about meaning nor did he engage in Wittgensteinian "grammatical" enquiries or Rylean "conceptual cartography". His significance was rather that—together with other humanists—he launched a new approach towards the study of Latin, which emphasized the careful examination of the language, starting from the premiss that language is essentially a social phenomenon and hence should be studied against the background of the shared rules that govern its use. But it had its philosophical significance and implications: a turn towards language led to a growing awareness that language is a shaping force of our thinking about the world as well as an instrument in shaping other people's ideas and feelings about the world. With a grounding in human conventions, meanings—in all their variety—become glasses through which the world is seen.

# References

Ashworth, E. J. (1981). '"Do Words Signify Ideas or Things?" The Scholastic Sources of Locke's Theory of Language', *Journal of the History of Philosophy*, xix: 299–326 (repr. in E. J. Ashworth, *Studies in Post-Medieval Semantics* (Aldershot: Variorum, 1985), no. VII).
Austin, J. L. (1962). *Sense and Sensibilia*, ed. G. Warnock. Oxford: Oxford University Press.
Austin, J. L. (1979). *Philosophical Papers*, ed. J. O. Urmson and G. Warnock. Oxford: Oxford University Press.
Camporeale, S. I. (1972). *Lorenzo Valla: Umanesimo e teologia*. Florence.
Camporeale, S. I. (1986). 'Lorenzo Valla, "Repastinatio, liber primus": Retorica e linguaggio', in O. Besomi and M. Regoliosi (eds), *Lorenzo Valla e l'umanesimo italiano. Atti del convegno internazionale di studi umanistici*. Padua: Antenore, 217–39.

Cave, T. (1979). *The Cornucopian Text: Problems of Writing in the French Renaissance*. Oxford: Oxford University Press.
Cesarini Martinelli, L. (1980). 'Note sulla polemica Poggio-Valla e sulla fortuna delle *Elegantiae*', *Interpres: rivista di studi quattrocenteschi*, 3: 29–79.
Gerl, H.-B. (1974). *Rhetorik als Philosophie. Lorenzo Valla*. Munich: Fink.
Hacker, P. M. S. (1996). *Wittgenstein's Place in Twentieth-Century Analytical Philosophy*. Oxford: Blackwell.
Henry, D. P. (1999). 'Review Article: The Philosophy of Abelard', *British Journal for the History of Philosophy*, 7: 141–5.
Kristeller, P. O. (1964). *Eight Philosophers of the Italian Renaissance*. Stanford: Stanford University Press.
Kristeller, P. O. (1979). *Renaissance Thought and its Sources*. New York: Columbia University Press.
McGinn, M. (1997). *Wittgenstein and the Philosophical Investigations*. London: Routledge.
Mack, P. (1993). *Renaissance Argument: Valla and Agricola in the Traditions of Rhetoric and Dialectic*. Leiden: Brill.
Monfasani, J. (1989). 'Was Lorenzo Valla an Ordinary Language Philosopher?', *Journal of the History of Philosophy*, 50: 309–23; repr. in J. Monfasani, *Language and Learning in Renaissance Italy: Selected Articles* (Aldershot: Variorum, 1994), no. IV.
Nauta, L. (2009). *In Defense of Common Sense: Lorenzo Valla's Humanist Critique of Scholastic Philosophy*. Cambridge, MA: Harvard University Press.
Nauta, L. (2011). 'Philology as Philosophy: Giovanni Pontano on Language, Meaning, and Grammar', *Journal of the History of Ideas*, 72: 481–502.
Nauta, L. (2012). 'Anti-Essentialism and the Rhetoricization of Knowledge: Mario Nizolio's Humanist Attack on Universals', *Renaissance Quarterly*, 65: 31–66.
Pinborg, J. (1976). 'Some Problems in Medieval Semantic Representations in Medieval Logic', in H. Parret (ed.), *History of Linguistic Thought and Contemporary Linguistics*. Berlin: de Gruyter, 254–78.
Rizzo, S. (2002). *Ricerche sul latino umanistico*. Rome: Edizioni di Storia e Letteratura.
Ryle, G. (1949). *The Concept of Mind*. London: Hutchinson.
Ryle, G. (1954). *Dilemmas*. Cambridge: Cambridge University Press.
Spade, P. V. (1982). 'The Semantics of Terms', in N. Kretzmann, A. Kenny and J. Pinborg (eds), *The Cambridge History of Later Medieval Philosophy*. Cambridge: Cambridge University Press, 188–96.
Struever, N. (1992). *Theory as Practice: Ethical Inquiry in the Renaissance*. Chicago: University of Chicago Press.
Tavoni, M. (1984). *Latino, grammatica, volgare: Storia di una questione umanistica*. Padua: Antenore.
Tavoni, M. (1986). 'Lorenzo Valla e il volgare', in O. Besomi and M. Regoliosi (eds), *Lorenzo Valla e l'umanesimo italiano. Atti del convegno internazionale di studi umanistici*. Padua: Antenore, 199–216.
Urmson, J. O. (1998). 'Austin, J. L.', in *Routledge Encyclopedia of Philosophy*. London: Routledge, i. 571–4.
Valla, L. (1982). *Repastinatio dialectice et philosophie*, ed. G. Zippel. 2 vols. Padua: Antenore.

Valla, L. (2012). *Dialectical Disputations*, ed. and trans. B. P. Copenhaver and L. Nauta. 2 vols. Cambridge, MA: Harvard University Press.
Waswo, R. (1979). 'The "Ordinary Language Philosophy" of Lorenzo Valla', *Bibliothèque d'Humanisme et Renaissance*, 41: 255–71.
Waswo, R. (1987). *Language and Meaning in the Renaissance*. Princeton: Princeton University Press.
Wittgenstein, L. (1958). *Blue and Brown Books*. Oxford: Blackwell.
Wittgenstein, L. (2009). *Philosophical Investigations*. 4th rev. edn, trans. G. E. M. Anscombe, P. M. S. Hacker, and J. Schulte. Oxford: Wiley-Blackwell.

# 8

# Medieval Theories of Signification to John Locke

E. Jennifer Ashworth

## Introduction

Locke wrote that "*Words*... came to be made use of by Men, as *the Signs of* their *Ideas*... The use then of Words, is to be sensible Marks of *Ideas*; and the *Ideas* they stand for, are their proper and immediate Signification" (*Essay*, 3.2.1).[1] Behind this brief and controversial passage lies a long development of interrelated discussions of the Aristotelian semantic triangle: the discussion of spoken words as signs, both of things and of concepts; the discussion of whether the things signified are natures (whatever their ontological status) or individual existents; and the discussion of ordering: do words signify things or concepts primarily? In this chapter I hope to do three things: (i) trace the history of developments from the thirteenth to the seventeenth century; (ii) throw some light on the issue of whether the theory of signification is a theory of meaning; (iii) illuminate the immediate background to Locke on language.[2]

My treatment is partly synoptic, partly chronological. Given the long period I am dealing with, and the complicated doctrinal history involved, I shall simplify my account by tracing just a few influential doctrines and focusing on just a few authors, though I shall make occasional references to other figures. The main path I intend to follow starts with Thomas Aquinas (1224/5–74), for, although he was not a logician, he had many things to say about language, and his views, particularly as found in his unfinished commentary on Aristotle's *Peri hermeneias*, were influential in the sixteenth and seventeenth centuries.[3] I shall then turn to the two fourteenth-century

---

[1] Quotations are taken from Locke (1975), but references will be given in standard format so that other editions can also be used.
[2] See Ashworth (1981, 1984, 1987) for discussion of the sixteenth- and seventeenth-century background.
[3] For a wider perspective on the earlier period, see Rosier (1994) and Rosier-Catach (2004). For more on Aquinas, see Ashworth (1999). References to Aquinas will be given in standard format, since there are many editions (and some translations) of his works.

nominalists, William of Ockham (c.1287-1347) and John Buridan (1295/1300-1358/ 61).[4] Both men were very influential at the University of Paris in the late fifteenth and early sixteenth centuries, though Thomism also had a role to play there. For my purposes, the most important product of the Parisian schools is the Dominican, Domingo de Soto (1494-1560), who, while absorbing many features of nominalist logic, is more properly described as an eclectic Thomist. He published his popular logical works after his return to Spain, where he retained a strong influence into the seventeenth century. Another important Iberian was the Portuguese Jesuit Petrus Fonseca (1528-99), whose work inspired the *Conimbricenses*, commentaries on Aristotle's works produced by the Jesuits at Coimbra. The volume on Aristotle's Organon was first published in 1606. Other significant Jesuit authors include the two Spaniards Franciscus Toletus (1533-96) and Antonius Rubius (1548-1615) and the Polish logician Martinus Smiglecius (1564-1618). The importance of these late Scholastic authors is twofold. First, they were all moderate realists in the Thomistic tradition, although they were well acquainted with nominalism and Scotism. Second, they were read throughout Europe and, in particular, were used at the University of Oxford. Descartes told Mersenne that he recalled reading the *Conimbricenses*, Toletus, and Rubius (AT III, 185),[5] and, when Locke was teaching at Christ Church, Oxford, he recorded in a notebook that his students bought works by Smiglecius (Ashworth 1981: 304).

## Background Assumptions about Human Language and its Origins

During the medieval and post-medieval periods a number of common assumptions were made about language, at least by those working within the Aristotelian tradition. Language was taken to be natural to human beings: as social animals, we have a need to communicate with each other, and we have been endowed with voices as an appropriate instrument for communication. Animals too can be both social and communicative, but their noises express only sensory and emotional states such as pain, hunger, and fear, and these noises, in the form of barking, neighing, and so on, are natural in the further sense that they are the same for all members of the species, and no choice or decision is involved. While humans do express bodily states through such natural signs as groans, we are rational animals and as such we form concepts, which we also wish to express. Moreover, in so far as the words we use to express our concepts were instituted or imposed by humans, those humans—the impositors— must have had concepts prior to their act of imposition, and their first interlocutors, like our current interlocutors, must also have had a sufficient conceptual framework

---

[4] For nominalism, see Biard (1989), Panaccio (2004), and Klima (2009).
[5] I give standard references to the Adam and Tannery edition (Descartes 1897-1913).

to interpret what they were hearing. A certain primacy was thus given to mental content.

How humans first came to use spoken language was a matter of discussion. Particularly in the sixteenth and seventeenth centuries, some logicians, including the *Conimbricenses* (Doyle 2001: 140), adopted the theory of divine infusion, whereby God infused language into Adam. In his commentary on Aristotle's *Peri hermeneias*, the earlier German logician and theologian Johannes Eckius (1486–1543) had gone even further, and argued that, whatever the case with Adam, after the destruction of the Tower of Babel, God had infused such languages as German into groups of human beings (Eckius 1516–17: fo. lxxi rb). Nonetheless, most logicians preferred the notion of an original human impositor of language, who endows particular vocal sounds with particular significations. In the medieval Christian tradition, Adam was often given this role, but logicians frequently spoke of unspecified people, groups, and entire communities as having the authority to impose.

The next question was what guided them in their imposition. Knowledge was the key here. Adam was supposed to have perfect knowledge, and even those who preferred not to speak of Adam agreed that language should be produced by those with an appropriate knowledge of what they intended to speak about. For instance, logical terms should be imposed by logicians, and grammatical terms by grammarians. But how did the term chosen relate to the thing spoken of? There was occasional discussion, for instance, by Henry of Ghent (d. 1293) in the late thirteenth century (Rosier 1995: 196–214)[6] and the *Conimbricenses* at the beginning of the seventeenth century (Doyle 2001: 132–42), of whether language could be natural in the sense that simply knowing the spoken word gave some kind of direct access to the nature of the thing spoken of. If this were the case, the impositor would have to match the sound chosen to the properties of the thing spoken of in accordance with the properties of the sound. However, no logician, at least in the predominant Aristotelian tradition, was ready to adopt such a view, and the general agreement was that language could not be natural in that sense. Simply knowing a sound can give us no access to what it signifies. Accordingly, the imposition of language was said to be *ad placitum* (or *secundum placitum*).

This phrase is often translated as 'conventional' or even 'arbitrary', but neither translation is entirely appropriate. 'Conventional' is not a helpful translation. In his translation of Aristotle, Boethius may have taken the phrase *secundum placitum* to mean something like "according to what is agreable", which fits in with the notion of convention, but later logicians seem to take the phrase to mean "at the pleasure of the impositor", and Buridan asked, in the obvious expectation of receiving a negative response, whether words could be newly imposed at my pleasure or at your pleasure (Buridan 1983: 16). Similarly Ockham said that the imposition of a word was "at the

---

[6] Rosier (1995) has a substantial discussion, pp. 145–91, and an edited text, pp. 192–253.

pleasure of the institutor".⁷ Conventions arose only when subsequent speakers adopted the original imposition as their own, and thus allowed the pleasure of the original impositor to persist.

'Arbitrary' is not a helpful translation either. Locke speaks of "a voluntary Imposition, whereby such a Word is made arbitrarily the Mark of such an Idea" (*Essay*, 3.2.1), and it is true that, once the idea of natural signification had been dismissed, the actual sound chosen would be arbitrary, not only in the original sense of related to the will, but also in the sense of being random. Nonetheless, particularly in the Thomistic tradition, the impositor was taken to be rationally motivated by his knowledge of the thing spoken of. That is, the sound chosen would be matched to a significate that reflected knowledge of the world, that cut the world up in the right way (Ashworth 2013: 262–3). It is important to stress here that, for all the logicians I am discussing, realist assumptions underlay their account of imposition. There is an external world with which we are acquainted through our senses and about which we speak. For non-nominalists there were also common natures, genera, and species that enjoyed some kind of existence, albeit not that of a Platonic Idea. Even nominalists such as Ockham believed that there were kinds of things in the sense that there were groups of maximally similar individuals to which we could successfully refer by means of common nouns, and about which we have a strong tendency to agree. Aristotle had claimed that concepts are the same for all, or, at least, all those with similar experiences, and this claim was not seriously questioned. Here Locke strongly differentiated himself from the Aristotelian tradition, for he preferred to emphasize the variability of human experience and human concepts.

The first imposition to take place was of what came to be called categorematic terms: nouns referring to individual objects in the external world, and most particularly medium-sized physical objects near at hand and easily identifiable. The model of Adam naming the animals is important here, for he started by imposing natural kind terms. Words signifying mental, fictional, and impossible entities such as chimeras—the medieval equivalent of round squares—raise problems that I shall not discuss here. Syncategorematic terms, those terms such as logical operators that perform a function in propositions, were imposed subsequently, and, given that one could not easily appeal to the process of pointing at something while uttering such a term, logicians usually shied away from the question of how their imposition took place. Moreover, in their main discussions of what words signify, and how they are related to concepts and to things, they tend to ignore syncategorematic terms.⁸

The view that imposition begins with categorematic terms was closely related to a compositionalist view whereby propositions acquire their signification from the individual terms that enter into them, and their interrelationships. At the same

---

⁷ Ockham (1978: 348): "Hoc tamen non est nisi ad placitum instituentis."

⁸ In part this is because the discussion of words, concepts, and things usually occurred in commentary on Aristotle's definition of the name in *De interpretatione* 16ª19–20. Note that the term used in the Latin translation is *nomen*, which means both noun and name.

time, it was also related to a theory about how the mind works. First we acquire simple concepts, then we make judgements that involve the formation of propositions, and finally we arrange propositions into arguments. If there are no simple concepts, then there is no beginning point, and judgements cannot be made, nor can reasoning take place.

Here the notion of 'simple concept' needs some explanation, especially in relation to the views of John Locke. In general, such terms as 'man' and 'horse' were accepted as simple terms, and were subordinated to simple concepts. These concepts were simple both because they were not initially formed by the combination of more primitive concepts and because, although they represented a complex reality, they did so in a confused manner. That is, the elements of the representation were not distinguished but fused together, and only later analysis would, in principle at least, bring us from the initial confused concept to the fully articulated concept revealed by an Aristotelian real definition. Given this approach, along with the belief that living things are indeed divided into natural kinds, we can understand why terms such as 'horse' were regarded as simple lexical and conceptual items, to be contrasted with terms such as 'father' whose definition includes a relationship to children, and with phrasal items such as 'bearded man'. Drawing a distinction between concepts that function as simple semantic items despite their confused representation of metaphysically complex objects, and concepts that are simple in the sense of being both primitive and non-complex in what they represent, actually or potentially, allows us to understand the difference between the Aristotelian–Scholastic and the Lockean account. For Locke, a concept such as 'horse' is not merely complex, but is formed by composition from more primitive concepts that are epistemologically prior.

We now need to explore the notion of signification in more detail.

## Signification and Meaning

The central notion for medieval and post-medieval logicians in their discussion of language is signification, and here we must consider three key texts, two from Aristotle in Boethius' Latin translation, and one from Augustine. Medieval and post-medieval logicians usually took Aristotle's texts as the starting point for their discussion of signification, and supplemented them by one or other of Augustine's definitions of sign, though in the sixteenth century reference was often made to similar definitions in other classical sources.

I will start with Augustine's definition of sign in *On Christian Doctrine*: "A sign is a thing that causes us to think of something beyond the impression (*species*) that the thing itself makes upon the senses."[9] He went on to explain that spoken words were one kind of sign, differing from other kinds, such as smoke as a sign of fire, or a groan

---

[9] Augustine (1962: II.i.1, p. 32): "Signum est enim res praeter speciem, quam ingerit sensibus, aliud aliquid ex se faciens in cogitationem uenire...".

as a sign of pain. Complications were introduced by the view, prevalent by the fourteenth century, though found earlier, that the concept was itself a sign. This led to the qualification that concepts were formal signs, whereas spoken words were instrumental signs, and that Augustine's definition applied only to the latter. In the thirteenth century Roger Bacon (d. c.1292) subordinated the notion of a linguistic sign to the notion of a sign in general, but other logicians, such as Peter of Spain,[10] focused on the spoken word. It was only in the sixteenth century that logicians, as opposed to theologians, returned to a full account of signs. Domingo de Soto and other logicians writing in early sixteenth-century Paris gave elaborate classifications, which were taken up by the *Conimbricenses*. Moreover, in the sixteenth century the Aristotelian and Stoic tradition of signs as natural indicators and the bases for inference was also well known, not only through its presence in rhetoric texts and in the 1564 Latin translation of Sextus Empiricus, but also through medical literature. Locke's reference to "semeiotike, or *the Doctrine of Signs*" (*Essay*, 4.21.4) seems to spring from the latter source.[11]

The first of the two key Aristotelian texts uses the notion of sign (or, at least, was so interpreted). It comes from *De interpretatione* $16^a 3$–5, which was read as saying "Spoken words are signs [*notae*] of concepts [*passiones*]".[12] This passage places the emphasis on the speaker who is expressing his own concepts. It is in the same passage ($16^a 6$–8) that Aristotle goes on to say that concepts are similitudes of things, and are the same for all.[13]

The third text is from *De interpretatione* $16^b 19$–21, which was read as saying that to signify is to generate or establish an understanding (*significare est intellectum constituere*).[14] This definition places the emphasis on the hearer who, in understanding what the speaker says, actualizes a concept he already has, or perhaps forms a new concept, if the speaker is pointing to a hitherto unnoticed object and uttering its name.

Each of these three key texts is tied to signification as a psychologico-causal property of words, and no mention is made of the semantic and syntactic functions of the significative term. In this respect, Ockham stands apart from other authors, for in his definitions he appeals to the theory of supposition that was used to specify the type and range of reference had by the subject and predicate terms of propositions.[15]

---

[10] Peter of Spain probably flourished in the 1230s and 1240s. There is a dispute about who he was, but it seems certain that he was not the person who became Pope John XXI.
[11] For further discussion of signs, see Ashworth (1990a, 1990b), Biard (1989), Demonet (1992), and Meier-Oeser (1997).
[12] Aristotle (1965: 5. 4–6): "Sunt ergo ea quae sunt in voce earum quae sunt in anima passionum notae."
[13] Aristotle (1965: 5. 8–9): "eaedem omnibus passiones animae sunt, et quorum hae similitudines, res etiam eaedem."
[14] Aristotle (1965: 7. 14–16): "Ipsa quidem secundum se dicta verba nomina sunt et significant aliquid—constituit enim qui dicit intellectum, et qui audit quiescit."
[15] Signification is generally speaking wider than supposition, since, for most authors, supposition was a property of terms in a proposition. This is why Ockham speaks of a term's being able to supposit rather than of its actually suppositing.

In his *Summa logicae*, after excluding the general sense of sign that embraces the circle outside a tavern as a sign of wine, he gives an initial definition of a verbal sign as either (i) what brings something to cognition and is able to supposit for that thing, or (ii) what, like syncategorematic terms and verbs, is able to be added to a suppositing term in a proposition, or (iii) what, like a phrase or sentence (*oratio*), is able to be composed of the two other kinds of sign.[16] This passage, however, needs to be supplemented by a later passage (Ockham 1974: 95-6) in which he distinguishes four definitions of signification, from the narrowest to the most general. Even there supposition plays a major role.

While we will return to supposition theory below, the most influential definition in the later period, especially at Paris, was not Ockham's but that given in the late fourteenth-century *Conceptus et insolubilia* by Peter of Ailly (1350-1420). He wrote that "to signify is to represent something, or some things, or in some way to a cognitive power by vitally changing it".[17] The explicit mention of representation was not new, for in the mid-thirteenth century the popular logician Peter of Spain had already defined signification as the representation of a thing by means of an utterance *secundum placitum*,[18] but reference to the effect on a cognitive power, already found in Augustine, now became standard. Soto wrote that "to signify, taken generally, is to represent something other than itself to a cognitive power",[19] and later Fonseca wrote that "to signify is nothing other than to represent something to a cognizing power".[20]

This emphasis on the psychologico-causal property of significant terms, and the lack of reference to their semantic and syntactic functions by authors other than Ockham, strongly suggests that the notion of signification cannot be treated as if it were precisely equivalent to the notion of meaning. Critics often point out that it is inappropriate to identify a meaning with a mental or physical thing or a set of behavioural responses, and criticize Locke in particular for a mistaken ideational theory of meaning. However, whether or not we agree that to give the meaning of a word is not to name some item to which the word is related in some way, we can sensibly say that a spoken word signifies or makes known an item, whether mental or physical, conceptual or real, universal or particular. Moreover, meaning is

---

[16] Ockham (1974: 9). "Aliter accipitur signum pro illo quod aliquid facit in cognitionem venire et natum est pro illo supponere vel tali addi in propositione, cuiusmodi sunt syncategoremata et verba et illae partes orationis quae finitam significationem non habent, vel quod natum est componi ex talibus, cuiusmodi est oratio." Panaccio (2004: 48-9), correctly argues against an interpretation of Ockham's words that would include "bring something to mind and" in clauses (ii) and (iii).

[17] Peter of Ailly (1498), sig. a 1 ra (and Spade 1980: 16): "Significare autem est potentie cognitive eam vitaliter immutando aliquid vel aliqua vel aliqualiter representare." He added 'in some way' (*aliqualiter*) in order to cover the case of syncategorematic terms.

[18] Peter of Spain (1972: 79): "Significatio termini, prout hic sumitur, est rei per vocem secundum placitum representatio." Cf. p. 2: "Vox significativa ad placitum est illa que ad voluntatem instituentis aliquid representat, ut '*homo*'."

[19] Soto (1529: fo. v ra): "significare, generaliter dictum, est potentie cognitive aliud a se representare."

[20] Fonseca (1964: 34): "significare nihil aliud est, quam potentiae cognoscenti, aliquid repraesentare."

not transitive, but signification was often so regarded. Thus Lambert of Auxerre (or Lagny[21]) wrote: "A spoken word that is a sign of a sign, that is, of an understanding, will be a sign of the significate, that is, of the thing. However, it is immediately a sign of the understanding but mediately a sign of the thing."[22] It is also relevant to note that proper names were taken to have signification, and provided one standard example of chance equivocals (homonyms) on the grounds that each proper name has many significates.[23] This is not to deny that medieval thinkers had a general notion of meaning. They did talk about sense (*sensus*), about the thought or content (*sententia*) of a phrase, about the force of a word (*vis verbi*), and about its force when used in its proper sense (*virtus sermonis*). Moreover, they often used the word *significatio* itself along with its cognates quite widely. For instance, Domingo de Soto drew a distinction between the common signification involved in our understanding of 'this man' in the context-free written sentence "This man is disputing", and the particular signification the phrase has if we utter it while pointing to Peter (Soto 1539–40: fo. xix rb). In the latter case, it simply signifies Peter.

If we return to the first text from Aristotle, we can see that we have now been presented with the semantic triangle formed by words, concepts, things, and their various relationships. While the notion of the spoken word is largely regarded as unproblematic here (though there is ample discussion in other contexts), exactly what was meant by 'concept' and by 'thing' was a matter of disagreement, as was the issue of exactly how the three elements of the triangle were interrelated. That is, do words signify just concepts, or just things, or both concepts and things, and, if the latter, is there an order of priority that can be established? In order to answer these questions in turn, we need to explore the various senses of 'concept' and of 'thing' (that is, the various senses of the words so translated).

## The Semantic Triangle: 1. What Is a Concept?

There was general agreement that concepts have a representative function, especially given Aristotle's remark that they are similitudes, and they were usually regarded as temporally limited mental acts, but there was a disagreement about what counted as a concept, expressed by the changing vocabulary used of mental contents. The study of this vocabulary begins with the passage from Aristotle quoted earlier that, in its Latin translation, uses the word *passio* or mental affection. In his commentary on the *Peri hermeneias* I.2.5 Aquinas asked why Aristotle had used this word, and he suggested that it was because people are moved to speak by such passions as love and hate, and

---

[21] There is a dispute about who Lambert was, and his dates are not known, but his logic text is thought to date from between 1250 and 1255.

[22] Lambert of Auxerre (1971: 206): "Vox que est signum signi, scilicet intellectus, erit signum significati, scilicet rei, sed immediate est signum intellectus, mediate autem signum rei."

[23] The view that proper names signify raises awkward questions about the possibility of singular concepts. For further discussion, see Ashworth (2004).

because concepts (*intellectus conceptiones*) themselves come from sensory impressions, which are also a kind of passion (or reception). Be that as it may, everyone, including Aquinas, agreed that neither of these senses is appropriate, and that some other word must be used.

In the mid-thirteenth century, the *passio* was generally identified with the intelligible species, produced by the intellect through abstraction from the sensible species received from an external object.[24] Lambert wrote that the signification of a term was the understanding (*intellectus*) of a thing, and that this understanding was a *species* or similitude (Lambert of Auxerre 1971: 205). Similarly John Duns Scotus (1265/6–1308) in the first of his two commentaries on the *Peri hermeneias* began with the question "Does a name signify a thing or a species in the soul",[25] and focused on intelligible species in both commentaries (Pini 1999: 26). However, in *Summa theologiae* Ia.85.2, Aquinas had already attacked the claim that the passions of the mind (*passiones animae*) are intelligible species. He argued that the intelligible species is that by which the intellect understands, and not what is understood. Accordingly, he distinguished between intelligible species and the conceptions of the intellect (*conceptiones intellectus*), and, quoting Aristotle, he frequently writes that the *ratio* that a name signifies is the intellect's conception of the thing signified by the name.[26] In other places he refers to an inner word. Thus in his commentary on St John's Gospel I.1.26 he writes of the inner word as that in which the understanding understands the nature of the thing understood. In *De potentia* 8.1 he remarks that a conception (*conceptio*) is the same as the inner word (*verbum*) but not the same as the intelligible species. Similar remarks are found in post-medieval Thomists. For instance, Rubius wrote that what we signify to others is the 'expressed' species (*species expressa*—so called because it is derived from the intelligible species) or concept (*conceptus*) or mental word (*verbum mentis*) (Rubius 1641: 365A).

Rubius used *conceptus* where Aquinas had used *conceptio*, and by the fourteenth century the word *conceptus* had become the preferred option. However, this is not as simple as it seems, since the word-form *conceptus* is both a noun and a perfect passive participle of the verb 'to conceive', and in the latter case it has an adjectival function, being able to characterize either something produced by the physical act of generation, or something conceived by the mind.[27] As Ockham argued, like Roger Bacon before him, this produces an ambiguity in the frequently used phrase 'concept of the mind' (*conceptus mentis*). The phrase can refer to a thought, but it can also refer to

---

[24] In this context, 'species' has a technical meaning that differs from that used in the context "Horse is a species of the genus animal." Scotus (1891a: 540B) explained that the intelligible species is an intelligible similitude, and the sensible species is the similitude of a sensible thing.

[25] Scotus (1891a: 540A): "Utrum nomen significat rem, vel speciem in anima."

[26] e.g., *ST* Ia.13.4: "Ratio enim quam significat nomen, est conceptio intellectus de re significata per nomen." The reference is to Aristotle, *Metaphysics* 1012$^a$24–25. The word *ratio* is not easily translatable. It can mean roughly the same as concept, or conceptual content, or essence, or common nature, or even Platonic Idea.

[27] For further discussion of the history of '*conceptus*', see Biard (2009).

"everything cognized by the intellect".[28] Ockham was interested only to reject the ambiguity, especially as he came to regard concepts as cognitive acts directly related to individual things without any need to postulate intentional objects as their contents or products, but it may lie behind the distinction that arose in the fourteenth century between the *conceptus formalis*, the concept conceived as an act of the mind, and the *conceptus obiectivus*, the object of the concept, the thing as thought. Thus the Franciscan Peter Aureol (c.1280-1322) had spoken of the *conceptus obiectivus* and said that a thing is called a *conceptus* because it is conceived of passively (*includit ipsum concipi passivum*) (cited in Nuchelmans 1983: 22).

This distinction relates back to Aquinas's distinction between the intelligible species and the inner word or conception, especially when we consider his identification of the universal concept with the form of the object understood,[29] and it was still very important for post-medieval writers in the Thomistic tradition.[30] For instance, in his commentary on Porphyry's *Isagoge*, Domingo de Soto wrote: "Note that there are two kinds of concept. One is the formal concept, which is the quality of the cognitive power by which we cognize a thing formally, and the other is the objective concept, which is formally the object immediately signified by the formal concept, that is, by the act of cognizing (*notitia*)."[31] He explained (Soto 1587: 114B) that the objective concept was the *ratio* signified in the things (*ratio significata in rebus*). Later Fonseca wrote that the *conceptus obiectivus* is the thing that is understood according to the form or nature conceived by the formal concept,[32] or the thing that is understood, in so far as it is represented by the formal concept.[33]

Obviously this notion of an objective concept raises a number of problems: is the thing as thought an intentional object, or a common nature that has some kind of existence independent of both the mind and external objects, or is it the external object itself seen as characterized by an essence and standing in a certain relationship to the thinking subject? Those in the Thomistic tradition in the sixteenth and seventeenth centuries were inclined to adopt the first view for two reasons. First, they held that nothing outside the mind exists as universal, so that the universal thing as thought could have only what was called objective existence (*esse*)—that is, existence as an internal object of thought. Second, the notions of objective concepts and objective existence allowed them to solve various problems of signification.

---

[28] Ockham (1979a: 50): "mentis conceptus aliquando vocatur omne cognitum ab intellectu." Cf. Bacon (1988: 70).
[29] See Klima, Chapter 6, this volume.
[30] See Ashworth (1997, 1998), and Nuchelmans (1983: 9-35).
[31] Soto (1587, 28B and 30B): "notandum est duplicem esse conceptum. Alius est formalis, qui est qualitas potentiae cognoscitivae, qua res formaliter cognoscimus; et alius est conceptus obiectivus, qui est formaliter obiectum immediate significatum per conceptum formalem, puta per notitiam."
[32] Fonseca (1615: vol. I, col. 711): "Conceptus obiectivus est res, quae intelligitur, secundum eam formam, naturamve quae per formalem concipitur."
[33] Fonseca (1615: vol. I, col. 712): "conceptus obiectivus respondet conceptui formali, cum sit nihil aliud, quam res quae intelligitur, quatenus per formalem repraesentatur…"

While the objective concepts of natural kind terms such as 'man' were directly derived from the real common natures that existed only as characterizing external individuals, the objective concepts of other terms, such as negations and privations, as well as fictitious terms such as 'chimera' and analogical terms such as 'being' (*ens*), could be explained without the postulation of any special kind of nature.[34] The notion of 'objective concept' has an obvious bearing on the construal of the third member of the semantic triangle, the thing, which is discussed in the next section.

The vocabulary used of concepts had changed completely by the time we reach Locke, who consistently used the word 'idea' for our mental contents. A theoretical point lay behind the seventeenth-century use of this word as it was popularized by Descartes, for in his *Replies to Objections* he had claimed that he chose it because it was the term used to refer to God's forms of perception (AT VII, 181), thus implicitly suggesting that he had chosen it in order to break with the Aristotelian account of concepts as related to our sensations of external objects. Unsurprisingly, given Locke's empiricism, his use of the word seems to be less ideologically motivated, since he said that he used the term 'idea' "to express whatever is meant by *Phantasm, Notion, Species*, or whatever it is, which the Mind can be employ'd about in thinking" (*Essay*, 1.1.8), especially as in Scholastic vocabulary phantasms were the result of imagination's processing of the sensible species.[35]

## The Semantic Triangle: 2. What Is a Thing?

When 'things' appear in the semantic triangle, it is natural to think primarily of individual physical objects, and this was reinforced by Aristotle's frequently quoted remark that we use words to refer to things, because we cannot bring actual things into disputations (*Sophistical Refutations*, 165$^a$6–10). However, while medieval and post-medieval logicians were insistent that the truth of ordinary propositions such as "A man is running" depended on reference to individuals in the world around us, they also recognized that signification must be independent of the physical objects that exist here and now if we want words to keep their signification through time. One set of solutions to this problem was approached through discussion of the relationship between theories of signification and theories of supposition, the type and range of reference to be ascribed to terms within a proposition. What a term signifies may or may not be identified with what a term supposits for. On the one hand, Lambert had expressed a view that was and remained widespread when he wrote that we must make a sharp distinction between signification and supposition, for a term must have signification before it can acquire supposition. Moreover, while the word 'man' signifies man as such or humanity, and can even supposit for these in

---

[34] For analogical terms, see Ashworth (1997, 1998).
[35] We have already seen how Scholastics used the word *species*. For *notio* as an alternative to *conceptus*, see Burgersdijck (1650: 9).

certain special contexts, it does not signify such individuals as Socrates and Plato, but only supposits for them (Lambert 1971, 206-7). This allows signification to endure even though individuals do not. On the other hand, Ockham, as we saw above, had linked signification to supposition, but he made it clear that, if we are to avoid a constant change in signification, we need to say that a term such as 'man' is a sign of the singular things that that term can supposit for in propositions about the past, present, future, or what may possibly be (Ockham 1974: 95).[36]

One of the things that differentiates Ockham from Lambert is the nominalist belief that only individual substances and their individual qualities (including their mental acts) exist, and that only concepts can properly be described as universal. Hence there are no common natures or essences that might serve as the 'things' signified by a spoken word, and there is no problem attached to the notion of 'thing', at least where natural kind terms are concerned. For those who accepted some kind of realism with respect to common natures, matters were more complicated, partly because there were differing views on whether individual physical objects could be known at all, and partly because the nature and the individual might both be said to be signified, especially for those in the Thomistic tradition who took it that common natures existed only in so far as they characterized individuals.

Aquinas, who did not want to give common natures any kind of intermediary existence independent of both concepts and singular things, nonetheless struggled with the issue of what would count as a thing signified. On the one hand, whatever it is that is understood through the universal nature abstracted by the mind must be independent of the mind. On the other hand, there are, according to Aquinas, epistemological and metaphysical reasons for denying that physical individuals are understood as individual. In the first place, even though natures exist outside the mind only as individualized, individuals that are composites of form and matter cannot be known directly because of their materiality (*ST* Ia.86.1), and, as a result, they cannot properly be said to be understood and hence signified. In the second place, Aquinas often claimed that the act of existence is what individualizes. In *De veritate* 2.11 he explained that *existing* as a man is not common to Peter and Paul, whereas humanity is, and that is why 'is a man' can be said of both univocally, yet apparently without any implication that 'man' signifies Peter and Paul. Generally speaking, Aquinas held that the thing signified (*res significata*) was a property or a nature as it characterized individual external objects, but with the emphasis on 'nature' rather than 'individual'.[37]

Other non-nominalist authors were more inclined to place the emphasis on individuals, while nonetheless allowing essences some kind of priority. The Franciscan

---

[36] A number of further qualifications need to be introduced here, to allow for the effect of a variety of propositional contexts on the type and range of reference permitted. For instance, in "'man' is a monosyllable" 'man' supposits for the word 'man' and its equiforms.

[37] See *In Perihermenias* I.1.5, *ST* Ia.13.1 ad 2. Cf. Rubius (1641: 368A).

Peter John Olivi (1247/8–98) wrote that, since names were instituted to signify things, 'man' first signifies the thing that is a man rather than anything else, and that this is proved not only by reference to the intention of the impositor, but also from the common meaning of locutions (*ex communi sensu locutionum*). When we say "A man is running" we intend to say that a concrete man, the composition of form and matter, is running, and not that his humanity is (Brown 1986: 346–7). However, he added that names are imposed according to the mode by which intellect wishes things to be signified so they are indifferent to past, present, and future until they receive the appropriate type of supposition in a propositional context (Brown 1986: 338). Here he is unlike his controversial Franciscan predecessor Roger Bacon, who had insisted that names were imposed only to signify whatever is present and actual, whether one is speaking of the essences of things (man, animal) or of individuals such as Caesar (Bacon 1988: 56–99).

Post-medieval authors in the Thomistic tradition were much more comfortable than Aquinas had been with the notion that spoken words signify individual things, whether they do so directly or not, and some also incorporated the theory of supposition in their discussions, perhaps as a result of nominalist influence. For instance, Fonseca held that words signify by means of concepts and hence were proximate signs of them (Fonseca 1964: 38), but he also held that, while the immediate significate of 'man' is a common nature, the mediate significate is an individual man, and that which significate is at issue depends on the context and the type of supposition involved. In "Man is a species" the significate of 'man' is a common nature, but not so in "A man is running". He added that one can also have the special case of "Man is animal" in which the significate is a common nature that is not thought of as abstracted and separate from individuals (Fonseca 1964: 690–6).

This desire to combine the signification of common natures with the signification of individuals is also revealed by the changing definition of univocal terms, and once more Fonseca provides a useful example: he defined a univocal name as one that signified all its significates by one and the same *ratio*, a term that seems to mean concept or definition here.[38] Up to the fourteenth century, the notion of a univocal term had been contrasted to that of an equivocal or homonymous term through the claim that univocal terms signify just one thing (whether a concept or an essence), whereas equivocal terms signify more than one,[39] but when the doctrine of one primary significate of a term had been replaced by the doctrine of the term as (also) a sign of individual things, it had become necessary to explain that there were several ways of signifying a plurality.[40] For nominalists, this was done by remarking that

---

[38] Fonseca (1964: 62): "Nomen univocum est, quod eadem omnino ratione sua significata significat, ut vox Homo comparatione omnium verorum hominum: omnes siquidem dicuntur homines, quia sunt animalia rationalia." Cf. Soto (1539–40: fo. 6 va); Soto (1587: 113A); Toletus (1615–16: 15).

[39] e.g., Scotus (1891b: 13A). "de ratione aequivoci est significare plura, sicut de ratione univoci significare unum."

[40] Ockham (1979a: 50; 1979b: 174–7).

while 'dog' (*canis*), the standard example of an equivocal term, signifies barking things, constellations, and marine animals by means of three concepts, a univocal term signifies many things under one concept.[41] Fonseca's definition is far closer to the nominalist definition than it is to the original Aristotelian definition in *Categories* 1ᵃ6–12. A little earlier, Soto had even used Ockham's terminology when he wrote that a univocal term signified its significates by means of the concept to which the term was subordinated. He then referred to natures, saying that that 'man' thus signifies men in so far as they agree in one human nature (Soto 1539–40: fo. vi va).

## The Semantic Triangle: 3. What Is the Relationship between Words, Concepts, and Things?

The last question raised by the semantic triangle is what kind of order obtains between word, concept, and thing, however the last two are construed. One could begin by asking whether a word signifies a concept or a thing, and if the answer was both, then one could also ask whether one was more primarily and immediately signified than the other. A range of answers to this final question was possible. The concept could have priority over the thing; the thing could have priority over the concept; or both could be signified on a more-or-less equal footing, but in different ways. The possible relationships are further complicated by the admission of both essences and individuals as things signified, and by the distinction between formal concepts or acts of mind and objective concepts or things as thought. It should also be noted that the decision made regarding whether concepts were intermediary in the process of signification had an important bearing on the issue of the relationship between knowing and signifying. If concepts are intermediary, we cannot signify something more distinctly and perfectly than we understand it, but if they are not, then we can do that. This issue was particularly important in theology, for it affected how we speak about God, of whom we can have only a confused and imperfect understanding.[42]

The problem of ordering was dealt with most easily by nominalists, since the thing spoken of, at least in the context of speech about natural kinds, was an ordinary individual, and the concept was a representative act of mind that was a necessary condition for signification. Nonetheless, Buridan and his near contemporary Ockham differed on this issue. Buridan held that words signify both concepts and things, and that they first signify concepts, because only then can we explain why terms such as 'being' and 'one' that have the same extension nonetheless differ in signification. He also appealed to the common distinction between univocal and equivocal terms,

---

[41] e.g., Buridan (2001: 832) (without the example *canis*).
[42] See Ashworth (1980, 2013). The topic was still discussed in the post-medieval period: see Ashworth (1997: 52–3), Fonseca (1615: vol. I, cols 407–411), and Smiglecius (1634: 440–2). I take the qualifications 'distinct' as opposed to 'confused', and 'perfect' as opposed to 'imperfect', from Smiglecius.

whereby equivocal terms have several significates, while univocal terms do not (Buridan 2001: 832). This claim could be justified only if concepts were taken to be the immediate significates in question. Ockham preferred to say that words signified only individual things and were subordinated to concepts without signifying them (Ockham 1974: 7–8). In order to support his view, he not only appealed to what he took to be the intention of the original impositor, but gave an ingenious reinterpretation of Aristotle's text. He argued that Aristotle had intended to say that words are instituted secondarily to signify, not concepts, but those things that the concepts primarily came to signify.[43] In other words, the ordering is merely temporal.

Turning to non-nominalists, we have already seen that the solution was reasonably simple for Lambert, who held that a word signified an intelligible species immediately and by virtue of that species signified an essence or common nature mediately. Aquinas's later doctrine seems reasonably simple as well. A word primarily signifies a conception of the mind, the inner word, and by means of that signifies an essence or common nature in so far as it characterizes individuals. However, some thirteenth-century authors presented an alternative interpretation of what Aquinas held, whereby what is primarily signified is not a conception of the mind but an external thing in so far as it is understood through its essence, as opposed to an actually existent individual (Pini 1999: 40–1, 49–50; 2001: 23). The two interpretations were developed at length by various late-thirteenth-century authors, and were reported on by Duns Scotus in his two commentaries on Aristotle's *Peri hermeneias*, though Scotus himself seems not to have reached a final conclusion about which view to accept (Pini 1999: 51; 2001: 21).

Scotus' second commentary on the *Peri hermeneias* presents us with yet another ingenious reinterpretation of Aristotle, in that he identified the *passio* with the thing as understood.[44] Whether or not Scotus took the thing as understood to be an external thing, other thinkers embraced that interpretation. Thus, three centuries later, in the longer of his two Aristotle commentaries, Rubius inveighed against those authors who claimed that when Aristotle said that words signified the passions of the mind, *passio* should be interpreted as *conceptus objectivus*. He wrote that

the exposition of the moderns, who assert that Aristotle designated by 'passions of the mind' not formal concepts as they signify things, but those very things signified, which they call objective concepts, is very far from Aristotle's intentions and the proper signification of the word, since the thing existing externally was never designated by the name 'passions of the mind' either by him or by anyone else.[45]

---

[43] Ockham (1974: 7–8; 1978: 347–8; 1979a: 47, 50).
[44] Scotus (1891a: 583): "Ad omnes auctoritates dico quod Aristoteles et Boetius intellexerunt per passiones, non similitudinem, quae est in anima, sed rem prout concipitur ab anima, et est illud in cujus notitiam perducitur intellectus per species."
[45] Rubius (1605: col. 22): "remota valde est, a mente Aristotelis et a propria verbi significatione, modernorum expositio, qui per se passiones animae, non conceptus formales, ut significant res, sed potius easdem res significatas (quas obiectivos conceptus appellant) designasse Aristotelem asseverant, non tamen res extra existens, nec ab eo, nec ab alio unquam nomine passionum animae fuerit designata."

In the post-medieval period Thomistic tradition, authors tended to combine the view that spoken words signify a concept in the sense of an intellectual conception, Aquinas's inner word, with the view that spoken words also signify both essences or common natures and individual existents. They were supported in this by the adoption of a moderate realism, whereby common natures can exist only as characterizing individuals, and of an epistemology that allowed knowledge of individuals. In their discussions, some further notions were introduced, particularly that of 'expressing concepts' either as a replacement for or as an explication of the phrase "signifying a concept". In the first edition of his *Summulae*, Soto argued that to say that spoken words are signs of passions in the soul does not mean that my utterance causes hearers to cognize my concept (though it can do so), but rather that I express the concept I have in order for hearers to form a similar concept (Soto 1529: fo. vi ra). This is, he said, compatible with the claim that words signify actual things, for signification has a dual function: it expresses concepts and signifies things (Soto 1529: fo. vii rb; cf. Rubius 1641: 366B). In the second edition of his *Summulae*, Soto repeated the point. He noted that ordinary language supports an appeal to concepts, for we talk about making our mind known to others, and concluded that his own view was compatible with authoritative texts, since Aristotle had suggested that concepts were expressed, and Peter of Spain had suggested that a thing was represented (Soto 1539–40: fo. iv va).

The *Conimbricenses* took up the notion of a double signification from Soto. They said that both the signification of concepts and the signification of things were immediate, and even argued that there was a double act of imposition involved (Doyle 2001: 97, 101). They also made a brief reference to supposition as distinguishing the two cases, but did not emphasize the point (Doyle 2001: 106). Other authors who focused on the distinction between signifying or making known a thing and expressing a concept employed the theory of supposition to clarify the difference. Toletus and Rubius both drew a distinction between manifestive and suppositive signs (Toletus 1615–16: 209A; Rubius 1641: 367B). A word that signifies manifests a concept, but it both manifests and supposits for the thing spoken of, at least when it appears in a proposition. This appeal to supposition underlines the point that the things at issue include, at least where natural kind terms are concerned, ordinary individuals, whether past, present, future, or possible. But the signification of concepts and of common natures was also included through further distinctions. For instance, using a Thomistic distinction between *ut quo* (that by which) and *ut quod* (that which), Rubius attacked 'certain moderns' who held that words only express concepts and only signify things. He argued that words signify concepts immediately *ut quo*, since it is by them that things are known, and they signify things immediately *ut quod*, since these are what the sign was instituted to signify. As a result, concepts are signified less principally, and things are signified principally (Rubius 1641: 366B–368A). He also argued, again following Aquinas, that words had to signify by means of concepts because they were imposed to signify universal natures, which are understood only as abstracted. In short, a spoken word signifies a concept in so far as the concept is a universal—that is, in so far as the concept is the understanding of a common nature, and, by means of that concept, both common natures and the things they characterize are signified. Which of these possibilities we emphasize in a given case depends on the propositional context, as Fonseca had pointed out.

Smiglecius had another approach (Smiglecius 1634: 436–8). He used the distinction between manifestive and suppositive signs, and insisted that 'man' and 'Peter' signify a true and real man outside the intellect. He went on to argue that words signify things primarily and immediately (*primo et immediate*) and they signify concepts only by means of things. This is because I can grasp what concept you are employing only if I know what the word you are using signifies. Of course, concepts are necessarily present as conditions for signification, so they are in a sense a medium, but this is not because they are immediate significates, but because they bring about signification. Impositors have to have a concept before they can carry out an act of imposition.

Although the works of Rubius and Smiglecius were printed in England, and other authors that I have mentioned, including Aquinas himself, were still read there in the seventeenth century, the more sophisticated discussions were very probably not studied by Locke, and they leave little trace in the ordinary logic texts that were used at Oxford, which were certainly known by him. In such texts, we find simple formulae and summaries of main points.[46] For instance, the popular Dutch logician Franco Burgersdijck (1590–1635) wrote: "Articulate utterances [*voces*] signify the concepts of the mind, primarily, that is, and immediately, for they also signify things, but by means of concepts."[47] Unfortunately, he adds no discussion of his reasons for taking this stand, but in earlier remarks about what the mind conceives in forming a concept, that is, a representative notion (*notio*), he gives human nature as his example of the thing conceived (Burgersdijck 1650: 9).

From the passage I quoted at the beginning of this chapter, it seems clear that Locke rejected the view that individual things are the primary significates of spoken words, and it is equally clear that he treated the suggestion that common natures or real essences could be signified as mere scholastic gibberish (*Essay*, 3.10.14). Nonetheless, he does not disallow the secondary signification of individual things. He seems to echo the view that concepts have priority but lead us to things when he writes that we need to make our own ideas known to others "Thereby *to convey* the *Knowledge* of Things" (*Essay*, 3.10.23). Moreover, he insists that our words must conform to things: "our Names of Substances being not put barely for our *Ideas*, but being made use of ultimately to represent Things, and so are put in their place, their signification must agree with the Truth of Things..." (*Essay*, 3.11.24; cf. 3.6.28,

---

[46] See Ashworth (1984: 63–4).
[47] Burgersdijck (1650: 157): "Voces articulatae significant animi conceptus, primò scilicet, atque immediatè. Nam res etiam significant, sed mediante conceptibus."

3.9.11). Accordingly, it makes sense to see Locke as standing in a long tradition, and as making reference to interpretations of Aristotle's semantic triangle that would have been familiar to his contemporaries, if not to us. However, although his view of the relationship between words, concepts, and things is closest to that of the nominalist Buridan, one cannot deny that the way in which he developed his account of concepts and things is quite different from that found in his Scholastic predecessors.

# References

Aristotle (1965). *Aristoteles Latinus II 1-2. De Interpretatione vel Periermenias, Translatio Boethii*, ed. L. Minio-Paluello. Leiden: E. J. Brill.

Ashworth, E. Jennifer (1980). '"Can I speak more clearly than I understand?" A Problem of Religious Language in Henry of Ghent, Duns Scotus and Ockham', *Historiographia Linguistica*, 7: 29-38.

Ashworth, E. Jennifer (1981). '"Do Words Signify Ideas or Things?" The Scholastic Sources of Locke's Theory of Language', *Journal of the History of Philosophy*, 19: 299-326; repr. in Ashworth, *Studies in Post-Medieval Semantics*, London: Variorum Reprints, 1985, and Udo Thiel (ed.), *Locke: Epistemology and Metaphysics*, Ashgate: Dartmouth, 2002.

Ashworth, E. Jennifer (1984). 'Locke on Language', *Canadian Journal of Philosophy*, 14: 45-73; repr. in Ashworth, *Studies in Post-Medieval Semantics*, London: Variorum Reprints, 1985; Richard Ashcraft (ed.), *John Locke: Critical Assessments*, London and New York: Routledge, 1991, iv. 235-58; and Vere Chappell (ed.), *Locke*, Oxford and New York: Oxford University Press, 1998, 175-98.

Ashworth, E. Jennifer (1987). 'Jacobus Naveros (fl. ca.1533) on the Question: "Do Spoken Words Signify Concepts or Things?"', in L. M. de Rijk and H. A. G. Braakhuis (eds), *Logos and Pragma: Essays on the Philosophy of Language in Honour of Professor Gabriel Nuchelmans*. Artistarium Supplementa III. Nijmegen: Ingenium Publishers, 189-214.

Ashworth, E. Jennifer (1990a). 'Domingo de Soto (1494-1560) and the Doctrine of Signs', in G. L. Bursill-Hall, Sten Ebbesen, and Konrad Koerner (eds), *De Ortu Grammaticae: Studies in Medieval Grammar and Linguistic Theory in Memory of Jan Pinborg*. Amsterdam and Philadelphia: John Benjamins, 35-48.

Ashworth, E. Jennifer (1990b). 'The Doctrine of Signs in Some Early Sixteenth-Century Spanish Logicians', in Ignacio Angelelli and Angel d'Ors (eds), *Estudios de Historia de la Logica. Actas del II Simposio de Historia de la Logica: Universidad de Navarra Pamplona 25-27 de Mayo de 1987*. Pamplona: Ediciones EUNATE, 13-38.

Ashworth, E. Jennifer (1997). 'Petrus Fonseca on Objective Concepts and the Analogy of Being', in Patricia A. Easton (ed.), *Logic and the Workings of the Mind: The Logic of Ideas and Faculty Psychology in Early Modern Philosophy*. North American Kant Society Studies in Philosophy, 5. Atascadero, CA: Ridgeview Publishing Company, 47-63.

Ashworth, E. Jennifer (1998). 'Antonius Rubius on Objective Being and Analogy: One of the Routes from Early Fourteenth-Century Discussions to Descartes's Third Meditation', in Stephen F. Brown (ed.), *Meeting of the Minds: The Relations between Medieval and Classical Modern European Philosophy*. Turnhout: Brepols, 43-62.

Ashworth, E. Jennifer (1999). 'Aquinas on Significant Utterance: Interjection, Blasphemy, Prayer', in Scott MacDonald and Eleonore Stump (eds), *Aquinas' Moral Theory*. Ithaca, NY, and London: Cornell University Press, 207-34.

Ashworth, E. Jennifer (2004). 'Singular Terms and Singular Concepts: From Buridan to the Early Sixteenth Century', in Russell L. Friedman and Sten Ebbesen (eds), *John Buridan and Beyond: Topics in the Language Sciences, 1300-1700*. Copenhagen: Royal Danish Academy of Sciences and Letters, 121-51.

Ashworth, E. Jennifer (2013). 'Aquinas, Scotus and Others on Naming, Knowing, and the Origin of Language', in Heine Jansen, Ana Maria Mora Marquez, and Jakob L. Fink (eds), *Logic and Language in the Middle Ages*. Leiden: E. J. Brill, 257-72.

Augustine (1962). *De Doctrina Christiana*. Corpus Christianorum, Series Latina XXXII. Turnhout: Brepols.

Bacon, Roger (1988). *Compendium Studii Theologiae*, ed. and trans. Thomas S. Maloney. Leiden, New York, Copenhagen, and Cologne: E. J. Brill.

Biard, Joël (1989). *Logique et théorie du signe au XIVe siècle*. Paris: Vrin.

Biard, Joël (2009). 'Verbe, signe, concept: L'Effacement du verbe intérieur au XIVe siècle', in T. Shimizu and C. Burnett (eds), *The Word in Medieval Logic, Theology and Psychology*. Turnhout: Brepols, 347-64.

Brown, Stephen F. (1986). 'Petrus Ioannis Olivi, "Quaestiones Logicales": Critical Text', *Traditio*, 42: 335-88.

Burgersdijck, Franco (1650). *Institutiones logicae*. Genevae.

Buridan, John (1983). *Questiones Longe super Librum Perihermeneias*, ed. Ria van der Lecq. Nijmegen: Ingenium Publishers.

Buridan, John (2001). *Summulae de Dialectica*, trans. Gyula Klima. New Haven and London: Yale University Press.

Demonet, Marie-Luce (1992). *Les Voix du signe: Nature et origine du langage à la Renaissance (1480-1580)*. Champion-Slatkine: Paris-Genève.

Descartes, René (1897-1913). *Œuvres de Descartes*, ed. Charles Adam and Paul Tannery. Paris: Cerf; rev. edn, Paris: Vrin/CNRS, 1964-1976.

Doyle, John P. (2001). *The Conimbricenses: Some Questions on Signs. Translated with Introduction and Notes*. Milwaukee, Wisconsin: Marquette University Press.

Eckius, Johannes (1516-17). *Aristotelis Stagyrite Dialectica... a Joanne Eckio Theologo facili explanatione declarata: Adnotationibus compendiariis illustrata: ac scholastico exercitio explicata*. Augsburg.

Fonseca, Petrus (1615). *Commentariorvm In Metaphysicorvm Aristotelis Stagiritae Libros*. Coloniae Agrippinae; facsimile repr., Hildesheim: Georg Olms, 1964.

Fonseca, Petrus (1964). *Instituições Dialécticas. Institutionum Dialecticarum Libri Octo*, ed. and trans. Joaquim Ferreira Gomes. Coimbra: Universidade de Coimbra.

Klima, Gyula (2009). *John Buridan*. Oxford: Oxford University Press.

Lambert of Auxerre (1971). *Logica (Summa Lamberti)*, ed. F. Alessio. Florence: La Nuova Italia Editrice.

Locke, John (1975). *An Essay Concerning Human Understanding*, ed. Peter H. Nidditch. Oxford: Clarendon Press.

Meier-Oeser, Stephan (1997). *Die Spur des Zeichens: Das Zeichen und seine Funktion in der Philosophie des Mittelalters und der Frühen Neuzeit*. Berlin and New York: Walter de Gruyter.

Nuchelmans, Gabriel (1983). *Judgment and Proposition: From Descartes to Kant*. Amsterdam, Oxford, and New York: North-Holland Publishing Company.

Ockham, William of (1974). *Summa Logicae*, ed. Philotheus Boehner, Gedeon Gál, and Stephen Brown. Opera Philosophica I. St Bonaventure, NY: Franciscan Institute.

Ockham, William of (1978). *Expositio in librum Perihermenias Aristotelis*, ed. Angel Gambatese and Stephen Brown. Opera Philosophica II. St Bonaventure, NY: St Bonaventure University.

Ockham, William of (1979a). *Scriptum in librum Primum Sententiarum Ordinatio. Distinctiones XIX–XLVIII*, ed. G. Etzkorn and F. E. Kelley. Opera Theologica IV. St Bonaventure, NY: St Bonaventure University.

Ockham, William of (1979b). *Expositio super libros Elenchorum*, ed. Francesco del Punta. Opera Philosophica II. St Bonaventure, NY: St Bonaventure University.

Panaccio, Claude (2004). *Ockham on Concepts*. Aldershot and Burlington, VT: Ashgate.

Peter of Ailly (1498). *Conceptus et insolubilia*. Parisius.

Peter of Spain (1972). *Tractatus Called afterwards Summule Logicales*, ed. L. M. de Rijk. Assen: Van Gorcum.

Pini, Giorgio (1999). 'Species, Concept, and Thing: Theories of Signification in the Second Half of the Thirteenth Century', *Medieval Philosophy and Theology*, 8: 21–52.

Pini, Giorgio (2001). 'Signification of Names in Duns Scotus and Some of His Contemporaries', *Vivarium*, 39: 20–51.

Rosier, Irène (1994). *La Parole comme acte: Sur la grammaire et la sémantique au XIIIe siècle*. Paris: Vrin.

Rosier, Irène (1995). 'Henri de Gand, le *De Dialectica* d'Augustin, et l'institution des noms divins', *Documenti e Studi sulla Tradizione Filosofica Medievale*, 6: 145–253.

Rosier-Catach, Irène (2004). *La Parole efficace: Signe, rituel, sacré*. Paris: Éditions du Seuil.

Rubius, Antonius (1605). *Logica Mexicana sive Commentarii in Universam Aristotelis Logicam*. Coloniae Agrippinae.

Rubius, Antonius (1641). *Commentarii in Universam Aristotelis Dialecticam*. Londini.

Scotus, John Duns (1891a). *In duos libros Perihermeneias quaestiones* and *In duos libros Perihermeneias quaestiones octo*, in Opera Omnia I. Paris: Vivès.

Scotus, John Duns (1891b). *In libros Elenchorum quaestiones*, in Opera Omnia II. Paris: Vivès.

Smiglecius, Martinus (1634). *Logica*. Oxonii.

Soto, Domingo de (1529). *Summulae*. Burgis.

Soto, Domingo de (1539–40). *Aeditio Secunda Summularum*. Salmanticae.

Soto, Domingo de (1587). *In Porphyrii Isagogen, Aristotelis Categorias, librosque de Demonstratione Absolutissima Commentaria*. Venetiis; facsimile repr., Frankfurt: Minerva, 1968.

Spade, Paul Vincent (1980). *Peter of Ailly: Concepts and Insolubles. An Annotated Translation*. Dordrecht, Boston, London: Reidel.

Toletus, Franciscus (1615–16). *Commentaria in universam Aristotelis logicam*. In Opera Omnia Philosophica I–III. Coloniae Agrippinae, facsimile repr., Hildesheim, Zurich, and New York: Georg Olms, 1985.

# 9

# Locke on the Names of Modes

*Benjamin Hill*

In the course of pursuing his epistemological reflections, Locke discovered that he had to consider language as well as ideas because "there is so close a connection between *Ideas* and Words; and our abstract *Ideas*, and general Words have so constant relation one to another, that it is impossible to speak clearly and distinctly of our Knowledge, which all consists in Propositions, without considering, first, the Nature, Use, and Signification of Language".[1] It is common to see Locke's principal reason for including philosophical reflections on language as the misleading and duplicitous nature of words.[2] But Locke's thoughts went far beyond a diagnosis and cure of the Idols of the Marketplace.[3]

In this chapter I wish to explore one such contribution—namely the importance Locke attached to the naming of the idea of a mode. According to Locke, "*in mixed Modes 'tis the Name that ties the Combination together, and makes it a Species*". This is a rich and intriguing suggestion. Why is it necessary that the name tie the combination together *and* make it a species? What does it mean to say that a name *ties* the combination together? How is it that a *name* is able to unite simple ideas together and provide it with its "lasting duration"? And, perhaps most importantly, how is it that a name is able to make the idea a *species*?

I shall argue that Locke was creating a brand-new kind of linguistic act. He created the "structuring thought" form of naming—the act of naming a mode quite literally makes the idea of the mode; the names of modes, in other words, make the thoughts of modes possible, not vice versa. This subtle move expands the variety of meanings floating around late-seventeenth-century philosophy of language and points towards an interesting new source for meaning, a linguistic act itself. Although this idea might be familiar now, it was quite radical back then. Before Locke, the standard view was that language was parasitic and dependent on thought. Although Locke himself may not have been fully aware of the power and significance of his conception, others,

---

[1] Locke (1975: II.xxxiii.19, 401). Quotations from Locke are from this edition.
[2] See, e.g., Guyer (1994) and Dawson (2007).
[3] Bacon (2004: §43, 81, and §§59–60, 93 and 95).

such as Condillac,[4] would soon explore just how deeply it cut across Locke's own conceptions of language, ideas, and species.

The aim of this chapter is to show the historical roots of the idea that language can have priority over thought. It has three main parts. The first introduces Locke's doctrine of modes and his naming thesis (NT). The second introduces the unity problem that modes have and explains why Locke's epistemology requires a solution to it. The third explores the significance of Locke's NT. It contrasts two readings of the NT, one emphasizing the priority of language (which I argue Locke ought to have endorsed) and the other emphasizing the priority of conception.

## 1. Locke on Modes and their Names

Modes are an important category within the schema of the *Essay*. Alongside ideas of substances and relations, they are one of three categories of complex ideas. They are an especially important category for Locke because the ideas of mathematics and morality are ideas of modes. And they are especially interesting because, according to Locke, the knowledge we build out of them is real, instructive, and certain. This is in marked contrast with what we can know about qualities and substances. For, on the one hand, the knowledge we build out of our simple ideas, according to Locke, is real and certain but trivial. And, on the other hand, those beliefs we build out of our ideas of substances, whenever real and instructive, are not certain.[5]

### 1.1. What are Lockean Modes?

Book II of Locke's *Essay Concerning Human Understanding* constitutes Locke's reply to Aristotle's *Categories*. By outlining the types of ideas we have, Locke also described the types of things there are.[6] There are simple ideas, which correspond to monadic, qualitative properties of substances (for example, colour, shape, solidity, and so on) and to monadic transcendental properties of objects (for example, existence and unity). There are also three types of complex ideas, which correspond to substances (for example, Socrates, elephants, humans, and so on), to polyadic properties that Locke called relations (for example, father, imperfection, cause, general, moral goodness, and so on), and to complex monadic properties that Locke called modes.

The category of modes is fascinating because of how it fits with the other categories. Unlike complex ideas of substance, ideas of modes are properly predicated of substances. In this regard, they are like qualities and relations. Yet, unlike relations

---

[4] Condillac (2001).   [5] IV.viii.8, 614; IV.viii.3, 609–12; and IV.viii.9, 615.
[6] Locke is often criticized for confusing ideas and properties and often slides between them. This description may give rise to a similar perception, but there is no confusion of the different categories here (or in Locke). The relationship between ideas of modes and modes qua properties of substances will be described in Section 3.4.

and like simple ideas, they are properly predicated of individuals,[7] which means that they have a singular subject and do not necessarily or conceptually connote another thing. This also means that modes have a kind of fundamental unity, like simple ideas but unlike ideas of relations. But, of course, this unity cannot be the same as simple ideas because simple ideas are simple and ideas of modes are complex. And modes are unlike simple ideas but like ideas of relations and substances in that they conceptually contain a plurality of elements. Yet their complexity is unlike that of relations and substances in that there are no elements that are necessary or constitutive for modes—ideas of substance must all contain a substratum to be an idea of substance and ideas of relations must contain a plurality of substance ideas functioning as relata to be an idea of a relation; modes, however, may contain many ideas of substances or none (for example, the ideas of number) and do not contain anything analogous to the idea of substance's substratum or the idea of relation's relata. And finally, unlike simple ideas and ideas of substance but like ideas of relations, ideas of modes are according to Locke their own archetypes, which means that they possess a kind of reality and adequacy not found in simple ideas and ideas of substance.

There are modes of space (distance, capacity, figure, place, and all the measures of space among others) and duration (ditto). All ideas of number are modes of unity. There are modes of motion (slide, roll, tumble, walk, creep, run, dance, leap, skip, and so on), modes of sounds (every distinct word, note, and tune), modes of colours (every shade of "*the same Colour*"), and tastes and smells. There are also various modes of thinking: recollection and contemplation; reverie, attention, study, and dreaming; reasoning, judging, volition, and knowledge; and remission. And numerous modes of pleasure and pain (love, hatred, desire, joy, sorrow, hope, and so on). Locke labels all these "simple modes", not because they are simple ideas, of course, but because they involve a plurality of ideas of the same type (that is, they are typologically simple). The most interesting and instructive are the types of "mixed modes", which involve the composition of ideas of different types.[8] Murder, triumph, beauty, apotheosis, hypocrisy, adultery, jealousy, sacrilege, drunkenness, obligation, a lie, parricide, any idea of any custom or practice, appeal, reprieve, consideration, assent, revenge, running, speaking, printing, etching, fencing, boldness, testiness, habit—it is quite a long and diverse list that Locke gives us! Although it is tempting to think of the category of mode as a hodge-podge consisting simply of everything

---

[7] I am deliberately taking care to avoid the term "substances" here because at the very least modes of space and numbers are properties predicated of non-substances—space and mereological sums or unities. But they still have individual logical subjects, i.e. the region of space and the mereological sum. I am dancing around it for now, but the close examination of particular modes requires attention to this issue and working out Locke's claim that modes "are considered as Dependences on, or Affections of Substances" (II.xii.4, 165).

[8] It is possible to take the distinction between simple and mixed modes to be semantically significant and to push the NT onto mixed modes only. I do not think that is correct and in this chapter will treat all modes as similar from a semantic standpoint.

that is not a substance, quality, or relation, we shall see that there is a deeper unity beneath the category in Locke's conception.[9]

It is generally recognized that the importance of the category of modes lies in Locke's placement of mathematical and moral properties within it. This has important epistemological ramifications for Locke in that it opens the possibility of differentiating the cases of mathematical and moral knowledge from knowledge of substances and their qualities. And, as we all know, Locke made important use of this difference to ground the reality, certainty, and instructive nature of moral and mathematical knowledge as opposed to the merely probable belief that we can have about substances, their qualities, and their causal interactions. Although important and extremely interesting, this feature of modes will not be a topic in this chapter. Now that we have seen what modes are, let us turn to the theoretical principles uniting the category of modes.

## 1.2. Locke's Naming Thesis

Locke's doctrine of modes consists of six principal theses:

(i) Modes do not "subsist by themselves" but are "Dependencies on, or Affectations of Substances".

(ii) The ideas of modes are "*very arbitrarily*" constructed by the mind "without reference to any real Archetypes, or standing Patterns, existing anywhere".

(iii) So, "not being intended for Copies of Things really existing", they are "Archetypes made by the Mind, to rank and denominate Things by".

(iv) Thus they "cannot differ from their Archetypes, and so *cannot be chimerical, unless*" containing "inconsistent *Ideas*".

(v) Having, moreover, no steady existence in nature, or even in men's minds, "'tis the Name which is, as it were the Knot" uniting them and giving them "*a constant and lasting existence*".

(vi) And finally, being themselves archetypes, their "*real* and *nominal* Essence is the same".[10]

Call thesis (v) Locke's 'naming thesis' (NT).

So what was Locke's NT? Let us begin with Locke's discussion of the names of numbers. Locke does not present NT itself there. But he was touching on it by arguing that names are "*necessary*" to the simple modes of number.

---

[9] One of the aims of this chapter is to push back against the notion that the category of Lockean modes is an unprincipled motley of everything that does not fit into the other categories. Of course, trivially it contains everything not contained in the others because the taxonomy is supposed to be exhaustive. What I am pushing against is the idea that it is an unprincipled motley.

[10] II.xii.4, 165; III.v.3, 429 and II.xxxi.3, 376; II.xxxi.3, 376; II.xxx.4, 373; III.v.10, 434, and II.xxii.8, 291; and finally III.v.14, 437.

§5. *Names necessary to Number*. By the repeating, as has been said, of the *Idea* of an Unite, and joining it to another Unite, we make thereof one collective *Idea*, marked by the Name *Two*. And whosoever can do this, and proceed on, still adding one more to the last collective *Idea*, which he had of any Number, and give a Name to it, may count, or have *Ideas* for several Collections of Unites, distinguished one from another, as far as he hath a Series of Names for following Numbers, and a Memory to retain that Series, with their several Names: All *Numeration* being but still the adding of one Unite more, and giving to the whole together, as comprehended in one *Idea*, a new or distinct Name or Sign, whereby to know it from those before and after, and distinguish it from every smaller or greater multitude of Unites. So that he, that can add one to one, and so to two, and so go on with his Tale, taking still with him the distinct Names belonging to every Progression; and so again by subtracting an Unite from each Collection retreat and lessen them, is capable of all the *Ideas* of Numbers, within the compass of his Language, or for which he hath names, though not, perhaps, of more...

§6. *Names necessary to Numbers*. This, I think, to be the reason why some *Americans*, I have spoken with, (who were otherwise of quick and rational Parts enough,) could not, as we do, by any means count to 1000; nor had any distinct *Ideas* of that Number, though they could reckon very well to 20. Because their Language being scanty, and accommodated only to the few necessaries of a needy simple Life, unacquainted either with Trade or Mathematicks, had no Words in it to stand for 1000; so that when they were discoursed with of those greater Numbers, they would shew the Hairs of their Head, to express a great multitude, which they could not number; which inability, I suppose, proceeded from their want of Names...[11]

The key points here are (*a*) that the distinctness necessary to have a proper idea of a number is determined by the name attached to it, so much so that no ideas of numbers are possible where there are no names for them and (*b*) that the reason why the native Americans cannot properly reason or think about numbers greater than twenty is because they lacked names for them.

The NT proper is introduced in the chapter "Of Mixed Modes".

§4. *The Name ties the Parts of the mixed Modes into one* Idea. Every *mixed Mode* consisting of many distinct simple *Ideas*, it seems reasonable to enquire, *whence it has its Unity*; and how such a precise multitude comes to make but one *Idea*, since that Combination does not always exist together in Nature. To which I answer it is plain, it has its Unity from an Act of the Mind combining those several simple *Ideas* together, and considering them as one complex one, consisting of those parts; and the mark of this Union, or that which is looked on generally to compleat it, is one name given to that Combination. For 'tis by their names, that Men commonly regulate their account of their distinct Species of mixed Modes, seldom allowing or considering any number of simple *Ideas*, to make one complex one, but such Collections as there be names for.[12]

Locke returned to the point a few short sections later.

§8. *Mixed Modes, where they exist ... mixed Modes*, which being fleeting, and transient Combinations of simple *Ideas*, which have but a short existence any where, but in the Minds of

---

[11] II.xvi.5–6, 206–8.  [12] II.xxii.4, 289–90.

Men, and there too have no longer any existence, than whilst they are thought on, *have not so much any where the appearance of a constant and lasting existence, as in their Names*: which are therefore, in these sort of *Ideas*, very apt to be taken for the *Ideas* themselves. For if we should enquire where the *Idea* of a *Triumph*, or *Apotheosis* exists, it is evident, they could neither of them exist altogether any where in the things themselves, being Actions that required time to their performance, and so could never all exist together: and as to the Minds of Men, where the *Ideas* of these Actions are supposed to be lodged, they have there too a very uncertain existence; and therefore we are apt to annex them to the Names, that excite them in us.[13]

The NT is also alluded to in II.xxxii.12: "the Essence of each Species [of mixed modes], being made by Men alone, whereof we have no other sensible Standard, existing any where, but the Name it self, or the definition of that Name."[14]

The most extensive discussion of the NT occurs in III.v, "*Of the Names of mixed Modes and Relations*".

4.... We must consider *wherein this making of these complex* Ideas *consists*; and that is not in the making any new *Idea*, but putting together those which the Mind had before. Wherein the Mind does these three things: First, It chuses a certain Number. Secondly, It gives them connexion, and makes them into one *Idea*. Thirdly, It ties them together by a Name.

6.... To see *how arbitrarily these Essences of mixed Modes are made* by the Mind, we need but take a view of almost any of them. A little looking into them, will satisfie us, that 'tis the Mind, that combines several scattered independent *Ideas*, into one complex one; and by the common name it gives them, makes them the Essence of a certain Species, without regulating it self by any connexion they have in Nature.

§10, 11. *In mixed Modes 'tis the Name that ties the Combination together, and makes it a Species.* 10.... it is the Name that seems to preserve those *Essences*, and give them their lasting duration. For the connexion between the loose parts of those complex *Ideas*, being made by the Mind, this union, which has no particular foundation in Nature, would cease again, were there not something that did, as it were, hold it together, and keep the parts from scattering. Though therefore it be the Mind that makes the Collection, 'tis the Name which is, as it were the Knot, that ties them fast together. What a vast variety of different *Ideas*, does the word *Triumphus* hold together, and deliver to us as one *Species*! Had this Name been never made, or quite lost, we might, no doubt, have had descriptions of what passed in that Solemnity: But yet, I think, that which holds those different parts together, in the unity of one complex *Idea*, is that very word annexed to it: without which, the several parts of that, would no more be thought to make one thing, than any other shew, which having never been made but once, had never been united into one complex *Idea*, under one denomination... §11. Suitable to this, we find, that *Men speaking of mixed Modes, seldom imagine or take any other for Species of them, but such as are set out by name*: Because they being of Man's making only, in order to naming, no such *Species* are taken notice of, or supposed to be, unless a *Name* be joined to it, as the sign of Man's having combined into one *Idea* several loose ones; and by that *Name*, giving a lasting Union to the Parts, which would otherwise cease to have any, as soon as the Mind laid by that abstract *Idea*, and ceased actually to think on it. But when a Name is once annexed to it, wherein the

---

[13] II.xxii.8, 291.  [14] II.xxxii.12, 388.

parts of that complex *Idea* have a settled and permanent Union; then is the *Essence*, as it were established, and the *Species* look'd on as compleat...[15]

Clearly, what we have here is an appeal to language—to names and naming—to unite the components of ideas of modes. But why? Why does Locke have a problem with the unity of ideas of modes? And why do they not possess such unity intrinsically as ideas of substance seem to? And why is it necessary that the name tie the combination together?

## 2. Locke's Unity Problem with Ideas of Modes

Why must ideas of modes be unitary? According to Locke, all ideas are in fact unitary: "*Existence* and *Unity*, are two other [simple] *Ideas*, that are suggested to the Understanding by every Object without, and every *Idea* within... whatever we can consider as one thing, whether a real Being, or *Idea*, suggests to the Understanding, the *Idea* of *Unity*."[16] The reason why Locke requires the unity of all ideas is not too hard to find. It is built into his definitions of knowledge and belief. More precisely, it is due to the propositional nature of knowledge and belief states.

### 2.1. The Unity of All Ideas

By defining knowledge and belief or judgement as comparisons of ideas,[17] Locke was modelling those cognitive states on the standard, well-formed propositions of Aristotelian logic.[18] For Locke, as indeed for anyone steeped in the traditional logics of the seventeenth century, propositions had a basic structure of categoremata linked by syncategorematic terms. This was the default, pre-Fregean conception of propositions and persisted for a long time, at least through Mill.[19] Standard form for that tradition was <quantifier, subject term, copula, and predicate term>, and Locke's usual examples reflected this (for example, all centaurs are animals; all men are animals; and so on).

---

[15] III.v.4, 6, and 10–11, 429–31 *passim*, and 434–5.
[16] II.vii.7, 131. I leave it to others to determine whether Locke's use of modal rather than indicative language ("whatever we *can* consider..." rather than "whatever we consider...") is significant. It does not seem so to me, although I can see how some might take it to be and build a "possibilist" interpretation around it. But I see no reason why the points being developed in this chapter require taking a stand on that.
[17] "*Knowledge* then seems to me to be nothing but *the perception of the connexion and agreement, or disagreement and repugnancy of any of our Ideas*" (IV.i.2, 524) and "*Judgment*, which is the putting *Ideas* together, or separating them from one another in the Mind, when their certain Agreement or Disagreement is not perceived, but *presumed* to be so" (IV.xiv.4, 653). For discussion of the proposition nature of this definition of knowledge, see Hill (2008).
[18] In addition to the passage with which this chapter opened (II.xxxiii.19, 401), consider: "Knowledge: Which being conversant about Propositions, and those most commonly universal ones, has greater connexion with Words, than perhaps is suspected" (III.i.6, 404) and "But when having passed over the Original and Composition of our *Ideas*, I began to examine the Extent and Certainty of our Knowledge, I found it had so near a connexion with Words, that unless their force and manner of Signification were first well observed, there could be very little said clearly and pertinently concerning Knowledge: which being conversant about Truth, had constantly to do with Propositions" (III.ix.21, 488).
[19] Mill (1963: I.ii.2 and I.iv.1–4).

But, for Locke, not everything that appeared before the mind appears *as* a single, unitary idea. There are mental acts that involve ideas but are not the perceptions of an idea. Knowledge is one such example: it is a complex cognitive state involving two distinct ideas and an act of comparison. There is no reason to think Locke considered this a single complex idea, and plenty against it. But not even every collection of ideas appearing before the mind was itself an idea in Locke's system. A sensory episode, for example, often encompasses a variety of ideas that do not present themselves as unitary.[20] When I look at my desk, for example, I *discern* several distinct ideas simultaneously and without considering them unitary—the idea of my desk; the messiness of the papers scattered across it; the orange I will snack on later; and so on. Some of these are unitary complex ideas, like the idea of the desk or the idea of its messiness, but the collection as a whole is not. And, most importantly, it is not perceived to be so.[21]

If we can come to see that sense perception was not a unitary mental state for Locke through consideration of the psychological faculty of discernment, we can also come to see it through consideration of Locke's discussion of sensitive knowledge. In having sensitive knowledge, I come to know that my desk exists by comparing my currently sensed idea of the desk with the idea of existence. It is always the case that the objects serving as the subjects of sensitive knowledge are individuals and never the collective whole of a sensory episode.[22]

Thus we should say that not everything that appeared before the mind could serve as a term in a mental proposition simply by virtue of appearing before the mind.[23] This seems right generally, and seems rightly attributed to Locke. Only mental items that were properly unitary could. Whether they were given as unitary or made unitary by the mind does not matter; what mattered was that they be properly unitary. So, for Locke there was a real question as to what constitutes a unitary idea capable of functioning as a categorematic term in a mental proposition.

---

[20] "Unless the Mind had a distinct Perception of different Objects, and their Qualities, it would be capable of very little Knowledge; though the Bodies that affect us, were as busie about us, as they are now, and the Mind were continually employ'd in thinking. On this faculty of Distinguishing one thing from another, depends the *evidence and certainty* of several, even very general, Propositions" (II.xi.1, 155). Cf. Hall (1987). Hall was concerned with a different question, whether simple ideas qua simples were sensed according to Locke. He concluded that Locke believed that they were, but that he ought not to have done so. During the course of his analysis, however, Hall suggests that a sensory episode was, for Locke, a complex idea rather than a disunited group of complex ideas. I say otherwise because there is no compounding (II.xi.6, 158) of the elements of the sensory episode and thus the elements are discerned (II.xi.1, 155-6) as separate ideas. The key here really is discernment.

[21] Taking seriously the "object" talk in Locke's "official" definition of idea is what drives this line of interpretation, or so I would argue were I to defend this claim in detail. Locke's "official" definition is at I.i.8: "whatsoever is the Object of the Understanding when a Man thinks."

[22] Representative is IV.xi.9, where he identified the "Collection of simple *Ideas*" that we observe and know really to exist as an individual substance: "If I saw such a Collection of simple *Ideas*, as is wont to be called *Man*..." (IV.xi.9, 635).

[23] As he said in I.i.8, it is only that which appears as an object to the understanding that has the unity requisite for an idea.

## 2.2. The Problem of Unity for Ideas of Modes

So, why is there a problem with the unity of modal*[24] ideas for Locke? In the passages quoted in Section 1.2, Locke clearly identified the reason for such a problem as the possibility that such a "Combination does not always exist together in Nature".[25] Locke's unity problem with ideas of modes is rooted in the metaphysical nature of modes, I argue. With ideas of substances and simple ideas of qualities, Locke can hook the unity of those ideas onto the unity of those substances and their qualities. The unity in those ideas reflects the unity in those objects they represent, which those objects possess *per se* because they are unitary metaphysical subjects (in the case of substances) or because they inhere* in such subjects (in the case of qualities). Modes, however, are different in that they are not, for Locke, properties that inhere* in their subjects.[26]

Locke indentified many things as modes that traditional Cartesian and Scholastic philosophers would not—creeping and sliding; dozen and theft; beauty and hope; drunkenness and obligation, and so on. One of his favourites was the Roman triumph. This was a complex religious procession that essentially depended on a whole host of different individuals and substances. For example, it was not a triumph if the Senate did not invite the conquering general in for the parade. And it was not a triumph if the general did not enter the city with his prisoners and representatives of his army. In discussing this example, Locke focused on the temporal spread of the triumph.[27] At the very least, Locke was saying here that being momentary is a necessary condition for inhering* in a logical subject and he was saying that these two modes fail to satisfy that. I suggest that we should take this claim as a hint towards understanding the general non-inherence* of modes. Locke's claim here should be taken as a hint that modes cannot ever be "in" an object.

---

[24] I will * the terms "modal" and "inherent" to mark that they are being used in a technical Lockean or historical sense that is different from what we now usually understand those terms to mean. Modal* does not have anything to do with necessity or possibility, but rather signifies Locke's distinctive notion of modes. And inherent* concerns a particular relationship between a property and its subject—namely, that the property is a part of the substance and is rooted in the substance's being in some way; inherent* is meant to be contrasted with imposed or adventitious.

[25] II.xx.4, 289.

[26] It is perhaps easiest to see the non-inherence* of Lockean modes through their contrast with the traditional, Suarezian–Cartesian conception of modes. Suarezian–Cartesian modes were characterized in terms of non-mutual separability. They were the sorts of things that could not be separated from their substances, even though their substances could be separated from them. For them, the key metaphysical contrast was between substances, on the one hand, and modes, on the other. Locke, however, was consciously bucking this trend when he introduced his conception of mode (see II.xii.4, 165) because as a physician and natural philosopher he was more interested in the contrast between inherent* and non-inherent* properties than in the more abstract, metaphysical notion of existential dependence and the subsistent/non-subsistent divide.

[27] "If we should enquire where the *Idea* of a *Triumph*, or *Apotheosis* exits, it is evident, they could neither of them exist altogether any where in the things themselves, being Actions that require time to their performance, and so could never all exist together" (II.xxii.8, 291).

Not all of Locke's modes are "Actions that require time to their performance", however. Beauty, for example, hope, and dozen are all properties that exist at a given moment, like Lockean qualities. Yet he still classified them as modes. How do they differ from qualities? Non-inherence* helps here. Beauty was a mixed mode because it compounded simple ideas of several kinds, specifically colour, figure, and the relation of causing delight in a perceiver, for example.[28] The key for Locke, however, was that there was no reduction of the various qualities to a single power inherent* in the beautiful thing, which is another necessary condition for inherence*. The property of beauty is not unified in the beautiful object because it is not reducible to an inherent* power, as it would have to be to be inherent* like a quality. Why not? Because for Locke what was central to the notion of an inherent* power was the capacity "to produce various Sensations in us by their *primary Qualities*".[29] As Locke conceived it, this notion of being produced by their primary qualities was such as to generate a *dependence* relation between the power and the primary qualities[30] and it was mediated by the mechanical interaction of *impulse*.[31] Such is not the case for beauty. Beauty relies also on a judgement by the perceiver.

For Locke, modes and qualities were mutually exclusive categories divided by the property of metaphysical inherence*. And this was the reason why modes posed a peculiar unity problem. In the case of modes that are "Actions that require time to their performance", it is obvious why the mind must impose boundaries not there in nature. But because of non-inherence*, the same applies in the cases of modes that exhibit all of their essential characteristics simultaneously. And, because modes do not inhere* in substances, as qualities do, they cannot derive their unity from the unity of the substances to which they are attributed. Their unity, in other words, cannot be given, like the unity of our ideas of substances or our simple ideas of qualities, and so they require that unity be pushed onto them. This is where Locke's commitment to the NT comes from:

For the connexion between the loose parts of those complex *Ideas*, being made by the Mind, this union, which has no particular foundation in Nature, would cease again, were there not something that did, as it were, hold it together, and keep the parts from scattering. Though therefore it be the Mind that makes the Collection, 'tis the Name which is, as it were the Knot, that ties them fast together.[32]

---

[28] II.xii.5, 165.
[29] II.viii.10, 135. Non-reducibility also explains why Locke curiously identified shades of colours as modes—they are not reducible to the primary quality itself (the primary colour), but come about because of some mixture of two primary colours or the mixing of the primary colour with greys or whites.
[30] II.viii.14, 137.
[31] II.viii.11, 135–6. Locke's revision to accommodate gravitational attraction is well known and widely thought to create tensions within his mechanism. I am not going anywhere near that debate in this chapter.
[32] III.v.10, 434.

We have gone quite some distance towards answering our first major question here. We can see why Locke had a unity problem with regard to ideas of modes and we can understand to a certain extent why he appealed to the NT to solve it. We can see, at least, why Locke needed to say something about the unity of our ideas of modes. But we cannot yet see why Locke appealed to *naming* as the tie binding the ideas parts rather than the act of thinking.

## 3. Why Names and not Minds? The Meaning of Locke's Naming Thesis

A bit of reflection reveals that the NT can be taken in one of two directions. It can be understood in terms of a commitment to the priority of the mental over the linguistic in that the ideas' unity is ultimately derived from the unity of the act of perception and that the name merely helps the unity persist. Or it could be understood in terms of a commitment to the priority of the linguistic over the mental in that the ideas' unity is ultimately derived from the name, or from some distinctively linguistic act, and that the mental act of perceiving the idea is dependent on and consequent to that linguistic act. Each possibility entails deeper commitments to fundamentally opposed theses regarding the nature of ideas.

### 3.1. What the Mental Reading of the NT Is

The first option is the mental reading (MR), which has a strong Kantian flavour to it.[33] According to it: the mind brings together the various elements of an idea of mode, and, *by virtue of bringing these elements together*, treats them as a single object of cognition, thereby creating the idea of the mode. It is, in other words, the culmination of the gathering process alone that creates the idea of a mode. The name, then, gets appended to the already formed idea, and the name assists memory, which is what gives the idea its *"constant and lasting existence"*. Thus, the name *perfects* the idea of a mode, and makes it useful, but it does not play any role in creating the idea and does not, strictly speaking, accord the essential unity to the idea of a mode. According the essential unity to the idea is accomplished by the act of cognizing alone. Names simply help to maintain the modal* idea and have no role in its creation.

The MR rests on four theses.

(1) A Formation Thesis: A Lockean modal* idea is formed by an act of understanding alone.
(2) A Cognition Thesis: Any mode may be cognized independently of the name of the mode or in the absence of any linguistic act relating to the mode.

---

[33] The unity of a Lockean modal idea is synthetic and follows from the formal unity of the act of thinking about the mode. See, e.g., Kant, *Critique of Pure Reason* (1933), B131-143 and A335-341.

(3) An Existence Thesis: Every modal idea exists independently of the name of the mode or the linguistic act of naming the mode.
(4) A Perfection Thesis: Naming a mode plays no role in creating the idea of the mode; at most, it "compleats" the process of idea-formation only in the sense that it makes the idea more useful or better functioning or better able to fulfil its purpose as an idea.

Thesis (1) is the key. Everything else follows from it. Thesis (1) revolves around two conditions, (*a*) the simultaneous existence of the idea-elements in the mind and (*b*) the ability of the mind to attend to the collection of the idea-elements *as a group*. The unitary idea is formed if and only if each of the elements simultaneously exists in the mind and the mind accepts or perceives them as a single object of the understanding. As we have seen above, these were the two conditions that were lacking with regard to Lockean modal* properties because of their non-inherence*. But, according to this interpretation, these two conditions are satisfied by the understanding gathering up the idea-elements and attending to them as a collective whole.

Thesis (2) follows from this: it is possible to think about a mode independently of its name. Independently means conceptually and temporally prior to the name, or the linguistic act of naming the mode. It also means in the absence of the name.[34] So, an individual could think of a mode in ignorance of the name it may have within her linguistic community. Or, she may think of it even though there is no name for that mode in her linguistic community. And, even more radically, she could, presumably, think of the mode even if no linguistic community, past, present, or future, ever gave it a name. Independence here means that the name is unnecessary for the cognition of the mode.

Thesis (3) is yet another corollary of thesis (1). It states that the idea *exists* independently of the name or any linguistic act of naming. The kind of independence at stake here is just like that described above—the name is unnecessary for the existence of the idea.

The fourth and final thesis describes the role names have according to the MR. As it turns out, their role is important, but not essential to the ideas of modes. It is important *for us* because with names we are better able to use the ideas of modes because we are better able clearly and distinctly to fix them in memory. The ideas of modes are thus *perfected* by names but not implicated in the formation of the ideas.

Below we will consider the case that can be made for attributing this to Locke. For now it should be noted that this analysis is consonant with the usual understanding of Lockean ideas, their cognition, and their creation.

---

[34] Something like "habitual knowledge" may give Locke some more wriggle room here. But such a form of habitual knowledge, in so far as it is Lockean habitual knowledge, would require a prior linguistic act of naming, if a linguistic reading were the correct interpretation of the NT.

## 3.2. What the Linguistic Reading of NT Is

The second option for understanding the NT is the linguistic reading (LR), which has a strongly Condillacian flavour.[35] According to it the mind does not accord unity to the idea by virtue of bringing all the idea-elements together. Another distinctively linguistic act is also required. Quite literally, it is the name—or better yet, *the act of naming*—that forges the idea-elements together and creates the idea itself. Simply collecting the elements together is insufficient according to the LR. Why? Because the elements cannot be attended to as a single object of the understanding without the name! That is the key difference between the two readings—without the name, or the linguistic act of naming, attention cannot be directed at the elements *collectively* or *as a whole*. It is the name that allows for the understanding to attend to the elements as a group, that allows for the group to function as an idea, and that allows it to be discerned from all other ideas.[36] It is naming that allows the collection of elements to appear to the mind as an object. The name, then, "compleats" the idea in the strict sense. Names do much more than simply maintain the modal* idea—they play a role in the very construction of the idea.

In the LR, we have mirror images of the four earlier theses because of the crucial difference regarding the formation of the idea.

(1′) Formulation Thesis: An idea of mode is formulated by a linguistic act working in conjunction with an act of the understanding.

(2′) Cognition Thesis: No mode can be cognized independently of the name or without an act of naming.

(3′) Existence Thesis: No idea of mode can exist independently of the name of the mode or the linguistic act of naming it.

(4′) Perfection Thesis: Names do not merely perfect the idea of a mode, they do not merely help us use ideas of modes; names are what make the ideas of modes possible; they complete the process in the literal sense.

As before, thesis (1′) is the central one, and the others follow from it as corollaries. The difference concerns a limitation seen in the mind's power of attention. On the MR, the mind's powers of attention are autonomous: the mind is able to attend to *things* as objects even though those things are neither given to the mind as objects nor do they contain any kind of *per se* unity. On the LR, however, attention is not autonomous. The understanding requires unity in order to attend to the thing as an object, and, as was seen before, this was problematic for modes qua properties.[37]

---

[35] Condillac (2001).

[36] If we want to push this harder, we can speculate regarding reasons for thinking that attention requires this: because discernment, which is necessary for attending, requires being able to contrast the idea from others, identifiable boundaries are a prerequisite for attention; thus they cannot result from attending.

[37] It is really important to note that the point here is not about the imagination. The imagination can create ideas of fictional substances because the idea of substance or substratum is able to unify the

According to the LR, Locke had to solve the unity problem *before* the idea of a mode could even be formed. Without unity, the elements would be discerned as distinct from one another and the group as a whole would fail to be discerned from anything or everything else precisely because it would not be recognized as a group. The claim behind the NT, according to this reading, is that language is the crucial power that allows for the possibility of discerning the modal idea from all other complex ideas, as well as the jumble of idea-elements presently before the mind.

Certainly this model is dissonant with the usual impressions of Locke according to which the mental takes priority over the linguistic.[38] No one can dispute that as Locke's general semantic orientation. I, for one, am not about to consider any such thing. But we should consider the narrower question of whether Locke's reflections on modes carve out an exception to the general impression of the linguistic–mental relationship that III.ii.2 suggests.

*3.3. Why Attribute the LR to Locke? The Textual Evidence*

I am defending the thesis that the LR is a more proper and better reading of Locke's NT than the MR. I am defending the idea that naming is part of the creation of Lockean modal* ideas and that they do much more than simply assist in the creation of the ideas. What I will show here is that the textual evidence is a wash between the two readings, that the texts cut both ways and so cannot determine the issue. Then I will discuss other evidence that, I shall argue, determines the question more conclusively.

Let us begin with the textual evidence for the MR. In II.xxii.2, we find a nice expression of thesis (1), the Formulation Thesis: "to form such *Ideas*, it sufficed, that the Mind put the parts of them together, and that they were consistent in the Understanding, without considering whether they had any real Being."[39] Note in particular the assertion that this *suffices* to form ideas of modes and the absence of any reference to names or naming. This seems pretty clear and compelling.[40]

We can also find what appear to be assertions of the Perfection Thesis, thesis (4) of the MR:

---

idea-elements (which consist of various ideas of qualities). The point here concerns the doctrine of modes itself—there is nothing that can function as the idea of substance or substratum does for modes. The problem here concerns the formal nature of modes, which has nothing to do with the imagination.

[38] "*Words in their primary or immediate Signification, stand for nothing, but the Ideas in the Mind of him that uses them*" (III.ii.2, 405).
[39] II.xxii.2, 288.
[40] Reasons will be given in Section 3.4 against taking this as expressing Locke's considered view on the formation of ideas of modes. In interpreting this passage, we should recognize the limited purpose Locke has here—namely, emphasizing how mixed modes themselves are "*Made by the Mind*", rather than explaining in detail the formation process for ideas of modes. In addition to the considerations discussed below, one might wish to note that this passage is inconsistent with II.xxx.4, where Locke suggests that fantastical ideas of modes, such as the idea of a round square, are possible.

It is plain, it has its Unity from an Act of the Mind combining those several simple *Ideas* together, and considering them as one complex one, consisting of those parts; and the mark of this Union, or that which is looked on generally to compleat it, is one name given to that Combination.[41]

Because they being of Man's making only, in order to naming, no such *Species* are taken notice of, or supposed to be, unless a *Name* be joined to it, as the sign of Man's having combined into one *Idea* several loose ones; and by that *Name*, giving a lasting Union to the Parts, which would otherwise cease to have any, as soon as the Mind laid by that abstract *Idea*, and ceased actually to think on it. But when a Name is once annexed to it, wherein the parts of that complex *Idea* have a settled and permanent Union, then is the *Essence*, as it were established, and the *Species* look'd on as compleat.[42]

The thing to notice here is that the name is being presented simply as a "mark" or a "sign" of the union that is "annexed" to the union, presumably after the fact. This is, of course, a very different concept from the name as *constituting* or *causing* the union. And it strongly implies that the role of the name is the lesser one of merely facilitating our thinking and use of the idea rather than literally constituting the idea in any way. At best, in other words, the name helps to perfect the idea by allowing the idea to become an "Essence" and complete the "species-ification" of the idea. In both passages, "compleat" is getting read in the "perfection" sense rather than in the literal sense of culminating or ending the process of creation. This all points directly back to the Existence Thesis, of course, and we should turn to the textual evidence for that now.

It is quite clear that Locke committed himself to the MR's Existence Thesis in the text. In II.xviii.5–7 he says plainly that we have ideas of modes for which there are no names in either own our language or in any human language whatsoever:

All *compounded Tastes and Smells*, are also Modes... but they being such, as generally we have no names for, are less taken notice of, and cannot be set down in writing... Though they are in themselves many of them very distinct *Ideas*; yet [they] *have ordinarily no distinct Name*, nor are much taken notice of, as distinct *Ideas*, where the difference is but very small between them. Whether Men have neglected these modes, and given no Names to them, as wanting measures nicely to distinguish them; or because when they were so distinguished, that Knowledge would not be of general, or necessary use, I leave it to the Thoughts of others... Thus we see, that there are great varieties of simple *Ideas*, as of Tastes and Smells, which have no Names; and of Modes many more.[43]

But perhaps even clearer and more compelling is III.v.15, where Locke gives an argument against the possibility of names contributing to the creation of ideas of modes.

---

[41] II.xxii.4, 289.   [42] III.v.11, 435.   [43] II.xviii.5–7, 224–6 *passim.*

In the beginning of Languages, it was necessary to have the *Idea*, before one gave it the Name: And so it is still, where making a new complex *Idea*, one also, by giving it a new Name, makes a new Word.[44]

*Necessarily*, the idea precedes the name; a necessary condition for naming is there being something to be named in other words. Thus, it is impossible to deny that Locke explicitly expressed widespread and substantial agreement with three of the four core theses that make up the MR.

But before we accept the MR, we need to recognize that these passages are balanced by equally clear and extensive expressions of agreement with the core theses of the LR of the NT.

At III.v.4–6 we find Locke's "official" description of the formation process for ideas of modes.[45]

The Mind does these three things: First, It chuses a certain Number. Secondly, It gives them connection, and makes them into one *Idea*. Thirdly, It ties them together by a Name... No body can doubt, but that these *Ideas* of mixed Modes, are made by a voluntary Collection of *Ideas* put together in the Mind independent from any original Patterns in Nature, who will but reflect, that this sort of complex *Idea* may be made, abstracted, and have names given them, and so a Species be constituted, before any one individual of that Species ever existed... 'tis the Mind, that combines several scattered independent *Ideas*, into one complex one; and by the common name it gives them, makes them the Essence of a certain Species, without regulating it self by any connexion they have in Nature.[46]

We also find commitments to thesis (2′), the Cognition Thesis of the LR, in II. xvi.5–7. Locke was arguing here that the reason why certain people fail to think about or are unable to conceive of certain numbers is because they do not possess names for such numbers.[47] The underlying reason for the necessity of the names is the complexity of our ideas of numbers and the minuteness of the difference between any two ideas of number, especially larger and larger ones. The only way to prevent such ideas from being confused and indistinct messes is through the role that the names play in differentiating them.

In addition, we should recognize that this point ought not to be restricted to the simple modes of number. Almost every idea of mode is very complex. Indeed, according to Locke our ideas of mixed modes are generally much more complex and more prone to being confused and indistinct than our ideas of numbers.[48] So, if it is the case that for numbers names are necessary to formulate their ideas of their complexity, it ought also to apply to modes generally, *mutatis mutandis*.

---

[44] III.v.15, 437.
[45] It deserves to be considered the "official" description because it occurs in a section entitled "*How this* [modes being made arbitrarily and without Pattern] *are done*" and begins with the claim that "To understand this aright, we must consider *wherein this making of these complex* Ideas *consists*".
[46] III.v.4, 429.   [47] II.xvi.5–7, 206–8 *passim*.   [48] III.v.13, 436 and III.v.8, 433.

Evidence for a commitment to the linguistic version of the Existence Thesis (3′) may be found in II.xvi.5–7 as well. It is the claim that names are *necessary* for numbers and their ideas. "Names or Marks for each distinct Combination, seem more necessary than in any other sort of *Ideas*... [For without them] the whole business of Numbering will be disturbed, and there will remain only the confused *Idea* of multitude, but the *Ideas* necessary to distinct numeration, will not be attained to." Such a necessity undercuts any claim to the independence of the idea from the name. The same point seems to be implied in III.v.15 as well. According to Locke, "it is convenient, if not necessary, to know the Names, before one endeavour to frame these complex *Ideas*".[49] Reading this as evidence for a commitment to thesis (3′) depends on how one takes the concessive force of the "if not necessary", of course. But it dovetails nicely with II.xvi.5–7 and could in principle be pushed.

The final bit of textual evidence concerns (4′), the linguistic version of the Perfection Thesis. The same passages cited in evidence of (4) are appealed to here, only now the interpreter provides reason against taking Locke's talk of "marks" and "signs" as diminishing them or their role. These reasons include how Locke spoke of ideas as signs in II.xvi.5–7, already noted, which clearly was not meant to diminish them or their role in the formation of our ideas of numbers. If we do not read such a diminution into the texts supporting the Perfection Thesis, we can easily and much more naturally read them as supporting the LR rather than the MR, because "compleat" is naturally taken in the usual sense of creating or formulating.

So the textual situation looks to be a wash. Some passages clearly and compellingly point to the MR. Most important here seem to be commitments to the Existence Thesis expressed in II.xviii.5–7 and III.v.15. But other passages clearly and compellingly point to the LR. Most important here seem to be commitments to the alternative Formation Thesis in III.v.4–6 and to the alternative Cognition Thesis in II.xvi.5–7. And it seems possible naturally to read some passages in both ways, such as II.xxii.4 and III.v.11.

It would seem, then, that the text is ambiguous and Locke himself confused, conflicted, or uncommitted on this key point. Perhaps we should, strictly speaking, conclude that he took no position on it. Fine—*concedemus*—but who cares about that? I did not go into this business simply to understand the psychological state of historical figures. I went into it to understand the philosophical systems and visions that those figures strove to devise, develop, and defend. So the interesting question is not what Locke himself *really* believed, but rather "what did his philosophical vision require?" or "what should Locke have held?" And to approach that we need to go beyond the textual evidence and identify which theoretical features were more important or central to Locke's philosophical vision and ascertain how the two sets of theses affect or enable these theoretical features.

---

[49] III.v.15, 437. On the LR, the force of the "if not necessary" is not, obviously, concessive.

## 3.4. Why Attribute the LR to Locke? The Theoretical Evidence

I shall now argue that on this basis we ought to attribute the LR to Locke's philosophical system. I first undercut the importance of the most compelling textual evidence for the MR, the support of thesis (2), the MR's Existence Thesis. Then I argue that the theoretical heart of Locke's doctrine of modes was the claim that our ideas of modes are their own archetypes.[50] Within Locke's system, this was the key to unlocking their reality, certainty, and informativeness. And the only way to support this claim, I argue, is by adopting the linguistic reading of the NT. This is the only way possible because only this way satisfies two conditions for functioning as an archetype, a persistence condition, and an universalizability condition.

The first thing we ought to recognize, however, is that the mentalistic version of the Existence Thesis is an outlier. It plays no role in Locke's doctrine of modes and could be dropped without loss to anything else within the doctrine of modes. Nothing else Locke says hangs on it, or on the "in the beginnings of languages" argument of III.v.15.

But the same cannot be said of the LR. In particular, because of the conceptual connections between names, essences, and archetypes, if Locke were to accept the mentalistic interpretation of the NT, he would not be able to claim that ideas of modes are their own archetypes, and would lose the central claim that our knowledge of modes is real, instructive, and certain.

I take it that the claim that the central point of the doctrine of modes was to secure real, instructive, and certain knowledge of mathematics and morality, among other things, is uncontroversial.[51] Certainly, it is difficult to see the point of postulating this category if such knowledge collapses. I also take it as clear that Locke could not have compromised on the claims that ideas of modes are their own archetypes and that their real and their nominal essences are identical. Our real question here concerns the conceptual connection between names, essences, and archetypes.

The key lies in the archetypal *function* of ideas of modes. They can perform that function only *via their names*. Thus, those names are necessary for the ideas being archetypes, which, as already mentioned, was not something Locke or any Lockean could compromise on and which constitutes the essence of modal* ideas.

---

[50] For some old discussions of whether Locke truly could have, and should have, adopted the doctrine that ideas of modes are their own archetypes and that the nominal essences and real essences of modes are identical, see Perry (1967: 223-4); Aronson and Lewis (1970: 195-7); Mackie (1976: 90-1). This is also implied by more recent criticisms of Locke's claim that ideas of modes may be formed without reference to reality. See Ayers (1991: ii. 98) and Jolley (1999: 159).

[51] I do not mean to suggest here that naming or the doctrine of modes would be unimportant for other things, such as coordinated or collaborative action or communication. My point here is that the central focus in Locke's thinking and in the philosophical system he is constructing is the epistemological issue of grounding the certainty of our knowledge about mathematics, morality, and other modal* properties.

My argument goes like this:

(A) To be an archetype is to *regulate* predications and the attribution of properties to a thing.
(B) Therefore, archetypes are inherently normative, and perform an essentially normative, prescription function.
(C) In order to perform such a function, it is necessary that these ideas satisfy the following three conditions:
   1. Abstraction Condition: The ideas apply to a variety of instances of phenomena, at least in principle and generally in practice.
   2. Persistence Condition: The idea must persist in order to regulate predications and ascriptions of properties to things.
   3. Universalizability Condition: The idea must be capable, at least in principle, of being used by any number of other thinkers.
(D) Ideas without names cannot satisfy all three (in particular, they cannot satisfy conditions 2 and 3).
(E) Language and names allow all three conditions to be satisfied.
(F) Therefore, the MR ought not be accepted by a Lockean.
(G) Therefore, the LR ought to be.

Let us look at the argument in detail.

(A) Locke did not provide any definition of archetypes, but he did make a couple of illuminating comments about them. First, he defined the reality of ideas in terms of them.[52] Here, archetypes are placed on a par with "Nature" and said to ground reality by exhibiting a conformity with a particular tokening of an idea. Second, Locke also defined the adequacy of ideas in terms of archetypes: "Those I call *Adequate*, which perfectly represent those Archetypes, which the Mind supposes them taken from; which it intends them to stand for, and to which it refers them."[53] Here, we see three characteristics involving the archetype—idea connection: the tokening of the idea is supposed to be *taken from* the archetype; it is intended to *stand for* the archetype; and it is *referred to* the archetype. These characteristics point to the idea that the archetype regulates predications and ascriptions of a property to a thing; the archetype lays out the satisfaction conditions for being that sort of thing, in other words. It is because a token idea signifies the elements contained within the archetype that the idea is entitled to the name of the thing and said adequately to represent it. That there be an idea—archetype connection is necessary for the idea's being real—and that that connection exemplifies certain semantic and referential characteristics are necessary for the idea's being an adequate representation of the archetype.

---

[52] "By *real Ideas*, I mean such as have a Foundation in Nature; such as have a Conformity with the real Being, and Existence of Things, or with their Archetypes" (II.xxx.1, 372).

[53] II.xxxi.1, 375.

(B) We can see, then, that the archetype is supposed to perform at least two crucial functions, grounding the reality of the idea and its adequacy. Moreover, we can see that both of these functions are inherently prescriptive and normative. The archetypes govern the idea-tokenings; that a particular idea-tokening is an idea *of that* is due solely to the conformity of the idea-tokening with the archetype. In other words, the archetype lays down the norms for being an idea *of that*.

(C) In order to be normative in that way, it is necessary that the archetype transcend the particular idea-tokening. It is necessary, in other words, that the archetype be at the very least abstract and general in a way that the idea-tokening is not. Caesar's triumph, for example, was Caesar's. But the archetype of *triumph* does not contain Caesar as an element, because Anthony's triumph was just as much of a triumph as Caesar's. Caesar's triumph was a triumph because the idea of it conformed to the abstract, general idea of triumph. Archetypes must be abstract and general if they are to serve as the grounds for the semantic properties rolled into the concept of adequacy–inadequacy, which includes the identification of satisfaction conditions whereby things really existing are to be ranked and denominated.[54]

But that is not all. Archetypes also require being extensive. That is to say, they require the possibility of encompassing more than one tokening of the idea, if they are supposed to regulate predications. Being extensive can take two forms, both of which generally obtain. They can extend interpersonally—they can apply to idea-tokenings of a variety of different individual thinkers. We call this "universalizability". The archetypes should at least in principle apply to and regulate the idea-tokenings of several different thinkers. Or they can extend temporally. They can apply to idea-tokenings spaced at different moments. We call this "persistence". The archetypes should at least in principle persist across several moments. Generally, archetypes will exhibit both sorts of extensiveness.

These three features follow analytically from the notion of regulation. Regulation requires some difference from that which is regulated. What precisely that difference is, and how great it must be, are not material for our discussion; only that there must be a difference. It makes no sense to say that something *individual and momentary* regulates anything, including itself, because there is no basis for any conformity relation to obtain. When something can be said to regulate itself, it is only because a conformity relation obtains between its present state and a past or future one. Furthermore, nothing regulates by virtue of its individual and momentary characteristics. Something regulates by virtue of its abstract, general features, or characteristics. As any reader of the passages pertaining to the NT can see, Locke is more focused on the issues of persistence and generality than on interpersonal extent. But the key here is to recognize that these characteristics are necessarily bound up with the idea that archetypes are normative and regulate predications and ascriptions.

---

[54] II.xxxi.3, 376.

And in the discussions pertaining to the NT, Locke recognized and pushed this very point.

(D) Bare ideas cannot satisfy the conditions necessary for archetypal functioning. According to Locke, "our *Ideas* [are] nothing but actual perceptions in the Mind", which means that they are "fleeting, and transient Combinations... which have but a short existence any where, but in the Minds of Men, and there too have no longer any existence, than whilst they are thought on".[55] We nowadays recognize this as meaning that ideas are purely subjective entities. Perhaps purely subjective entities can be abstract and general.[56] But it would seem difficult for such entities to satisfy the two conditions related to archetypal extent. It would be impossible for a purely subjective entity to satisfy the universalizability condition. And subjective ideas cannot satisfy the persistence condition either.

Subjective ideas become nothing the moment that they are not thought of. And no idea lasts long in a person's cognitive gaze, according to Locke. The fleeting and transient character of ideas is a running theme throughout the *Essay*. Sometimes, with great intellectual effort, an idea can be held in contemplation and retained for a time. But Locke is talking about minutes here, which is far short of the persistence required of his archetypes. Locke requires ideas of modes to persist for years and decades, not mere minutes.

One might think that perhaps memory and retention could be called upon to help here. That seems unlikely for a Lockean, however. Memory itself is fraught. Locke's main focus in II.x is on the failings and limitations of memory.[57] Such a constant wearing-down and fading of our ideas is inconsistent with the sort of stability and persistence required to function as true archetypes. Archetypal function requires long-term, stable persistence.[58]

(E) Language and naming are just the right support for ideas here. Language and naming can rather easily satisfy all three characteristics. The close connection between words and abstract, general ideas is often remarked on by Locke, as was mentioned at

---

[55] II.x.2, 150 and II.xxi.8, 291.

[56] The general drift of seventeenth-century thinking about language and abstract seems to be that language is at least a sign or mark of the ability to abstract. Locke argued in just this way in II.xi.10–12. While there is considerable evidence that Locke believed there to be a strong correlation between abstraction and language, it is not clear that he believed language to be necessary for or prior to abstraction.

[57] "There seems to be a constant decay of all our *Ideas*, even of those which are struck deepest, and in Minds the most retentive," Locke declared in II.x.5, 151.

[58] It is possible that some individuals possess truly prodigious memories, whose ideas do not constantly decay. Locke recognized this possibility and noted the stories told of M. Pascal's retentive abilities. "'Tis reported of that prodigy of Parts, Monsieur *Pascal*, that, till the decay of his health had impaired his memory, he forgot nothing of what he had done, read, or thought in any part of his rational Age. This is a privilege so little known to most Men, that it seems almost incredible to those, who, after the ordinary way, measure all others by themselves" (II.x.9, 154). Perhaps someone like him could be said to satisfy the persistence condition without falling back on names. But the archetypal function of ideas of modes is open to us all, according to Locke, and not just the exceedingly rare folks with photographic memories. Ordinary minds require something other than memory to ground the persistence of our ideas of modes, if we are to have something stable enough to serve as a norm for other idea-tokenings. Bare ideas need help here.

the beginning of this chapter. Such a close connection might easily suggest that names are necessary for abstraction, although it is not a point that Locke himself seemed to develop or push. Of more interest is the way that names and language satisfy the more difficult universalizabilty and persistence conditions. They are able to do this because language is inherently a shared, normative system, as Locke recongized. We do not just prescribe things within language or via language; speaking itself is a form of prescription. Whenever we speak, we not only express support for the norms and regulations of common use; we reassert them. It is by our tacit agreement with other members of our linguistic communities that we continue codifying the linguistic and semantic prescriptions of old. And, in the case that we should attempt to coin a new name, we project those linguistic and semantic norms forward as fully-fledged members of the linguistic community. This is no guarantee that such prescriptions will be taken up by the linguist community, but that is not the point. The point is that in performing the linguistic act we intend them to be taken up by the community and intend that they persist indefinitely. And that is the key to names having a regulative function—they are bound up within an inherently normative activity, the activity of speaking.

This grounds universalizability because other speakers—the whole linguistic community, in fact—are implicated in our speech acts. But more is at stake. This also grounds the persistence of the idea of mode. It grounds it via "common use". Common use is a concept that is clearly and importantly present in Locke's thinking about language and ideas, but that is relatively neglected in analyses of Locke's philosophical system. But here is one place where appreciating the importance of the concept of common use is crucial—an idea of a mode persists through the common use of a name. Just so long as the tacit agreement of the linguist community with regard to the use of a name persists, so long does that modal* idea persist. Common use does not refer to any particular set of speech acts; it refers to the propriety rules that govern speech acts within the linguistic community. Just so long as the community members would recognize certain speech acts involving names of mode to be proper, the idea of the mode persists within that linguistic community. Of course these norms can change,[59] but this is not a constant and general decay like an individual's memory. Lockean common use is able to ground the persistence of an idea for years, decades, even centuries, as his understanding of archetypal function would seem to require.

Locke also hinted at an interesting argument that connected the purpose of forming ideas of modes with the purpose of language. "For to what purpose should the Memory charge it self with such Compositions, unless it were by Abstraction to make them general? And to what purpose make them general, unless it were, that

---

[59] II.xxi.7, 291.

they might have general *Names*, for the convenience of Discourse, and Communication?"[60] This refers back to an argument in III.iii.3:

> If it [having a distinct peculiar name for every particular thing] were possible, *it would yet be useless*; because it would not serve to the chief end of Language. Men would in vain heap up Names of particular Things, that would not serve them to communicate their Thoughts. Men learn Names, and use them in Talk with others, only that they may be understood: which is then only done, when by Use or Consent, the Sound I make by the Organs of Speech, excites in another Man's Mind, who hears it, the *Idea* I apply it to in mine, when I speak it. This cannot be done by Names, applied to particular Things, whereof I alone having the *Ideas* in my mind, the Name of them could not be significant, or intelligible, to another, who was not acquainted with all those very particular Things, which had fallen under my Notice.[61]

What is driving the process is language, according to this argument. Language drives the formation of abstract ideas, and abstraction drives the formation of ideas of modes. What this suggests is that non-human, non-linguistic animals do not and cannot formulate ideas of modes, even though they may "observe" modes just as well as we do. They may observe them, but they do not conceptualize them, which is just to say that their observations of modes do not attain the level of ideas or archetypes. Why not? Because animal cognition cannot achieve the normativity required to function archetypically. Non-human animals have the same kind of perceptions, the same kind of basic ideas that humans have.[62] The difference between humans and other animals is language, which makes a very material difference when it comes to the types of ideas each may possess (simple qualitative ideas and ideas of substances versus simple qualitative ideas, ideas of substances, *and* ideas of modes and relations).

This is the fundamental reason why, for Locke, the essences of modes have a much tighter connection to their names than the essences of substances do.[63] "*The near relation* that there is *between Species, Essences, and* their *general Names*, at least in *mixed Modes*, will farther appear, when we consider, that it is the Name that seems to preserve those *Essences*, and given them their lasting duration,"[64] said Locke. This might suggest that it is the sustaining of the essence that is crucial to the especially near relation between names, species, and essences of modes. But that cannot quite be right, as III.iii.19 reveals. In III.iii.19, Locke argued that the eternality of essences is

---

[60] III.v.11, 435.  [61] III.iii.3, 409–10.  [62] II.ix.12, 148.

[63] "*Men speaking of mixed Modes*, seldom imagine or *take any other for Species of them, but such as are set out by name*: Because they being of Man's making only, in order to naming, no such *Species* are taken notice of, or supposed to be, unless a *Name* be joined to it, as the sign of Man's having combined into one *Idea* several loose ones; and by that *Name*, giving a lasting Union to the Parts, which would otherwise cease to have any, as soon as the Mind laid by that abstract *Idea*, and ceased actually to think on it. But when a Name is once annexed to it, wherein the parts of that complex *Idea* have a settled and permanent Union; then is the *Essence*, as it were established, and the *Species* look'd on as compleat" (III. v.11, 435) and "There being no *Species* of these ordinarily taken notice of, but what have Names; and those *Species*, or rather their Essences, being abstract complex *Ideas* made arbitrarily by the Mind, it is convenient, if not necessary, to know the Names, before one endeavour to frame these complex *Ideas*" (III.v.15, 437).

[64] III.v.10, 434.

rooted in the sort of persistence according them by names, and he said that this applied to substances just as easily as it applies to modes.[65]

The key for modes, however, is not the possibility of the essence persisting after the loss of all individuals of that kind. The key is a different kind of independence from instantiations, the possibility of the real essence being formulated, obtaining, and persisting even though *there never was, is, or will be any individuals of that kind*.[66] The truly peculiar nature of the name–essence relation for modes is rooted in the distinctive kind of persistence that the name accords the essence. In the case of substances, that persistence requires at the very least a past instance of the essence for there to be a species. In the case of modes, however, even that rather thin requirement is rejected. Ideas of modes may be real, talked about, and known despite the non-existence of any instances of the mode. Language, and language alone, makes this possible for Locke.

The pair of conclusions, (F) and (G), follow immediately. The mentalistic conception of the NT cannot be sustained once we focus on the archetypal nature of idea of modes. That archetypal nature is possible only through language and the names of modes. This is why a Lockean must accept the LR. And this is why we should attribute the LR to Locke himself. Locke conceived that the archetypal nature of ideas of modes was inseparable from them; he believed that all ideas of modes, by their very nature, were archetypes.[67] This would suggest that it is impossible to have an idea of a mode that was not an archetype, and since being an archetype is necessarily connected with language and having a name, it would follow that no modal idea could be formulated without being named. Hence, the LR must be the right way to conceive of Locke's naming thesis.

## 4. Conclusion

What we have seen here is the emergence of a new form of linguistic use, the emergence of the idea that certain kinds of naming literally create new thought. In the case of Lockean modes, it is the name that makes the idea possible, rather than

---

[65] "That such *abstract* Ideas, *with Names to them*, as we have been speaking of, *are Essences*, may farther appear by what we are told concerning *Essences, viz.* that they are all ingenerable, and incorruptible. Which cannot be true of the real Constitutions of Things, which being and perish with them... But *Essences*, being taken for *Ideas*, established in the Mind, with Names annexed to them, they are supposed to remain steadily the same, whatever mutations the particular Substances are liable to. For whatever becomes of *Alexander* and *Bucephalus*, the *Ideas* to which *Man* and *Horse* are annexed, are supposed nevertheless to remain the same; and so the *Essences* of those Species are preserved whole and undestroy'd, whatever Changes happen to any, or all of the Individuals of those *Species*. By this means the *Essences* of a *Species* rests safe and entire, without the existence of so much as one Individual of that kind" (III.iii.19, 419).

[66] "We cannot doubt, but Law-makers have often made Laws about Species of Actions, which were only the Creatures of their own Understanding; Beings that had no other existence, but in their own Minds." Nevertheless, "these Species of mixed Modes... might be as well discoursed of, and reasoned about, and as certain Truths discovered of them, whilst yet they had no being but in the Understanding" (III.v.5, 430).

[67] See II.xxx.4, 373–4 and II.xxxi.3–5, 376–8.

vice versa. The name makes the idea possible because language, in so far as it is an inherently normative system, makes it possible for the idea to function as an archetype. And, in the case of ideas of modes, it is necessary that they function as archetypes, because they can be real, truths can be known about them, and informative discoveries can be made about them, even though no modes have ever or will ever obtain in nature. Indeed, functioning as an archetype is the heart of the very essence of a modal* idea. The radical independence modes have from nature means that there is nothing else to ground these truths about modes except for the ideas themselves. And the archetypal function that is required of this cannot be performed by fleeting and fragile, subjective ideas. It can be performed only by ideas codified in and protected by language and the norms of a linguistic community. Hence, the need for names.

Condillac would soon take up this Lockean idea and stretch it far beyond the bounds that Locke had set for it. Whether or not that is a fair extension of Locke's thinking is best left for another day. But we can now see that the seed for Condillac's enthusiastic extension was in fact contained in Locke, and that it was, at least while contained within those bounds, a properly Lockean doctrine.

# References

Aronson, C., and Lewis, D. (1970). 'Locke on Modes, Substances, and Knowledge', *Journal of the History of Philosophy*, 8: 193–9.
Ayers, M. (1991). *Locke: Epistemology and Ontology*. New York: Routledge.
Bacon, F. (2004). *Novum organum*, trans. Graham Rees with Maria Wakely. Oxford: Clarendon Press.
Condillac, E. de (2001). *Essay on the Origin of Human Knowledge*, trans. Hans Aarsleff. Cambridge: Cambridge University Press.
Dawson, H. (2007). *Locke, Language, and Early Modern Philosophy*. Cambridge: Cambridge University Press.
Guyer, P. (1994). 'Locke's Philosophy of Language', in *The Cambridge Companion to Locke*, ed. Vere Chappell. Cambridge: Cambridge University Press.
Hall, R. (1987). 'Locke and Sensory Experience: Another Look at Simple Ideas of Sensation', *Locke Newsletter*, 18: 11–31.
Hill, B. (2008). 'Locke on Propositions and Assertion', *Modern Schoolman*, 85: 187–205.
Jolley, N. (1999). *Locke*. Oxford: Oxford University Press.
Kant, I. (1933). *Critique of Pure Reason*, trans. Norman Kemp-Smith. London: Macmillan and Co.
Locke, J. (1975). *An Essay Concerning Human Understanding*, ed. Peter H. Nidditch. Oxford: Clarendon Press.
Mackie, J. L. (1976). *Problems from Locke*. Oxford: Oxford University Press.
Mill, John Stuart (1963). *System of Logic, Ratiocinative and Inductive* (1843), in *Collected Works of John Stuart Mill*, ed. J. M. Robson. Toronto: University of Toronto Press, vii–viii.
Perry, D. (1967). 'Locke on Mixed Modes, Relations, and Knowledge', *Journal of the History of Philosophy*, 5: 219–35.

# 10

# Herder's Doctrine of Meaning as Use

*Michael N. Forster*

Philosophers have long pondered the nature of meanings or concepts. During the first 2,000 years or more of the discipline, the predominant tendency was to equate them with items that are in principle independent of language—for example, objects referred to, Platonic Forms, or the subjective mental "ideas" favoured by the British Empiricists and others in the seventeenth and eighteenth centuries.[1] More recently, though, a radically different sort of doctrine has won favour: a doctrine that equates them instead with the *use of words*. This doctrine is most famously associated with the name of Wittgenstein in the twentieth century. But it did not first emerge with him and it does not come in only one version. The present chapter will therefore first explore its genesis,[2] then consider the question of what specific form the doctrine should take.

## The Doctrine in Herder and his Predecessors

One of the central figures in the early development of the doctrine was J. G. Herder (1744–1803). Herder argued against theories that equate meanings or concepts with referents, Platonic Forms, or subjective mental "ideas". He instead held that they consist in the use of words. For example, as early as *On Diligence in Several Learned Languages* (1764) he writes:

Whoever learns to express himself with exactness precisely thereby gathers for himself a treasure of determinate concepts. The first words that we mumble are the most important foundation stones of the understanding. (Herder 1985: i. 27)

---

[1] For an excellent account of this last position, the "way of ideas", see Hacking (1993: chs 2–5).
[2] I shall not here attempt to pursue its history further back than the early modern period, though it is reasonable to suppose that such a longer story could be told, which would include medieval nominalism, for instance. Other chapters in the present volume may contain helpful information here.

And already in the *Fragments on Recent German Literature* (1767–8) he insists on the "adhesion of the thought to the word" or the "expression"; writes concerning the understanding of concepts that "the question is not how an expression can be etymologically derived and analytically determined, but how it is *used* [*gebraucht*]"; and accordingly advocates that, in order, for example, to understand the changing nature of people's moral concepts over the course of history, one must closely scrutinize their changing word-usages (Herder 1985: i. 421–3, 322). Later, in *On the Spirit of Hebrew Poetry* (1782–3), he writes: "Let us seek the word's concept not from etymologies, which are always uncertain, but according to the clear use [*Gebrauch*] of the name [i.e. the word] in its various times" (Herder 1985: v. 1007).[3]

Herder's mentor J. G. Hamann (1730–88) has sometimes been credited with inventing a doctrine about meanings or concepts of this general sort and then passing it on to Herder (for example, by Isaiah Berlin).[4] Hamann does indeed eventually embrace such a doctrine. This is perhaps clearest from his *Metacritique on the Purism of Reason* from 1784. There he opens with warm praise of Hume's praise of Berkeley's attack on abstract ideas—which Hamann evidently (mis)understands as an attack on any conception of meanings or concepts that takes them to be subjective ideas (Hamann 1820: vii. 3). Hamann then implies that, instead of concepts being independent of, and actively governing, language, the opposite is in fact true ("Receptivity of language and spontaneity of concepts!" he writes sarcastically); that language is "without any other source of authority than tradition and usage [*Usum*]"; and that words get elevated from being mere objects of the senses to constituting "understanding and concepts" simply by the "spirit of their employment [*Einsetzung*] and application" (Hamann 1820: vii. 6, 13; cf. 14). However, as I have argued in detail elsewhere, it actually seems probable that, instead of Hamann being the source of this doctrine and Herder the borrower, the truth is the other way round (Forster 2010a: chs 2, 9).

On the other hand, if Herder was probably not indebted to Hamann here, there are other people to whom he *was*. Spinoza (1632–77) had already held in the *Tractatus theologico-politicus* (1670) that "words gain their meaning [*significationem*] solely from their usage [*ex solo usu*]", and that it was therefore a primary task of an interpreter of ancient texts to determine what the relevant word-usages were at the time when the texts were written (Spinoza 1951: 167, 101). Herder seems not to have come under the *direct* influence of the *Tractatus* until several years after he first began implying commitment to this doctrine in 1764; his enthusiasm for the work seems to date only from around 1768 (see Forster 2012). So his original commitment to the doctrine was probably not *directly* influenced by Spinoza. However, it *was* in all

---

[3] This doctrine, besides being fundamental to Herder's philosophy of language, also had profound implications for his theories of interpretation and translation (see Forster 2010a: esp. chs 2, 4).
[4] Berlin (1976: 165): "Herder had derived from Hamann his notion that words and ideas are one" (cf. pp. 166–7).

likelihood *indirectly* influenced by him. For already by the late 1750s and early 1760s there was a movement afoot in German biblical hermeneutics that was ultimately influenced by Spinoza, and that emphasized the fundamental importance of word-usage for meaning. For example, Wettstein writes in a work on biblical hermeneutics first published in 1756:

The true meaning [*significatio*] of words and phrases is not so much to be sought from etymology or from single words taken separately, but rather from usage [*ex usu*] and examples. (Wettstein 1766: 120)[5]

And Ernesti's *Institutio interpretis Novi Testamenti* from 1761 holds that a word's meaning depends on its usage, and that interpreting a word therefore essentially turns on determining its usage:

It is evident that the signification [*sensum*] of words depends upon the *usage of language* [*ab usu loquendi*]; and that the latter being known, the former is known also. (Ernesti 1832: i. 27; cf. 63)

Like Wettstein, Ernesti especially contrasts this approach to determining meaning with a focus on etymology, which he considers unreliable (Ernesti 1832: i. 91, 97, 161). Herder, who was a great admirer of Ernesti's work, was pretty clearly drawing on this school of biblical hermeneutics in his early commitment to the doctrine.[6]

What, if anything, did Herder's version of the doctrine *add* to it, though? The exact force of Spinoza's version is obscure, but Ernesti at least was basically advancing a doctrine about what determines, and hence how to discover, which meaning a word bears rather than a doctrine about what meaning *is*. Or, as one might alternatively put it, he was advancing an *epistemological* doctrine rather than an *ontological* one. Thus, despite making the points just cited, he nevertheless still conceived the nature of word-meaning in conventional Enlightenment terms as consisting in *a connection between a word and an idea* (he was a great admirer of Locke) (Ernesti 1832: i. 15–17, 27).[7] By contrast, Herder, and then following him Hamann, developed Ernesti's merely epistemological doctrine into a corresponding and explanatory *ontological* one: a word's meaning depends on its usage, so that discovering word-usage is the key to discovering word-meaning, because *meaning just consists in word-usage*.

This still leaves the question of the *justification* for such a doctrine, though. Hamann nowhere gives one, as far as I can see; he merely rejects the various traditional models of meaning in a more or less unargued way and opts instead for

---

[5] Concerning Spinoza being the ultimate source of this doctrine, notice that this passage is almost identical to the passage already quoted from Spinoza not only in semantic content but also in wording.

[6] Notice, for example, that Herder echoes, not only Wettstein's and Ernesti's idea that meaning depends on word-usage and their consequent injunction to determine meaning by determining word-usage, but also their insistence that this is superior to a focus on etymologies, which are unreliable as a guide to meaning.

[7] The same may be true of Wettstein (though this is less clear); Wettstein was also an admirer of Locke, especially of Locke's close attention to word-usage when interpreting the Pauline Epistles.

equating meaning with word-usage again in a more or less unargued way. But Herder's position is more interesting, and makes an important contribution. In *Ideas for the Philosophy of History of Humanity* (1784–91) he explicitly rejects the notion that a word's meaning or concept is its referent:

> No language expresses things [*Sachen*] but only names [i.e. words/concepts]. Also no human reason therefore has cognition of things but it has only characteristic marks of them which it signifies with words. (Herder 1985: vi. 348; cf. 348–50)

Moreover, if one surveys his writings more broadly, one finds that he has at least three powerful reasons justifying that rejection: (1) Already in the *Fragments* (1767–8), then especially at the start of the *Treatise on the Origin of Language* (1772), he argues that the original and fundamental roots of human language are *expressive* in nature rather than referential or descriptive—namely, the expressive "language of sensation" that human beings share with animals[8]—a position that would be incompatible with equating meanings with referents. (2) Implicitly in the *Treatise*, then more explicitly later in *A Metacritique on the Critique of Pure Reason* (1799), he argues that even the meanings of singular referring terms essentially and fundamentally involve *general* concepts[9]—which again seems to block equating meanings with referents. (3) As can be seen from an early draft of the *Treatise* in which he criticizes our tendency to accept uncritically "linguistic concepts" that we receive from tradition but that are in fact empty (Herder 1877: v. 152–3), Herder (like almost anyone who has a significant knowledge of the history of thought) is acutely aware of the phenomenon of meaningful referring-terms (proper names, terms for general kinds, and so forth) that happen to lack referents (e.g. "Zeus" and "centaurs")—a phenomenon that is again incompatible with equating meanings with referents. This complex Herderian case against equating meanings with referents anticipates much important subsequent philosophy of language that has taken a similar position, including work by Frege and Wittgenstein.[10]

Herder also hints at a powerful argument for rejecting both the Platonic theory of Forms and the equation of meanings with subjective mental "ideas", and for equating them with word-usages instead. Already implicitly in 1765, then more explicitly later, he alludes approvingly to some lines from Edward Young's poem *Night Thoughts*:

> Speech, Thought's Canal! Speech, Thought's Criterion too.
> Thought, in the Mine, may come forth Gold or Dross;
> When coin'd in Word, we know its *real* Worth.[11]

---

[8] The *Treatise* famously resists attempts such as Condillac's to derive the whole of human language from this expressive "language of sensation", but it also insists that this is an original and fundamental *part* of human language.

[9] H. S. Reimarus had already argued for a priority of general concepts over particular concepts in his *Allgemeine Betrachtungen über die Triebe der Tiere* (1760).

[10] For more details, see Forster (2010a: 69–70).

[11] See Herder (1985: i. 39; 1877: xviii. 385).

What Herder finds attractive in these lines is the suggestion that how one uses words is the decisive criterion for what thoughts and concepts one has. Herder also says things that divide up that generic point into two more specific points: (A) that using words in certain ways is *necessary* for having corresponding thoughts and concepts; and (B) that it is also *sufficient* for having them. For example, concerning (A), he writes in the *Fragments*:

Who can express himself about all subjects... in the language of common life more fluently and correctly than the common man of good healthy understanding? But now, try in his case to separate the *thought* from the *expression*—you do not understand the word. (Herder 1985: i. 395; cf. 556–7)

And concerning (B), as we have already seen, he writes in *On Diligence*:

Whoever learns to express himself with exactness precisely thereby gathers for himself a treasure of determinate concepts.

These passages already suggest a powerful line of argument against the Platonic theory of Forms and the equation of meanings with subjective mental "ideas", and in support of equating them with word-usages instead—a line of argument that would later be developed more elaborately by Hegel and Wittgenstein.[12] The line of argument in question focuses on our ordinary criteria for ascribing semantic understanding to people, and goes roughly as follows. First, as Herder's (A)-passages already suggest: if, as Platonism or the theory of subjective "ideas" holds, meaning consisted in a mental connection to a Platonic Form or in possessing a subjective idea, then one would expect that, in cases where we assume that this occurs for a person, our ordinary criteria for ascribing semantic understanding would tell us to ascribe it to him no matter how wayward his linguistic behaviour might be. But, in fact, we find that, if we assume that it occurs but also that he engages in very wayward linguistic behaviour, our ordinary criteria dictate that we should *deny* him such understanding. Conversely, as Herder's (B)-passages already suggest: if Platonism or the theory of subjective "ideas" were true, then one would expect that, in cases where we assume that a person engages in all the linguistic behaviour that is typical of someone who semantically understands but that he lacks the relevant mental connection to a Platonic Form or possession of a subjective "idea", our ordinary criteria would dictate that we should deny him semantic understanding. But, actually, we rather find that they dictate that we should *ascribe* it to him. By contrast, these two facts concerning our ordinary criteria for ascribing semantic understanding accord *perfectly* with an equation of meaning with word-usage.

---

[12] Wittgenstein's version of this line of argument is well known. For a discussion of Hegel's much less well-known version of it, see Forster (1998: chs 2, 4).

## The Doctrine in Herder's Immediate Successors

As we have already noted, after Herder had adopted, radicalized, and justified the doctrine of meaning as use, it was taken over from him by his friend Hamann. But there were also several other important philosophers of language in the next generation who took it over.

Hegel (1770–1831) already assumes a version of the doctrine in his *Phenomenology of Spirit* (1807). For instance, he writes there:

> Although it is commonly said that reasonable men pay attention not to the word but to the thing itself, yet this does not give us permission to describe a thing in terms inappropriate to it. For this is at once incompetence and deceit, to fancy and to pretend that one merely has not the right word, and to hide from oneself that really one has failed to get hold of the thing itself, i.e. the concept. If one had the concept, then one would also have the right word. (Hegel 1977: 198)[13]

Friedrich Schlegel (1772–1829), the founder not only of German Romanticism but also in his work *On the Language and Wisdom of the Indians* (1808) of "comparative grammar" and thereby of modern linguistics, adopted a version of the doctrine as well. For example, he already writes in 1798–9 that "every spirit has its word, the two are inseparable" (Schlegel 1958: xviii. 289), and in lectures from 1804–6 he says that "each concept must be a word" (Schlegel 1846: ii. 83).

Wilhelm von Humboldt (1767–1835), another early founder of modern linguistics, also adopted a version of the doctrine. For example, he writes in the preface to his translation of Aeschylus's *Agamemnon* (1816): "A word is so little a sign for a concept that the concept cannot arise, let alone be held fast, without the word" (Humboldt 1903: viii. 129).

Likewise, Schleiermacher (1768–1834), the early nineteenth century's great developer of both hermeneutics and the theory of translation, espoused a version of the doctrine. For example, he is expressing an elaborated version of it when he writes in his lectures on hermeneutics:

> The... meaning of a term is to be derived from the unity of the word-sphere and from the rules governing the presupposition of this unity. (Schleiermacher 1977: 50)

## The Doctrine in the Later Wittgenstein

The most important philosopher of language of the twentieth century, Wittgenstein (1889–1951), subsequently espoused a version of the doctrine in his later period as well. For example, he writes in the *Philosophical Investigations* (1953):

---

[13] Translation slightly modified. For more details about the important role this doctrine plays in the *Phenomenology of Spirit*, see Forster (1998, 2011).

For a *large* class of cases—though not for all—in which we employ the word 'meaning' [*Bedeutung*] it can be defined thus: the meaning of a word is its use [*Gebrauch*] in the language. (Wittgenstein 1958: § 43)[14]

Michael Dummett, who characterizes Frege generally as "the father of 'linguistic philosophy'" (Dummett 1981a: 683), seems in particular to believe that Wittgenstein's doctrine that meaning consists in the use of words can be traced back to Frege. For in "Was Frege a Philosopher of Language?" (Dummett 1981b) he argues that Frege held a position that amounted to, or was at least consistent with, such a doctrine. However, Frege's position was in fact completely inconsistent with such a doctrine. For Frege was committed to a form of Platonism, according to which senses generally, including thoughts (that is, the senses of whole sentences), are eternal objects entirely independent of us and our languages.

We should, therefore, ask how the later Wittgenstein *really* came by the doctrine. The short answer, I believe, is that he acquired it from the Herder–Hamann tradition. In particular, he did so via a certain rich and enthusiastic source of information about that tradition and its commitment to the doctrine that he had read—namely, Fritz Mauthner's *Contributions to a Critique of Language* (first published in 1902). Wittgenstein read this book even before writing his *Tractatus logico-philosophicus* (1921), where he alludes to it at 4.0031 (albeit critically). Mauthner's book contains a prominent discussion of the doctrine near its beginning (Mauthner 1925: i. 24–5), as well as copious discussions of Herder, Hamann, and other people influenced by them.[15]

## Closer Specification of the Doctrine, I: Atomism versus Holism

Having sketched the history of the doctrine of meaning as use, I would like now to turn to the question of the more exact form that the doctrine should take. For, although, as it has been discussed so far, it is clearly far from platitudinous or vacuous, it remains vague and would allow of competing precisifications, between which choices need to be made.

In what follows I shall consider four issues in connection with which such choices arise, and I shall try to say something in each case about what an optimal version of the doctrine ought to hold. The first issue concerns *atomistic versus holistic* versions of the doctrine; the second the involvement of *rules* in the constitution of meaning and the character of the rules involved; the third the role of *society* in constituting

---

[14] The qualification Wittgenstein implies here ("though not for all") is probably not intended to be a big one, as some of the secondary literature has supposed. See on this Forster (2004: 213).

[15] As I have argued elsewhere, there is actually good reason to believe that the later Wittgenstein took over not only this doctrine but also a much broader range of doctrines from the Herder–Hamann tradition via Mauthner's work (see Forster 2011: 269).

meaning; and the fourth the role of *psychological* processes such as sensation in meaning.

Let us begin with the question of atomism versus holism. In continuity with a predominant tendency of the Enlightenment (for example, Locke and Hume), Herder and Hamann tended to think of meanings or concepts *atomistically*. More specifically, they tended to think of the meanings of individual words as more fundamental than the meanings of whole sentences, and they tended to think that the meaning of an individual word was constituted by the use of that word alone.

However, shortly after Herder and Hamann, people whom they influenced began to think of the sort of use that constitutes meanings in much more *holistic* terms. In fact, Herder himself already prepared the ground for this development in certain ways: in particular, from an early period he at least espoused an emphatic principle that *interpretation* should be holistic (a sort of epistemological anticipation of the ontological principle in which we are interested), and in his relatively late work *Ideas for the Philosophy of History of Humanity* (1784–91) he began to emphasize that *grammatical structures* play a fundamental role in languages, as well as that they are diverse in character. Friedrich Schlegel in *On the Language and Wisdom of the Indians* (1808) then developed these Herderian contributions into the position that languages constitute "organisms" or "systems" whose character is defined above all by their distinctive grammars. This position was subsequently taken over by Schleiermacher, Humboldt, and many others. Schleiermacher also developed a further sort of holism (reflected in his recently quoted expression "the unity of the word-sphere"): a doctrine that the several different uses that are typically associated with a "single" word, and that we might be tempted to think of as constituting several quite discrete meanings that really make the word multiple, in fact constitute a sort of unity, omission, or modification of any part of which necessarily affects all the rest as well. (An example would be "impression" in "He made an impression in the clay", "My impression is that he is reluctant", and "He made a big impression at the party".) In addition, Schleiermacher (in his lectures on dialectic) developed yet another sort of holism: a doctrine that the meaning of a descriptive general term is in essential part constituted by its relation not only to superordinate genus-terms (for example, "dog" by its relation to "animal"), but also to subordinate species terms and to coordinate species terms that fall under the same genus-terms. A similar sort of inter-word holism was also adopted by Humboldt and others. Finally, yet another holistic doctrine had its origins in Kant and was later famously championed by Frege (as his "context principle"), but was also taken over by several thinkers in the meaning-as-use tradition, including Humboldt and the later Wittgenstein: a doctrine that individual words have meanings only in the context of whole sentences. The later Wittgenstein indeed developed this into the even more ambitious doctrine that they have meanings only in the context of whole *languages*.

These several forms of holism constitute important and plausible developments in the doctrine of meaning as use. However, defining the *exact* forms and degrees of holism that are involved in meaning remains a tricky matter. For example, certain extreme forms of holism—such as the ambitious Wittgensteinian doctrine just alluded to (at least on one reading of it), and its more recent adoption by Donald Davidson—seem to lead to the conclusion that *any* change in the use of any part of a language, however modest, changes the use and therefore the meaning of all the rest, so that, for example, if in my computing life I acquire the new concept of "spamming" today, then I no longer mean quite the same by the word "dog" as I did yesterday, and my poor mother who has not yet acquired the new concept of "spamming" as I have can no longer quite understand me when I tell her that I am taking the dog for a walk. But this seems an unacceptably counterintuitive conclusion, a sort of *reductio ad absurdum* of the strong form of holism in question.[16]

## Closer Specification of the Doctrine, II: Rules and their Character

Let us turn now to the question of rules. Herder's original version of the doctrine that meaning consists in word-use arguably already implies that the word-uses that constitute meanings must be *rule-governed*. For his equation of meaning with a word's *Gebrauch*, or use, implies an association with *Brauch*, or *custom*.[17] Schleiermacher's version of the doctrine makes the essential involvement of rules more explicit: "The...meaning of a term is to be derived from the unity of the word-sphere and from the rules governing the presupposition of this unity." Wittgenstein's version of the doctrine likewise explicitly incorporates the idea that the word-uses that constitute meanings must be *rule-governed*.[18] This is a fundamental aspect of his distinctive conception of "grammar" or "grammatical rules". "Grammatical rules" are for him rules that govern the use of words and thereby constitute their meanings. Such rules in particular include all of the principles that we normally think of as *necessary*. For example, in Wittgenstein's view, the necessary principle "$2 + 2 = 4$" prescribes that one should never endorse "Here are two $X$s" and "Here are another two $X$s" without also being prepared to endorse "Here are four $X$s", and by doing so it makes a contribution to constituting the very meanings of the words "two" and "four". Wittgenstein's assumption that it is *rule-governed* word-use that constitutes meaning also lies behind his running analogy between linguistic practices and games such as chess, as well as his closely related conception of a "language game". In addition, it

---

[16] Davidson's position in Davidson (1986) that our usual notion of meaning is indefensible and that there are instead only myriad "passing theories" of meaning can be seen as a way of biting the bullet on this absurdity and thereby breaking one's theoretical teeth.

[17] Indeed, these two German terms were not even clearly distinguished before the nineteenth century as they are today.

[18] This point is fundamental to any real understanding of the later Wittgenstein. Surprisingly, though, it is controversial (e.g. Stanley Cavell and his followers have denied it). For more on this subject, see Forster (2004: ch. 1).

lies behind his development of the famous "rule-following argument" in the *Philosophical Investigations*, whose interest for him lies precisely in the fact that it throws light on the nature of the rules that constitute meaning.

Now this insistence that the use of words that constitutes meaning must be rule-governed seems clearly right. For one thing, if just *any old* use of a word were to constitute its meaning, that would preclude characterizing certain employments of the word as violating its meaning and hence as mistakes, which is of course something we routinely do and reasonably believe it to be part of the nature of meaning to warrant. (To put the point in current philosophical jargon, it would preclude the essential *normativity* of meaning.)

How, though, ought we to conceive the rules in question more precisely? Herder's avoidance of explicitly talking about rules in this connection probably derives in part from his rejection of *one* rather natural way of thinking about what the rules in question would have to be like: roughly, the Socratic–Platonic–Aristotelian conception that they consist in formulated, or at least formulable, *definitions*—that is, sets of non-trivial essential necessary and sufficient conditions of application for the words involved.[19] Herder's rejection of this can already be seen clearly in his early essay *On Being* (1764), where he insists that certain fundamental concepts (including Being, Space, Time, and Force) are indefinable. It can also be seen in his discussions of the concepts of a literary genre and of specific literary genres, such as the ode or the tragedy, where he is invariably sceptical about both the possibility and the need to provide definitions of them.[20] His implicit stance thus seems to be that, while rule-governedness of *some* sort is required for meaning, this should not be thought of as necessarily a matter of following formulated or formulable definitions. This stance seems to me philosophically deep, even if still inchoate.

In order to pursue it a bit further, it may be helpful to explore a similar but more fully developed line of thought in the later Wittgenstein. As the arithmetical example of a "grammatical rule" recently mentioned ("2 + 2 = 4") illustrates, Wittgenstein believes that the rules that constitute meanings are sometimes explicitly formulated. However, he does not believe that this is always the case. For example, he already says in lectures from 1930–2 that "correct use does not imply the ability to make the rules explicit" (Wittgenstein 1982: 53). Likewise, in *On Certainty* (written 1950/1) he writes concerning a certain class of grammatical rules that "their role is like that of rules of a game, and the game can be learned purely practically, without learning any explicit rules", and that, although these are rules that "I do not explicitly learn", nevertheless, "I can discover them subsequently like the axis around which a body rotates" (Wittgenstein 1977: §§95, 152). Indeed, as time went on he became

---

[19] "Non-trivial" here precludes, for example, defining *speed* as *speed* or as *quickness*. "Essential" precludes, for example, defining *creature with a heart* as *creature with kidneys*.

[20] See, e.g., *Of the Ode* (1764/5) (Herder 1985: i. 77–8), and *Shakespeare* (1773) (first draft) (Herder 1985: ii. 522–4).

increasingly inclined to say, not only that the rules in question sometimes fail to be explicitly formul*ated*, but also that they sometimes fail even to be explicitly formul*able*. For example, at another point in *On Certainty* he writes:

> Am I not getting closer and closer to saying that in the end logic [i.e. grammar] cannot be described? You must look at the practice of language, then you will see it. (Wittgenstein 1977: §501)

It is this more radical and surprising idea that the rules in question are not even always explicitly formul*able* that I would like to pursue here. What led Wittgenstein to espouse this position? One important line of argument that did so concerned his discovery of *family resemblance concepts*.[21] His account of this class of concepts has a strong negative thrust: *contrary* to a certain picture of how all general concepts work, according to which they always apply to their particular instances in virtue of some single common feature that all the instances share and that can be captured in a definition, certain general concepts, for example, the concept "game", apply in virtue of multiple features that not all of their instances share and that defy capture in a definition; instead, they apply in virtue of features that are shared only by sub-sets of their instances in a "criss-crossing" or "overlapping" manner (like the overlapping fibres of a thread) (see Wittgenstein 1958: §§65–7).

The thesis that there are concepts that work in this way involves a sharp rejection of the familiar Socratic–Platonic–Aristotelian picture according to which whenever we have a univocal general term it always works by picking out some single common feature in such a way that the feature in question can be captured in a set of non-trivial essential necessary and sufficient conditions (for example, "*Bachelors* are unmarried men"). Wittgenstein can thus be seen as vindicating Herder's scepticism about that picture here.

Wittgenstein intends much of the force of his thesis that some concepts work in this alternative way to come from close scrutiny of the specific examples he gives, such as "game", "language", and "number" ("Don't think, but look!" (Wittgenstein 1958: §66)). Considered in the light of such examples, the model of a family resemblance concept does indeed have considerable plausibility, and poses a strong challenge to the Socratic–Platonic–Aristotelian theory of the nature of general terms. Just try to give a strict definition of "game" that covers all cases, for example!

However, on further reflection it may come to seem doubtful that there really *could* be concepts that worked in this way after all. For while, as we have seen, Wittgenstein himself plausibly holds that all meanings or concepts are by nature *rule*-governed, the family resemblance model seems to conflict with rule-governedness. It is therefore no accident that in the *Philosophical Investigations* his consideration of family resemblance concepts at §§65 ff. is followed almost immediately afterwards by his famous discussion of rule-following. For it is evidently one of the purposes of this discussion

---

[21] For a fuller treatment of his subject, see Forster (2010b).

to show that family resemblance *is* in fact compatible with rule-following, and hence with genuine meaning or concepthood (see Wittgenstein 1958: §§68, 70–1). Indeed, the apparent conflict between family resemblance as a characteristic of concepts and the rule-governed nature of all concepts, together with the resulting task of resolving it, seem to constitute one of Wittgenstein's main reasons for being interested in family resemblance concepts in the work in the first place.

What exactly is his original worry here, though? Obviously enough, it is that the model of a family resemblance concept *seems* to conflict with rule-governedness. However, in order to see the real force of this worry, it is important to distinguish more clearly than Wittgenstein himself does between (1) the issue of a single common feature and (2) the issue of definability by non-trivial essential necessary and sufficient conditions for application; and it is important to realize that Wittgenstein's denial of such definability for the relevant cases is meant to be quite unrestricted, to preclude even definitions that involve complicated disjunctions. For the problem here lies not so much in the absence of any single common feature, but rather in the unavailability of any statement of non-trivial essential necessary and sufficient conditions for application, and that problem's full force depends on the unavailability in question being *unrestricted*, precluding even a complicated disjunctive statement of such conditions. It is *this* that really seems to bring the model of a family resemblance concept into conflict with the principle that any term that expresses a concept must be governed by a rule.

There really does *seem*, then, to be a deep conflict between the insight—based on close scrutiny of how such concepts as "game", "language", and "number" actually work—that certain concepts function in a family resemblance manner and the principle that all concepts are of their very nature constituted by rules. Nonetheless, Wittgenstein denies that there really is in the end. How can there not be?

In a way, the answer to this question lies in the fact that, while Wittgenstein certainly is committed to the principle that meanings or concepts are of their very nature constituted by rules, he is *not* committed to any rigid preconception about exactly how this principle should be understood, but is rather engaged in an attempt to pin down an apt sense for it.[22] His discovery of family resemblance concepts in particular shows that the rules in question must not (as might initially have seemed natural or even inevitable) be equated with, or even conceived as requiring the possibility of, *specifications of non-trivial essential necessary and sufficient conditions for application*.

What, then, *are* they? Wittgenstein is rather tentative and vague about this in the *Philosophical Investigations*, but one of his key ideas there is that they may be something more like *perceptually recognizable patterns*. This is part of the significance of his remark that "meaning is a physiognomy" (Wittgenstein 1958: §568). It is

---

[22] Cf. Wittgenstein's question at Wittgenstein (1958: §82): "What meaning is the expression 'the rule by which he proceeds' supposed to have left to it here?"

also part of the significance of his long exploration in the second part of the book of the visual experience of "noticing an aspect" (as in the famous duck–rabbit example or the example of the double cross). For he says that this experience is akin to experiencing the meaning of a word (Wittgenstein 1958: 230), implies that its philosophical interest largely lies in precisely that kinship (p. 214), and in particular opens his discussion of it with an allusion to the phenomenon of family resemblance: "Two uses of the word 'see'. The one:... The other: 'I see a resemblance [*Ähnlichkeit*] between two faces'" (p. 193).

What more exactly is Wittgenstein's thought here? A key part of it at least is that "noticing an aspect", like understanding a meaning, while it may superficially have the phenomenology of a simple, immediate experience, in fact implicitly involves an ability to classify together as similar an open class of cases (for example, an ability to classify the rabbit that one comes to notice in the duck–rabbit picture together with the class of all rabbits or all rabbit pictures),[23] but that this ability need not be capturable in any algorithm, any set of non-trivial essential necessary and sufficient conditions, and indeed in cases such as that of recognizing the facial resemblance between members of a family typically is not.

Accordingly, switching to a slightly different perceptual analogy, Wittgenstein writes in *Zettel* concerning one of the family resemblance concepts that he identifies, "to think":

> I cannot enumerate the conditions under which the word 'to think' is to be used—but if a circumstance makes the use doubtful, I can say so, and also say *how* the situation is deviant from the usual ones... It could very well be imagined that someone knows his way around a city perfectly... and yet would be quite incompetent to draw a map of the city. (Wittgenstein 1967: §§118–21)

Finally, this reconception of the type of rule-governedness that is constitutive of family resemblance concepts also serves Wittgenstein as a sort of model for reconceiving the rule-governedness that constitutes concepts *generally*. The line of thought concerning family resemblance concepts that I have just explained, beginning as it does at *Philosophical Investigations*, §65, anticipates and illustrates by means of an especially dramatic example a broader lesson that emerges in the subsequent rule-following argument—namely, that grasping a rule is not fundamentally a matter of being able to give an "interpretation" of it, in particular an explicit formulation of it (even in cases where that can be done), but rather of being able to conform to it and recognize violations of it in particular cases:

> There is a way of grasping a rule which is *not* an *interpretation*, but which is exhibited in what we call 'obeying the rule' and 'going against it' in actual cases. (Wittgenstein 1958: §201; cf. §198)

---

[23] "What I perceive in the dawning of an aspect is not a property of the object, but an internal relation between it and other objects" (Wittgenstein 1958: 212; cf. 194–7).

In the area of family resemblance concepts, the failure of a conception of grasping rules as fundamentally a matter of being able to give an "interpretation", or an explicit formulation, is especially dramatic because here it turns out that there *is no* adequate "interpretation" at all. In this area, "what we call 'obeying the rule'... in actual cases" is just applying the term in question correctly to instances of the various particular collections of features that relate to one another in the appropriate "crisscrossing" or "overlapping" fashion. But even in the case of concepts for which an "interpretation", or an explicit formulation, *can* be given, a similar sort of competence in the actual application of the words involved still turns out to be fundamental. The phenomenon of family resemblance concepts thus serves as a paradigm example for Wittgenstein's subsequently developed position concerning conceptual rule-following generally. Conversely, the more general position at which he eventually arrives in the rule-following argument reinforces his foregoing treatment of family resemblance concepts by defusing any residual scepticism concerning his position there that family resemblance concepts can dispense with definitions and instead ultimately rest on brute patterns of response to particular collections of features: this, or at least something very much like it, is ultimately the basis of *all* conceptualization, *all* rule-following.

## Closer Specification of the Doctrine, III: The Question of Sociality

A further difficult question concerning the exact form that a doctrine of meaning as word-use should take has to do with *sociality*. Herder already argued in works such as the *Treatise on the Origin of Language* (1772) and especially *On the Cognition and Sensation of the Human Soul* (1778) that the grasp of linguistic meanings is deeply dependent on participation in a linguistic community. However, he represented the dependence in question as merely efficient-causal and/or functional, rather than *essential*. Hegel then came along and, especially in the *Phenomenology of Spirit* (1807), strengthened Herder's thesis into the more ambitious thesis of an essential dependence. Moreover, Hegel has been followed in this position by many philosophers since, including the later Wittgenstein of the *Philosophical Investigations* and more recent philosophers of language such as Robert Brandom and John McDowell. We should, therefore, consider which, if either, of these two versions of a doctrine of meaning as use is correct: the Herderian version, which incorporates the thesis of a dependence on society that is only efficient-causal and/or functional, or the Hegel–Wittgenstein–Brandom–McDowell version, which incorporates the thesis of a dependence that is essential. My inclination is to think that the former, Herderian version is the superior one.

Among the champions of the stronger thesis of an essential dependence, there is an important distinction to be drawn. A thesis that the rules of word-use that constitute meanings are *essentially* social ought to strike one as highly counterintuitive. For example, if there had existed only a single intelligent being in the whole universe, a sort of cosmic Robinson Crusoe put together by a chance confluence of atoms or whatnot, and he had systematically made marks on his cave wall corresponding to the different species of animals he kept (one mark for pigs, another for goats, and so on) together with strokes corresponding to their numbers, would (or at least could) those marks and strokes not have had *meanings*? Hegel and Wittgenstein (as Saul Kripke has plausibly reconstructed his position) are both deeply aware of this counterintuitiveness, and consequently realize that a powerful argument of some sort would be needed in order to overcome it in favour of the thesis of meaning's essential sociality. Accordingly, as I have argued in detail elsewhere, Hegel in the *Phenomenology of Spirit* tries to show that each of the specific ways in which someone might attempt to cash out the intuitive assumption that would allow meaning to be achieved by one individual alone, each individualistic theory of meaning, turns out to be incoherent and unacceptable, and that a defensible theory of meaning therefore needs to posit a community of language-users in order to constitute meaning (Forster 1998: ch. 4). And, as Kripke (1982) has shown, Wittgenstein can be read as developing a similar argument in the rule-following and private-language sections of the *Philosophical Investigations*. These sophisticated versions of the thesis of an essential dependence of meaning on society that Hegel and Wittgenstein advance are superior to the more dogmatic versions of such a thesis that have been offered more recently by Brandom and McDowell, who overlook or at least seriously underestimate the counterintuitiveness of the thesis and therefore fail even to attempt to provide a cogent argument for it, instead more or less taking it for granted (albeit while in Brandom's case *elaborating* on it copiously).

To say that the Hegel–Wittgenstein version of the thesis of meaning's essential sociality is superior because it includes a forceful argument is not, however, to say that the argument in the end succeeds or that the thesis is correct. In fact, I believe that the argument fails and the thesis is incorrect. This is a complicated subject about which I have written in more detail elsewhere (see esp. Forster 2004: 96–102; 2011: 229–31). Here I shall just consider one important aspect of it.

It seems to me that the most promising way of cashing out our common-sense individualistic intuition that an understanding of meanings could in principle be achieved by a single individual alone is by means of some version of the idea that understanding meanings consists in having certain *real dispositions* to patterns of behaviour, especially linguistic behaviour. (The function of the word "real" here is to insist that the dispositions in question are something over and above the patterns of behaviour, not merely reducible to them.) Herder in effect already held just such a position. For he identified all mental conditions, including the understanding of meanings, with real *forces* [*Kräfte*], in the sense of underlying conditions that manifest their presence in patterns of physical behaviour that they produce.

Hegel attempted to refute such a conception of force in a perfectly general way—most famously in the section of the *Phenomenology of Spirit* called "Force and the Understanding". In particular, he objected that it (1) failed to account for the *necessity* of the connection between a force and the patterns of behaviour that it produced, and (2) posited something unknowable. It seems reasonable to doubt that these objections succeed. I shall not here pursue that question further, though.

Instead, I would like to turn to Wittgenstein's rather different critique of the notion that understanding meanings consists in having real dispositions, and is consequently the sort of thing that could in principle be achieved by a single individual alone.

Wittgenstein himself considers and rejects such a notion in the course of his rule-following argument in the *Philosophical Investigations*, where he employs "knowing the ABC" as a sort of stand-in for the grasp of a rule that constitutes meaning:

> If one says that knowing the ABC is a state of the mind, one is thinking of a state of a mental apparatus (perhaps of the brain) by means of which we explain the manifestations of that knowledge. Such a state is called a disposition. But there are objections to speaking of a state of mind here, inasmuch as there ought to be two different criteria for such a state: a knowledge of the construction of the apparatus, quite apart from what it does. (Wittgenstein 1958: §149)

What exactly is Wittgenstein's objection to the real-disposition account here? Part of it is evidently that, whereas an account of understanding a meaning as a sort of real disposition identifies it with a state of the brain or of some putative mental apparatus, all that we ever really know about in this area is the agent's observable *behaviour*. Consequently, when we know that someone understands a meaning, this must in fact be knowledge concerning his observable behaviour, not knowledge of some state of his brain or of his putative mental apparatus.

This objection is not very compelling, however. For one thing, Wittgenstein is assuming here that one never has direct knowledge of the states of a person's brain or mental apparatus, whereas this may well be wrong, in particular when the person in question is *oneself*. For another thing, even if *direct* knowledge of such states were impossible, why could we not have *indirect* knowledge of them? If not knowledge by acquaintance, why not knowledge by description? For example, why could we not know them under some such description as "the state that produces this pattern of behaviour"?[24]

Kripke has recently developed another line of criticism of a dispositional account of meaning that we should also consider briefly. Kripke raises two main objections against such an account, of which I shall consider only the most important one here.[25] This is the objection that the concept of a disposition cannot account for the

---

[24] There is actually a little more to Wittgenstein's line of thought than this, but it does not enable it to fare any better in the end. For a fuller discussion, see Forster (2004: 96–9).

[25] For a more complete treatment, see Forster (2004: 99–103).

*normativity* of meaning.²⁶ According to Kripke, the notion of grasping a rule or understanding a meaning essentially allows for the possibility of a *discrepancy*, indeed even a *systematic* discrepancy, between the subject's grasp of a rule or understanding of a meaning, on the one hand, and his actual (linguistic) behaviour, on the other, whereas the concept of a disposition does not allow for any such (systematic) discrepancy.

However, this objection is mistaken. On the contrary, it is an essential part of our ordinary concept of a disposition that someone's or something's being in a disposition to X is perfectly consistent with his/its non-manifestation, indeed even with his/its *systematic* non-manifestation, of the behaviour that is typical of the disposition to X, provided only that one or more of an indefinitely large set of possible explanatory-excusing conditions is realized. This essential feature of our ordinary concept of a disposition is evident even in the case of mundane physical dispositions, such as salt's water-solubility. For example, a particular piece of salt may be water-soluble but yet fail, indeed even systematically fail, to dissolve when put in water because it happens to be coated with a thin film of plastic.²⁷ Consequently, the concept of a real disposition, once properly analysed, far from excluding, precisely includes the sort of possibility of (systematic) discrepancy that Kripke quite rightly takes to be essential to grasping rules or understanding meanings. Far from being an embarrassment for the dispositional theory, therefore, the normativity of grasping rules and understanding meanings, and the possibility of (systematic) discrepancy that this essentially involves, turn out on closer examination to constitute a strong argument in *favour* of the theory.²⁸

The good prospects of accounting for grasping rules and understanding meanings in individualistic terms by reference to Herderian real "forces", or real dispositions, strongly suggest that the elaborate arguments that Hegel and Wittgenstein develop against the possibility of individualistic meaning and for meaning instead being essentially social, for all their ingenuity and interest, in the end fail. Our strong common-sense intuition that individualistic meaning is not metaphysically impossible—that a cosmic Robinson Crusoe who understood meanings is a metaphysical possibility—turns out to have been right after all. Consequently, if meaning is deeply social, as it probably still is, then it will be so in something more like the way that Herder

---

²⁶ This is an ambiguous and slippery term that has led to much confusion in recent philosophy, but Kripke himself is not guilty of such confusion.
²⁷ To put the point in a slightly different way: it is crucial to draw a distinction here that Kripke overlooks between behaviour that is *typical* of a disposition and behaviour that is *consistent* with a disposition. An object that is in a certain disposition cannot indeed fail to behave in ways that are *consistent* with the disposition, but it can very well fail, indeed even systematically fail, to behave in ways that are *typical* of the disposition.
²⁸ To put the point in a slightly different way again: the concept of a disposition *itself* turns out to be a normative concept in a sense that is strikingly similar to that in which the concepts of grasping rules and understanding meanings are normative concepts, and therefore looks very promising as a candidate for explaining the nature of the latter concepts.

originally envisaged: its deep dependence on a linguistic community will be an efficient-causal and/or functional dependence, not an essential one.

## Closer Specification of the Doctrine, IV: The Question of Anti-Psychologism

Another important question concerning the exact form that a doctrine of meaning as word-use should take is whether or not psychological processes such as having perceptual or affective sensations play any essential role in meaning and in the understanding thereof.

Herder's original version of the doctrine of meaning as word-use was not meant to preclude such a role. On the contrary, he himself held a quasi-empiricist doctrine to the effect that meanings or concepts must of their very nature be anchored in perceptual or affective sensations. (His doctrine was only *quasi*-empiricist because it differed from more traditional forms of concept-empiricism, such as Locke's or Hume's, in two significant ways: first, it also affirmed a converse dependence—namely, of human sensations on concepts; and, second, it allowed for metaphorical extensions of concepts beyond their sensuous foundations.)

By contrast, Wittgenstein's version of the doctrine that meaning is word-use normally incorporates a strict *denial* that any such psychological processes as having perceptual or affective sensations play an essential role in meanings or in the understanding thereof. This denial is continuous with a similar denial by his predecessor Frege. The main difference between the two of them is that, whereas Frege casts the denial in terms of his Platonism about meaning and the understanding thereof, Wittgenstein recasts it more naturalistically as a denial concerning the physical behaviour, especially the linguistic physical behaviour, that he takes to constitute meaning and the understanding thereof.

Which of the versions of a doctrine of meaning as word-use is superior, the Herderian psychologistic version or the Wittgensteinian anti-psychologistic version? This is another large and difficult topic. However, I want at least to suggest that Herder's psychologism is more plausible than Wittgenstein's anti-psychologism. The following two points are important in this connection.[29]

First of all, it must be conceded that, in comparison with Frege's metaphysically extravagant Platonist version of anti-psychologism, Wittgenstein's naturalistic version of it seems more attractive at first sight. He supports it by developing arguments in terms of the criteria that we actually use for ascribing conceptual understanding to people: he argues that what is decisive here is always their linguistic competence, construed in narrowly behavioural terms, not whatever sensations or other psychological processes they may happen to have. However, there are two sides to this case

---

[29] For a somewhat fuller treatment of this issue, see Forster (2010b: ch. 4).

that need to be distinguished and that are very different in their levels of plausibility: On the one hand, he argues that such linguistic competence is *necessary* for conceptual understanding—and this side of his case seems *entirely* plausible. But, on the other hand, he also argues that such linguistic competence is (at least in a way) *sufficient* for conceptual understanding, in particular that there is no need of any psychological processes such as having sensations in addition—whereas this side of his case seems much less plausible. Suppose, for example, that someone had never had any sensations of redness and could not generate any images of redness (say, because he was congenitally blind or colour-blind), but that we nonetheless managed to teach him to make all of the right intra-linguistic statements about redness—concerning its being a colour, its position on the colour spectrum, its phenomenological characteristics, and so on—and also, by implanting a fancy electronic device in his brain (say, one that caused an audible buzzing in his head whenever he focused on something red), enabled him to apply the word "red" when and only when presented with something red. Would we in such a case want to say that he fully understood the word "red"? It seems at least very plausible to say that we would *not*. A similar thought-experiment leads to a similar conclusion when the sensations in question are affective rather than perceptual ones. For example, could someone who was entirely bereft of emotions all his life (like Spock in *Star Trek* minus the mawkish lapses) be brought to a full understanding of words such as "love", "hate", and "anger" just by being trained to make the same sorts of intra-linguistic statements using them as the rest of us and to apply them to particular cases with equal competence? Arguably *not*.

Second, an anti-psychologist who listened sympathetically to such an objection might still be tempted to question whether Herder's quasi-empiricism deserves the sort of *generality* that he gives it, to complain that there are at least some cases of meanings or concepts for which sensations and the like play no essential role. One class of candidate counter-examples would be terms like "chiliagon" (thousand-sided figure) or "God". However, it seems likely that the Herderian can accommodate this sort of apparent counter-example without much difficulty by deploying a strategy of analysis into sensorily instantiated sub-concepts that was already familiar to earlier concept-empiricists such as Locke (recall Locke's distinction between "simple" and "complex" ideas). For example, even if I have never sensorily encountered an intelligent being who is infinitely knowledgeable, powerful, and good (God), I *have* sensorily encountered intelligent beings, knowledge, power, goodness, and progressions that can in principle be continued without end. Another class of candidate counter-examples would be logical connectives, such as "and" and "not". However, on reflection, these too fail to be convincing. For instance, whenever one observes a certain state of affairs added to another (say, a chair being red and (then) having a cat sitting on it), one has a sensory illustration of "and"; and whenever one observes a certain state of affairs ceasing to obtain (say, a cat initially sitting on the chair but then jumping off it), one has a sensory illustration of "not".[30] In short, it is at least much less easy to restrict the range of meanings for which Herderian psychologism is plausible than one might think.

In sum, it may well be that Herder's psychologistic version of the doctrine that meaning consists in word-use is in the end superior to Wittgenstein's anti-psychologistic version of it.

## Conclusion

I have attempted in this chapter to sketch the history of the revolutionary doctrine in the philosophy of language that meanings or concepts consist in the use of words. As we saw, the doctrine was first adumbrated by Spinoza, then taken over from him by the eighteenth-century German biblical scholars Wettstein and Ernesti, then adopted from them and also significantly revised by Herder, who in particular both radicalized and justified it, then passed on by him to Hamann, then transmitted from the two of them to Hegel, Friedrich Schlegel, Wilhelm von Humboldt, and Schleiermacher, and then eventually channelled into twentieth-century philosophy of language largely through Fritz Mauthner's communication of it from the Herder–Hamann tradition to Wittgenstein.

I have also pointed out, though, that the generic doctrine still leaves much room for different specific versions, and that anyone who is attracted to it therefore has a number of further questions to answer—in particular, questions concerning atomism versus holism; the role and character of rules in meaning; meaning's dependence on society; and the relation of meaning to psychological processes such as sensation.

Concerning these questions, I have adumbrated cases that some form of holism is no doubt superior to atomism, but that it needs to be formulated carefully; that rules do play an essential role in meaning, but "rules" construed in a somewhat surprising and unusual way; that meaning is dependent on society, but only in a causal and/or functional way, not essentially; and that psychological processes such as sensation do play an essential role in meaning.

In the course of pursuing these issues we have also seen reason to believe that it is by no means always the later versions of the doctrine of meaning as word-use that are philosophically best. Indeed, overall, it was perhaps the first great champion of the doctrine, Herder, who got things most nearly right.

---

[30] Notice that, because Herder's quasi-empiricism itself incorporates a claim that human sensations depend on concepts (not only conversely), it would not be an apt objection here to point out (plausibly enough) that one could not have the sorts of sensations mentioned in these examples without also having the concepts in question.

# References

Berlin, I. (1976). *Vico and Herder*. New York: Viking Press.
Davidson, D. (1986). 'A Nice Derangement of Epitaphs', in *Truth and Interpretation*, ed. E. LePore. Oxford: Blackwell.
Dummett, M. (1981a). *Frege: Philosophy of Language*. Cambridge, MA: Harvard University Press.
Dummett, M. (1981b). 'Was Frege a Philosopher of Language?', in M. Dummett, *The Interpretation of Frege's Philosophy*. Cambridge, MA: Harvard University Press.
Ernesti, J. A. (1832). *Ernesti's Institutes*, ed. C. H. Terrot. Edinburgh: Thomas Clark.
Forster, M. N. (1998). *Hegel's Idea of a Phenomenology of Spirit*. Chicago: University of Chicago Press.
Forster, M. N. (2004). *Wittgenstein on the Arbitrariness of Grammar*. Princeton: Princeton University Press.
Forster, M. N. (2010a). *After Herder: Philosophy of Language in the German Tradition*. Oxford: Oxford University Press.
Forster, M. N. (2010b). 'Wittgenstein on Family Resemblance Concepts', in A. Ahmed (ed.), *Wittgenstein's Philosophical Investigations: A Critical Guide*. Cambridge: Cambridge University Press.
Forster, M. N. (2011). *German Philosophy of Language: From Schlegel to Hegel and Beyond*. Oxford: Oxford University Press.
Forster, M. N. (2012). 'Herder and Spinoza', in E. Förster and Y. Melamed (eds), *Spinoza and German Idealism*. Cambridge: Cambridge University Press.
Hacking, I. (1993). *Why does Language Matter to Philosophy?* Cambridge: Cambridge University Press.
Hamann, J. G. (1820). *Hamanns Schriften*, ed. F. Roth. Berlin: G. Reimer.
Hegel, G. W. F. (1977). *Phenomenology of Spirit*, trans. A. V. Miller. Oxford: Oxford University Press.
Herder, J. G. (1877). *Johann Gottfried Herder Sämtliche Werke*, ed. B. Suphan et al. Berlin: Weidemann.
Herder, J. G. (1985). *Johann Gottfried Herder Werke*, ed. U. Gaier et al. Frankfurt am Main: Deutscher Klassiker Verlag.
Humboldt, W. von (1903). *Wilhelm von Humboldts Gesammelte Schriften*, ed. A. Leitzmann et al. Berlin: B. Behr.
Kripke, S. A. (1982). *Wittgenstein on Rules and Private Language*. Cambridge, MA: Harvard University Press.
Mauthner, F. (1925). *Beiträge zu einer Kritik der Sprache*. 3rd edn (1st edn, 1902). Berlin: Felix Meiner.
Reimarus, H. S. (1762). *Allgemeine Betrachtungen über die Triebe der Tiere, hauptsächlich über ihre Kunsttriebe. Zum Erkenntniß des Zusammenhanges der Welt, des Schöpfers und unser selbst vorgestellet*. Last rev. edn (1st edn, 1760). Hamburg: Johann Carl Bohn.
Schlegel, F. (1846). *Friedrich Schlegels philosophische Vorlesungen aus den Jahren 1804 bis 1806*, ed. C. J. H. Windischmann. Bonn: Eduard Weber.
Schlegel, F. (1958). *Kritische Friedrich Schlegel Ausgabe*, ed. E. Behler et al. Munich: F. Schöning.

Schleiermacher, F. D. E. (1977). *Hermeneutics: The Handwritten Manuscripts*, ed. H. Kimmerle. Atlanta, GA: Scholars Press.

Spinoza, B. de (1951). *A Theologico-Political Treatise; A Political Treatise*, trans. R. H. M. Elwes (first published under a different title). New York: Dover.

Wettstein, J. J. (1766). *Libelli ad crisin atque interpretationem Novi Testamenti*. 2nd edn (1st edn, 1756). Halle, Magdeburg: I. G. Trampe.

Wittgenstein, L. (1958). *Philosophical Investigations*, ed. G. E. M. Anscombe. 2nd edn (1st edn, 1953). Oxford: Blackwell.

Wittgenstein, L. (1967). *Zettel*, ed. G. E. M. Anscombe and G. H. von Wright. Oxford: Blackwell.

Wittgenstein, L. (1977). *On Certainty*, ed. G. E. M. Anscombe and G. H. von Wright. Oxford: Blackwell.

Wittgenstein, L. (1982). *Wittgenstein's Lectures: Cambridge, 1930–1932*, ed. A. Ambrose. Chicago: University of Chicago Press.

# 11
# Thomas Reid on Language

*Patrick Rysiew*

## 1. Introduction

While he is best known for his rejection of 'the theory of ideas' and his role as a central figure in the 'Scottish school of Common Sense', Thomas Reid (1710-96) made important contributions to the study of language and linguistic communication. Throughout his works, Reid's ultimate interest is in contributing to the development of a careful and accurate 'anatomy' (*IHM*, Introduction, 98a, 12[1]) of the human mind, a delineation of its basic powers and principles; and this, not coincidentally, was ultimately to be in service of the anti-sceptical claims for which he is most famous. Whatever one's degree of interest in the latter, however, there is no denying that Reid's work affords plenty of rich material for those interested in language and the history of philosophy of language. Thus, interpreters have found in Reid anticipations of both 'ordinary language philosophy' (Jensen 1979) and modern speech act theory (Schuhmann and Smith 1990). As well, Reid's writings on language include: proto-Gricean, pragmatic explanations of the (in)felicity of certain forms of speech; foreshadowings of later 'direct reference' theories of proper names, and referential theories of linguistic meaning in general; an important discussion of the origins of language; claims about the relation of language to thought, and the connection between communication (linguistic and otherwise) and our capacity to 'read' the minds of others; and treatment of the origin, meaning, and acquisition of general terms.

Reid was not a very systematic writer: his remarks on language (and on many of the other central topics he addresses) are spread across his substantial body of work, and this, of course, can make it harder to grasp and appreciate his views. The goal of

---

My thanks to Margaret Cameron, Rob Stainton, and participants in the 2012 History of the Philosophy of Language Workshop at UWO, for extremely valuable guidance and feedback.

[1] In-text references to Reid provide indication of the relevant work (see Abbreviations, at end of this chapter) and passage (essay, chapter, section, etc.), followed by relevant page numbers in both the Hamilton and Edinburgh editions of Reid. Thus, the above citation refers to the "Introduction" to Reid's *Inquiry*; p. 98a of Hamilton ('a' refers to the left-hand column, 'b' to the right-hand side), p. 12 of the Edinburgh version.

this chapter is to isolate, extract, and introduce Reid's principal claims in and contributions to the philosophy of language, as it is known today. Along the way, the connections among these elements and their more salient points of contact with Reid's other philosophical views, and with the views of some other key figures in the history of philosophy, will be discussed. We will begin by considering Reid's views on why the philosopher should be concerned with language in the first place.

## 2. On the Importance of Language to Philosophy

According to Henning Jensen (1979), "Reid's position represents an extremely pivotal stage in the upgrading of the importance of language in philosophy". In particular, Jensen is impressed by Reid's appeals to the everyday meaning of various terms, which would later figure centrally in 'ordinary language' philosophy of G. E. Moore and the later Wittgenstein, for example. However, while Jensen is correct that Reid gives language more attention than many of his predecessors, his concern with language, and with ordinary language in particular, is driven by his broader philosophical project of contributing to a better understanding of the human mind. In pursuit of this goal, language is seen by Reid both as a vital source of evidence and as a possible hindrance to theoretical progress.

In the first Essay of Reid's 1785 *Essays on the Intellectual Powers of Man* ('Preliminary'), Reid makes explicit some of the fundamental substantive and methodological assumptions he is making in carrying out his project. Much of the discussion here concerns linguistic matters. Thus, the *Essays* begins: "There is no greater impediment to the advancement of knowledge than the ambiguity of words" (*EIP* I.1, 219a, 17). (Reid does not intend anything technical by 'ambiguity' here; he means simply a lack of clarity and precision in what is meant.) This, he thinks, is not a problem that can be solved by providing rigorous definitions of all terms: "it is evident that every word cannot be defined; for the definition must consist of words; and there could be no definition, if there were not words previously understood without definition" (*EIP* I.1, 219b, 18). The solution is to use common words "in their common acceptation" (*EIP* I.1, 219b, 18); and, "when we have occasion to enlarge or restrict the meaning of a common word, or to give it more precision than it has in common language, the reader ought to have warning of this, otherwise we shall impose upon ourselves and upon him" (*EIP* I.1, 230a, 38).

It is because "use is the arbiter of language" (*EIP* I.1, 228b, 35) for Reid that he freely intermingles observations concerning the various faculties of the mind, statements and defences of various fundamental principles, and so on, with explicitly linguistic observations about the ordinary use of key terms. One important instance of this is Reid's "ordinary language analysis" of 'common sense' (*EIP* VI.2, 421b–426a, 423–34), as Jensen (1979: 360) calls it. Another is Reid's discussion of Hume's use of the term 'impression' to describe the sensations occasioned in us by material objects (*EIP* I.1, 227b ff., 33 ff.). This example also serves to illustrate the essential role that analogy—"the judg[ing] of things less known, by some similitude [we] observe, or think [we] observe, between them and things more familiar or better known" (*EIP* I.4, 236b, 52)—plays in human thought and language.

Our natural love of analogy, according to Reid, accounts for the ease with which we acquire language (*Lett.* 71a, 193). It also explains many of the particular names we give to things, a notable case in point being our terms for various mental operations. Almost all the words we have for talking about mental operations—'apprehend', 'conceive', 'imagine', 'comprehend', 'deliberate', and so on—are borrowed from our talk about the non-mental realm (*EIP* I.4, 237b–238a, 54). In itself, this is natural and harmless. The danger is that, having been led by analogical thinking to the employment of certain words and certain familiar ways of thinking and talking, we will in turn be led by *that* to suppose certain similarities that, in fact, we have no evidence to suppose are real (*EIP* I.4, 237b–238a, 54; cf. *EAP* I.2, 515b–516a, 14–15). For instance, in the case of 'impression', we know, for example, that a seal cannot make an impression upon wax unless there is "contact and pressure" (*EIP* I.4, 237b, 54); in the same way, Reid thought, many philosophers had taken it for granted that in perception material objects can affect the mind only mediately, via the interposition of some mental object. This is one source of 'the theory of ideas'—the view that the immediate object of thought (perception, memory, reasoning, consciousness, and so on) is always some specifically mental object (see *EIP* II.14, 301a–302a, 175–8). Among the eventual consequences of this view, of course, is that the familiar processes we started out wanting to explain become problematic. In Hume, for instance, the mental *act* of sensing an object (the "impression") becomes the *object* of my thought (*EIP* I.1, 228b, 35–36); and that object quickly usurps the worldly thing, the mind's interaction with which philosophers want to understand. Thus, it is early on in the *Treatise* that Hume (1978: 67) tells us that " 'tis impossible for us so much as conceive or form an idea of any thing specifically different from ideas and impressions". Hence Reid's saying that "ideas seem to have something in their nature unfriendly to other existences" (*IHM* II.6, 109a, 33):

> They [ideas] were first introduced into philosophy, in the humble character of images or representatives of things; and in this character they seemed not only to be inoffensive, but to serve admirably well for explaining the operations of the human mind understanding. But since men began to reason clearly and distinctly about them, they have by degrees supplanted their constituents, and undermined the existence of every thing but themselves. (*IHM* II.6, 109a, 33–4)

Part of Reid's response to the theory of ideas[2] is to point out that, while it is perhaps encouraged by the language we (quite understandably) use to talk about such things, we have no good grounds to grant the presumed analogy between physical and

---

[2] But *only* part; Reid objects to the theory of ideas on other, purely non-linguistic grounds as well—for instance, that "if we should admit an image in the mind, or contiguous with it, we know as little how perception may be produced by this image as by the most distant object" (*EIP* II.14, 302a, 178; cf. *Orations*, 52–67).

mental phenomena, any more than we have good grounds to think that the mind needs a hand to apprehend or a womb to conceive (*Orations*, 75).

A final example of the importance of attending to language as a way of avoiding philosophical error concerns the term 'idea' itself. (This example will prove important later on.) Reid, of course, denies the theory of ideas just mentioned. Does this mean that he wants to deny something as obvious as that we have ideas? Locke, for instance, thought that their existence was something so obvious as hardly to need remarking upon (Locke 1959: Introduction 8; i. 32–3). And Reid grants as much: in common language, 'to have an idea' of $x$ means simply to think of $x$—an idea (or thought) is an act of the mind (*EIP* I.1, 226b, 31); and no one denies that we think (have thoughts). As philosophers use the term, however, 'idea' refers (as above) to the immediate *object* of thought. And, Reid says: "I believe *ideas*, taken in this sense, to be a mere fiction of philosophers" (*EIP* I.1, 226b, 31; cf. *EIP* II.14). Once again, then, for Reid determining the theoretical significance of the naturalness of a certain way of speaking requires understanding what ordinary speakers do and do not mean by the term or phrase in question.

The preceding is enough to make it clear that, as much as Reid's attention to ordinary language might prompt thoughts of the later 'linguistic turn' (Rorty 1967) in philosophy, or the mid-twentieth-century 'ordinary language' movement,[3] the concern with language should not be overstated. For Reid the interest is never in language for its own sake—"Disputes about words belong rather to grammarians than to philosophers" (*EIP* I.1, 227a, 32), he says; and there is no suggestion that Reid thinks, for example, that philosophical problems are *merely* linguistic[4]—an idea sometimes associated (incorrectly, I believe) with the later Wittgenstein. For Reid, the attention to ordinary language is to a great extent prophylactic—it is the *abuse* of language, it would seem, that he is on guard against.

But Reid's concern goes deeper than this: as the preceding examples also make clear, Reid thinks that we must be cautious in inferring, even from the *correct* use of a given term or phrase, some substantive philosophical claim.[5] Nor is this just because some of our terms ('impression', 'conceive', and so on) have an analogical origin. Rather, it is because of *pragmatics*, which concerns the information arising from utterances, as opposed to that encoded in the words uttered. In several places, Reid provides some rather strikingly Gricean (Grice 1989) examples wherein it is perfectly appropriate to speak as we do, even though what we say (and do not say), if taken entirely at face value, could easily lead to bad theory.

---

[3] Chappell (1964) is a good introduction to the latter.
[4] At the same time, however, one might disagree with Schuhmann and Smith's claim (1990: 52) that "we do not find examples of passages where Reid dismisses philosophical problems as *caused* by improper uses of language"—he certainly thinks that such misuses can *abet* and *encourage* philosophical problems.
[5] This is something of which the best of the 'ordinary language' philosophers—for example J. L. Austin (1975)—were quite aware.

Thus, for example, while judgement is an essential element in *many* mental acts, including perception, we seldom will *say* 'I see *x* and judge it to be real', because that would be pleonastic—a "superfluity of speech" (*EIP* VI.1, 415a, 410); and, just because our adding 'I judge' is unnecessary, were we to do so we would naturally be taken to mean something *more* than what is literally expressed—most likely, Reid says, the effect would be 'dogmatical' (*EIP* I.1, 223a, 25). 'I conceive' or 'think', by contrast, is naturally used to express an opinion modestly, though of course when we say such things we typically *do* mean more than merely that we have a thought—that is, a 'simple apprehension', without any "belief or judgment at all", which is all that conception involves (*EIP* I.1, 223a, 24). Or, to take another example, the evidence we have that there is such a city as Rome is probable, not demonstrative. "Yet, in common language, it would sound oddly to say, it is probable that there is such a city as Rome, as that would imply some degree of doubt or uncertainty" (*EIP* VII.3, 482b, 557).[6] As these examples show, Reid is well aware that language has the potential to mislead, even when it is not being used sloppily or being abused by the philosopher. To put the point anachronistically, Reid is aware of the dangers of inferring semantic facts merely on the basis of the (im)propriety of certain claims—of the dangers, that is, of committing the 'pragmatic' (Salmon 1991) or 'speech act' (or 'assertion') (Searle 1969) fallacies.

Overall, then, Reid regards language as a potential obstacle to carrying out the sort of 'anatomy' of the human mind he wishes to promote. And yet, at the same time, he also sees it as a vital source of information in that study.[7] For example, he takes it to be a sign that something is a 'first principle' that it is somehow embedded in our language: "[some] opinions appear to be universal, from what is common in the structure of all languages" (*EIP* I.2, 233b, 45). In fact, he goes further, saying:

Language is the express image and picture of human thoughts; and from the picture we may draw some certain conclusions concerning the original. (*EIP* VI.5, 440b, 466; cf. *Log.* 691b–692a, 112)

every distinction to be found in the structure of a common language, is a real distinction... I know nothing that can give so much light to the human faculties as a due consideration of the structure of language. (*Lett.* 78b, 185)[8]

---

[6] Compare Grice (1961: 124): "When someone makes such a remark as 'It looks red to me' a certain implication is carried, an implication which is disjunctive in form. It is implied either that the object referred to is known or believed by the speaker not to *be* red, *or* that it has been denied by someone else to be red, *or* that the speaker is doubtful whether it is red, *or* that someone else has expressed doubt whether it is red, *or* that the situation is such that though no doubt has actually been expressed and no denial has actually been made, some person or other might feel inclined towards denial or doubt if he were to address himself to the question whether the object is actually red."

[7] The primary such source, Reid thinks, is "accurate reflection upon the operations of our own minds" (*EIP* I.5, 238b, 56; *IHM* I.1, 97a–98b, 11–12). But such reflection has its own difficulties (*EIP* I.6, *IHM* I.2), and the reliance upon linguistic data cannot be lightly dismissed.

[8] While, as in such passages, Reid regards thought as prior to language, in other places he makes it clear that language can shape and influence thought: "our thoughts take their colour in some degree from the language we use; and... although language ought always to be subservient to thought, yet thought must be,

Such claims may seem to contradict the sort of careful handling of linguistic data that, as we have seen, Reid recommends. But it does not.[9] Particular forms of speech can mislead, or can mask substantive and controversial theoretical assumptions. In terms of its most general features, however—those that all languages share—language can provide us insights into the workings of the human mind. Thus, Reid thinks, we find in all languages a distinction between nouns and adjectives, between active and passive verbs (*EIP* I.2, 233b, 46); a distinction between mind, its operations, and the objects of thought (*EIP* I.1, 223b–224a, 26); certain rules of syntax or grammar; and so on (*EIP* VI.5, 440b, 466; *EIP* I.1, 224a, 26; *EIP* I.2, 233b, 45–6; *EIP* I.5, 238b, 56; *EIP* II.19, 322b, 218; *EAP* I.2, 515a–517a, 13–17). From this, we may infer such things as that we naturally conceive of the world in terms of subjects and qualities, that perception and other operations are taken to have mind-independent objects, that we have a notion of active power, and so on. Such inferences are defeasible—such general features *may* be explained as merely accidental, or the result of some widely held 'prejudice' (see, e.g., *EIP* VI., 440b, 465–6). In the absence of such a debunking explanation, however, they are perfectly reasonable and may be presumed to be correct.[10] So, whereas his immediate predecessors' investigations of the human mind were driven largely by introspection, Reid sees language as an important and equally legitimate resource in developing a science of the mind. Reid's view of the importance of language to philosophy, then, is far from exclusively negative.

## 3. Language and its Basis: Artificial and Natural Signs

Now that we have considered Reid's position on the importance of language, it is important to understand his views on language itself, and on what we today would call 'natural language', in relation to the rest of his philosophy. (As we shall see in this section, what we call 'natural language(s)', Reid sees as 'artificial language'.) The recent rediscovery of Reid has centred on his views concerning epistemology—his response to the sceptic, his fallible foundationalism, and so on—and perception— notably, his rejection of 'the theory of ideas' in favour of 'direct realism'. An essential element in the latter is the distinction Reid draws between sensation and perception— something that J. J. Gibson (1966: Introduction) takes as the jumping-off point for his own theory of human perceptual systems. The sensation–perception distinction, however, is not fundamental for Reid: it is an instance of what D. D. Todd (1987) has called "Reid's semiotic", his theory of signs, which was the alternative he

---

at some times and in some degree, subservient to language" (*EIP* VI.8, 474a, 539); and "When language is once learned, it may be useful even in our solitary meditations; and by clothing our thoughts with words, we may have a firmer hold of them" (*EIP* I.8, 245a, 69).

[9] Jensen (1979: 361–2) is very good on the close but imperfect correspondence between human language and thought, as Reid sees it.

[10] Obviously, this claim connects with the more general issue of Reid's defense of common sense and its deliverances; see Rysiew (2002).

proposed to the ideal theorist's way of thinking about some of the mind's fundamental operations.

Sensations for Reid are distinctive among mental acts in that a sensation "hath no object distinct from the act itself" (*EIP* I.1, 229a, 36)—"there is no difference between the sensation and the feeling of it" (*EIP* II.16, 310a, 194). The tactile sensation I have upon touching a hard object, for example, is like a pain, in that to have it *just is* to feel a certain way. In most instances of perception, for Reid, sensations serve as *signs* of material objects' qualities.[11] By this, Reid means no more than that, owing to our constitution (and indirectly, 'the will of our maker'), upon having a certain sensation we are led naturally to form a conception (thought) of and belief in the existence of the relevant quality existing in an object. (It is at this point that we have *perception*; see *EIP* II.5, *IHM* VI.20.) As Reid otherwise describes it, the sensation "suggests" to the mind a certain worldly object or quality. As with signs generally, there is no necessary connection between sign and thing signified here,[12] and no intrinsic feature of a sign that *makes it* the sign of some quality rather than another. Nor do our sensations resemble the qualities they signify—Berkeley, in Reid's view, was entirely correct in insisting that an 'idea' can be like nothing but another idea (Berkeley 1996: *Principles*, I.8, p. 27; *Second Dialogue*, 146). And yet, upon having a certain sensation, we find ourselves with an immediate conception and belief of a quality existing in some object. To say that the former 'suggests' or 'signifies' the latter does not "explain the manner of their connection";[13] it does, however, "express a fact, which every one may be conscious of" (*IHM* V.8, 131b, 74; cf. *IHM* II.7, 111a, 38)—namely, that, by a law of our constitution, the one immediately "introduces" (a conception of) the other (*IHM* V.2, 120a, 56).[14]

Clearly, Reid's use of 'sign' (signification) fits comfortably Aristotle's characterization of signification as generating an understanding—as putting something in the mind, as it were (*de Interpretatione* $16^b19$–21). As Jennifer Ashworth (Chapter 8, this volume) explains, this conception of signs in terms of their "epistemological impact" was retained in Augustine in his *On Christian Doctrine*;[15] and, like Augustine,

---

[11] The visual perception of figure is the exception: visible figure, which is not a sensation but a real 'external object' (*IHM* VI.7, 142b ff., 95 ff.), is the sign of real figure.

[12] Visible figure once again provides an exception: see *IHM* VI.7, 142b ff., 95 ff.

[13] The use of signs in Reid's theory differs importantly from their employment by contemporary 'teleosemanticists' such as Millikan (1984) and Dretske (1988), who try to *explain* intentionality. Reid takes the 'aboutness' of thought for granted, and makes no attempt to explain it.

[14] That talk of sensations as signs is not meant to be doing any real explanatory work is one difference between Reid's semiotic and the theory of ideas; another is that there is no presumption that the sign must resemble what it signifies; another still is that such signs, unlike other philosophers' 'ideas', are *not* the immediate object of thought. Granted, by attending to it, I can *make* a sensation an object of awareness. But when I touch a hard surface, the *hardness* is the immediate object of my conception (thought); the sensation qua sign is part of the psycho-causal story of what occasions that thought.

[15] Augustine writes that "a sign is a thing which, over and above the impression it makes on the senses, causes something else to come into the mind as a consequence of itself" (*On Christian Doctrine*, book II, trans. O'Donnell).

Reid distinguishes between natural and artificial signs—between signs that signify what they do by nature, and those that do so "by habit and custom" (*IHM* V.3, 121b ff., 58 ff.).[16]

As to natural signs, Reid says that they fall into three classes: first, those whose connection to the thing signified is discovered only by experience; second, those whose connection to the thing signified "is discovered to us by a natural principle, without reasoning or experience"; and, third, those that, "though we never before had any notion or conception of the thing signified, do suggest it, or conjure it up, as it were, by a natural kind of magic, and at once give us a conception, and create in us a belief in it" (*IHM* V.3, 121b–122b, 58–61). It is the business of science to investigate the first class of natural signs—for example, to discover through experience that certain spots on the skin are a sign of measles. To the third belong the sensations that figure in perception in the manner sketched above—a given tactile sensation is a sign of hardness, for instance.[17] For our purposes, however, it is the second class of natural signs that is of interest: it comprises what Reid calls "*the natural language of mankind*" (*IHM* V.3, 121b, 59).

Now, Reid uses 'language' to refer to "all those signs which mankind use in order to communicate to others their thoughts and intentions, their purposes and desires" (*IHM* IV.2, 117b, 51). What is distinctive about the signs of *natural* language—certain "modulations of voice, gestures, and features" (*IHM* IV.2, 118a, 52)—is that qua natural signs they "have a meaning which every man understands by the principles of his nature" (*IHM* IV.2, 117a, 51): without reasoning or reflection, when we see/hear them we immediately pass to a conception and belief of others' thoughts and intentions. Thus, an infant hears an angry voice and immediately begins to cry; a certain gesture is naturally read as ostensive, another as indicating assent; and so on.

Crucially, Reid claims that the 'common', 'natural language of mankind', though "scanty", is "the seed of [artificial] language" (*Lett.* 71a, 192). The terminology here invites misunderstanding. For by 'artificial language' Reid means precisely what *we* would call '*natural* language(s)' (English, Dutch, Korean, and so on); the latter are examples of artificial language, in Reid's terms, because *words* are 'artificial signs'—their connection to the thing signified is established, not by nature, but by convention ('compact or agreement'; 'habit and custom'). Reid's claim then is that 'the natural

---

[16] In terms of contemporary invocations of the relevant distinction, one thinks, for example, of Grice's distinction (1989) between non-natural and natural meaning, and Dretske's discussion (1988) of symbols *versus* natural signs.

[17] Such perception is *original* perception. In *acquired* perception, the outputs of original perception or some quality of things comes, *through experience*, to serve as the sign of some other objectual quality or state of affairs. So, for example, original perception acquaints me with the sound of the passing coach; after sufficient experience, upon hearing the same sound I can learn (perceive) that a coach is passing (this example is at *IHM* IV.1, 117b, 50; Reid provides discussion of the general phenomenon at *IHM* VI.20-3 and *EIP* II.21-2).

language of mankind' provides the necessary basis for the invention and deployment of such artificial signs:

> all artificial language supposes some compact or agreement to affix a certain meaning to certain signs; therefore there must be compacts or agreements before the use of artificial signs; but there can be no compact or agreement without signs, now without language; and therefore there must be a natural language before any artificial language can be invented. (*IHM* IV.2, 117b–118a, 51)

As Todd (1987) notes, one obvious target of Reid's argument here is Locke, who held that language was purely an invention of men. According to Locke, to enable the "communication of thoughts", humans, by a mutual and "voluntary imposition", invented words to serve as "sensible marks of ideas" (Locke 1959: *Essay* III.2.1–2; ii. 8–9).[18] As we shall see, Reid rejects the latter, 'ideational' view of linguistic meaning—the view that the meaning of a word is the mental act or object it expresses or to which it corresponds. For now, however, Reid's claim is that people cannot have invented language so as to "bring out their ideas, and lay them before the view of others" (Locke 1959: *Essay* III.2.2; ii 9). *Artificial* language, of course, is developed so as to *hone* and *extend* our communicative powers, but, if our thoughts, intentions, purposes, and so on were not already to some degree 'out in the open'—if we had no prior grip on others' intentional states—we would lack a communicative medium in which to undertake the necessary compact. It is the job of natural language to give us that initial communicative ability.

Some might wonder whether Reid's argument here is too quick. Condillac, for example, drew a distinction similar to Reid's, among different types of sign—in Condillac's case, between accidental, natural, and artificial signs. According to Condillac, however, while natural signs (such as a "natural cry") are (as in Reid) instinctively produced without any explicit communicative intention, we must *learn* their signification through being exposed to their characteristic association with what they signify (Condillac 2001: *Essay* I.2.4 and II.1.1, §§1–4; Falkenstein 2010: section 6). (In terms of Reid's tripartite division, Condillac appears to assimilate 'the natural language of mankind' to the *first* type of natural sign.)

To such a suggestion, Reid has two objections. First, he claims, it "contradict[s] all experience": we observe that children *learn* that flames will burn and knives will cut, and they do so at different rates and at different points in their lives; whereas "we know that an angry countenance will fright a child in the cradle" immediately, before they have had exposure to repetitions of the relevant pattern, and that this is "common to the whole species" (*EIP* VI.5, 449b, *EAP* V.6, 665a). Second, when we experience both a sign and the thing signified, experience can instruct us how the sign is to be interpreted—this is what happens with the first class of natural signs; but, in

---

[18] "words, in their primary or immediate signification, stand for nothing but *the ideas in the mind of him that uses* them" (Locke 1959: *Essay* III.2.2; ii. 9).

the case at hand, we see the signs only, and so *cannot* learn of their connection to others' "thoughts and passions" by experience; therefore, "there must be some earlier source of this knowledge" (*EIP* VI.5, 449b–450a, 485–486; cf. *EAP* V.6, 664b–665a, 330–1).[19]

## 4. Linguistic Meaning: Reference and the Role of Conception

In many ways, it is fair to say that Reid regards humans as distinctively 'sign-minded' creatures.[20] In terms of linguistic meaning, or 'artificial' signs and language, throughout his works, Reid consistently speaks of words as 'signs', and of 'signification', with 'meaning' occasionally being used in place of the latter. As artificial signs, words in themselves are merely "empty sounds" (*EIP* V.2, 391b, 359) or insignificant marks on the page. As Susan V. Castagnetto (1992: 42) writes, for Reid "a word does not have meaning for the user unless that user has an understanding or conception of what the word is being used to signify".[21] Phillip Cummins (1976: 66) puts Reid's view this way: "To say that a word signifies is really to say that a person signifies something by it. If a word is used with meaning or is understood by somebody, that person intends a thought-object which is what the word signifies."

As the discussion of the previous section would lead one to expect, it is *not* Reid's view that the speaker is free to mean whatever he or she likes by a given term: while artificial (versus) natural signs owe their signifying power—their power to give rise to an understanding, the occurrence of a thought, in the hearer—to humans' communicative intentions, there is also an important *conventional* element to linguistic meaning. Communication requires that speaker and hearer "affix the same meaning or notion—that is, the same conception to them" (*EIP* IV.1, 364a, 303; cf. *EIP* V.2, 391b, 359); and "the *common* meaning is the standard by which such conceptions are formed" (*EIP* IV.1, 364a, 303; emphasis added): "The meaning of the word is the

---

[19] Much the same position has recently been endorsed by Sperber (1995), albeit in rather different terms. According to Sperber, it is a mistake to think that what enables communication is the possession of a common language—a code that provides a mapping between sounds(/shapes) and ideas, with inference sometimes providing an in-principle-dispensable shortcut. Rather, it is 'inference'—i.e., the ability to grasp others' intentional states—that grounds (linguistic) communication, with language being the in-principle-optional add-on. Recasting this in Reid's terms: language is not, and cannot be, exhausted by 'artificial signs' (what *Sperber* calls 'language'); it is preceded and enabled by 'the natural language of mankind', which affords us a pre-reflective, pre-conventional understanding of others' intentional states.

[20] At least in terms of degree. At *EAP* V.6 (665b, 333), for example, Reid seems to allow that a grasp of natural signs is exhibited in "social intercourse among brute-animals, and between some of them and man". Reid's 'semiotic' is evident as well in his account of acquired (versus 'original') perception (see n. 17), and in the analogy he draws between perception and the credit we give human testimony (*IHM* VI.24), discussion of which would carry us too far afield here.

[21] The 'or' here is, plausibly, read as expressing identity for Reid. He, like Hobbes (1991: ch. 5, 30), appears to be of the view that "*Understanding* [is] nothing else, but conception caused by speech".

thing conceived; and that meaning is the conception affixed to it by those who best understand the language" (*EIP* IV.1, 364b, 303).

Notice: the meaning of the word is *the thing conceived*—the *thought-object*, in Cummins's phrase. Conceptions and intentions *are* important here, for two reasons. They are important, first, because we are talking about signs, and understanding them as things that express and prompt thoughts and understanding ("conceptions", to use Reid's term). And, second, because, as just noted, the *source* of artificial signs' signifying power, and their having the *particular* meaning that they do, are to be explained in terms of "some compact or agreement" among language-users (*IHM* IV.2, 117b, 51). So again: conceptions and intentions matter to language and linguistic communication. But, except when we are talking about the mind, thoughts are not what terms *signify*. They signify whatever object is the object of the conception expressed by the speaker and understood by the hearer. There is a very real sense, then, in which Reid is to be taken literally when he says that individuals are "expressed in language" (*EIP* IV.1, 364b, 303).[22] And, except when we are deliberately and explicitly using a common word with an 'enlarged' or 'restricted' meaning (*EIP* I.1, 230a, 38), what it signifies is a function of *ordinary* use, such use being "the arbiter of language" (*EIP* I.1, 228b, 35).[23]

In short, Reid appears to be operating with a straightforward, referential theory of meaning (cf. Jensen 1979: 363): while they serve to express and communicate thoughts, and while they mean what they do because of the intentional activities of language-users, words signify *objects* (things, properties, and so on), and not anything mental (ideas, conceptions, and so on). Or perhaps it would be better to say that, for his purposes, Reid is content to operate with such an unremarkable, seemingly commonsensical view of meaning; certainly he does not further discuss the nature of linguistic meaning *per se*. He does, however, address important linguistic phenomena beyond those already discussed. Among the latter, what gets perhaps the greatest attention from Reid, and a case that can seem to place the view of meaning just outlined under serious stress, is the nature of general terms.

---

[22] For Reid, recall, sensation is unique among our mental acts in that it "hath no object distinct from the act itself" (*EIP* I.1, 229a, 36). The rest of our mental operations, including conception, always have an object distinct from themselves (*EIP* II.11, 292b, 161; *EIP* I.1 223b–224a, 26)—they are, as we would say, *intentional* acts. It bears emphasizing as well that having a conception of *x*, in Reid's sense, is not to be understood as subsuming *x* under a concept or entertaining a proposition about *x*; it is, rather, to *apprehend x*, to *have it in mind*, to *have a mental grip* on it (see Wolterstorff 2001: 9–12; Van Cleve 2004: 107).

[23] There is no conflict between this idea and the claim, just made, that "meaning is the conception affixed to it by those who best understand the language". For, in the case of ordinary as opposed to technical terms, ordinary speakers are those who best understand the language.

## 5. On General Terms and Conceptions

While Reid's views, including his views on language, depart in important ways from those of his immediate predecessors, they also converge on many points, linguistic and otherwise. On the matter discussed in Section 2, for example—Reid's concern that language, and unclear and non-standard uses thereof in particular, can be an "impediment to the advancement of knowledge" (*EIP* I.1, 219a, 17)—there are clear echoes of Berkeley, who is moved to preface his own views with discussion "concerning the nature and abuse of language" (Berkeley 1996: *Principles*, Introduction, 9, para. 6).

As Berkeley saw it, the chief cause of philosophical confusion is the Lockean doctrine of abstract ideas and the assumptions about language that help motivate it. Locke arrives at that view by combining several theses: first, that "words, in their primary or immediate signification, stand for nothing but *the ideas in the mind of him that uses* them" (Locke 1959: III.2.2; ii. 9); second, that everything that exists is particular; and third, that if language and linguistic communication are to be possible, there must be general terms—terms that signify, not individuals, but kinds of things, essences, 'universals' (that is, qualities that can be had by more than one thing), and so on. Locke's answer to the resulting tension, of course, is to claim that "words become general by being made signs of general ideas: and ideas become general, by separating from them the circumstances of time and place, and any other ideas that may determine them to this or that particular existence" (Locke 1959: III.3.6; ii. 16–17). The latter process Locke calls 'abstraction', and the general ideas to which it gives rise, 'abstract ideas'.

Berkeley shares Locke's commitment to the three theses just described. But he finds Locke's own solution to the problem of how they can all be true deeply problematic. Not only is Lockean abstraction impossible; according to Berkeley, Locke is quite wrong to think that it is necessary for explaining certain phenomena—in particular, our capacity to think and talk about *types* of things. As to the former: *any* idea is particular—one cannot think of brown, for example, without thinking of a particular shade of brown; if one strips away all particularity from an idea, one ends up with no idea at all (Berkeley 1996: *Principles*, Introduction, 11, para. 10; *First Dialogue*, 131-2). As to the latter, Berkeley offers the following alternative to Locke's unsatisfactory view of how we come to have general ideas: "an idea, which considered in itself is particular, becomes general, by being made to represent or stand for all other particular ideas of the same sort" (Berkeley 1996: *Principles*, Introduction, 13–14, para. 12). Since words signify ideas, general terms signify such general ideas; and so we can, Berkeley thinks, explain what needs explaining without recourse to abstraction and abstract ideas.

Against this background, Reid's discussion of general terms (and conceptions) is a notable example of the characteristic combination of orthodox and heterodox claims alluded to above. Before considering Reid's positive views, however, it is important to note that, as he sees it, both Locke and Berkeley only *appear* to be explaining what is at issue. For both of their accounts are obviously regressive: Locke's requires that we already know which features of an idea determine it to this or that existence and which do not; Berkeley's requires that we already know which other ideas are "of the same sort". In either case, what is being presumed is precisely what the theorist is claiming to have explained—namely, our capacity for general thoughts (e.g. *EIP* V.6, 409a, 397).

As just discussed, Reid is operating with a referential view of linguistic meaning. In the case of proper names, they "are intended to signify one individual only" (*EIP* I.1, 389a, 354), and none of the relevant parties regards *this* type of case as particularly problematic—in Reid's case, he mentions proper names only so as to immediately set them aside. Granted, Reid's view of proper names as signifying individual things, rather than ideas, both separates him from Locke and anticipates Mill (1963). However, what merits attention for him, as for Locke and Berkeley, is not proper names but the apparent generality at least implicit in most of our talk: "*All* other words of language [besides proper names]", Reid says, "are general words, not appropriated to signify any one individual thing, but equally related to many" (*EIP* V.1, 389a, 354; emphasis added). In addition, Reid agrees that everything that exists is a particular (e.g. *EIP* V.1, 389a–b, 355). So, what do general terms signify for Reid?

Obviously, they will not, and cannot signify ideas in the sense intended by Locke, Berkeley, or any other proponent of 'the theory of ideas'—since, as we have seen, Reid thinks "*ideas*, taken in th[at] sense, to be a mere fiction of philosophers" (*EIP* I.1, 226b, 31). It might appear, however, that Reid's own view here *is* ideational, in the sense that it takes general terms, if not proper names, to signify specifically mental objects. As we saw in Section 2, Reid (of course!) allows 'ideas' in the sense of *thoughts* ("conceptions"); and there are places in Reid's discussion of general terms that suggest that *these* are what general terms signify. At first blush, the following passage in particular seems clearly to support this reading: "every attribute, common to several individuals, may be expressed by a general term, which is the sign of the general conception" (*EIP* V.3, 395b, 368; cf. *EIP* IV.1, 364b, 304).

And, surely, it *must* be conceptions, or *something* mental, to which such terms refer. After all, what else *could* they signify? Universals? Qua non-particular things, they do not by Reid's lights exist! Natural though it may be, however, it would in fact be a mistake to think that Reid's account of general terms has it that their meaning is the thoughts or conceptions they express—that Reid's view is, as it were, a kind of watered-down Lockean view, an ideational view without the ideas. Once again, this way of reading Reid is very natural. But there are very good reasons for thinking that this is not Reid's position, and that the naturalness of so reading him is really evidence of the distinctiveness of his actual view.

While in the passage above Reid says that general terms are signs of general conceptions, there are many more places where he says that what they signify is something *non*-mental. For instance: that it is *attributes* that "must...be expressed by general words" (*EIP* V.1, 389b, 355); that *classes* are what "are called kinds and sorts; and, in the scholastic language, *genera* and *species*" (*EIP* V.1, 390a, 356); and that general terms (unlike proper names) "signify not any individual thing, but attributes common to many individuals" (*EIP* V.3, 396b, 370).[24] Or again:

> To conceive the meaning of a general word, and to conceive that which it signifies, is the same thing. We conceive distinctly the meaning of general terms, therefore we distinctly conceive what they signify. But such terms do not signify any individual, but what is common to many individuals; therefore, we have a distinct conception of things common to many individuals—that is, we have distinct general conceptions. (*EIP* V.2, 393b, 363)

Words, then, can be said to be "the signs of our thoughts" (*EIP* VI.8, 474a, 538), or to *express* our thoughts; so too, we can say that, when they are used successfully to communicate, what words signify "is conceived by the mind of both the speaker and hearer" (*EIP* V.2, 391b, 359). These are perfectly harmless claims: they immediately follow from the fact that we use such terms to communicate, to cause conceptions to arise in others, and that qua artificial signs they communicate what they do in virtue of the thoughts, intentions, and so on, of languages-users (Section 4). Again, though, a term is "called a general word" only "because that which it signifies is general" (*EIP* V.2, 391b, 359); and no *conception* is general—a conception is "an individual act" (*EIP* V.2, 391b, 360).

Reid says that there is *one* sense in which "most words (indeed all general words) are the signs of ideas"—namely, if ideas are understood simply to be "general objects of conception" (*EIP* V.6, 404a-b, 387). But, of course, the objects of conception are not the conceptions themselves. Why then would Reid *say* in the passage just cited that "a general term ... is the sign of the general conception" (*EIP* V.3, 395b, 368)? Well, as Reid was at pains to emphasize, our terms for various mental operations suffer from an act/object ambiguity. And, in the case at hand, we have further evidence that Reid's is not an ideational view; for it is only qua *object* of the relevant mental act that a conception can be said to be what a general term signifies:

> We must here beware of the ambiguity of the word *conception*, which sometimes signifies the act of the mind in conceiving, sometimes the thing conceived, which is the object of that act. If the word be taken in the first sense, I acknowledge that very act of the mind is an individual act; the universality, therefore, is not in the act of the mind, but in the object or thing conceived. The thing conceived is an attribute common to many subjects, or it is a genus or species common to many individuals. (*EIP* V.2, 393b-394a, 364)[25]

---

[24] One could hold that such items (attributes, classes, etc.) just *are* general conceptions, but it is obvious that this is not Reid's view—see later in this section.

[25] Here is one passage in which Reid himself switches from conception-as-act to conception-as-object in midstream, as it were: "To begin with the conceptions expressed by general terms—that is, by such general words as may be the subject or the predicate of a proposition. They are either attributes of things, or they are the *genera* and *species* of things" (*EIP* V.2, 391b-392a, 360).

The words notion and conception, in their proper and most common sense, signify the act or operation of the mind in conceiving an object. In a figurative sense, they are sometimes put for the object conceived. I think they are rarely, if ever, used in this figurative sense, *except when we speak of what we call general notions or general conceptions.* (*EIP* V.5, 403b, 385; emphasis added)

So, when Reid says that "every attribute, common to several individuals, may be expressed by a general term, which is the sign of the general conception" (*EIP* V.3, 395b, 368), he is speaking figuratively. Properly speaking, Reid's real view is that general terms signify the non-mental items that are the *objects* of such acts.

But how is that possible? Reid says that "every creature which God has made, in the heavens above, or in the earth below, or in the waters under the earth, is an individual" (*EIP* V.1, 389a–b, 355). So there *are no* universals, no attributes, no *genera* or *species*—in short, no general objects—to serve as the objects of our general conceptions, and so the meanings of general terms. To this, Reid's answer is straightforward. It is not the answer that has come to be associated with Meinong (1960)—namely, that there is a sense in which such non-actual objects *do* exist. Reid's answer, rather, is to insist that "we have power to conceive things which neither do nor ever did exist. We have power to conceive attributes without regards to their existence" (*EIP* V.5, 403b, 385).[26] The error, as Reid sees it, of both Locke and the Platonists is to suppose that *attributes* (universals) or *kinds* of things *must* exist—either as mind-independent Forms, or as abstract ideas—in order for us to be able to conceive of them.[27]

So how *are* general thoughts (conceptions) possible, on Reid's view? In one sense, the question is perfectly answerable. Such thoughts are made possible by three operations of the mind: analysing a subject into its known attributes, and giving a name to each; observing one or more of these attributes to be common to many subjects; and combining into a whole several of these attributes and giving that combination a name. The first two underlie our capacity to think of universals; the third is what underlies the formation of conceptions of *genera* and *species* (*EIP* V.2, 394a–b, 365–6). There is no special training required for the performance of such operations—"the invention and use of general words...is not a subtile invention of philosophers, but an operation which all men perform by the light of common sense" (*EIP* V.1, 390b, 357). But neither does one always, or even typically, acquire one's general terms by carrying out the relevant operations oneself. Sometimes one learns the meaning of such a word by being presented with a definition. Most often, however, such terms are acquired "by a kind of induction, by observing to what individuals they are applied by those who understand the language. We learn by habit to use them as we see others do, even when we have not a precise meaning annexed to them" (*EIP* V.2, 393a, 363). Thus, as Reid puts it, "the labour of forming abstract

---

[26] There is good reason to think that, contrary to how he is customarily interpreted, this is in fact Meinong's view as well; see Van Cleve (1996) and Nichols (2002).

[27] See Cummins (1976: esp. 71), where supporting passages from Reid are given.

notions, is the labour of learning to speak, and to understand what is spoken" (*EIP* V.6, 409b, 398). Coupled with Reid's claim that "the meaning of the word is the thing conceived; and that meaning is the conception affixed to it by those who best understand the language" (*EIP* IV.1, 364b, 303), there is obviously a natural home here for the notion of 'the division of linguistic labor', as Putnam (1975) calls it.[28] More broadly, as Susan Castagnetto (1992: 55–6) points out in her fine discussion of Reid's views on general conceptions, Reid's remarks on the acquisition of general conceptions depict it as in many cases a decidedly *social* process: we do not start with our own ideas, abstract away some of their features, and arrive at a general conception that may or may not match those that others associate with a given term; rather, we start with public language and public objects, and learn by 'habit' and 'a kind of induction' that some of these things' shared features, but not others, are what are signified by a given general term.

This is indeed a noteworthy feature of Reid's view. But, of course, it leaves unanswered the *hard* version of the question posed above: while it depicts their creation and acquisition as the result of various operations, both solitary and public, it does not yet tell us how general conceptions are possible *at all*.[29] To this question, Reid does not give or attempt to give an answer. In general, he regards it as a mistake, albeit an extremely natural and tempting one, to attempt to explain our most fundamental cognitive abilities.[30] His attitude towards our capacity for general thoughts, and so for having general terms in our language, is no different:

As to the manner how we conceive universals, I confess my ignorance. I know not how I hear, or see, or remember, and as little do I know how I conceive things that have no existence. In all our original faculties, the fabric and manner of operation is, I apprehend, beyond our comprehension, and perhaps is perfectly understood by him only who made them. (*EIP* V.6, 407b–408a, 394)

Briefly to summarize the discussion of this section: Reid maintains a referential theory of meaning, not just for proper names, but for words generally. He does so, even though he believes that, while all terms excepting proper names refer to (signify) kinds, attributes, classes, and other non-particulars, only particular things exist. The apparent tension here is relieved, not by (for example) adopting an ideational view of meaning, but by acknowledging our apparent—that is, obvious—ability to think and speak of non-existent things.[31]

---

[28] The connection with Putnam is noted by Coady (2004: 191); one passage that strongly suggests the idea in Reid is *EIP* V.2, 393a–b, 362–3. See too *Lett.* 70b–71a, 191–3, where Reid compares language to both "a huge and complicated machine" and "a tree", with various individuals and successive generations effecting changes and improvements, contributing to its overall state.

[29] Castagnetto (1992) is very clear about this as well.

[30] "It is genius, and not the want of it, that adulterates philosophy, and fills it with error and false theory" (*IHM* I.2, 99b, 15).

[31] Is most of our talk false then, according to Reid, since *most* terms are general and so involve reference to non-existent things? No. When I say that there is a red apple on the table, for example, I do indeed refer

## 6. The Social Operations of the Mind

Since we typically use language to communicate with others, there is a sense in which everyone must admit that language and its users are social. At several points in our consideration of Reid's views on language, however, we have seen Reid making points that depict language, and us, as more deeply and interestingly social. One instance of this is the importance of ordinary use as setting the standard for correct use; another is the significance of language as affording evidence of the general character of our thought; another is our possessing a natural means of automatically grasping others' intentional states; and another still is the essentially social process by which we have come to have most of the words we possess and to form most of the conceptions we do. In all of these respects, Reid's orientation is decidedly anti-individualistic. Whereas, of course, if one adheres to the theory of ideas, for example, *everything* begins at home, as it were, with one's own stock of ideas; from there, the task is (for the individual) to recover and (for the theorist) to explain engagement with the familiar world of things and persons.

Yet another example of Reid's anti-individualism, his commitment to a view of humans and language as deeply social from the first, is his discussion of 'social operations of the mind', "such operations as necessarily suppose an intercourse with some other intelligent being" (*EIP* I.8, 244b, 68); they "can have no existence without the intervention of some other intelligent being, who acts a part in them" (*EAP* V.6, 664a, 330). These "social intellectual operations" (*EIP* I.8, 244b, 69) include asking or receiving information, giving or receiving testimony, asking or accepting a favour, and giving or receiving a promise. Such operations, Reid says, are as natural as "solitary" operations such as judging, conceiving, perceiving, remembering, imagining, willing, and so on—they "are found in every individual of the species, even before the use of reason" (*EAP* V.6, 664b, 331; cf. *EIP* I.8, 244b–245a, 69). So, too, they are "simple", or unanalysable in terms of some more basic operation(s). Thus, just as it is a mistake to try to reduce one or more solitary operations to another, as the ideal theorist does when he tries to reduce memory, perception, imagination, and so on to consciousness (the perception of ideas in one's mind) (*IHM* VII, 206b, 210), it would be a mistake to try to reduce social operations to solitary ones. "To ask a question", for example, "is as simple an operation as to judge or to reason; yet it is neither judgment nor reasoning, nor simple apprehension, nor is it any combination of these" (*EIP* I.8, 244b, 68; cf. *EAP* V.6, 664a–b, 331).

---

to redness and (the kind) apples. But I do not (falsely) assert the existence of these non-existent things. Rather, I assert/imply the existence (and location) of an individual thing having features shared by (that is, that is similar to) both certain other fruits and other red things, where 'fruits' and 'red things' (etc.) need have no reality beyond various individuals grouped according to similarity relationships.

Unsurprisingly, the distinction between solitary and social operations[32] shows up in language. First, the expression of solitary acts "by words, or any other sensible sign, is accidental": one may reason, remember, perceive, and so on, without expressing one's conclusion, memory, or perception, in words. By contrast, just because they are social, and because they necessarily involve interaction with another intelligent agent, in the social operations "the expression is essential" (*EAP* V.6, 664a, 330), and that expression demands investigation: "an analysis of such speeches, and of the operations of the mind which they express, would be of real use, and perhaps would discover how imperfect an enumeration the logicians have given of the powers of human understanding" (*Log.* 692a, 113; cf. *Lett.* 72a, 195).[33]

However, while "the expression of a question, or of a promise, is as capable of being analysed as a proposition is" (*EIP* I.8, 245b, 70), it is instead the *proposition*—the complete sentence, which can be true or false, and which is the expression of the solitary act of judgment (*EIP* I.8, 245a, 70)[34]—that has preoccupied philosophers.[35] Thus, for example, while Aristotle recognizes the existence of other kinds of speech—prayers and wishes, for example—he "remits them to oratory or poetry" (*Log.* 692a, 112). Centuries later, Hobbes would do the same: recognizing "divers kinds of speech" (prayers, promises, threats, commands, complaints, and so on), Hobbes says that, "in philosophy, there is but one kind of speech useful, which ... [is called a] proposition" (quoted in Hungerland and Vick 1973: 469).

In the mid-twentieth century, of course, J. L. Austin would begin his *How to do Things with Words* with precisely the same complaint as Reid's about the neglect of certain forms of speech:[36] "It was for too long the assumption of philosophers that the business of a 'statement' can only be to 'describe' some state of affairs, or to 'state some fact', which it must do either truly or falsely" (Austin 1975: 1). The development of 'speech act theory', by Austin himself, John Searle (1969), and P. F. Strawson

---

[32] Coady, for one, thinks that Reid assumes too neat of a distinction between the two. For example, he says, "making a judgment can serve a solitary or social purpose" (Coady 2004: 198). So too, of course, while social operations as such might not be *reducible* to some combination of solitary acts, they may very well include and presume various of the latter. Clearly, there is much more to be said here.

[33] In a letter to James Gregory (*Lett.* 70a ff., 191 ff.), Reid says that the 'natural' unit of speech is a sentence (or proposition—see note 34), in the sense that that is what we intend to communicate, even when we do so with one complex sound. But, Reid thinks, it is incredible to suppose that language would have begun with a conception and invention of the parts of speech, which were then assembled into wholes. Much more likely that, beginning with complex individual sounds, "the parts of speech [were] cut out of words that signif[ied] whole sentences".

[34] A 'proposition', for Reid, is not an abstract object but "a kind of speech" (*Log.* 692a, 112), "kind of sentence" (*EAP* V.7, 671b, 346), "a complete sentence" (*EIP* VI.1, 414a, 408). As to 'judgement', Reid means "every determination of the mind concerning what is true or false" (*EIP* VI.1, 415b, 411). Most of our judgements are formed naturally and unreflectively, and many of the mind's operations have judgement as either a component or a natural consequence. So, for example, he speaks of "the senses, memory and consciousness" as "judging faculties" (*EIP* VI.1, 414a, 410).

[35] In a similar fashion, and as part of his critique of abstract ideas, Berkeley complains that Locke (and others) simply assume that "language has no other end but the communication of ideas"; see Berkeley (1996: *Principles*, Introduction, 19 ff., paras 19 ff.).

[36] Reid's affinity with Austin here has been noted by others: see Coady (2004: 202 n. 7).

(1964), for example, was intended precisely to counter this assumption and remedy the neglect of the various other things we do with words, besides expressing truth-evaluable judgements. There is, in Reid, nothing approaching the kind of systematic treatment of speech acts ('speeches', as Reid calls them) that these later theorists would propose. But the connection is unmistakable (see Schuhmann and Smith 1990). And Reid's views on two types of social operation in particular—namely, testimony and promising—have recently got focused attention.[37]

However, to see Reid's remarks on the social operations as significant *merely* because they anticipate contemporary speech act theory would be a mistake. While the phenomenon is importantly linguistic, the implications of Reid's views on 'social operations' go beyond philosophy of language. For it is not just that a treatment of language that dismissed or ignored questions, commands, promises, and so on, or that tried to reduce them either to 'solitary' operations or to other forms of speech (for example, simple assertions of propositions) would be incomplete linguistic theory. A failure to appreciate the social operations, and to see that they are "specifically different from the solitary" (*EAP* V.6, 664a, 330), would lead to an impoverished picture of "the powers of human understanding" (*Log.* 692a, 113; emphasis added). After all, these social operations—which it is "the primary and direct intention of language" to express—are social operations *of the mind*; and, as we have seen, Reid thinks that "in the social operations the expression their expression is essential"—"[they] can have no existence without the intervention of some other intelligent being, who acts a part in them" (*EAP* V.6, 664a, 330). They are, as Coady (2004: 186) puts it, "social mental" acts (cf. Yaffe 2007: 284–5); and it is part of Reid's point in stressing their reality, importance, and irreducibility that some of our most fundamental mental acts essentially involve other people—the power we have of engaging in them is "a distinct faculty given by our Maker, and a part of our constitution, like the powers of seeing and hearing" (*EAP* V.6, 664b, 331).[38] In this way, it is a deeply social view, not just of language, but of persons and the mind as well, that Reid is promoting.[39]

---

[37] In addition to Schuhmann and Smith's more general discussion, both Yaffe (2007) and Coady (2004), for example, discuss Reid's views on promises; Coady's (1992), which has been largely responsible for the recent spate of work on testimony, develops at length a broadly Reidian account thereof.

[38] These words of Reid's, and his observation that the social operations "suppose a conviction of the existence of other intelligent beings" (*EIP* I.8, 244b, 68), once again clearly anticipate Austin (1946: 115): "believing in other persons, in authority and testimony, is an essential part of the act of communicating, an act which we all constantly perform. It is as much an irreducible part of our experience as, say, giving promises, or playing competitive games, or even sensing coloured patches."

[39] The preceding stands in stark contrast to what Schuhmann and Smith (1990) say in assessing Reid's views. While crediting Reid with anticipating many points of twentieth-century speech act theory, Schuhmann and Smith (1990: 58) nonetheless think that what they call Reid's "Cartesianism" about the mind "thwarts any claims which might be made on his behalf to the effect that he had a full-blown theory of speech acts in the modern sense". On the current reading, whatever Reid's stance on the relation between mind and body, part of the point of his discussion of the social operations of the mind is to counter the individualism and extreme introversion evident in Descartes', and many others', thinking about the

## 7. Conclusion

In his writings, Reid's primary target is an improved understanding of the mind, and his remarks on language and various linguistic phenomena are spread throughout his works. Nevertheless, it is clear that Reid made important contributions to its study and that on several points he anticipated later developments. Like Reid's views themselves, the significance of his contributions is not easily summarized. That Reid came at language, approaching it both as a source of data and as an important subject in his efforts towards an anatomy of the human mind, however, is significant. Indeed, two important themes that have emerged here are, first, that language should not be studied in isolation from a consideration of the mind and various other non-linguistic phenomena; and, second and relatedly, that to understand thought and language will include seeing how they relate us to the objects, persons, and society that surround us.

## Abbreviations

EAP   Thomas Reid, *Essays on the Active Powers of the Human Mind* (1788) [*PW* 509–679], ed. Knud Haakonssen and James A. Harris. Edinburgh: Edinburgh University Press, 2000.

EIP   Thomas Reid, *Essays on the Intellectual Powers of Man* (1785) [*PW* 213–508], ed. Derek R. Brookes. Edinburgh: Edinburgh University Press, 1997.

IHM   Thomas Reid, *An Inquiry into the Human Mind on the Principles of Common Sense* (1764) [*PW* 93–211], ed. Derek R. Brookes. Edinburgh: Edinburgh University Press, 1997.

Lett.   *The Correspondence of Thomas Reid* [see *PW* 39–92], ed. Paul Wood. Edinburgh: Edinburgh University Press, 2002.

Log.   *Thomas Reid on Logic, Rhetoric, and the Fine Arts* [see *PW* 681–713], ed. Alexander Broadie. Edinburgh: Edinburgh University Press, 2004.

Orations   Thomas Reid, *The Philosophical Orations of Thomas Reid*, ed. and with an introduction by D. D. Todd, trans. from the Latin by S. D. Sullivan. Carbondale and Edwardsville: Southern Illinois University Press, 1989.

PW   Thomas Reid, *Philosophical Works*, 8th edn, ed. William Hamilton. New York: Georg Olms Verlag, 1885.

---

mind. (Coady (2004: 191) is very good here, as is Castagnetto (1992: 59 n. 14), who responds to similar remarks by Jensen (1979: 373).) See, e.g., Reid's talk of "the intercourse of human minds, by which their thoughts and sentiments are exchanged, and their souls mingle together, as it were" (*EAP* V.6, 665a, 332–3). Coady (2004: 191–2) also suggests that Reid's views on the social operations of the mind foreshadow recent views in philosophy of mind and semantics that feature 'wide content'; the same connection can be seen, of course, with Reid's account of linguistic meaning and the object-directedness of conceptions generally (see Section 4, including note 22).

# References

Aristotle (1984). *Complete Works*, ed. Jonathan Barnes. Princeton: Princeton University Press.
Augustine (1992). *On Christian Doctrine*, ed. and trans. James J. O'Donnell. *Select Library of Nicene and Post-Nicene Fathers* <http://www9.georgetown.edu/faculty/jod/augustine/ddc.html> (accessed 1 November 2012).
Austin, J. L. (1946). 'Other Minds', *Proceedings of the Aristotelian Society*, Supplementary Volume XX. Repr. in Austin (1979), 76–116.
Austin, J. L. (1975). *How to Do Things with Words*. 2nd edn (first edn, 1962, from 1955 lectures). Cambridge, MA: Harvard University Press.
Austin, J. L. (1979). *Philosophical Papers*, 3rd edn. Oxford: Oxford University Press.
Berkeley, George (1996). *Principles of Human Knowledge* [1710] *and Three Dialogues* [1713], ed. and with an introduction and notes by Howard Robinson. Oxford and New York: Oxford University Press.
Castagnetto, Susan V. (1992). 'Reid's Answer to Abstract Ideas', *Journal of Philosophical Research*, 17: 39–60.
Chappell, V. C. (1964) (ed.). *Ordinary Language*. Englewood Cliffs, NJ: Prentice-Hall.
Coady, C. A. J. (1992). *Testimony: A Philosophical Study*. Oxford: Oxford University Press.
Coady, C. A. J. (2004). 'Reid and the Social Operations of the Mind', in Cuneo and Woudenberg (2004), 180–203.
Condillac, Étienne Bonnot de (2001). *Essay on the Origin of Human Knowledge*, trans. and ed. Hans Aarsleff. Cambridge: Cambridge University Press.
Cummins, Phillip D. (1976). 'Reid on Abstract General Ideas', in Stephen F. Barker and Tom L. Beauchamp (eds), *Thomas Reid: Critical Interpretations*. Philadelphia: Philosophical Monographs, 62–76.
Cuneo, Terence, and Woudenberg, René. (2004) (eds). *The Cambridge Companion to Thomas Reid*. Cambridge and New York: Cambridge University Press.
Dretske, Fred (1988). *Explaining Behavior: Reasons in a World of Causes*. Cambridge, MA: MIT Press.
Falkenstein, Lorne (2010). 'Étienne Bonnot de Condillac', in *The Stanford Encyclopedia of Philosophy (Fall 2010 Edition)*, ed. Edward N. Zalta <http://plato.stanford.edu/archives/fall2010/entries/condillac/> (accessed 1 November 2012).
Gibson, J. J. (1966). *The Senses Considered as Perceptual Systems*. Boston: Houghton Mifflin.
Grice, H. P. (1961). 'The Causal Theory of Perception', *The Aristotelian Society: Proceedings, Supplementary Volume*, 35: 121–52.
Grice, H. P. (1989). *Studies in the Way of Words*. Cambridge, MA: Harvard University Press.
Hobbes, Thomas (1991). *Leviathan* (1651), ed. Richard Tuck. Cambridge: Cambridge University Press.
Hume, David (1978). *A Treatise of Human Nature* (1739–40), introduction and index by L. A. Selby-Bigge, revisions and notes by P. H. Nidditch. 2nd edn. Oxford: Oxford University Press.
Hungerland, Isabel Payton Creed, and Vick, George R. (1973). 'Hobbes's Theory of Signification', *Journal of the History of Philosophy*, 11/4: 459–82.
Jensen, Henning (1979). 'Reid and Wittgenstein on Philosophy and Language', *Philosophical Studies*, 36: 359–76.

Locke, John (1959). *An Essay Concerning Human Understanding* (1690), ed. A. C. Fraser. New York: Dover.
Meinong, Alexius (1960). 'The Theory of Objects' (1904), trans. Isaac Levi, D. B. Terrell, and Roderick M. Chisholm, in *Realism and the Background of Phenomenology*, ed. Roderick M. Chisholm. Glencoe, IL: Free Press, 76–117.
Mill, John Stuart (1963). *System of Logic, Ratiocinative and Inductive* (1843), in *Collected Works of John Stuart Mill*, ed. J. M. Robson. Toronto: University of Toronto Press, vii–viii.
Millikan, Ruth G. (1984). *Language, Thought and other Biological Categories*. Cambridge, MA: MIT Press.
Nichols, Ryan (2002). 'Reid on Fictional Objects and the Way of Ideas', *Philosophical Quarterly*, 52: 582–601.
Putnam, Hilary (1975). 'The Meaning of "Meaning"', *Minnesota Studies in the Philosophy of Science*, 7: 131–93.
Rorty, Richard (1967) (ed.). *The Linguistic Turn: Essays in Philosophical Method*. Chicago and London: University of Chicago Press.
Rysiew, Patrick (2002). 'Reid and Epistemic Naturalism', *Philosophical Quarterly*, 52/209: 437–56; repr. in *The Philosophy of Thomas Reid: A Collection of Essays*, ed. John Haldane and Stephen Read. Oxford: Blackwell, 2003, 24–43.
Salmon, Nathan (1991). 'The Pragmatic Fallacy', *Philosophical Studies*, 63: 83–97.
Schuhmann, Karl, and Smith, Barry (1990). 'Elements of Speech Act Theory in the Work of Thomas Reid', *History of Philosophy Quarterly*, 7/1: 47–66.
Searle, John R. (1969). *Speech Acts*. Cambridge and New York: Cambridge University Press.
Sperber, Dan (1995). 'How do we Communicate?', in John Brockman and Katinka Matson (eds), *How Things Are: A Science Toolkit for the Mind*. New York: Morrow, 191–9.
Strawson, P. F. (1964). 'Intention and Convention in Speech Acts', *Philosophical Review*, 73: 439–60.
Todd, D. D. (1987). 'Thomas Reid's Semiotic', in *In a Word: Essays in Honour of Steven Davis*. Burnaby: Philosophy Department Special Publication, Simon Fraser University, 126–44.
Van Cleve, James (1996). 'If Meinong is Right, is McTaggart Wrong?', *Philosophical Topics*, 24/1: 231–54.
Van Cleve, James (2004). "Reid's Theory of Perception", in Cuneo and Woudenberg, eds., pp. 101–33.
Wolterstorff, Nicholas (2001). *Thomas Reid and the Story of Epistemology*. Cambridge and New York: Cambridge University Press.
Yaffe, Gideon (2007). 'Promises, Social Acts, and Reid's Argument for Moral Liberty', *Journal of the History of Philosophy*, 45/2: 267–89.

# 12

# Meaning in Action: Anton Marty's Pragmatic Semantics

*Laurent Cesalli*

Anton Marty (1847–1914) belongs to the first generation of Franz Brentano's pupils. His main work, the *Untersuchungen zur Grundlegung der allgemeinen Grammatik und Sprachphilosophie* (*Investigations into the Foundations of General Grammar and Philosophy of Language*), appeared in 1908.[1] Marty's theory of meaning may be labeled a "pragmatic semantics" in the sense that it conceives of linguistic meaning primarily in terms of speakers' intentions to act upon hearers' minds. The present chapter is structured in four parts: in Section 1, I provide some background elements regarding Brentano's psychology and scholastic philosophy of language and mind (Marty and Brentano very often take scholastic positions as starting points); in Section 2, I present the central claims of Marty's theory of linguistic meaning; in the third section, I give an outline of the metaphysics that underlies Marty's theory of linguistic meaning; the last section is devoted to the reception and influence of Marty's *Sprachphilosophie*.

## 1. Background Elements

Among the many pupils of Brentano—Carl Stumpf, Alexius Meinong, Edmund Husserl, Christian von Ehrenfels, and Kasimierz Twardowski, just to name a few others—Marty is the one who most spectacularly developed the ideas of the Master in the field of philosophy of language. More precisely, Marty's "descriptive theory of meaning" is directly dependent on Brentano's psychology. Besides this common interest for psychology—or, as we would say nowadays: for philosophy of mind—Brentano and Marty share a significant biographical element: both were Catholic priests (although not for a very long time),[2] which means that they were originally

---

[1] On Marty's philosophy of language, see Funke (1924); Landgrebe (1934); Raynaud (1982); Mulligan (1990); Smith (1990); Spinicci (1991); Baumgartner et al. (2009); Rollinger (2010).

[2] Marty and Brentano both abandoned the priesthood in 1873 as a consequence of the promulgation of the dogma of papal infallibility by the first Vatican Council in 1870.

trained as philosophers in the neoscholastic tradition. Thus, for example, the notion of intentionality itself, as well as the idea that a theory of meaning has an essential psychological component, two fundamentals in Brentano's and Marty's philosophies, have their roots in the scholastic tradition.

## 1.1. Brentano's Psychology

Brentano defines psychology as the science of mental (or psychic) phenomena (Brentano 1924: 24).[3] What singles out mental from physical phenomena is the "intentional (or mental) inexistence of an object" (Brentano 1924: 115), where 'inexistence' means 'to exist *in*' (and not '*not* to exist'). Mental phenomena are of three (and only three) kinds: presentations (*Vorstellungen*), judgements (*Urteile*), and phenomena of interest (*Phänomene des Interesses* (Brentano 1924: 33–6)). The idea is that *in* a presentation *something* is presented, *in* a judgement, *something* judged, and *in* a phenomenon of interest, *something* loved or hated. For example, the two mental phenomena of hearing a sound, or seeing a colour, *contain* an object, whereas the sound heard or the colour seen (that is, the physical phenomena) do not.

Presentations are basic in the sense that any mental phenomenon either is itself a presentation, or is based on a presentation: there are no judgements without a presentation, nor are there any phenomena of interest without a presentation (Brentano 1924: 112–20). Take the case of a judgement, which is of central importance for the philosophy of language: judging amounts to accepting (or rejecting, in the case of a negative judgement) a presented object. This is a crucial feature of Brentano's psychology, for it takes part with the traditional (and scholastic) view of judgement as consisting in the composition or division of presentations.[4]

Although judgements are (most of the time) expressed in sentences consisting in a subject, a predicate, and a copula (i.e. in expressions displaying a propositional form), this is not to be taken as corresponding to the structure of the mental act of judging. In that sense, Brentano's theory of judgement is non-propositional: to judge is not to compose a subject with a predicate, but to have a certain attitude with respect to a presented object, which amounts to saying that every judgement is reducible to an existential one: to accept a presented object is to accept its existence (Brentano 1924: 276–95).[5] Such a conception is quite intuitive in the case of what Brentano calls "thetic" judgements such as "God exists". But how does it work in the case of "categorical" judgements such as "God is just"? Brentano maintains that categorical judgements are based on thetic ones (and, thus, that every judgement comprises an existential moment), but he explains the adjunction of the predicate as a kind of

---

[3] On Brentano's philosophy, see Jacquette (2004), in particular the contributions of Jacquette, Parsons, Simons, Mulligan, Chrudzimski and Smith, and Rollinger.

[4] The traditional conception of judgement is paradigmatically expressed by Aquinas in the *De veritate*, q. 14, a. 1: "There is another operation of the intellect <i.e. judging> according to which it composes and divides in affirming and negating."

[5] See Section 2.3.2.

second judgement supervening on the first one (he then talks of "double judgements"): what is expressed in a sentence like "God is just" is, first, the accepting (*Anerkennen*) of the object God, and, second, the ascribing of the predicate "just" (*Zuerkennen*) (Brentano 1924: 150-8).

Judgements stand out as mental phenomena for being the bearers of truth-values. Brentano defended successively at least two theories of truth. The first one, developed in the conference "On the Concept of Truth" (1889), consists in a peculiar interpretation of the traditional characterization of truth as an *adaequatio intellectus et rei* (correspondence of the intellect and a thing): in order to maintain the idea of correspondence, Brentano acknowledges objects that are not things (they are non-real entities, or *irrealia*), and that can serve as correlates for true negative judgements (for example, the judgement 'there is no centaur' is true in virtue of its corresponding to a non-real entity—that is, the lack or privation of centaurs), to the effect that what corresponds to a true judgement is not a thing properly speaking, but an *object* (Brentano 1930: 24-5). Later (from 1914 onward), Brentano abandoned the correspondence theory to defend a conception of truth based on evidence: "truth pertains to the judgement of the person who judges...about a thing in the way in which anyone whose judgements were evident would judge about the thing" (Brentano 1930: 139).[6]

## 1.2. The Scholastic Tradition

Both Brentano's psychology and the philosophy of language Marty developed out of it have their roots in the scholastic tradition. When introducing the distinctive feature of mental phenomena as the "intentional or mental inexistence" of an object in them, Brentano explicitly refers not only to the medievals, but also to Aristotle himself as forerunners.[7] Thomas Aquinas, for example, writes in his commentary on Aristotle's *De anima* (II, lect. 24, n. 3) that, when a thing is perceived by the senses, the form of the thing perceived has intentional being (*esse intentionale*) in the sense. As Aristotle puts it, the sense can receive the object without its matter (*De anima* III.2); thus, for example, "it is not the stone which is present in the soul but its form" (*De anima* III.8). And, when Marty formulates what turns out to be his final account of intentionality, he describes it as a relation of "ideal assimilation (*ideelle Verähnlichung*) of a subject to an object" (Marty 1908: 421), an idea that clearly echoes the Scholastic principle according to which every cognition occurs in virtue of an assimilation of the knower to what is known ("omnis cognitio fit per assimilationem cognoscentis ad cognitum").[8] In that connection, it has to be noted that the very term *intentionalitas* appears in a technical sense in medieval philosophical literature.

---

[6] All translations are the author's.
[7] For a recent study of Brentano's conception, see McDonnell (2006).
[8] Formulated, for example, by Aquinas in his commentary on Peter Lombard's *Sentences*, I, dist. 36, q. 1, arg. 3.

However, it refers not to a property of some mental act or states, but to a relation holding between the thing cognized (*res cognita*) and the act of cognizing.[9]

As for the intimate relation between philosophy of mind and semantics, it is constitutive of medieval semantic theories throughout, a feature that derives directly from its foundational text, the beginning or Aristotle's *De interpretatione* (c. 1), where one reads that spoken words are signs of concepts (or affections of the soul, as Aristotle puts it), and concepts in turn are likenesses of things. The difference between being a sign and a likeness is that a sign is conventionally related to what it signifies, whereas a likeness is naturally related to what it is a likeness of. Through the translation and interpretation of Boethius (sixth century), the Latin Scholastics will eventually give a uniform interpretation of the relations of being a sign and of being a likeness. As Lambert of Lagny (or of Auxerre) puts it in the middle of the thirteenth century: "since an utterance is a sign of a concept, and a concept is a sign of a thing, in this way, the utterance is a sign of a thing as well" (Lambert of Lagny 1971: 206). As a result, words were said to signify things by means of concepts (*mediantibus conceptibus*), and concepts were seen as semantic mediators. The exact nature of the role played by the concepts in the account of linguistic meaning is controversial among the medievals, however. The main alternative was that of semantic subordination, as it is most famously advocated by William of Ockham in the 1320s: words do not first signify concepts, and through them, things; rather, words signify things because they are associated with concepts that signify the very same things: both words and concepts are signs, but both signify directly things, and there is no relation of signification between words and concepts (Ockham, *Summa logicae* I.1, in Loux 1974: 49–51).[10] One even finds a combination of the two approaches in someone like John Buridan (first half of the fourteenth century), who writes that "spoken words do not signify extra-mental things unless through the mediation of the concepts to which they are subordinated" (Buridan 1998: 9).

One should also underscore that a certain pragmatic dimension is not absent from medieval semantics. For example, some authors present linguistic meaning as resulting from the way a speaker makes use of vocal sounds as communication instruments: 'to signify', says an anonymous logician of the late twelfth century, predicates an action on the side of the speaker (and a relation to things on the side of the word uttered), namely the action of using a word as an instrument "with the intention to make a sign of a thing" (*cum intentione faciendi signum de re* (De Rijk 1967: 710)). In his *De signis* (1267), Roger Bacon radicalizes such an instrumental conception of language in claiming that language users re-impose words *while uttering them* so that the semantic value of a word is directly linked to the intentions of speakers;

---

[9] The term appears several times in Hervaeus Natalis' tract *On second intentions*; see Dijs (2012: 133). On medieval theories of intentionality, see Perler (2001, 2002), as well as Lagerlund (2007).

[10] On Ockham's philosophy of mind and its relation to semantics, see Panaccio (2004: ch. 9). On the different ways the medievals conceived of the semantic role of concepts, see also Cesalli (2014b).

furthermore, Bacon insists that a sign is not first and foremost a sign *of something*, but a sign *for someone*, thus stressing the link between linguistic meaning and communication (Bacon 2013: 35).

Besides its manifest mentalist orientation and the presence of a certain pragmatic component, there is a further feature present in the medieval tradition that deserves to be mentioned as a relevant background element—namely, the idea that there is something like a formal or general grammar, transcending the specific grammars of the different languages. This is the core idea of the tradition of the so-called speculative grammar (*grammatica speculativa*) whose most famous theory describes different modes of signifying or *modi significandi* (the idea being that the different parts of speech are distinguished on the basis of different modes of signifying, which are derived from modes of understanding or *modi intelligendi*, which, in turn, are grounded in modes of being or *modi essendi*).[11] As a matter of fact, Marty also characterizes his descriptive theory of meaning as a general grammar (*allgemeine Grammatik*), the principles of which, being based on the functioning of the human mind, transcend the specificity of particular languages.[12]

## 2. Marty's Pragmatic Semantics

Marty's conception of linguistic meaning is directly derived from his view of language as being essentially a means of communication: what it means for a given expression *to have meaning* is determined by its being used by speakers with the intention to communicate. As for the relation between language and meaning, Marty describes meaning as being what he calls "the matter" of language ("the form" of language, in turn, is whatever belongs to *expression*, as opposed to meaning). Meaning itself is a complex notion and displays two related components: one pertains to what a speaker intends to do in uttering some expression (it is the *pragmatic* component of meaning), the other pertains to the contents or objects of the mental phenomena associated with the expression at stake (it is the *semantic* component of meaning). Furthermore, depending on the kind of mental phenomenon associated with a given expression, what is meant in the *semantic* sense will be of a different nature: *things* falling under a certain concept in the case of *names* (that is, expressions associated with presentations), *states of affairs* in the case of *statements* (that is, expressions associated with judgements), *states of values*, which parallel states of affairs in the "practical" realm, in the case of *Emotive* (that is, expressions associated with emotions).

---

[11] On this tradition, see the most recent study of Rosier-Catach (2010).
[12] In a seminal study of 1926 on the medieval logic of language (*Sprachlogik*) M. Grabmann (already, and rightly) associated speculative grammar with Marty's universalist theory of language (see Cesalli 2010). Note, however, that Marty does not share another central idea of the speculative grammarians according to which there is a kind of isomorphism between the structure of the world, that of thought, and that of language.

## 2.1. What Is Language?

Language is essentially a means of communication. If one wants to understand the principles and laws governing language, one always has to start from this basic fact. This claim has two remarkable implications: first, language is primarily spoken (and accidentally written), but in no case is there something like a mental language ("speaking silently in one's mind" is an instance of self-directed communication, but such an internalized form of language is not an instance of mental language)[13]; second, language can be apprehended—and thus understood— only as a specific type of human action: "Voluntary speech is a special kind of action whose ultimate aim is to trigger certain mental phenomena in other beings."[14]

Accordingly, linguistic expressions are communication tools that are developed and refined over time by trial and error and assume a precise function. The text just quoted suggests that language has a further, non-ultimate aim. As we shall see in Section 2.3.1, Marty distinguishes between two ordered linguistic functions: indicating a mental phenomenon (*kundgeben*) and triggering a mental phenomenon (*bedeuten*). Both are aimed at realizing (and are parts of) the action/communication process. Triggering presupposes indicating, and indicating is made in order to achieve triggering. Marty offers the following general definition: language is

> the intentional indication [*Kundgabe*] of <one's> mental life by means of sounds, in particular by sounds which are not understandable by themselves, but only in virtue of convention and habit.[15]

This definition has to be read against the background of Marty's first book, *Über den Ursprung der Sprache* (*On the Origin of Language*, 1875).[16] There, he shows in a complex thought experiment—the only possible "empirical" approach to the origins of language—that language could develop step by step in the interaction between humans. The only (and minimal) condition to be presupposed by the experiment is that the "primitive" human beings are capable of intentionally performing some movements that, originally, followed automatically (or mechanically) some mental states or acts (Marty 1875: 64).[17]

---

[13] Internalized speech always belongs to a determined language (e.g. "thinking in French"), but the "words" constituting mental language are, as Augustine pointed out in *De Trinitate*, XV, x, 19, "of no tongue" (*nullius linguae*); for the medieval conception of mental language, see William of Ockham, *Summa logicae* I, 1; on that topic, see also Panaccio (1999).

[14] Marty (1908: 284).

[15] Marty (1940: 81). See also Marty (1875: 61; 1908: 3, 53). In this passage, 'intentional' means not only that indication is deliberated, but also that it is performed with respect to a certain goal (namely, triggering).

[16] For an English translation of this book, see Rollinger (2010).

[17] The process described by Marty is analogous to the one observed in small children who *first* cry instinctively because they are hungry, and *then* learn to use the act of crying in order to communicate that they are hungry (or want something, etc.).

The resulting picture is the so-called empirico-teleological conception of language, a position that Marty develops in a critical discussion of the nativists of his time (Wilhelm Wundt, Moritz Lazarus, Heymann Steinthal), who conceive of language as a kind of natural, spontaneous emanation of the mind. For sure, language is not conceivable without thought (in a sense, language always expresses thought), but it does not follow that language is something like the external, perceptible form of thought. Rather, language was developed with the concrete intention to communicate (this is the teleological moment), but without any precise plan or global strategy (this is the empirical moment):

> Every single step of language formation was performed consciously insofar as it was yielded by the intention of communication... however, each of the language-builders thought but of the immediate need <to communicate>, and none of them... had an idea, neither of the whole, nor of the final result, and even less of the method... followed during the construction. In that sense, the building of language was performed unconsciously. The whole of language was there, and none of those who contributed to its accomplishment knew the inner structure of the work, its different parts, and their special functions.[18]

When it comes to the question of how exactly language does function as a means of communication—how is the *efficiency* of words as communication tools to be explained?—one has to turn to the heart of Marty's *Sprachphilosophie*—namely, to his theory of linguistic meaning.

## 2.2. What Is Linguistic Meaning?

### 2.2.1. FORM AND MATTER IN LANGUAGE AND MEANING

Marty's theory of linguistic meaning is structured according to a division of its subject matter into what he calls "matter" and "form". Although matter and form immediately evoke the basic components of substance in Aristotelian metaphysics, Marty uses those technical terms in a different sense: the form of language is to be understood as playing the role of a "container" (*Gefäß*), and the matter as being what is contained in it (one can think of a bottle giving its form to the liquid it contains, for example).[19] Marty applies the distinction between matter and form at two nested levels: first, whatever belongs to *expression* constitutes the form of language, and whatever belongs to *meaning* constitutes its matter; second, meaning itself is analysed in terms of matter and form: what Marty calls *Autosemantie* makes up the matter of meaning, while *Synsemantie* makes up the form of meaning (Marty 1908: 203–4). Figure 12.1 summarizes this double subdivision.

---

[18] Marty (1916b: 157).
[19] See Marty (1908: 101–20). On this subject, see Majolino (2003). For a different usage of the couple "matter and form" in the medieval tradition of speculative grammar see Marmo (1994: 484).

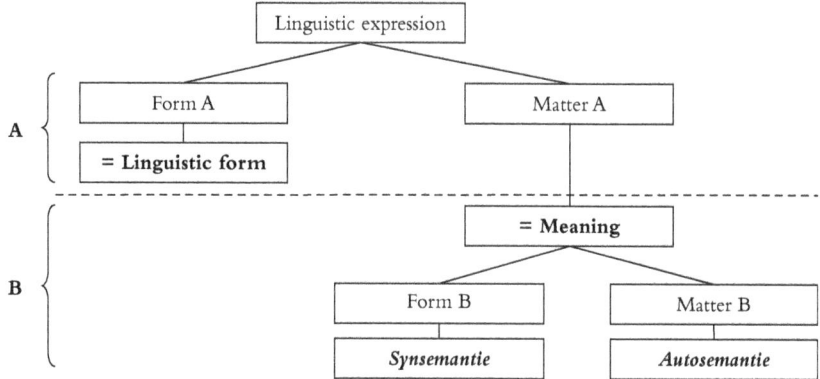

Figure 12.1

The terms *Autosemantie* and *Synsemantie* refer respectively to the semantic contribution of corresponding types of expressions:

<In every language, there are> in part means of designation that, even considered in themselves, are the expression of autonomously communicable mental phenomena, <and> in part ones for which such is not the case. *Autosemantic* and *synsemantic* seem to be the most suitable designations for the two fundamental classes under consideration here.[20]

Autosemantic expressions are able to express (and are used to trigger) mental phenomena properly speaking (that is, presentations, judgements, or phenomena of interest): they are, respectively, names, statements, and expressions of interest, the so-called *Emotive* (Marty 1908: 224–7). By contrast, synsemantic expressions contribute to express a mental phenomena only in association with autosemantic expressions: compare the two autosemantic expressions 'Socrates' and 'Socrates is a philosopher', the latter containing two synsemantic parts ('is' and 'a').

The general structure of the whole of Marty's *Untersuchungen* (the book published in 1908 is only the first volume of the work) is governed by this opposition between matter and form. Taking into account the volumes published posthumously, we have (roughly) the following thematic repartition: in Marty (1908), after the introduction of the nested distinctions or matter and form (*A* and *B*), the book deals mainly with

---

[20] Marty (1908: 205–6). The distinction recalls the medieval one between *categoremata* and *syncategoremata*, but it is not identical with it. The medievals had two ways of formulating the opposition: *categoremata* are described as those expressions that are either subject or predicate, or, alternatively, as those expressions whose meaning is complete (paradigmatically: names and verbs); *syncategoremata*, by contrast, cannot be subjects or predicates, and their meaning is incomplete (paradigmatically: logical constants such as *si*, *non*, *omnis*, etc.). Marty's criterion is designed to distinguish not types of words, but types of expressions—that is words, but also parts of words or complexes of words that, according to their semantic value in their actual use in communication, can be either auto- or synsemantic (for example, an expression like 'dass Du mir dies gesagt hast' (that you told me that) is autosemantic as an exclamation, but synsemantic as a subordinate proposition).

the semantics of *Autosemantika* (names, statements, expressions of interest or *Emotive*); in Marty (1940), the semantics of *Synsemantika* is at stake; in Marty (1950), (resulting) problems of syntax are discussed.[21]

2.2.2. THE INNER LINGUISTIC FORM

When meaning is considered as the matter of language (this is level A in Figure 12.1), the corresponding forms are *forms of expression* of this matter. On the descriptive level,[22] Marty distinguishes two so-called differences of the linguistic form.[23]

The first differences concern the *external* linguistic form, which consists in whatever elements contribute to the expression of a meaning and *are perceivable by the senses* (for example, the difference between written and spoken expressions, or between equivalent expressions of different languages). The second differences regard the *inner* linguistic form, that is: whatever contributes to expression but *is not perceivable by the senses* (those features are grasped by inner perception alone).

The inner linguistic form is twofold: we have, on the one hand, what Marty calls the 'figurative inner linguistic form' and, on the other, what he labels the 'constructive inner linguistic form'. Both are constituted by auxiliary presentations *that do not make up the meaning*, that is: presentations that are *not* the ones indicated (or to be triggered) by linguistic expressions. Their function is not to "constitute" meaning in the sense just explained, but to lead to it, or to facilitate the link between what is heard and what is indicated (or to be triggered). Here is an example of inner *figurative* linguistic form: the understanding of the verb 'to grasp' in the expression 'to grasp an idea' involves the image of a hand grasping an object. This image is an auxiliary presentation leading to what is meant by 'to grasp' here, but it is not part of what is meant (it is not part of the meaning of the expression). As for the *constructive* inner linguistic form, the auxiliary presentations at stake are expectations and anticipations generated in the process leading to the complete understanding of a complex expression. For example, while hearing the sequence of words 'After that she began to...', certain expectations and anticipations are generated that will facilitate the grasping of the expression's complete meaning once totally pronounced.

That being said, Marty repeatedly insists on the importance of distinguishing sharply between what pertains to meaning, and what belongs to the inner linguistic form. The reason is that the confusion of the two leads unavoidably to philosophical mistakes. For example, and to mention only the two most striking cases: the (mistaken)

---

[21] For a detailed exposition of the genesis and structure of the *Untersuchungen*, see Funke (1940).
[22] Following Brentano, Marty distinguishes the descriptive and the genetic approach of psychology (and meaning). Brentano introduced the distinction at the end of the 1880s. The genetic perspective considers the origins and development of a given phenomenon (e.g. linguistic meaning), whereas the descriptive one considers the structures and laws governing a given phenomenon as they exist now. See Marek and Smith (1987: 37–8), as well as Chrudzimski (2001: 19; 2004: 133).
[23] For a general presentation of the linguistic forms, see Marty (1893: 68–75; 1908: 121–50; 1918: 62–101). On that subject, see Funke (1924).

belief that the canonical form of judgement is propositional (something like *A is B*) is due to the image of an accident inhering in a substance that is involved in the understanding of the verb 'to predicate' (as well as in the understanding of the words 'subject' and 'predicate' (Marty 1918: 256–7)); further, the idea that presentations have an immanent object, something like a fictive duplicate of the transcendent (or external) object, a misleading idea that probably goes back to the relation subject–object in the case of ocular vision (Marty 1908: 415–16).

The origin of the inner figurative linguistic form is closely linked with the empirico-teleological nature of language (see Section 2.1). A conventional system of signs (as language exists nowadays) could emerge out of signs that were understandable by themselves (and this is, according to Marty, how language actually originated (Marty 1875: 79–106)) only in virtue of a process of semantic transfer such that what was originally meaning became progressively inner figurative linguistic form. And if, in some cases, the original meaning is still "alive" in the actual use of language (think of 'to grasp' in 'to grasp an idea'), in other cases, it has been fully forgotten, as the (real) etymologies of words often reveal (think, for example, of the original images that must have led to the apparition of a word like 'information').

## 2.3. Meaning in the Broader and in the Narrower Sense

Marty distinguishes between two senses of linguistic 'meaning'. In its most fundamental, primary (and broader) sense, meaning is the function of triggering certain mental states in a hearer (a function that is mediated by the function of indicating certain mental states in the speaker); according to its derived, secondary (and narrower) sense, meaning is the *content* of the mental acts indicated and to be triggered:

Linguistic means do not merely indicate the speaker's mental life in their subjective–immediate function; they are primarily aimed at mediately triggering corresponding mental states in the hearer; and this function, but also, further, the content of the mental states to be triggered, is what we call their meaning (*Bedeutung*).[24]

Because meaning in the broader sense has to do with what a speaker intends to induce in a hearer in saying something, I suggest calling it 'meaning in the pragmatic sense'; and, because meaning in the narrower sense has to do with the grasping of a certain content (and not with an intended action), I suggest calling it 'meaning in the semantic semantic sense'.[25]

---

[24] Marty (1908: 495–6). For an example, see Section 2.3.2.

[25] Note that Marty presents this hybrid notion of linguistic meaning as a kind of compromise between a subjective and an objective approach: according to a purely subjective approach, meaning would consist only in what a speaker intends (primarily and secondarily); according to a purely objective approach, meaning would be explained in terms of a relation holding between linguistic expression and ideal or abstract meanings (such as Bolzano's *Sätze an sich* or Husserl's *Bedeutungen in specie*).

## 2.3.1. THE CORE IDEA: MEANING IN THE BROADER (I.E. PRAGMATIC) SENSE

Just as Herbert Paul Grice will do some fifty years after him, Marty develops an intentionalist account of meaning. In other words, meaning is primarily "speaker meaning" and, thus, depends primarily on speakers' intentions:

> We said that language...is primarily understood as the intentional indication of inner life. However, what is primarily intended in this indication is a corresponding influence of others' inner life. As a rule, one indicates one's own presentations, judgements, emotions etc., in order to trigger presentations, judgements and emotions in another psychic being [*psychisches Wesen*], and indeed, ones which are analogous...to one's own.[26]

Meaning is analysed in terms of a twofold intention: on the one hand, the (speaker's primary) intention to influence others' inner life; on the other, the (speaker's secondary) intention to indicate his inner life. The latter intention leads to what Marty calls *Kundgabe* (indication), the former to what he calls *Bedeutung* (triggering), and triggering is mediated by indication. The triggering of mental phenomena in someone else is made possible by the indication of one's own inner life:

> in the case of voluntary speech...we always have to do with a twofold way of meaning: something which is primarily, and something which is secondarily intended, and correspondingly, something which is mediately intended, and something which is immediately intended. And just as we use the term 'to express' [*Ausdrücken*] or 'to intimate' [*Äußern*] for the latter, so, we want (as a rule) to use the term 'to trigger' [*Bedeuten*] and 'triggering' [*Bedeutung*] in order to designate the mediately and primarily intended sign-giving [*Zeichengebung*].[27]

Thus, according to the broader or pragmatic sense of 'meaning', linguistic expressions do not mean any *thing*, but rather something like *an intended action* (that is, something like "that a certain person should perform a certain mental act").

## 2.3.2. MEANING IN THE NARROWER (I.E. SEMANTIC) SENSE

Unlike meaning in the broader (or pragmatic) sense—which is described in terms of speakers' intentions to act upon hearers' mental life in one way or another—meaning in a narrower sense is characterized in terms of *contents* of mental phenomena:

> We said that, in a broader sense, a statement means as a rule that the hearer should form a judgement of the same matter [i.e. about the same object] and quality [i.e. affirmative or negative] as the one which is *indicated* by the statement as occurring in the speaker. In a narrower sense...one also calls something else the meaning of a statement. Who says: 'A exists'...considers A as an existent, and expects also of the hearer that he...considers A as

---

[26] Marty (1908: 22).
[27] Marty (1908: 286; see also 490–501). On Marty's notion of sign (and its comparison to Bühler's), see Majolino (2014). In this passage, 'Ausdrücken' and 'Äußern' are synonyms of 'Kundgeben', i.e. meaning 'to indicate'.

an existent. In that respect, one also says that the statement indicates the existence of A ... and *means* it in that sense. And since one also often designates the existence of A ... as being the content of the judgement 'A exists', one also may say: the statement indicates the *judgement content* and means it in that sense.[28]

In order to illustrate the different points established until now, let us consider the concrete example of the statement *P*: 'Socrates exists'. *P* expresses the judgement *J*: ¦Socrates exists¦, or, as Marty puts it, by pronouncing *P* a speaker *S* indicates *J* as occurring in herself. In the broader (i.e. pragmatic) sense, the meaning of *P* is that which is primarily (but mediately) intended by *S*—namely, that a hearer *H* should form a judgement analogous to *J*, that is, having Socrates as its object (or matter), and being affirmative, just as *J* is. In the narrower (that is, semantic) sense, by contrast, the meaning of *P* is the *content* of *J*.

Here it should be reminded that judging, according to Marty (and Brentano), is a non-propositional act: to judge does not amount to joining a subject and a predicate by means of a copula—as the traditional, that is, Aristotelian–scholastic tradition had thought—but to accept or reject (*annehmen/verwerfen*) a presented object.[29] Thus, the canonical form of a judgement is not something like "subject–copula–predicate", but rather something like* (*X*), where '*' stands for the act of accepting or rejecting, and '*X*' for a presented object. Such a discrepancy between the "logical" (that is, the psychological) form of judgements and the "linguistic" (that is, grammatical) form of statements clearly shows, as Marty often insists, that, although language and thought are intimately related, there is *nothing like a parallelism between the two*: spoken language is not something like "thought in a perceptible cloth".[30]

Returning to our example: *J* (that is, the judgement ¦Socrates exists¦) is based on the presentation *p*: ¦Socrates¦; when *S* forms *J*, she accepts the object presented in *p*—that is, Socrates. And when this occurs, *S* is mentally related not only to a presented object, but also to a judgement content or state of affairs *C*: [the existence of Socrates], a judgement content that, as we saw, is the meaning of *P* in the narrower (i.e. semantic) sense.[31]

Taking a step back and looking at the mechanisms described by Marty in his general analysis of linguistic meaning, one can say that two nested mediations are at work in this complex process: first, the mediation of triggering (*Bedeutung*) by

---

[28] Marty (1908, 291–2; see also Marty 1918, 70).
[29] For the Brentanian–Martyian theory of judgement, see Marty (1908: 229–30; 1918: 36–8); Brentano (1924: 44–8, 199–201). On that subject, see Mulligan (1989) as well as Rollinger (2004). The non-propositional theory of judgement is opposed not only to the scholastic one, which conceived of the affirmative judgement as a *compositio*, and of the negative as a *divisio*, but also to "contemporary" theories such as the ones of Husserl or Frege, which are both propositional. Meinong, by contrast, sides with Brentano and Marty.
[30] On that subject, see Marty (1893).
[31] See Marty (1908: 276, 371). For Marty's metaphysics of judgement contents (or states of affairs), see Section 3. For a comparison between different modern and medieval theories of states of affaires (including Marty's), see Cesalli (2012).

indication (*Kundgabe*); second, the mediation of meaning in the narrower or semantic sense (in the case described above: C) by meaning on the broader or pragmatic sense (that is, by indication and triggering).

## 2.4. The Semantics of Names and Statements

### 2.4.1. THE SEMANTICS OF NAMES: MEANING AND NAMING

According to Marty's account of linguistic meaning, a name means (in the broader, pragmatic sense) *that a hearer should form a certain presentation*, something that happens by the mediation of what the name indicates—namely, the occurrence of a certain presentation in the mind of the speaker.[32] However,

through the intermediary of the functions of indicating and of triggering, names also acquire that which we call naming [das *Nennen*]. We speak of naming in relation to the objects which possibly do correspond in reality to the presentations brought about by the names, or at least can correspond to them (without contradiction). These <objects of presentations> are that which is named [*das Genannte*].[33]

Thus, a name means (in the narrower, semantic sense) what it names. For example: a name like 'white' means (in the broader, that is, pragmatic sense) *that a hearer should form the presentation ¦white¦*, and names (that is, means in the narrower, semantic sense) white things (clouds, snow, and so on). In this context, Marty says that he fully agrees with the (late) scholastic principle according to which *voces significant res mediantibus conceptibus* (words signify things by means of concepts),[34] although, as the passage just quoted makes clear, Marty's idea (contrary to what the Scholastics thought) is *not* that words mean concepts, which, in turn, mean things.

But Marty makes a further distinction here. Just as one has to distinguish, in the case of judgements (which are indicated and triggered by statements), between object and content, analogously, one has to distinguish, in the case of conceptual presentations[35] (which are indicated and triggered by general names such as 'human being' or 'white'), between object and content: the *object* of a conceptual presentation is its extension—that is, whatever falls under the concept at stake (white things for the presentation ¦white¦, human beings for the presentation ¦human being¦); its *content*, by contrast, is what can be truly and equally predicated of anything falling under the concept at stake: something like the universal "white" (Marty 1908: 448). As we shall see, however (see Section 3), there is an important ontological difference between the content of a judgement and the content of a conceptual presentation: whereas the

---

[32] See Marty (1908: 384-5).   [33] Marty (1908: 436).
[34] For a passage where Marty uses this Latin phrase, see Marty (1908: 436, n. 1). Although the idea of the mental mediation of meaning is omnipresent in the medieval tradition thanks to Boethius' second commentary on Aristotle's *De interpretatione* (16a1-2)—see Boethius (2010: 25-7)—the slogan "voces significant etc." seems to emerge as such only quite late, i.e. in the fifteenth century (on that point, see Meier-Oeser 1997). On that subject, see Cesalli (2014b).
[35] As opposed to perceptual presentations like seeing a horse, for example.

former is a genuine (though non-real) entity, the latter is a mere counter-factual object (judgement contents exist, universals do not).

2.4.2. THE SEMANTICS OF STATEMENTS: THE THEORY OF TRUTH

Judgement contents, for Marty, cumulate two functions: that of being the significates of statements (in the narrower, semantic sense) *and* that of being the truth-makers of statements. A statement is true iff it expresses (and indicates) an act of judgement that is actually correlated to its content—and, in that sense, Marty can say, alluding to the classical definition of truth (*veritas est adaequatio intellectus et rei*), that truth is nothing but an *adaequatio cogitantis et cogitati*:

> When the judgement is conformed to the content in the sense of being actually correlated to it, that is: when the content which is conformed to it is given [i.e. exists], then we call <such a judgement> true or correct... If one labels the act of judging with the Latin *cogitare*, and the judgement content (or that which is judged) with *cogitatum*, one can appropriately speak of an *adaequatio cogitantis et cogitati* in which the correctness of the judgement consists in this strict sense [i.e. in the sense of an actual correlation].[36]

The obvious problem linked with such a combination of functions—namely: false propositions *must* have a significate (otherwise, they could not have a truth-value at all) but *cannot*, per definition, have a truth-maker—is solved by Marty in saying that the truth of a judgement is an *actual* correlation between the judgement and its content—say, between ¦Socrates exists¦ and [the existence of Socrates]—whereas, when the judgement is false, there is only a *possible* correlation between a judgement and its content, something Marty calls a "relative determination" (*relative Bestimmung*):

> We said that a judgement is true when an *adaequatio cogitantis et cogitati* in the sense of an actual correlation is the case. By contrast, when the content which is conformed to <the judgement> is missing in reality... and we nonetheless say... that 'it has a content' and that the statement expressing it has a meaning, this can only be justified with respect to the fact that this judgement possesses the harmony or conformity with a possible content in the *sense of a relative determination*. Correlates cannot exist without each other. When a judgement occurs without the existence of its content, 'to have a content' can only mean that *if*, in addition to this mental behavior [i.e. of judging], *that* would *also* exist, which we call its content, then a certain correlation (the one of adequacy or correctness) would necessarily be given as well.[37]

Thus, the content of the false judgement ¦Socrates exists¦ is that which, *if it existed*, would make it true—namely, a counter-factual entity. The false judgement is actually

---

[36] Marty (1908: 426). On the origins of the classical definition in the Middle Ages, see Muckle (1933). For its classical character, see Thomas Aquinas, *De veritate*, q.1, a.1. The notions of conformity and adequacy are technical expressions for the central notion of ideal conformity (*ideelle Verähnlichung*), which is how the mature Marty (i.e. after 1906) describes the intentional relation. On that topic, see Chrudzimski (1999) as well as Cesalli and Taieb (2013).

[37] Marty (1908: 426–7); see also Marty (1908: 411; 1916a: 148–59).

and effectively determined by such a counter-factual entity in the sense that it is true to say that nothing but [the existence of Socrates], if it existed, would make it true. In that sense, a counter-factual entity can exert an actual constraint on acts of judging and statements expressing them (they determine them *actually*, but only *relatively*).[38]

## 3. The Underlying Metaphysics

Looking at the different kinds of meaning distinguished by Marty, it appears that different ontological categories are at play in his "descriptive theory of meaning". And since the analysis of meaning is primarily made in terms of mental phenomena, the categories at stake coincide with the ones needed in order to account for the common and constitutive feature of mental phenomena—namely, intentionality. Let us first establish a list of the different types of entities involved in the theory, and then turn to the question of their ontological status.

First of all, we have the *mental phenomena* themselves—that is, presentations, judgements, and phenomena of interest; then, we have their *objects*—that is, things we think about, say something of, love or hate; finally, we have the *contents* of mental phenomena—that is, what is thought, what is judged, what is loved or hated. Recall that those three "functional" categories appear in the analysis of linguistic meaning in its broader (that is, pragmatic), as well as in its narrower (that is, semantic) sense: in the pragmatic sense, meaning is the triggering of some mental phenomenon in a hearer (by means of the indication of some analogue phenomenon by, and in, the hearer); in the semantic sense, meaning is the content of the mental phenomena at stake.

Leaving aside the more complex case of phenomena of interest, consider the following two examples:[39] the conceptual presentation ¦human being¦ (indicated/triggered by the name 'human being');[40] its object is whatever falls under the concept of human being (that is, its extension)—namely, individual members of the human species; and its content, were it to exist, would be something like "the human nature"—namely, that which would belong uniformly and equally to each member of the species (the Scholastics would say: the *natura communis*). Consider further the

---

[38] For Marty's theory of the *relative Bestimmung*, see Cesalli (2008). For an alternative reading of Marty's theory of truth—and thus of his conception of the relative determination, see Chrudzimski (2014), who rejects the counter-factual interpretation and advocates an adverbial one (the relative determination is not relational in any sense).

[39] Remarkably, Marty treats phenomena of interest in a way that, in many respects, is analogue to his treatment of judgements. For example: just as judgements are true or false depending on their being correlated to judgement contents (or states of affairs, *Sachverhalte*), phenomena of interest are correct or incorrect depending on their being correlated to value contents (or states of value, *Wertverhalte*); see Marty (1908: 425–7, 370).

[40] Not every presentation is a conceptual one, of course. Seeing a tree is a sense-based presentation, i.e. a perception. But, in such a case, there is no distinction between content and object (or, as one might put it, both coincide).

judgement ¦God exists¦ (indicated/triggered by the statement 'God exists'): its object is God, and its content is the state of affairs [the existence of God].

In order to determine the ontological status of mental phenomena, their objects and contents, one has to consider the fundamental distinction at work in Martyian ontology—namely, the distinction between the real and the non-real.

For Marty, whatever there is *exists* (there is nothing like non-existent objects, as, for example, Meinong admits them) and whatever exists does so in time (there is nothing like abstract entities, as Bolzano, Husserl, or Reinach admit them). However, that which exists is divided into the real and the non-real. The criterion for the distinction is that of the involvement in causal relations (or the absence of such an involvement): what is real is involved in causal relations, whereas what is non-real is causally inert. Examples of real entities are material substances and their accidents (Socrates, his paleness), but also mental entities like acts of presenting, judging, loving, and hating. Non-real entities, by contrast, are, for example, relations, collectives (a forest, an army, the French people), states of affairs (judgement contents), privations, past and future and merely possible things. Besides being causally inert, non-real entities are also singled out by their dependence on real ones: whereas real entities come into being and pass away for themselves (they have a proper *Werden* and *Vergehen*, as Marty says), non-real entities are always "consequences" (*Folgen*) of real ones (they have only a *Mitwerden* and *Mitvergehen* (Marty 1908: 316–21)).

Let us go through two simple examples. Consider, first, the statement 'Socrates exists'. The pronounced sounds (or the written marks) are real objects; so are the mental phenomena involved in the analysis—namely, the act of presenting Socrates and the act of accepting him (the act of judging affirmatively), but also the object of the judgement—namely Socrates himself; its content, by contrast, that is: [the existence of Socrates], is a non-real entity, a "consequence" of real Socrates; both Socrates and its existence exist in the same way—namely, objectively, that is: independently of what we think and say:

> If...the notion of judgement content is to have an intrinsic justification, then it must mean something which is independent from the existence of a judging subject, but which itself constitutes the condition for the possible correctness of an act of judging. In other words: it seems to me that what is naturally grasped in the notion of judgement content is that which objectively grounds the correctness of our acts of judging, or, more precisely: that without which this behaviour [i.e. judging] could not be correct or adequate.[41]

Our second example will be the name 'human being'. Here again, the sounds pronounced (or the written marks) are real entities, just as the act of presenting indicated (and triggered) by this name. But what about its object and content? As we saw earlier (see Section 2.4.1), general names like 'human being' indicate (and trigger) conceptual presentations—that is, presentations that have not only an object,

---

[41] Marty (1908: 295).

but also a content. The object at stake is a real entity, or, more precisely, several real entities—namely, individual members of the human species (the extension of the concept "human being"); unlike judgement contents, however, contents of conceptual presentations are not entities (not even non-real ones). They do not exist at all and exert only a semantic or cognitive function, without being taken ontologically seriously: the content of the presentation ǃhuman beingǀ is what one has in mind when using the expression 'human being', something that, *if it existed*, would be the universal "human being". In other words, it is a counter-factual universal, which is not an entity of any kind, but a mere "thought-object".

In that respect, the contents of conceptual presentations play a systematic role analogous to the one played by contents of false judgements (see Section 2.4.2), but also to the one played by what is meant by empty names;[42] with one important difference, however: whereas contents of false judgements might exist at some point in time (namely, when the judgements at stake have a different truth-value), counter-factual universals never exist. Whereas the difference between truth and falsity is a compelling reason to admit a difference in ontology (that is, to consider judgement contents as existing entities), this is not true of the difference between singularity and generality. Thus, Marty turns out to defend a remarkable ontology in which there are states of affairs, but no universals.

## 4. The Reception and Influence of Marty's *Sprachphilosophie*

Although the reception of Marty's *Sprachphilosophie* was not exactly a spectacular one,[43] Marty exerted an influence in the field of linguistics—mainly on the Linguistic Circle of Prague through his pupils Mathesius and Landgrebe,[44] as well as in the philosophy of language—mainly on (and through) Karl Bühler, who himself appears to have been a decisive source for Wittgenstein's conception of language.[45] Marty discussed and influenced the works of many of his contemporaries, and was influenced by them as well—Stumpf, Twardowski, Meinong, and Bühler to name just the

---

[42] Consider for example the following passage: "We call... <the object of a presentation> a real object of a presentation when it is the objective term of a presentational correlation. When, by contrast, there is actually no such correlation... one talks about an object *tout court* (*Gegenstand schlechtweg*). In that sense, the presentation 'Pegasus' does not have any real object, but it does have an object *tout court*... in the case of presentations, 'to have an object' <means> often merely: if what is at stake would exist, then it would be the object of this presentation" (Marty 1908: 432).

[43] See the impressive bibliography of works of and on Marty compiled by Bokhove and Raynaud (1990); see also Cesalli and Friedrich (2014a).

[44] See Holenstein (1976) and Raynaud (1982).

[45] See Mulligan (1997, 2011, 2012); Cesalli (2014a). As Mulligan (1997) has shown, the beginning of Wittgenstein's *Investigations* are directly dependent on the extended review of Marty's *Untersuchungen* Karl Bühler wrote in 1909, a text in which Bühler elaborates the central idea of his later *Sprachtheorie* (1934)—namely, the idea that, besides the functions of *Kundgabe* and *Bedeutung*, there is a third (and essential) linguistic function: *Darstellung* (representation).

most famous ones.[46] Furthermore, it has recently been convincingly argued that Marty's theory of meaning, in which the notions of intention and action play a crucial role, presents remarkable similarities with Grice's intentionalist semantics.[47]

The systematic relevance of Marty's theory of meaning can be best appreciated from the perspective of (some of) the latest developments in analytic philosophy of language in the post-Gricean tradition:[48] Marty's theory has the particularity of combining semantic and pragmatic elements, for mental phenomena have objects (and contents) that make up the semantic component of the words or sentences expressing those phenomena. But this "objective" (or one would perhaps want to say "objectual") component alone is not sufficient to account for the phenomenon of linguistic meaning; to be sure, it is a necessary component, but, according to Marty, it is not the essential one. Meaning is not an object (or a content)—it is not an entity at all; nor is it a property of words: words *do not have* meaning properly speaking. However, and this is Marty's key idea, words *are used in order to generate* meaning. In that sense, one could say that Marty would subscribe to the principle that "meaning is use"—with the following additional (and essential) clause, though: far from wanting to evacuate psychology from the account of meaning, Marty entirely bases his theory on (speakers') intentions and mental phenomena occurring in the speakers' and hearers' minds. In that sense, Marty's theory has the particularity of being at the same time a "pragmatic semantic" and a "philosophy of mind *and* language". From a historical point of view, Marty developed his main ideas just before (and while) the "referentialist paradigm" of meaning was set up by thinkers such as Frege, Russell, and the early Wittgenstein. Remarkably, however, his theory anticipates later challengers of this very referentialist paradigm such as the later Wittgenstein, Grice, Austin, and Searle. Thus, Marty's theory is at the same time a powerful elaboration of Brentanian psychology, and a remarkable anticipation of the analytic philosophy of language as it developed in the second half of the twentieth century.

## References

Albertazzi, L., Libardi, M., and Poli, R. (1996) (eds). *The School of Franz Brentano*. Dordrecht: Kluwer.

Bacon, R. (2013). *On Signs (Opus maius, part 3, chapter 2)*, trans. Th. Maloney. Toronto: Pontifical Institute of Medieval Studies.

Baumgartner, W., Fügmann, D., and Rollinger, R. (2009) (eds). *Die Philosophie Anton Martys*. Dettelbach: J. H. Röll [Brentano Studien 12].

---

[46] See Smith (1994); Albertazzi et al. (1996); Benoist (1997, 2001, 2002); Rollinger (1999); Cometti and Mulligan (2001); Cesalli (2009); Mulligan (2011, 2012).

[47] See Liedtke (1990, 2014); Cesalli (2013).

[48] See, e.g., Recanati (2008), but also Searle (1969) and Sperber and Wilson (1986).

Benoist, J. (1997). *Phénoménologie, sémantique, ontologie: Husserl et la tradition logique autrichienne*. Paris: Presses Universitaires de France.
Benoist, J. (2001). *Représentations sans objet: Aux origines de la phénoménologie et de la philosophie analytique*. Paris: Presses Universitaires de France.
Benoist, J. (2002). *Entre acte et sens: Recherches sur la théorie phénoménologique de la signification*. Paris: Vrin.
Boethius (2010). *On Aristotle On interpretation 1-3*, trans. Andrew Smith. London: Duckworth.
Bokhove, N. W., and Raynaud, S. (1990). 'A Bibliography of Works by and on Anton Marty', in Mulligan (1990), 237-83.
Brentano, F. (1924). *Psychologie vom empirischen Standpunkt. Erster Band*, ed. O. Kraus, Hamburg: Meiner.
Brentano, F. (1930). *Wahrheit und Evidenz*, ed. O. Kraus. Hamburg: Meiner.
Bühler, K. (1909). 'Anton Marty, *Untersuchungen zur Grundlegung der allgemeinen Grammatik und Sprachphilosophie*', *Göttingische gelehrte Anzeigen*, 171: 947-79.
Bühler, K. (1934). *Sprachtheorie. Die Darstellungsfunktion der Sprache*. Jena: Gustav Fischer.
Buridan, John (1998). *Summulae. De suppositionibus*, ed. R. van der Lecq. Turnhout: Brepols.
Cesalli, L. (2008). '*Relative Bestimmung*: Une relation martyienne', in C. Erismann and A. Schniewind (eds), *Compléments de substance: Études sur les propriétés accidentelles offertes à Alain de Libera*. Paris: Vrin, 215-29.
Cesalli, L. (2009). 'Anton Martys philosophische Stellung in der österreichischen Tradition', *Brentano Studien*, 12: 121-181.
Cesalli, L. (2010). 'Medieval Logic as *Sprachphilosophie*', *Bulletin de philosophie medieval*, 52: 117-32.
Cesalli, L. (2012). 'States of Affairs', in J. Marenbon (ed.), *Handbook of Medieval Philosophy*. Oxford: Oxford University Press, 421-44.
Cesalli, L. (2013). 'Anton Marty's Intentionalist Theory of Meaning', in D. Fisette and G. Fréchette (eds), *Themes from Brentano*. Amsterdam: Rodopi, 139-163.
Cesalli, L. (2014a). 'Marty, Bühler, and Landgrebe on Linguistic Functions', in Cesalli and Friedrich (2014a), 59-75.
Cesalli, L. (2014b). 'M&Ms. Mentally Mediated Meanings', in A. Reboul (ed.), *Mind, Values, and Metaphysics. Philosophical Essays in Honor of Kevin Mulligan*. London: Springer, 449-66.
Cesalli, L., and Friedrich, J. (2014a) (eds). *Between Mind and Language: Anton Marty and Karl Bühler*. Basel: Schwabe.
Cesalli, L., and Friedrich, J. (2014b). 'Introduction', in Cesalli and Friedrich (2014a).
Cesalli, L., and Goubier, F. (forthcoming). 'Anton Marty on Meaning (*Bedeuten*) and Naming (*Nennen*): A Comparison with Medieval Supposition Theory', in Ch. Kann, B. Löwe, Ch. Rode and S. Uckelman (eds), *Medieval and Modern Applied Logic*. Leuven: Peeters.
Cesalli, L., and Taieb, H. (2013). 'The Road to *ideelle Verähnlichung*: Anton Marty's Theory of Intentionality in the Light of its Brentanian Background', *Quaestio*, 12: 25-86.
Chrudzimski, A. (1999). 'Die Intentionalitätstheorie Anton Martys', *Grazer Philosophische Studien*, 57: 175-214.
Chrudzimski, A. (2001). *Intentionalitätstheorie beim frühen Brentano*. Dordrecht: Kluwer.
Chrudzimski, A. (2004). *Die Ontologie Franz Brentanos*. Dordrecht: Kluwer.
Chrudzimski, A. (2014). 'Marty on Truth-Making', in Cesalli and Friedrich (2014a).

Cometti, J.-P., and Mulligan, K. (2001) (eds). *La Philosophie autrichienne de Bolzano à Musil: Histoire et actualité*. Paris: Vrin.
De Rijk, L. M. (1967). *Logica Modernorum*, vol. II.2. Assen: Van Gorcum.
Dijs, J. (2012). *Hervaeus Natalis 'De secundis intentionibus'. Distinctiones I & 2. Critical Edition with Introduction and Indices*. Zutphen: Koninklijke Wöhrmann.
Funke, O. (1924). *Innere Sprachform. Eine Einführung in A. Marty's Sprachphilosophie*. Reichenberg i. Br.: Sudetendeutscher Verlag Franz Kraus.
Funke, O. (1940). 'Planskizzen und Etnwürfe: Zur Genesis von A. Martys *Untersuchungen zur Grundlegung der allgemeinen Grammatik und Sprachphilosophie*', in Marty (1940), 45–73.
Grabmann, M. (1926). 'Die Entwicklung der mittelalterlichen Sprachlogik', in M. Grabmann, *Mittelalterliches Geistesleben*, Bd. 1, Munich: M. Huber, 104–46.
Holenstein, H. (1976). 'Jakobson und Husserl: Ein Beitrag zur Genealogie des Strukturalismus', in Parret (1976), 772–810.
Jaquette, D. (2004) (ed.). *The Cambridge Companion to Brentano*. Cambridge: Cambridge University Press.
Lagerlund, H. (2007) (ed.). *Representation and Objects of Thought in Medieval Philosophy*. Burlington: Ashgate.
Lambert of Lagny (of Auxerre) (1971). *Logica (Summa Lamberti)*, ed. Franco Alessio. Florence: La Nuova Italia Editrice.
Landgrebe, L. (1934). *Nennfunktion und Wortbedeutung: Eine Studie über Marty's Sprachphilosophie*. Halle: Akademischer Verlag.
Liedtke, F. (1990). 'Meaning and Expression: Marty and Grice on Intentional Semantics', in Mulligan (1990), 29–49.
Liedtke, F. (2014). 'Ausdrücken und Bedeuten: Anton Martys Sprachphilosophie im Lichte der Kritik Karl Bühlers', in Cesalli and Friedrich (2014a).
Loux, M. (1974). *Ockham's Theory of Terms. Part I of the Summa logicae*. Translated by M. J. Loux. Notre Dame: Notre Dame University Press.
Mcdonnell, C. (2006). 'Brentano's Reevaluation of the Scholastic Concept of Intentionality into a Root-Concept of Descriptive Psychology', in *Yearbook of the Irish Philosophical Society*, 124–71 <http://www.irishphilosophicalsociety.ie/> (accessed 3 March 2014).
Majolino, C. (2003). 'Remarques sur le couple forme/matière: Entre ontologie et grammaire chez Anton Marty', *Les Études Philosophiques*, 1: 65–81.
Majolino, C. (2014). 'Par delà la suppléance: Contributions à une sémiotique phénoménologique: Bühler et Marty', in Cesalli and Friedrich (2014a).
Marek, J., and Smith, B. (1987). 'Einleitung zu A. Martys *Elemente der deskriptiven Psychologie*', *Conceptus*, 21: 33–47.
Marmo, C. (1994). *La semiotica e linguaggio nella scolastica. Parigi, Bologna, Erfurt 1270–1330: La semiotica dei Modisti*. Rome: Istituto Storico Italiano per il Medio Evo.
Marty, A. (1875). *Über den Ursprung der Sprache*. Würzburg: A. Stuber.
Marty, A. (1893). 'Über das Verhältnis von Grammatik und Logik', in *Symbolae Pragenses: Festgabe der Deutschen Gesellschaft für Alterskunde in Prag zur 42. Versammlung deutscher Philologen und Schulmänner in Wien*. Vienna: Tempsky [also in Marty (1920: 57–99)].
Marty, A. (1908). *Untersuchungen zur Grundlegung der allgemeinen Grammatik und Sprachphilosophie*. Halle: Niemeyer.

Marty, A. (1916a). *Raum und Zeit*. Aus dem Nachlass des Verfassers herausgegeben von J. Eisenmeier, A. Kastil, and O. Kraus. Halle a. S.: M. Niemeyer.
Marty, A. (1916b) [1884–92]. 'Über Sprachreflex, Nativismus und absichtliche Sprachbildung' [10 articles], in *Anton Marty: Gesammelte Schriften*, ed. J. Eisenmeier, A. Kastil, and O. Kraus, Bd I.2. Halle a. S.: Max Niemeyer, 1–304.
Marty, A. (1918) [1884–95]. 'Über subjectlose Sätze und das Verhältnis der Grammatik zu Logik und Psychologie' [7 articles], in *Anton Marty: Gesammelte Schriften*, ed. J. Eisenmeier, A. Kastil, and O. Kraus, Bd II.1. Halle a. S.: Max Niemeyer, 3–101, 116–307.
Marty, A. (1920). *Gesammelte Schriften*, Bd II.2, ed. J. Eisenmeier, A. Kastil, and O. Kraus. Halle a. S.: Max Niemeyer.
Marty, A. (1940). *Psyche und Sprachstruktur*, ed. Otto Funke. Bern: A. Francke [Nachlass I].
Marty, A. (1950). *Satz und Wort*, ed. O. Funke. Bern: A. Franke [Nachlass II].
Meier-Oeser, S. (1997). *Die Spur des Zeichens: Das Zeichen und seine Funktion in der Philosophie des Mittelalters und der frühen Neuzeit*. Berlin: De Gruyter.
Muckle, J. T. (1933). 'Isaac Israeli's Definition of Truth', *Archives d'histoire doctrinale et littéraire du Moyen Âge*, 8: 5–8.
Mulligan, K. (1989). 'Judgings: Their Parts and Counterparts', in *La Scuola di Brentano*. Dordrecht: Kluwer, 117–48 (supplement to *Topoi*, 6/1 (1986)).
Mulligan, K. (1990) (ed.). *Mind, Meaning, and Metaphysics: Anton Marty's Philosophy and Theory of Language*. Dordrecht: Kluwer.
Mulligan, K. (1997). 'The Essence of Language: Wittgenstein's Builders and Bühler's Bricks', *Revue de Métaphysique et de Morale*, 2: 193–215.
Mulligan, K. (2011). 'Wittgenstein et ses prédécesseurs austro-allemands', *Philosophiques*, 38/1: 5–69.
Mulligan, K. (2012). *Wittgenstein et la philosophie austro-allemande*. Paris: Vrin.
Panaccio, C. (1999). *Le Discours intérieur: De Platon à Guillaume d'Ockham*. Paris: Le Seuil.
Panaccio, C. (2004). *Ockham on Concepts*. Burlington: Ashgate.
Parret, H. (1976) (ed.). *History of Linguistic Thought and Contemporary Linguistics*. Berlin: Walter de Gruyter.
Perler, D. (2001) (ed.). *Ancient and Medieval Theories of Intentionality*. Leiden: Brill.
Perler, D. (2002). *Theorien der Intentionalität im Mittelalter*. Frankfurt: Klostermann.
Raynaud, S. (1982). *Anton Marty, Filosofo del Linguaggio: Uno strutturalismo presaussuriano*. Rome: La goliardica editrice.
Recanati, F. (2008). *Philosophie du langage (et de l'esprit)*. Paris: Gallimard.
Rollinger, R. (1999). *Husserl's Position in the School of Brentano*. Dordrecht: Kluwer.
Rollinger, R. (2004). 'Austrian Theories of Judgment: Bolzano, Brentano, Meinong, and Husserl', in A. Chrudzimski and W. Huemer (eds), *Phenomenology and Analysis: Essays on Central European Philosophy*. Frankfurt: Ontos, 257–84.
Rollinger, R. (2010). *Philosophy of Language and Other Matters in the Works of Anton Marty*. Amsterdam: Rodopi.
Rosier-Catach, I. (2010). 'Grammar', in R. Pasnau (ed.), *The Cambridge History of Medieval Philosophy*. Cambridge: Cambridge University Press, i. 196–218.
Searle, J. (1969). *Speech Acts: An Essay in the Philosophy of Language*. Cambridge: Cambridge University Press.

Smith, B. (1990). 'Brentano and Marty: An Inquiry into Being and Truth', in Mulligan (1990), 111-149.
Smith, B. (1994). *Austrian Philosophy: The Legacy of Franz Brentano*. Chicago: Open Court.
Sperber, D., and Wilson, D. (1986). *Relevance. Communication and Cognition*. Oxford: Blackwell.
Spinicci, P. (1991). *Il significato e la forma linguistica. Pensiero, esperienza e linguaggio nella filosofia di Anton Marty*. Milan: Franco Angeli.

# Name Index

Ibn ʿAdī, Yaḥyā 82, 86–7
Ammonius 41, 51
Aristotle 4, 7–9, 24, 33, 40, 48–53, 56, 59–63, 65, 71, 74–9, 84, 89–92, 101, 104, 140, 142, 147–9, 156–66, 170–1, 173, 177, 229, 240, 247–8
Ashworth, E. J. 229
Augustine 55n, 160–2, 229, 250n
Austin, J. L. 137–8, 146, 150, 152, 226n, 240, 262

Bacon, Robert 108
Bacon, Roger 161, 164, 168, 248–9
Berkeley, G. 5, 9, 202, 229, 234–5
Berlin, I. 202
Boethius (Anicius Manlius Severinus) 62–3, 66, 85n, 104–5, 140, 158, 160, 248, 257n
Bolzano, B. 260
Brandom, R. 214–15
Bühler, K. 261
Burgersdijck, Franco 172
Buridan, John 5, 13, 113–15, 117, 118, 157, 158, 169, 173, 248

Camporeale, S. 149
Castagnetto, S. V. 232, 238
Chrysippus 55, 60–62, 67
Cicero 55n, 138, 142, 147
Condillac, E. de 177, 188, 200, 204n, 231
*Conimbricenses* 157, 158, 161, 171
Cummins, P. 232–3

Davidson, D. 2, 116, 209
Democritus 38
Descartes, R. 5, 12, 121, 127, 157, 166, 241n,
Dummett, M. 116, 207

Eckius, Johannes 158
Erasmus, Desiderius 142
Ernesti, J. A. 203, 220

al-Fārābī, Abū Naṣr Muḥammad 82–6
Fonseca, Petrus 157, 162, 165, 168–9, 172
Frede, M. 52n, 59–60
Frege, G. 2, 39n, 40n, 44, 182, 204, 207–8, 218, 256n, 262; Fregean 182

Gibson, J. J. 228
Grice, H. P. 9, 230n, 255, 262; Gricean 223, 226, 262

Hamann, J. G. 202, 203, 206–8, 220
Hegel, G. W. F. 205, 206, 214–17, 220
Henry of Ghent 111–12, 158
Herder, J. G. 5, 8, 201–5, 207–20 *passim*
Hobbes, T. 5, 240
Humboldt, W. von 206, 208, 220
Hume, D. 5, 81n, 202, 208, 218, 224, 225
Husserl, E. 245, 256n, 260

Jensen, H. 224
al-Jurjānīʿ, ʿAbd al-Qāhir 93–4

Kirchhoff, R. 103

Lambert of Auxerre (or Lagny) 163–4, 166, 167, 170, 248
Locke, John 5, 7, 67, 134, 156, 157, 159, 160–2, 166, 172–3, 176–200, 203, 208, 218–19, 226, 231, 234–7

MacFarlane, J. 101, 115
Marty, A. 9, 245–62
Mattā, Abū Bishr 76–82, 91–4
Matthew of Orléans 112–3
Mauthner, F. 207, 220
McDowell, J. 214–15
Meinong, A. 237, 245, 256n, 260, 261
Mersenne, M. 157
Mill, J. S. 182, 235
Moore, G. E. 224

Nicholas of Paris 106

Olivi, Peter John 168

Panaccio, C. 121–4, 127, 162n
Peter Abelard 6, 55, 61–71, 117
Peter Aureol 165
Peter of Ailly 114, 162
Peter of Spain 105–12, 114, 161–2, 171
Plato 4–9 *passim*, 16–32, 34–48, 52, 61, 83; Platonist/Platonic 60, 70, 77, 159, 202, 204–5, 218, 237
Porphyry 62n, 84, 141, 165
Priscian 101, 104
Putnam, H. 121, 125, 127, 129, 133–4, 238

Reid, T. 5, 7, 9, 223–42
Rubius, Antonius 157, 164, 170–2
Ryle, G. 150–3

Schlegel, F. 206, 208, 220
Schleiermacher, F. D. E. 206, 208–9, 220
Scotus, John Duns 164, 170
Searle, J. 240, 262
al-Sijistānī, Abū Sulaymān 76
al-Sīrāfī, Abū Saʿīd 76, 79–82, 87–94
Smiglecius, Martinus 157, 169n, 172
Soto, Domingo de 13, 157, 161, 163, 165
Spinoza, B. de 202–3, 220
Stoics, the 5, 33, 55–61, 69–71
Strawson, P. F. 240

al-Tawḥīdī, Abū Ḥayyān 76
Thomas Aquinas 5, 121–2, 128, 130–4, 156, 163–5, 167–8, 170–2, 246n, 247, 258n
Todd, D. D. 228, 231
Toletus, Franciscus 157, 171

Valla, Lorenzo 5, 8, 136–53

Wettstein, J. J. 203, 220
William of Ockham 5, 7–8, 113, 121–7, 133–4, 157–9, 161–5, 167–70, 248, 250n
William of Sherwood 103
Wittgenstein, L. 6, 40n, 116, 137, 149–53, 201, 204–20

# Subject Index

act(s)
  mental 114-16, 122-3, 131-2, 163, 183, 227, 229, 231, 233n, 236, 241, 248
ambiguity 24, 69, 90, 91-3, 164-5, 224
  act/object ambiguity 236
  see also equivocity
analogy 94, 225
anti-psychologism 218-20
archetype 178-9, 193-200
argument/argumentation 7, 16, 47, 111, 113, 137-8, 160
  form of 102, 114-15, 117-18
attention 188
  *attentio* 64
attitude 57, 66-7, 246
  force 57, 66-7
*Autosemantie* (autosemantic expression) 251-2

being (in an ontological sense) 27, 30, 41, 44, 47, 53, 65
  *esse intentionale* 129
  *esse reale* 129

common sense 224-5, 237
  Scottish school of 223
communication 13, 19, 88, 101, 157, 193n, 198, 223, 231-4, 240n, 248-252
concept 3, 4, 8, 16-18, 20-8, 30-2, 44, 56n, 60-1, 62-5, 69-70, 101, 104, 108, 113-14, 122-8, 131-4, 137, 140, 142, 150-3, 156-7, 159, 163-73, 201-2, 204-6, 208-13, 217n, 218-19, 229, 248-9, 257, 259
  *formalis* 165
  function (Fregean) 2
  general 204
  identity 122
  linguistic 24-5, 31, 45, 204
  mental word 164
  moral 16, 17, 19n
  *objectivus* 165
  *passio* (i.e., passion of the soul) 161
  simple 127, 160
conception (i.e. understanding) 229, 232-9
consequence, medieval theories of 114-15, 117
content
  descriptive 22
  intentional/conceptual 31, 60, 164n
  linguistic/semantic 1-9, 18, 55-6, 74, 121, 124-34, 137, 203n

mental 74-5, 77-94, 121, 125, 158, 163, 166, 249, 254-8
phenomenal 123-34
propositional, *see* proposition
convention (arbitrary, linguistic agreement) 4, 7-9, 22, 34, 48, 60, 79, 86-7, 122-3, 132, 138, 140-2, 153, 158-9, 203, 228-32, 248, 250, 254
  linguistic community 32, 144, 187, 197, 200, 214-15, 218
  *secundum/ad placitum* 48, 158, 162
copula 44, 50-1, 91, 104n, 114, 182, 246, 256

definition 16-32, 40, 61, 86, 90, 92, 94, 160, 168, 181, 210-12, 224, 237
  *logos* 25, 29-30
dialectic 208
  dialectical method 17, 20, 24, 27
  Dialecticians (Peripatetics) 104
*dicibile* (sayable), *see lekton*
*dictum*, *see* proposition
disposition 107, 215-18
division, method of 10, 16, 24-8, 30-1

*elenchus* 16-18, 26, 28, 30
empiricism 166, 218-20
equivocity 59, 112, 163, 168-70
  *see also* ambiguity
essence 17-18, 21-2, 31, 67, 132, 140, 150, 164n, 165, 167-70, 179, 181, 190, 193, 198-9, 234
  common nature 133, 159, 164n, 165-72
etymology 22, 34, 36, 43n, 44, 45, 70n, 83, 202-3, 254
extension 101, 127, 132-4, 169, 257
externalism (linguistic and/or epistemic) 121-34

falsity 27-8, 65, 68, 70, 79, 104, 110, 261
  not-being 40, 45, 52-3, 110, 113
force 57, 66-7, 163, 182n, 216
  ampliative 112
  inferential 111
  *Kräfte* 210, 215-7
  *vis* (*verbi*) 163
  *see also* attitude; meaning, dispositional
forms
  Platonic Ideas/Forms 16, 18-21, 23, 27-32, 60, 70, 159, 164n, 201-2, 204-5

grammar 52, 66, 74-90, 94, 101, 103-5, 118, 136-8, 141-53, 158, 206, 208, 226, 228, 245, 249, 256
speculative grammarians 249n, 251n

hearer 35, 57, 62, 65, 140, 161, 171, 232-3, 236, 245, 254-7, 259, 262

idea(s) 3, 5, 9, 77, 84, 88, 91, 126, 132, 157, 159, 166, 172, 176-200, 201, 204-5, 219, 223-41
Platonic, *see* form(s), Platonic
imitation, *see* etymology
imposition (dubbing, act of naming) 65n, 123, 157-9, 168, 170-2, 231
impression 7, 8, 208, 226
  rational 56, 60
  sense 160, 164, 224-5, 229n
ineffability 23n
intelligible species, *see* species
intension 127, 132-4

judgement 3, 47n, 57, 116, 127, 160, 182, 185, 227, 240n, 246-7, 249-60

knowledge 18, 20-3, 28-31, 79, 83, 86, 91, 150, 158-9, 171-2, 176, 179, 182-3, 187n, 190, 193, 216, 224, 232, 234

language
  common 143-6, 151-3, 224-7, 232n
  conventional, *see* convention (arbitrary, linguistic agreement)
  natural, *see* sign(s), natural
  *lekton* (sayable) 53, 55-61, 69-71
  *see also* proposition
letters (written, spoken) 23, 30, 34, 38
likeness 4-5, 8, 62n, 124, 248
  similitude 161, 163, 164, 225
  *see also* resemblance
logic 53, 55, 58-61, 61-62, 67, 69-71, 75-94, 101-3, 105, 111, 113, 116-18, 133, 142, 146, 157-60, 160-3, 172, 182, 248
logical constant 101-2, 115-18, 252n
*logos* 25, 29-30, 34-5, 37, 42-3, 46-8, 83
  *see also* definition

meaning
  *Bedeutung* 207, 254, 255-6
  as concept, *see* concept
  dispositional 215-18
  ideational theory of 162, 231, 235, 238
  normativity of 210, 217
  pragmatic, *see* pragmatics (pragmatic semantics)
  semantic, *see* signification
  theory of 7, 75, 134, 139, 156, 215, 233, 245, 259
  as use 201-20

metaphor 82, 91-2, 218
metaphysics/ontology 2, 16, 18-19, 24, 30, 55, 56n, 59-61, 69-71, 86, 110-15, 133, 140, 184-5, 218, 247, 251, 259-61
  ontological/metaphysical ground/foundation 1-9, 18, 23n, 24, 27, 28, 30, 41, 61, 71, 137, 139-41, 259-61
modes 2, 109, 114
  mixed 176-200
  *modi essendi* (mode of being/existence) 71, 128, 132
  *modi intelligendi* (mode of predicating/understanding) 249, 168

name(s), *see* noun(s)
natural kind, *see* term
negation 25, 27-8, 58, 107-8, 110, 147, 166
nominalism 67-8, 121-34, 157, 159, 167-70
noun(s) 39-40, 57, 59, 62, 80, 84, 92, 101, 104, 106-7, 108n, 110, 137, 148, 228
  common 22, 34, 41, 48, 159
  proper 22, 34, 48

*onoma*, *see* noun; name
ordinary language 6, 16, 19, 27, 28, 30, 146-7, 171, 226
  ordinary language philosophy 137, 143, 145-6, 149, 150-3, 223-4, 226

perception 20-1, 28-30, 124, 130-1, 150-2, 166, 182n, 186, 196, 198, 225, 227-30, 232n, 239-40, 253, 259n
pragmatics (pragmatic semantics) 136-7, 223, 226, 245-62
predicate (v. subject) 2-7, 28, 31, 36-40, 46, 49, 51-3, 57-69, 101, 103n, 104-7, 110-14, 161, 182, 236n, 246-8, 252n, 254, 256
predication 49-51, 55, 62, 66-7, 69-70, 108n, 177-8, 194-5, 254
property 49, 100, 112, 161, 167, 184n, 185, 194, 213n, 262
proposition 2, 6, 53, 89n, 101-18, 133, 147, 150, 159-62, 166-8, 171-2, 176, 182-3, 233n, 236n, 240-1, 246, 254, 256n, 258-9
  *axioma* 57-61, 69-71
  *dictum propositionis* 63-9, 69-71
  mental 78, 83
psychologism 218-20

quality 46, 60, 105-8, 131, 140, 147-9, 152-3, 179, 185, 229, 230n

reference 2, 4, 16, 20, 22-3, 28, 31, 94, 137, 140, 161, 166, 167n, 232, 238n
  direct 223
representation 1, 4, 5, 7, 21, 23n, 31, 123, 131n, 133, 139, 160, 162, 194, 261n

resemblance 3-4, 7, 81
  family resemblance 211-14
*rhema, see* verbs; predicate
rhetoric 22, 34, 76n, 82, 92n, 103, 136-43, 161
rule(s) 2, 83, 106n, 112, 137, 142, 150, 197, 206-7, 209-14, 220
  grammatical 88, 142, 146, 150, 228
  rule-following argument 214-17

Scholasticism 136-8, 140, 142-8, 153, 157, 166, 172, 184, 236, 245, 247-9
  Aristotelian-Scholastic tradition 140, 160
  Neoscholasticism 246
sensation 86, 150, 166, 185, 208, 218-20, 224, 228-30, 233n
  language of 204
sense (i.e. semantic) 2, 16, 21, 137, 141, 163
  common, *see* common sense
  proper (*virtus sermonis*) 163
sentence 2-4, 6, 27, 33-5, 38-53, 59, 84, 88, 101n, 162-3, 208, 240
signification (*significare*)
  by convention (*ad placitum*), *see* convention (arbitrary, linguistic agreement)
  by nature, *see* sign(s), natural
  'semantic triad' (Aristotle 16$^a$3-9) 5, 62, 78, 132, 161, 257
sign(s)
  artificial, *see* convention (arbitrary, linguistic agreement)
  conventional, *see* convention (arbitrary, linguistic agreement)
  natural 33-4, 36, 77, 79, 87, 90, 123-4, 133, 157, 159, 228-32
similitude, *see* likeness; resemblance
social 3, 149, 153
  animal 157, 214
  compacts 9
  concept acquisition 238
  meaning 214-15
  mental operations 239-41
society 142, 207, 214-15, 220
sound 20, 56n, 129, 178, 230n, 232, 246
  vocal/linguistic 4, 5, 7, 9, 23, 38, 42, 43n, 48, 56n, 74, 77-8, 122, 139-42, 158-9, 198, 240n, 246, 248, 250, 260
speaker(s) 24, 35, 43, 45-6, 57, 58n, 62, 65, 77n, 80-1, 122, 125, 140, 143, 145, 159, 161, 197, 226, 227n, 232-3, 236-7, 245, 248-9, 254-7, 262
species 25, 27, 60, 65, 111, 123-5, 131, 133, 157, 159, 166, 170, 176-7, 180-2, 190-1, 198-9, 208, 215, 231, 236-7, 239, 259, 261
  as concept or similitude 160, 164
  intelligible 164-5, 170
  sensible 164, 166

speech 28, 30, 34, 37, 42, 56n, 59, 78, 81, 83-4, 88, 139, 144, 198, 204, 227-8, 232n, 240, 250, 255
  parts of 34, 104, 137, 249
  see also *logos*
speech-act(s) 3, 57-8, 197, 241
  speech-act theory 223, 241
*Sprachphilosophie* 246, 261-2
state(s) of affairs 6, 56, 68, 109, 127, 219, 230n, 240, 249, 256n, 260-1
*status* 64-8
subject (v. predicate) 39, 40, 43n, 46, 48-53, 57-61, 66, 70, 101, 103-7, 110-13, 161, 182, 184, 228, 236-7, 246, 252n, 254, 256
substance 65, 71, 106-8, 110, 115, 140-1, 148-9, 152-3, 167, 172, 177-85, 188n, 198-9, 251, 254, 260
supposition (doctrine of) 114, 137, 161-2, 166-8, 171
syllables 22-3, 30, 34, 37
*syncategoremata* (consignificate expressions) 2, 6-7, 59, 100-18, 137, 159, 162, 252n
*Synsemantie* (synsemantic expressions) 251-2
syntax 36, 40, 46, 52, 61, 143, 161-2, 228, 253

term(s)
  categorematic 59, 101-2, 126-7, 133, 137, 159, 182-3, 252n
  equivocal, *see* equivocity
  general 24, 49, 52, 108, 208, 211, 223, 233, 234-8,
  natural kind 65n, 67, 122-6, 159-60, 166, 169, 171
  syncategorematic, *see syncategoremata*
  univocal, *see* univocity
Thomism 157
thought experiment 219, 250
  brains-in-a-vat 121, 125-7, 132
  demon-skepticism 121, 125-33
Tower of Babel 158
trivium 103
truth 2, 17, 23-4, 31, 36, 45n, 47, 53, 58-9, 65, 67-70, 76, 79, 81-3, 89, 101-5, 109, 111-12, 116-17, 151, 166, 172, 182n, 199n, 200, 241, 247, 258-61
  *adaequatio intellectus et rei* 247, 258

understanding (the act/faculty of) 19, 21, 24, 27-8, 31-2, 57, 59, 62-6, 69-70, 79, 81, 133, 140, 147, 152-3, 161-4, 169, 172, 182, 186, 188, 199n, 201-2, 205, 226, 229, 241, 249, 253
  suspense criterion 57
  *modi intelligendi, see* modes
universal(s) 65, 67, 77, 133, 165, 167, 171-2, 182n, 234-8, 257-8, 261

universal(s) (*cont.*)
  universal generalization 61
universality
  of logic 79, 82, 84–6, 90
  of grammar 80
univocity 167–70, 211

vagueness 24
verb(s) 23–4, 28, 34–53, 57, 59, 62–3, 66–8, 80, 84–5, 100, 104, 106–10, 137, 148–9, 151–2, 162, 228

substantive 66
*rhemata* 6, 33–52

word(s)
  spoken 4, 5, 8, 56n, 156, 158, 160–3, 167–72, 248
  written 5, 8, 9, 62n, 78, 114, 122, 163, 250, 253, 260
  inner/mental 5, 7, 113–14, 164, 250
  *verbum* 35, 37, 56, 138, 142, 164